PENGUIN BOOKS

THE RIDDLES OF THE SPHINX

David J. Bodycombe (born 1973) is a puzzle author and games consultant. In the UK, over two million people a day read his puzzles, and internationally his work is syndicated to over 300 newspapers. The British public know him best as the author of the popular puzzle columns in publications such as the *Big Issue*, the *Daily Mail*, the *Daily Telegraph* and *Metro*.

He also consults on many television game shows, including hits such as *The Crystal Maze*, *Codex*, *The Mole* and *Treasure Hunt*. On BBC Radio 4 he regularly appears on the quiz *Puzzle Panel* and provides the cryptic clues for *X Marks the Spot*. He has written and edited over forty books, including *The Mammoth Book of Brainstorming Puzzles*, *How to Devise a Game Show*, *Number Crunchers* and *Visual Vexations*. In 2005 he became a leading author of sudoku puzzles, and he was the first person to have sudokus published in several major territories, including India and Scandinavia. As well as the classic 9 × 9 puzzle, David has pioneered a number of alternative designs which have proved popular with readers all over the world. His games, puzzles and questions also appear in many other magazines, websites, board games and advertising campaigns, and on interactive television.

He qualified in mathematics from the University of Durham in north-east England and he currently lives in Surrey.

WEBSITE: *www.labyrinthgames.com*

THE RIDDLES
of
THE SPHINX

... and the **PUZZLES, WORD GAMES,
BRAINTEASERS, CONUNDRUMS, QUIZZES,
MYSTERIES, CODES** *and* **CIPHERS** *that have*
BAFFLED, ENTERTAINED *and* **CONFUSED**
the world over the last 100 years

DAVID J. BODYCOMBE

PENGUIN BOOKS

PENGUIN BOOKS

Published by the Penguin Group

Penguin Group (USA) Inc., 375 Hudson Street, New York, New York 10014, U.S.A.

Penguin Group (Canada), 90 Eglinton Avenue East, Suite 700, Toronto,
Ontario, Canada M4P 2Y3 (a division of Pearson Penguin Canada Inc.)

Penguin Books Ltd, 80 Strand, London WC2R 0RL, England

Penguin Ireland, 25 St Stephen's Green, Dublin 2, Ireland
(a division of Penguin Books Ltd)

Penguin Group (Australia), 250 Camberwell Road, Camberwell,
Victoria 3124, Australia (a division of Pearson Australia Group Pty Ltd)

Penguin Books India Pvt Ltd, 11 Community Centre,
Panchsheel Park, New Delhi – 110 017, India

Penguin Group (NZ), 67 Apollo Drive, Rosedale, North Shore 0632,
New Zealand (a division of Pearson New Zealand Ltd)

Penguin Books (South Africa) (Pty) Ltd, 24 Sturdee Avenue,
Rosebank, Johannesburg 2196, South Africa

Penguin Books Ltd, Registered Offices:
80 Strand, London WC2R 0RL, England

Published simultaneously in Penguin Books (UK)
and Penguin Books (USA) 2007

1 3 5 7 9 10 8 6 4 2

ISBN 978-0-14-311275-4
CIP data available

Printed in the United States of America
Set in TheAntiqua & TheSans
Designed and typeset by Richard Marston

Contents

For Sofia

Acknowledgements

I would like to extend my thanks to: Sam Loyd, Henry Dudeney, Hubert Phillips and Lewis Carroll – gone but not forgotten; Gaby Martin at Knight Features, Gill Hudson at Puzzlemakers, Albie Fiore and Loyd King for their additional contributions; David Singmaster and Angela Newing for their help in tracking down information for Chapter 1; Paul Sloane of destination-innovation.com, Lloyd King of ahapuzzles.com and Albie Fiore for taking time out to be interviewed; the team at Penguin UK; John Woodruff for his eagle-eyed editing; Richard Marston for wrangling 150 years of puzzles into a coherent format; and Sofia Lorenzana for her invaluable contributions and support.

ILLUSTRATION CREDITS

Illustrations on the following pages are reproduced with permission: p. 2 – George Grantham Bain Collection/Library of Congress; pp. 66 and 128 – Getty Images; p. 248 – W. W. Norton & Co.; p. 343 – Alinari/TopFoto; p. 379 – Robert Gilhooly. Picture research by Zooid Pictures Ltd.

Introduction

The telephone rings. 'Have you got a minute?' asks my mother. 'Capital of Saint Helena, nine letters.' Damn and blast – I'm sure I should know that one. Kingston? No, that's not it. 'What letters have you got?' I plead. 'Hang on a minute,' she says, as her mildly myopic eyes squint at the magazine. 'J blank M then six blanks.' 'Jamestown!' I cry. A warm smugness creeps over me as I thank my brain for not failing me against the might of the *Sunday Express* general knowledge crossword.

As a devisor of puzzles and games myself for many publications and game shows, I realize that our job is to tease the solver just enough: they should be able to get there in the end, but not without a fight. However, how can I justify my decision of giving up a well-paid middle management job at the age of twenty-four to become a full time enigmatologist?

The truth is that puzzles are important. We are solving puzzles every day of our lives: how to drive from Oxford to Brighton by the quickest route; how to program the DVD recorder so that it doesn't cut off halfway through *Countdown*; how to find the perfect strategy on the Internet poker table. No matter how time-wasting a puzzle may seem, there is always something to be gleaned from it – a quickness of hand and eye, an expanded vocabulary, a killer nugget for the pub quiz.

Puzzles have medical benefits too. Doing a puzzle a day is now thought to stave off Alzheimer's disease and brings positive mental benefits in that, no matter what the rest of the day brings, you've got off to a good start thanks to the sudoku. Research carried out by Professor Ian Robertson from Trinity College, Dublin has shown that the brain is like a mental muscle in that it retains more of its strength into later life the more you use it. As evidence accumulates on the benefits of improving body and mind in tandem, perhaps we can view the quick crossword as the equivalent of a quick jog around the block – over in ten minutes, but we feel good for having done it.

From the most secret cryptography to simple household tasks, puzzles are all around us. Despite labour-saving technology, our lives seem more complicated, not less, and one could argue that puzzles are even more relevant to today than ever before. The three questions that this new collection of puzzles aims to answer are therefore: where have these puzzles emerged from, who are the largely anonymous people who create them, and what are the best puzzles ever devised? To this end, each of the book's nine chapters begins with an introduction to the history and background of one type of puzzle, followed by a generous selection of examples from that genre.

WHAT DO YOU DO ALL DAY?

Most compilers have an interest in puzzles before they even know it. I seem to recall making marble runs out of cardboard tubes and board games out of pieces of paper before I was a teenager. My grandfather was a vicar who also turned his hand to magic when the occasion called, and my curiosity was piqued by my early exposure to the ingenious principles behind feats of apparent mind-reading. I enjoyed game shows on television, and I had my first game submission accepted by an independent production company when I was just eighteen. As you'll see in the pages ahead, many other puzzle writers have been influenced by games, puzzles and magic at an early age.

Puzzle setters tend to specialize in particular genres. This is certainly the case with crossword compilers, a very individual breed who have to be at ease with the minutest nuances in language. Specialists in mathematical and logic puzzles also tend to keep themselves to themselves, as these too have very particular techniques that do not transfer well to other areas. A third, rarer, category contains the generalists who'll have a go at anything. I consider myself one of this final group, as I feel that being a polymath allows me to work in many different media. I've been lucky to work in such diverse worlds as TV and radio shows, magazines, syndicated newspaper columns, advertising campaigns, interactive television, board games and the Internet. Oh, and books.

So once they've been bitten by the bug, how do potential writers turn their enthusiasm into useful puzzles? Compilers are on the lookout for unusual words or logical situations that allow the greatest amount of information to be deduced from the minimum of clues – or, to put it bluntly – a short puzzle that has pleasing depth. I asked a fellow puzzle writer, Albie Fiore, for a second opinion. 'There are different techniques for different types,' he told me. 'For a mathematical problem, for instance, I'd work out a general algebraic formula before specifying any numbers. From the equation, it can then be seen what effect different values would have and whether there is one particular set that is unique in some way. Logic problems usually develop in a need-to-know fashion; other types require flow diagrams or exhaustive analysis of all possibilities. However, the objective is usually the same – to spot any unique circumstances that can be used as the key to the puzzle.'

From Albie's quote, you can appreciate that in order to devise a puzzle, it is sometimes necessary to have a higher level of understanding than is required to solve it. This is particularly the case with logical and mathematical puzzles. Some of the puzzles in this book can be easily solved using a pencil and five minutes of thinking time, but they needed degree-level mathematics to set them. This is one reason why puzzles are useful teaching tools to demonstrate complicated principles to new students.

A COMPILER'S LOT

Despite the millions of games and puzzles printed and manufactured each year, one of the most surprising facts is that many compilers do it for the love of the sport rather than for any serious financial gain. Full-time puzzle professionals, I would estimate, account for less than 10 per cent of all those in the industry. There are many more compilers than there are opportunities to publish, and this oversupply further depresses prices and makes it harder to carve out a full-time career. Did Albie Fiore ever think that he could make a living out of puzzles alone? 'Quite honestly, I never thought so. A good puzzle may take some time to perfect, but the payments are not necessarily commensurate with the time involved. It is possible to make a living if, and only if, you're in a field that is reaching a mass market, or develop a puzzle that can be manufactured and marketed. Personally, I couldn't survive on income from games and puzzles alone. I also do other work – research, writing and so on.'

When a new slot becomes available, it can be a rare opportunity – and a compiler has to grab it and hang on for as long as possible. There is a long waiting list to become a regular compiler for national newspapers, and it's a sad-but-true fact that, most likely, you'll have to wait for one of the existing contributors to pass away before you get your turn.

Those who do manage to make puzzles pay the mortgage often specialize in one particular genre, for which they become the 'go-to guy'. A handful of crossword compilers earn a decent crust, but it's real nose to the coalface stuff: probably six or seven puzzles a day.

SHURELY SHOME MISHTAKE?

Apart from possible economic uncertainty, there are few risks to being a puzzle compiler other than that of making a potential mistake. One can be driven to paranoia by worrying about one's latest creation. Is the wording watertight? Is there more than one solution? Is there enough information to deduce the answer? Furthermore, puzzles need to be presented in new and interesting ways to avoid looking like re-treaded tyres.

I'll spare the blushes of the original compiler of this little gem by keeping them anonymous: 'You have brown, blue, black and green socks in your drawer in the ratio of 2 to 3, to 4, to 5 pairs. How many socks must you take out to be sure of having a pair?' The immediate criticism is that this is a puzzle type that has virtually been done to death, and it is very unusual for any surprises to be sprung. At the very least, couldn't it have been something other than socks for a change? Next: what's to stop you just looking in the drawer and picking out two matching socks to wear? Of course, what the compiler meant to add was the usual rigmarole about drawing socks at random (or in the dark), but that wasn't actually mentioned in the question. The final nail in the coffin is the published answer: twenty. Surely the answer is five – in the worst case scenario you pick out four differently coloured socks, but the fifth must match with something you already have. It's quite an interesting exercise to work out what question the compiler originally intended. My best guess is this: 'How many socks must you take out to be sure of having a green pair?' In this circumstance, the worst you could do is to take out all the brown, blue and black socks (that's $4 + 6 + 8 = 18$ so far) followed by two green socks, giving 20 in total. However, even that isn't totally satisfactory because there aren't necessarily 2, 3, 4 and 5 pairs – that was just the *ratio* according to the question, so there's no reason why there shouldn't be 20, 30, 40 and 50 pairs, say.

Puzzle compilation is a tricky business, and I've made a few blunders in my time. However, to prevent faulty puzzles putting off puzzlers of the future, the puzzle writer needs to tread very carefully. This situation becomes even more fraught when the devisor has to ensure that a unique solution can be found from hundreds of billions of possibilities. Another of Albie Fiore's roles is to check a new Rubik's puzzle before it is launched. How does he keep his head above water when trying to ascertain whether such a difficult puzzle is solvable? 'The secret is pencil and paper. To solve these puzzles, I get as far as

I can with them by eye and then devise a notation for moves and make notes as to what effect individual short combinations have. These can then be applied to have the desired effect. For instance, with Rubik's Cube, once I had the top layer completed, I reasoned that it must be possible to move the other pieces around by removing a piece from the completed layer and then putting it back. I experimented with different ways of doing this and noting the moves and their effect. I soon found a few sequences that moved pieces to the middle layer and others that rearranged the bottom layer. It was then easy to pick an appropriate sequence to complete the puzzle step by step.'

A DOZEN WAYS TO BECOME A BETTER SOLVER

Before we set you off on the hike up Puzzle Mountain, here's some general advice:

Read the question properly As with any test, read the rubric carefully to avoid giving the right answer to the wrong puzzle!

Read between the lines This is a vital skill for lateral-thinking puzzles. Look at what the compiler *hasn't* said as well as what they have. Is there a loophole lurking in there somewhere that provides the necessary insight?

Get off to a good start Most puzzles of any decent size try to suggest an obvious starting point. Even the most difficult cryptic crosswords contain a few easier clues deliberately included to get the solver out of the starting blocks.

Try out a few possibilities If there doesn't appear to be an obvious place to start, don't be afraid of trying your luck. Sometimes a puzzle will require you to try two or three different routes of attack until either you complete it or reach a contradiction and have to backtrack and try another option. However, resist the temptation to tackle a puzzle through a root-and-branch search of every possibility. You'll more than likely get tangled up in knots, the puzzle will end up in a flurry of pencil marks, and most importantly you won't enjoy it.

Look at the big picture Avoid getting caught up in the small battles. Think like a general and strategize a master plan. Is there a particular area of the puzzle that would be useful to solve? If so, how can you reach that area? Sometimes it's easy to avoid dead ends if you keep the ultimate aim in mind.

Is there a clue? If you're really stuck, look for the hidden extra that is present in the very best puzzles. Is there a clue in the question? Are some of the answers themed? Is there a hidden message in the answer grid? Puzzle compilers often go the extra mile to make their puzzles memorable, and providing extra twists or hidden signatures like these can provide you with additional hints.

Track your progress It can be useful to narrow down what's remaining when you're halfway through a puzzle. If you've solved a crossword clue, cross out the clue number. If you're sure that you've extracted all the possible facts from a clue in a logic problem, cross it out so that you can concentrate on the remaining clues. If you've found all the 9's in a sudoku puzzle, make a note of it.

Try something simpler first If you can't solve, for example, a geometrical puzzle that's set on an 8 × 8 chessboard, consider transferring the problem to a 4 × 4 or even a 2 × 2 board instead. Although the puzzle will have changed, thinking about the simpler version may provide you with the key that you need to solve the full-scale puzzle.

Take a break If you're really stuck, put the puzzle down and come back to it later. This seems to work particularly well with cryptic crosswords, where it is easy to get sucked into the surface reading of the clue without properly analysing what the clue really means.

A problem shared is a problem halved Try solving puzzles with a friend or relative. In my experience, two people can work, bouncing ideas off each other, so much more efficiently than a singleton that, together, they are able to solve much harder puzzles than would otherwise be possible.

Generalize, don't specialize If you can, widen the range of puzzles that you attempt. If you're not very good at a particular type of puzzle, the chances are that you haven't done many of them. With practice, the majority of puzzles are within the reach of everyone.

If all else fails … If you didn't solve the puzzle and had to look at the answer, look on it as 'deferred success' (as it is euphemistically referred to in educational circles these days). The important thing is to analyse what went wrong and learn from it for next time. For cryptic crosswords, look at the answers in conjunction with the clues. Even if you succeed, look for a general formula or principle that will enable you to solve with ease all puzzles of that type in the future.

WHY *RIDDLES OF THE SPHINX?*

Arguably the most famous puzzle in history was the one asked by the mythological Greek Sphinx to anyone who passed by: 'Which creature in the morning goes on four feet, at noon on two, and in the evening upon three?' Anyone who didn't know the answer was strangled (the word 'sphinx' ultimately comes from the Greek *sphiggo*, meaning 'to strangle'). That clever chap Oedipus came along and worked out the solution: a man, because a man crawls on all fours (as a baby), walks on two feet (as an adult), then walks with a walking stick (in old age). The defeated Sphinx, being a sore loser, promptly committed suicide by throwing herself off a cliff.

That's *the* Riddle of the Sphinx, but why Riddles plural? Handily, Sphinx is a word synonymous with some of the greatest puzzle makers of all time. England's most famous enigmatist, Henry Dudeney, used the pseudonym Sphinx in one of his puzzle columns. His American equivalent, Sam Loyd, had many of his puzzles published in a magazine called *Sphinx*, which is also the name of a 1930s Belgian puzzle magazine that published the very first alphabetic arithmetic puzzle, called a cryptarithm. We'll meet both Dudeney and Loyd in the first chapter.

ABOUT THIS BOOK

I have put together what I hope is one of the most wide-ranging collections ever assembled. The book is divided into nine chapters, each one concentrating on one of the classic worlds of puzzles. They range from the earliest riddles to the latest Japanese crazes, although we have concentrated on the period from the late nineteenth century to the present day, where much of the interest lies.

Although this could be thought of as a 'classic' collection, I have used a number of criteria which, I hope, set this book apart from similar works that have gone before. First, much of the material has been especially devised and appears in print here for the first time, even if the underlying principles are age-old. I have striven to avoid most of the 'usual suspects' that seem to crop up time and again in puzzle books. Hopefully, even the most ardent fan will find much here which is new to their eyes.

As a rule, the contents of each chapter are organized in increasing order of difficulty. Puzzles appear in themed clumps, so that even if you don't succeed with the first problem, you'll usually have a few more to attempt. I have set the average difficulty level at what could be described as 'the approachable side of middling'. There are some real stinkers, but – with a few exceptions that are too noteworthy to omit – the most complicated material has been excluded. What has made it into these pages should provide a firm but fair test of your enigmatological skills. I have tried to provide full explanations wherever possible, particularly in the mathematics and logic sections.

A particular bugbear of mine is when a puzzle book expects the poor reader to construct complicated and unwieldy physical models. For this reason, anything remotely resembling a jigsaw puzzle doesn't get a look-in. I hope that the 'barriers to entry' have been lowered as much as possible – nearly all the puzzles can be solved by reading the question and writing your answer directly into the book, possibly with some scrap paper by your side.

I am confident that the nine chapters that follow provide a taste of all the major flavours of puzzle, but I am also well aware that many topics – such as chess, mazes and science puzzles – could have had dedicated sections to themselves. Perhaps an opportunity to cover these and other areas in proper depth will arise in a second volume.

BACK TO THE FUTURE?

What, then, for the future of the humble puzzle? By the looks of things, the recent sudoku craze shows that we're more puzzle-mad than ever before. New technology seems to be a benefit rather than a threat – mobile phones and web pages provide new interactive ways of puzzling, more than compensating for any loss of readership in the traditional media. Equally, puzzle crazes are nothing new – as you'll see from the stories in this book – but whether they are the flavour of the month or not, puzzles are so prevalent that they'll always be around, even if they're not hitting the headlines.

While some puzzles may seem trivial and are unlikely to bring their authors Pulitzer Prizes, their regular appearance in newspapers and magazines gives reassurance for commuters and, like the pleas for help from my mum at weekends, bring people together like nothing else can.

CHAPTER 1

The Puzzle Kings

The year is 1880. The place is the United States. General Robert E. Lee surrendered his army fifteen years ago, bringing the Civil War to an end. Despite the distraction of the ongoing Indian Wars, industrialization has taken root, as demonstrated by the emergence of electric lights and telephones. And yet the most pressing question for Americans in 1880 is this: 'How do I swap that 14 block for the 15?'

The man synonymous with the so-called Fifteen Puzzle was one Sam Loyd, a precocious talent who devised, collected, promoted and popularized some of the classic puzzles of the late nineteenth century. His commercial nous enabled him to turn newspaper columns and pieces of cardboard into money-spinning features and products, earning him and his family a comfortable lifestyle. Though many people before him had set puzzles, it could be argued that Loyd was the world's first full-time puzzle-setter. The chances are that you'll have seen at least one of his puzzles in some form or other – as a toy or a cracker novelty, or on the pages of a puzzle book – for his influence is still felt to this day.

Sam Loyd was born in Philadelphia on 30 January 1841, of 'wealthy but honest parents'. His father was a land developer and estate agent, and the family moved to New York in 1844.

Loyd, the youngest of eight children, was never afraid of a challenge, despite his father's very conservative, Quaker ethos. On one occasion his family went to a fair where the travelling showman issued a challenge that no one could outrun him in a 100-yard dash. Loyd, tall and slim and in the flush of youth, couldn't resist taking up the bet. His father was furious when he found out, but Sam had already entered his name and couldn't back out. As he desperately sprinted down the course he heard

Sam Loyd

his father shout, 'Go it, Sammy! Don't let him beat you!' He crossed the line first and collapsed, exhausted but happy.

Loyd's pastimes were typical of someone who would later become a puzzle-writer. He enjoyed chess, conjuring, and skilled activities such as silhouette-cutting and ventriloquism. He was able to imitate many musical instruments and animals, and couldn't resist using this talent for mischief. One of the servant-girls who attended the family's living quarters handed in her resignation because each time she cleaned the parlour, she could hear voices coming down the chimney!

A similarly ingenious wheeze was concocted much later in Loyd's life, when his own fifteen-year-old son was asked to demonstrate his powers of telepathy.* The family was on a steamboat voyage when the heavens opened and they went in out of the rain. Loyd asked his son to think of a playing card that Sam Snr had selected at random from the pack. Each time, to much astonishment, the boy would correctly name the card. Occasionally he would falter, but after much concentration he would always get it right. Loyd explained later how it was done: 'Of course, Sammy does not know what card I draw out, but simply moves his lips in reply to my questions, while I supply his voice by ventriloquism.' To make the illusion more convincing, Loyd often threw the wrong answer to the younger Sam and forced him to retry several times, under great strain, until the correct card was eventually identified. After one performance of this trick, a gentleman begged Loyd to give it up, fearing that the mental effort would injure his son.

*The son's birth name was Walther, but it seems that he was called Sammy in the family. He took over the Sam Loyd name after his father's death in 1911, and is usually referred to today as Sam Loyd Jr.

Loyd studied to become a steam and mechanical engineer. In the evenings he would while away the time with his brothers Thomas and Isaac at the Society Library in New York. Chess was the order of the day – the game was becoming increasingly popular. Thomas was sufficiently skilled to play with chess celebrities such as Miron J. Hazeltine, who had just been offered a column in the New York *Saturday Courier*, probably the USA's first newspaper column on chess. A year later, in 1856, Hazeltine's column began running in the New York *Clipper*, where it was published without fail for over fifty years.

The Loyd brothers were envious of Hazeltine's success and decided to contribute their own chess problems to the newspapers. The problems of the day usually featured the end of a game of chess, with few pieces remaining on the board. The solver had to work out how to force checkmate in a specified number of moves (e.g. 'White to play and mate in 2') or to rescue a draw from an unfavourable position. The correct solution had to be rigorous and achieve the desired result regardless of any countermeasures taken by one's opponent, who, as in a normal game, makes their move after each of your own. They are often inspired by endings from actual chess games, possibly with some minor tweaks to ensure a unique solution.

Of the brothers, Thomas Loyd had the earliest success when a problem of his devising appeared in *Albion* magazine. Sam's first problem appeared in the *Courier* on 14 April 1855, but he was unhappy with its logic and later disowned it. Isaac followed behind Sam two weeks later. Although Thomas only ever composed two or three puzzles, both Sam and Isaac continued to have puzzles accepted in newspaper chess columns, with increasing regularity.

Sam took great pride in his early successes – perhaps too much pride. He later boasted, 'I was one of those infant phenomena at chess. Here's a chess problem from the 1851 edition of the *Chess Monthly* that I worked out when I was ten. At that tender age I was playing in matches with the crack chess men of the country and sometimes beating 'em too.' Sadly for Loyd's credence, the *Chess Monthly* didn't begin publication until 1857. Loyd was certainly a young talent, but despite his claims he took up chess at the age of fourteen, not ten.

Many of Loyd's best puzzles were devised in his teenage years. In 1856 he entered the *Illustrated Newspaper*'s 'tourney', a newspaper competition where readers could submit chess problems which were evaluated, and the best won prizes. The judge of this particular competition, one W. J. A. Fuller, was encouraging of Loyd: 'He is quite a youth and can hardly fail to attain the highest excellence if he perseveres in this field of labour. His only fault is too great fecundity. He makes a problem almost every day – some good, some indifferent, and some, of course, bad. If he confined himself to one a month he would gain reputation faster.' Another tourney in the new *Chess Monthly* magazine became another outlet for Loyd's work. Ten sets of problems were received in time for the first competition, the first prize going to Loyd and the second prize to one Mr W. King – which, it turns out, was a pen name used by Loyd. All the other problems were deemed to have faulty logic.

The winning puzzle in *Chess Monthly* was composed for Paul Morphy, who complimented it highly as it demonstrated four entirely different tactics depending on how the Black player responded to White's initial threat. Morphy, a twenty-year-old American chess wunderkind, became a sensation, and interest in him brought much attention to the game of chess. *Chess Monthly* wrote that 'his genial disposition, his unaffected modesty and gentlemanly courtesy have endeared him to all his acquaintances'.

Morphy's celebrity was great news for Loyd's prospects. Suddenly, a mere two years after Hazeltine's debut in 1855, over eighty different American publications were now running a chess column. No compiler would be able to have the range of ideas required to service all these outlets, but Loyd managed to sell problems to twenty-five of them. By 1858, still only seventeen years of age, he became the most successful and widely celebrated composer of chess problems in the USA.

Loyd's chess problems were not always faultless, but they were exciting and inventive. In November 1860 he created a new variety of problem known as the helpmate, where both players attempt to bring the game to its quickest possible conclusion. Although it began as a curiosity, the helpmate problem has been studied by chess fans to such an extent that it is no longer considered to be trivial. Other ideas that Loyd popularized include problems where one move had to be retracted first, tricks involving *en passant* moves and half-completed castling, a breathtaking 'mate in 50 moves', and boards where the positions of the pieces formed a letter of the alphabet, a geometric shape or even a simplistic picture of an animal. From 1857 to 1859, Loyd published whole slews of his problems around the country, and by 1860 he was able to continue publishing problems that he had devised in previous years.

Throughout this period Loyd was still studying, but his interest in engineering waned and he announced to his lecturer that he would no longer be taking lessons. His lecturer remonstrated with him and suggested that he reconsider. At this point Loyd took a piece of cardboard from his pocket, bearing a picture of two donkeys, that was to change his life.

ONE-TRICK PONIES
... AND DONKEYS

Phineas T. Barnum, the showman and co-founder of Ringling Bros. and Barnum & Bailey Circus, had struck a deal with Loyd for a puzzle that was to be called 'P. T. Barnum's Trick Donkey'. The principle was amazingly simple – to place the moveable section over the larger diagram to make the donkeys come alive. The puzzle can still be found in novelty bags today, and it is not difficult to find an unknowing victim who can struggle with the puzzle for twenty minutes or more.

Barnum used the puzzle for publicity, selling copies for a buck apiece. Although it is one of Loyd's most famous puzzles, it is almost certainly not his invention. An 1857 title, *The Magician's Own Book*, used a similar principle with two dead dogs, the challenge being to make them come alive once more by the addition of four new lines. Although the idea was not his own, Loyd made a substantial $10,000 in royalties.

Another of Loyd's most commercial puzzles was created during a return voyage from Europe, where he had been selling US Bonds in aid of the Civil War effort. There was much discussion between passengers about the famous White Horse monument on Uffington Hill in Berkshire, England. The Governor of Pennsylvania had suggested that it might be a good topic for a puzzle, and Loyd wasted no time in producing the

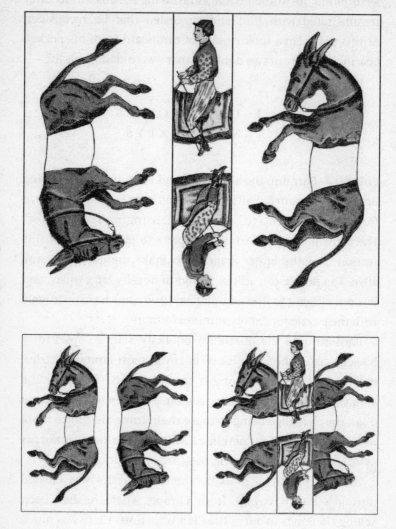

P. T. Barnum's Trick Donkey

Pony Puzzle. The idea was to rearrange the six pieces that made up one horse in such a way as to make a completely different type of horse. The solution involved using the spaces between the black pieces to form a white horse.

In 1876, Loyd accepted a job editing chess problems for *American Chess Journal*, and during 1878–81 spent much time editing chess columns for newspapers and magazines as well as a new book of his own, *Chess Strategy*. However, the book was distinctly flawed. In his excellent account *Sam Loyd and His Chess Problems*, Alain C. White writes: 'He had extraordinary intuition. His conclusions were often correct, even when his arguments were almost absurdly unsound. He seemed to form his opinions by instinct and afterwards to attempt their justification by appeal to reasoning, not always with success. He would express any idea that came to him, however particular its true application might be, in the form of a broad generalization; hence the contradictions, repetitions and general turmoil of style. He had not, in short, the patience to frame a carefully reasoned system nor expound a complex thought in simple words. He could tell a story admirably, and he could give suggestive hints briefly and to the point. But when it came to page after page of definition and criticism, he entirely lost his footing. The style of the *Strategy* reminds one of a runaway horse caught in quicksand.'

THE CRAZY CRAZE

In 1880, a combination puzzle spread throughout America and Europe and, according to Sam Loyd Jr, 'the Loyds were among its earliest victims'. Looking back in 1896, Loyd Snr wrote: 'The

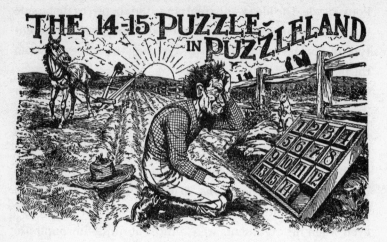

The 14–15 Puzzle

older inhabitants of Puzzleland will remember how in the early seventies [sic] I drove the entire world crazy over a little box of movable blocks which became known as the 14–15 Puzzle. The fifteen blocks were arranged in the square box in regular order, only with the 14 and 15 reversed, as shown in the ... illustration. The puzzle consisted in moving the blocks about, one at a time, so as to bring them back to the present position in every respect except that the error in the 14 and 15 must be corrected.'

Loyd mischievously added: 'A prize of $1,000, which was offered for the first correct solution to the problem, has never been claimed, although there are thousands of persons who say they performed the required feat. People became infatuated with the puzzle and ludicrous tales are told of shopkeepers who neglected to open their stores; of a distinguished clergyman who stood under a street lamp all through a wintry night trying to recall the way he had performed the feat. The mysterious feature of the puzzle is that no one seems to be able to recall the sequence of moves whereby they feel sure they succeeded in solving the puzzle. Pilots are said to have wrecked their ships, engineers rush their trains past stations and business generally became demoralized.' Loyd saw the potential of the puzzle straight away. It was exactly the kind of simple-at-first-glance yet intensely frustrating puzzle that he loved.

When the puzzle was rerun in a New York newspaper, the Sunday editor refused to shoulder the risk of the $1,000 prize reward, saying that he remembered very well that he had solved the puzzle once, and he wasn't going to throw away a thousand dollars. 'Before I could persuade him to offer the reward,' said Loyd, 'I had to bring the money to his office and deposit it in the safe. It was never claimed.'

Why? Because, in the form in which it is posed, the puzzle is completely impossible to solve. If one were to fill the blocks in the grid at random, there are some 21 thousand billion possible positions. It turns out that all the permutations fall into either of two groups – let's call them X and Y. If the puzzle is currently in an X configuration, sliding the tiles will move the puzzle into another group X configuration. It is impossible to move the puzzle from an X position to a Y position by sliding alone. However, if we exchange one pair of tiles (or perform any odd number of such swaps), the grid can change from X to Y and vice versa. Loyd's initial 13–15–14 set-up on the bottom row belongs to the opposite group to the 13–14–15 set-up required by the answer, so the puzzle cannot be solved by fair means. Various cheats and tricks are possible, such as turning the 6 and 9 tiles upside-down, or even turning the whole puzzle 90 degrees clockwise so that the numbers are in the correct places but they lie on their sides.

Loyd knew full well that his money was safe. However,

this backfired on him somewhat. As he did with many of his best puzzles, Loyd tried to patent the puzzle for legal protection. When demonstrating a working model to the Patent Commissioner, Loyd had to explain that the puzzle couldn't be solved. 'Then you can't have a patent,' exclaimed the Commissioner. 'If the thing won't work, how can you file a working model of it?'

DANIEL IN DENIAL

Loyd was amused and bemused by the poor souls who refused to be defeated by his con trick. 'There are thousands of persons in the United States who believe they solved that puzzle,' he said. 'I was talking with my shoemaker the other day, when a big Irishman, sitting not far away, who had overheard us, said, "Are ye the mon that invinted the Foorteen–Fifteen puzzle? Oi did that puzzle." I laughed and said that couldn't be, because it couldn't be done. "Don't you said oi didn't do it," he replied, "or oi'll flatten the nose on y'r face."'

If you believed the newspapers, people were literally driven mad by the game. 'The puzzle is filling the lunatic asylums of this country at the rate of about 5,000 a day,' exclaimed the Utica *Herald*. Various, mostly untrue, hearsay stories abounded, until the jocular tone changed on 23 March 1880 when one Daniel Conroy – a quiet family man – attempted to murder one of his children on a hot stove after becoming incensed with the 'Bothersome Three Blocks'. He was removed to the Dixmont Asylum, but released after two months – only to have another panic attack in church two weeks later, claiming that he was Daniel in the lions' den. From this we can perhaps assume that

Conroy and similar others 'driven mad' by the Fifteen craze may have been predisposed to madness, regardless of their puzzle addiction.

The puzzle became a drain on productivity. Employers had to display notices in offices, banning employees from playing it during office hours. In Germany the Reichstag was brought to a standstill, while the French considered the puzzle 'a greater scourge than alcohol or tobacco'. In 1904, the English puzzle compiler Henry Dudeney – whom we shall meet later – said that the game 'for a short period almost monopolized the attention of Europe and America. A London shop in Cheapside sold nothing else, and was besieged from morning till night, while hawkers at every street corner found it impossible to meet the demand.'

The craze ended after a few months, but modern versions of the game are still manufactured. And so Sam Loyd's greatest creation earned him a place in history … or did it?

STUMBLING BLOCKS

A few things don't stack up. Loyd's claimed date of creation skips around the 1870s depending on which interview you read, and he made no mention of the puzzle until 1891, more than ten years after the craze began. Loyd claimed that he had sold 10 million of the puzzles – one for every five people in the USA at the time – yet no examples of his model have ever been discovered.

The truth is that he didn't invent it, and had nothing to do with popularizing the game in its heyday. Despite this, he claimed ownership of it for twenty years. The claim became the accepted truth, and every obituary of Loyd included mention of 'his' Fifteen Puzzle.

So who did devise it? In 2006, a team led by puzzle historian Jerry Slocum managed to pin down the truth. An 1874 puzzle by a postmaster called Noyes Palmer Chapman was later copied by students at the American School for the Deaf, who began making the puzzle themselves. One of these puzzles was sold or given to a Boston-based woodworking shop owner, Matthias Rice, who repackaged it as the Gem Puzzle in December 1879. Various 'me too' products followed when a reward for a correct solution was offered by a dentist called Charles Pevey in January 1880. The prize was $100 in cash plus a $25 set of teeth.

OUT OF THIS WORLD

By the late 1890s, Loyd was living very comfortably. Although it was devised in what Loyd describes as 'a bad year', the Get off the Earth illusion of 1896 is one of his most famous and puzzling problems. When tasked by one Percy Williams to find a new advertising gimmick to promote his new pleasure resort at Bergen Beach, Loyd adapted a previously known linear illusion into a circular format.

When the puzzle is rotated from one marked position to the other, the number of men that can be counted around the Earth's edge changes by one. It is a most confusing effect. When Loyd showed it to the staff of the Brooklyn *Eagle* newspaper, they were immediately taken by it. However, Loyd had to let them down gently, explaining that he had already sold it, but the suitably impressed *Eagle* gave him a puzzle column on the paper for $50 a week.

The Get Off the Earth Puzzle

ENGLAND'S ENIGMATOLOGIST

While Sam Loyd has been dubbed the Puzzle King many times, the same title has also been conferred on England's greatest creator of puzzles. Henry Ernest Dudeney was born on 10 April 1857 in Mayfield, Sussex. For generations, the family had farmed sheep on the Sussex Downs. Of Henry's nine siblings, only four survived into adulthood.

Even at a very early age, Dudeney was bright and inquisitive. He recalled that when he was in his pram he was puzzled that it did not move when he pushed the handle, even though it worked for his nanny when she pushed. At a grandmother's house, he loved playing with her ornamental solitaire board and became fascinated with the strategy, later publishing several puzzles about the game.

Dudeney was delighted to make his first commercial sale at nine years of age. He had submitted some puzzles to a newspaper for boys, and received five shillings for each one published. Dudeney's adult interests developed along very similar lines to Loyd's: music, magic, ventriloquism and chess.

After completing his education, Dudeney took a job in the Civil Service as a clerk, but he lost interest and began to search for more creative outlets. In the late nineteenth century the market for weekly and monthly newspapers was booming, so there were opportunities to earn a living as a freelance writer. The problem was his choice of subject matter – recreational puzzles were still uncommon in periodicals.

Nevertheless, by 1896 Dudeney's profile had risen sufficiently that he secured two columns in the publications *Tit-Bits* and *Strand Magazine*. If the latter title sounds familiar, it may be because it was in this magazine's pages that Sir Arthur Conan Doyle first serialized many of his Sherlock Holmes stories. Doyle was two years younger than Dudeney, and, finding themselves in similar situations, they became good friends. Together with others from London's literary set, they founded a club called the Society of Authors. Writing under the pseudonym Sphinx, Dudeney wrote and later edited *Strand*'s puzzle column – 'Perplexities' – for thirty years.

In the meantime, Dudeney's personal life had moved on. He married in 1884, and the couple moved house to be reasonably close to both their friends in Sussex and Dudeney's publishing houses, chess club, writing friends and his beloved opera in London. Dudeney's wife, Alice Whiffin, later became a successful author herself under the monicker Mrs Henry Dudeney, and

Henry Dudeney

judging by historical newspaper clippings, her accessible tales of country life made her very popular at the time. She published many novels as well as short stories for *Harper's Magazine*, and her income was quite substantial.

In 1894, the New York State Chess Association held its summer meeting in Buffalo. One of the puzzles Sam Loyd contributed showed an unlikely-looking chess position. In addition to finding checkmate within four moves, many people wondered whether the position was in fact obtainable by open play. Loyd offered prizes for anyone who could better his answer, which was that it would take fifty-three moves to arrive at the position. Dudeney learned of this puzzle and sent off a fifty-move solution of his own. In a characteristic piece of cheek, it seems that Loyd may have later passed off Dudeney's answer as his own – when writing to a friend, he bragged: 'I enclose my latest Looking Backward problem, with the solution, which I consider the best thing I ever produced in the chess line.'

COLLABORATIVE EFFORTS

Through the fifty-move puzzle and other correspondence about puzzles Loyd had submitted to British magazines around that time, Loyd and Dudeney entered a collaboration, which lasted from 1896 to 1898. Loyd provided the bulk of the material for the columns in *Tit-Bits*, while Dudeney provided additional commentary and selected the competition winners.

This extract from one of Sam Loyd's personal letters from June 1896 gives an insight into his opinion of his new-found colleague: 'Mr Henry E. Dudeney of Five Oaks, who I have known for some time as a bright man and extremely clever fellow, kindly assists me in securing foreign copyrights. He has got up some very clever puzzles and games – but has somehow or other failed to put them in the catchy shape which takes with the public. He has a wonderful faculty for solving such matters – and has clever and original ideas.'

Since Loyd was doing most of the hard work compiling the puzzles, Dudeney repaid the compliment by sending some of his own material for Loyd's interest. Loyd was never a man to stand on protocol, and, as he had done with many other games and ideas, he passed them off as his own. Dudeney was distraught – he had meticulously credited Loyd with his many inventions (or claimed inventions, at least), and the thought that Loyd would dare not to mention Dudeney's name outraged him. The relationship between the two men broke down irrecoverably. According to Angela Newing's biography of Dudeney, his daughter Margery 'recalled her father raging and seething with anger to such an extent that she was very frightened and, thereafter, equated Sam Loyd with the devil'.

It is likely that Loyd was tempted to steal puzzles from his British counterpart because of Dudeney's much stronger ability in mathematics. One of Loyd's daughters later recounted that his 'mathematical puzzles were not always so easily perfected, and I recall once seeing him in a state of panic at the loss of what had been to him weeks and weeks of work. He was bringing out his Blind Luck game and he had filled any number of small note books with figures, the result of many hours of study. One night a burglar entered our house and cleared all his little books of figures … the loss of the note books and memoranda caused him terrible anxiety.' Fortunately the notebooks were found in the next yard later that day, where the burglar had dropped them in his flight, so Loyd was spared having to go over all his figures again.

Loyd found various wheezes by which he could avoid the most strenuous mathematical work. One way, for permutation-style puzzles for which there was surely a solution, was simply to ask for the smallest number of moves required to solve it. Loyd often published these puzzles with no clear idea of the solution; instead he offered large cash prizes as bait. Hundreds of solutions would be submitted to his office, and the secretaries were tasked with opening the correspondence and passing on the most likely-looking solutions for Loyd's personal attention.

He also sold on the names and addresses of his correspondents to advertising agencies for marketing purposes.

Dudeney's mood hit a downward spiral. He ignored his wife, who subsequently had an affair with one of his book illustrators. Dudeney returned to London and threw himself back into his favourite pastimes – music and puzzles. He became involved with the Church once more, and came to peace with his lot.

Mr and Mrs Dudeney reconciled their marriage after Alice's affair didn't work out, and at the onset of World War I they moved to Lewes in Sussex. The puzzle-writer's later life was sedentary but happy. He died in 1930, aged seventy-three. In addition to his main collections, his later material lives on thanks to posthumous anthologies organized by his wife. He is best remembered for solving what was known as the Haberdasher's Puzzle, where an equilateral triangle is cut into four pieces which are rearranged to form a square. In 1926, he created the first crossnumber (mathematical crossword) puzzle.

THE ULTIMATE HOAX

Though hardly anyone at the time suspected as much, Loyd's fame, confidence and sheer brazen cheek were such that by 1903 he had claimed many puzzle crazes as his own. His letter-head of that year read: 'Sam Loyd – Journalist and Advertising Expert. Original games, novelties, supplements, souvenirs, Etc., for newspapers. Unique sketches, Novelties, Puzzles, &c., for advertising purposes. Author of the famous Get off the Earth Mystery, Trick Donkeys, 15 Block Puzzle, Pigs in Clover,

Parcheesi, Etc. Etc. P.O. Box 826, New York.' The irony is that none of these claims are true. We have already seen this for the first three items listed. Pigs in Clover was a rolling-ball dexterity maze patented by Charles Crandall in 1889. Loyd claimed that he popularized the ancient Indian game for a flat fee of $10 when a company holding a huge pile of cardboard squares approached him to make a new puzzle to use up their stock – whereas John Hamilton registered his version of Parcheesi first, in 1867.

The year 1903 also saw Loyd's greatest hoax. He put out a book called *The Eighth Book of Tan Part I*, describing the history of a well-known seven-piece creative jigsaw puzzle called the tangram. The book contained hundreds of puzzles, and claimed that the game originated in China 4,000 years ago. Included in the book were comments by a Professor Chancellor on the relationship between the evolution of biological species and the huge variety of possible arrangements of the tangram's pieces.

Apart from the two-thirds of the puzzles that were Loyd's original inventions, the entire thing was tosh. There were no books 1 to 7 of Tan, and Professor Chancellor was a character of Loyd's making. In November 1908, Dudeney fell for the hoax, recounting Loyd's untrue story. The claims were proved to be untrue in 1911 by Sir James Murray of the *Oxford English Dictionary*. The tangram had a history dating back to the 1810s, for Napoleon is said to have owned a copy, but it was not ancient.

Despite this, Sam Loyd's influence lives on to this day. Many writers and reference sources still date the tangram back to the Song or Ming dynasty, and even the eminent puzzle historian Martin Gardner recounted the false history, in 1959.

A PUZZLING CHARACTER

So, was Loyd really a fly-by-night charlatan who, like the magpie, stole anything pretty from other people's nests and got rich quick? To reach this conclusion would be unfair. Loyd worked extremely hard – he had far too little time to analyse all his ideas in any great depth, and he grafted not only on the puzzle material but also on business correspondence and deals to keep the wolf from the door. Many of the early illustrations and puzzles he manufactured himself, working on handmade woodcuts and manual printing presses.

Although his big hits may have actually been reheated classics, the majority of his output was the result of his own intense concentration. On one occasion he was left in charge of the young Sam Jr, who was playing with a tin bucket. Shrieks were heard when the baby and bucket tumbled down the stairs. Loyd's daughter writes that her mother 'hurried back to find the child all in bruises at the foot of the back stairs, and father in his chair in the room at the top still immersed in his problem and oblivious to all the commotion'.

Nor was Loyd a con man. He had invented a mathematical game called Blind Luck to which he had devised a special answer key (the almost stolen notebooks) which enabled him to win regardless of his opponent's choice of move. A professor of Columbia College challenged him to a game for a bet of $100. Loyd refused, saying that he did not want to rob him. Nevertheless, they played a game, and the professor was put out when he lost.

News of Loyd's death broke on 10 April 1911 – ironically, Dudeney's birthday. Newspapers speculated that he had made millions from his inventions, but his estate was a very modest $15,000. His son took the Sam Loyd name and republished a collection of his father's work in the *Cyclopedia of Puzzles* (1914). Though flawed with copious typos, mistakes and missing answers, it remains one of the most varied, exciting and visually appealing sets of puzzles there has ever been.

Sam Loyd may have been an 'ideas vampire' at times, and many of his anecdotes and claims have to be taken at face value, but Loyd's opinion of Dudeney was quite correct: the Englishman did not share his own ability to make a puzzle entertaining, commercially successful and popular. Loyd may not have been the most honest character, but perhaps we can liken him to his early customer Phineas T. Barnum: he too was just giving the public what they wanted – cheap entertainment. Loyd held down a professional job as a popularizer and creator of puzzles for some forty years. Thanks to his pioneering career, many of the classic puzzles have remained in the public consciousness, and others have been able to follow in his footsteps.

The puzzles on the pages that follow are classics that have stood the test of the last century. They are reproduced here in their original form, though with a few minor corrections and abridgements. Some may be challenging, but, approached in the right frame of mind, their solutions are very obtainable. Enjoy your opportunity to pit your wits against Sam Loyd and Henry Dudeney – the puzzle kings.

The Puzzles

THE SQUAREST GAME
ON THE BEACH

My chum and I were taking in the side shows the other day, when we struck what the man told us was the squarest game in the world. There were ten little dummies which you were to knock over with base balls. The man said take as many throws as you like at a cent a piece and stand as close as you please. Add up the numbers on all the men that you knock out and when the sum amounts to exactly 50, neither more nor less, you get a genuine Maggie Cline cigar with a gold band, worth a quarter.

Our money gave out before we learned how to win, and we noticed that lots of people didn't smoke any more Maggie Clines than we did. Can you show how we might have made exactly 50 points, and won a Maggie Cline cigar with a gold band around it?

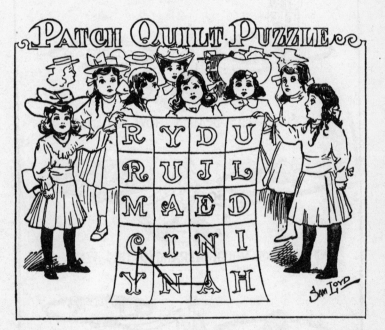

The children have worked all of their names into a wonderful patch quilt puzzle, which they are going to present to their teacher. Commence wherever you please and go from square to square, and see how many names you can discover. Beginning at N, for example, as shown by the lines, you can spell NANCY, but when you find all of the others you will know just how many scholars went to this school in Puzzleland.

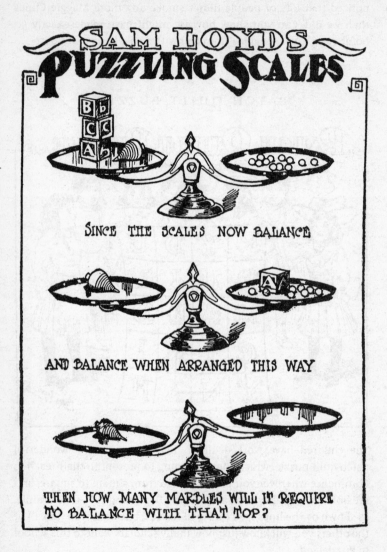

A PUZZLE IN OIL AND VINEGAR

'I started in business with an odd lot of oil and vinegar,' said a shrewd speculator. 'My first customer bought $14 worth of each, paying twice as much for oil as for vinegar per gallon, and left me but one barrel. Now, see if you can guess what that barrel was worth?'

REAL ESTATE PUZZLE

While the suburban boom is on we will take occasion to tell how a real estate speculator stopped off at a wrong station, and, having a couple of hours to wait for the next train, made a quick turn. He bought a piece of land for $243, divided it into lots, and sold them back to the original owners at $18 per lot, and cleaned up the whole transaction before his train arrived. He made a profit on the deal just equal to his first cost price of six lots, so you are asked to tell just how many lots were laid out in the town of Boomville.

MOTHER'S JAM PUZZLE

Mrs. Hubbard has invented a clever system for keeping tabs on her blackberry jam. She filled twenty-five jars and arranged the three sizes so as to have twenty quarts on each shelf. Can you guess her secret so as to tell how much one of the big jars contains?

It is not generally known that the celebrated piece of Venetian mosaic by Domechio, known as the Guido collection of Roman heads, was originally divided into two square groups, which were discovered at different periods. They were brought together and restored into what is supposed to be their correct form, in 1671. Considerable discussion was aroused regarding the possibility as well as appropriateness of uniting the collections of 25 heads into one square, as it now exists, when, apparently by accident, it was discovered that each of the two squares consisted of several pieces which would fit together into one 5 × 5 piece as shown.

It is a pretty puzzle, and as all puzzles, like mathematical propositions, can be worked backwards to advantage at times, we will reverse the problem, and ask you to divide the large square into the fewest number of pieces which can be refitted into two squares. In this puzzle we must cut on the lines only, so as not to destroy the heads.

I recently came across a vividly written description of the fifteenth century craze for gambling, wherein among other games of skill or chance upon which the cavaliers were wont to bet so recklessly, mention was made of the sport of laying eggs upon a cloth. Here possibly was the true solution of the Columbus egg story, which despite its clever moral has always seemed too tame for such a fierce period.

It is simply a game to be played between two opponents placing eggs alternately upon a square napkin in order to see who can win by placing the last egg. After an egg is placed it must not be moved or touched by another one, but as the size of the napkin or the eggs, as well as the variable distances which may occur between them, is of no importance, it would look as if the question of placing the last egg was a matter of luck or chance, and yet the winning trick, as the great navigator remarked, 'is the easiest thing in the world when you are shown how!'

So much has been said about the wonderful powers of teaching the deaf and dumb to carry on a wordless conversation by reading or interpreting the motions of the lips, that I propose to introduce a startling puzzle, which will at first appear almost incredible.

Here is a class of a dozen boys, who, being called up to give their names were photographed by the instantaneous process just as each one was commencing to pronounce his own name.

The twelve names were Oom, Alden, Eastman, Alfred, Arthur, Luke, Fletcher, Matthew, Theodore, Richard, Shirmer and Hisswald. Now it would not seem possible to be able to give the correct name to each of the twelve boys, but if you will practice the list over to each one, you will find it not a difficult task to locate the proper name for every one of the boys. The puzzle, of course, is to guess the names of the twelve boys correctly.

This odd puzzle is built upon the recent claim of a French astronomer to have located a new star of the first magnitude. He says that the popular impression held by scientists of there being no more stars is based entirely upon the discovery by a clever little puzzlist that the letters A-S-T-R-O-N-O-M-E-R-S form the pretty anagram 'no more stars'. We may mention that a still more appropriate anagram can be made with the same eleven letters.

The sketch shows the learned professor describing his new discovery to his brother astronomers. He has drawn the location of fifteen stars of different magnitudes, and is now going to show the position in the firmament of his new discovery.

See if you can draw the form of a five-pointed star which shall be larger than any of the others, and yet not touch one of them!

A schoolboy, who was one of those smart Alecs who think that they know it all, was quizzing a hod carrier about the weight of a brick, if a brick weighs three-quarters of a brick and three-quarters of a pound, when the man retorted by saying: 'Now, every one should stick to his trade; you are up on figures and I am up on the ladder, so I will agree to guess your puzzle if you will tell me the correct answer to mine. Just figure out the fewest number of steps one has to take to go up and down and up this ladder, so as to be twice on the ground and twice on the top. Every step must be of the same height and all of the steps must be used the same number of times?'

There is no catch or pun about this puzzle. It is straight goods, and yet it is safe to say that our young folks will have to go up and down that ladder many times before they hit upon the correct answer.

THE CANALS ON MARS

Here is a map of the newly discovered waterways in our nearest neighbor planet, Mars. See if you can make a tour of all of the towns and back to point of beginning without going through any one spot twice. Commence at the south pole from the letter T, spell a complete sentence, using each letter once. The puzzle was sent to a leading magazine, where over fifty thousand correspondents unanimously reported: 'There is no possible way,' and yet it is a very simple puzzle.

PUZZLING PRATTLE

Two school children, who were all tangled up in their reckoning of the days of the week, paused to straighten matters out over a circus poster, when little Priscilla, who was hinting for an invitation to the show, remarked to John: 'When the day after to-morrow is yesterday, "to-day" will be as far from Sunday as that day was which was "to-day" when the day before yesterday was to-morrow!' On what day of the week did this puzzling prattle occur?

To show how the clever people of Puzzleland, like everybody else all over the world, try to get the better of a bargain, it may be mentioned that gingerbread is always made in odd shapes, marked off in so many little squares for a penny. But there is always a puzzle connected with gingerbread in Puzzleland which gives purchasers a chance to win the whole cake for nothing. This puzzle is to find how to cut the cake on the lines in two pieces which can be fitted together so as to form an 8 × 8 square!

PUZZLE OF THE EDUCATED CATS

These trained cats have arranged their slates so as to spell the word SPARKLING. One cat picks up its slate and runs away, and the slates then spell an eight-letter word; then another slate is carried away, and then another, and so on until but one is left, but in each and every case the remaining letters without any changing spell a correct word. What are the different words?

THE MOTOR CAR RACE

I happened to be at a motor car race at Brooklands, when one spectator said to another, while a number of cars were whirling round and round the circular track:

'There's Gogglesmith – that man in the white car!'

'Yes, I see,' was the reply; 'but how many cars are running in this race?'

Then came this curious rejoinder:

'One-third of the cars in front of Gogglesmith added to three-quarters of those behind him will give you the answer.'

Now, can you tell how many cars were running in the race?

A REMARKABLE PLANT

Three-quarters of a cross, a circle next,
  Two semicircles then an upright meet;
A triangle upon two legs is set,
  Two semicircles, and a ring complete.

This will give you the name of a well-known plant, greatly appreciated by Thomas Atkins in the trenches.

THE CHALKED NUMBERS

We laughed greatly at a pretty jest on the part of Major Trenchard, a merry friend of the Squire's. With a piece of chalk he marked a different number on the backs of eight lads who were at the party. Then, it seems, he divided them in two groups, as shown in the illustration, 1, 2, 3, 4 being on one side, and 5, 7, 8, 9 on the other. It will be seen that the numbers of the left-hand group add up to 10, while the numbers in the other group add up to 29. The Major's puzzle was to rearrange the eight boys in two new groups, so that the four numbers in each group should add up alike. The Squire's niece asked if the 5 should not be a 6; but the Major explained that the numbers were quite correct if properly regarded.

THE THIRTY-THREE PEARLS

'A man I know,' said Teddy Nicholson at a certain family party, 'possesses a string of thirty-three pearls. The middle pearl is the largest and best of all, and the others are so selected and arranged that, starting from one end, each successive pearl is worth £100 more than the preceding one, right up to the big pearl. From the other end the pearls increase in value by £150 up to the large pearl. The whole string is worth £65,000. What is the value of that large pearl?'

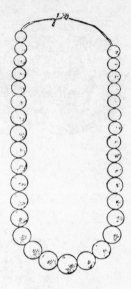

AN EASY DISSECTION PUZZLE

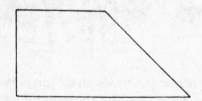

First, cut out a piece of paper or cardboard of the shape shown in the illustration. It will be seen at once that the proportions are simply those of a square attached to half of another similar square, divided diagonally. The puzzle is to cut it into four pieces all of precisely the same size and shape.

BICYCLE TOUR

The map shows twenty-three prominent cities of the State of Pennsylvania connected by bicycle routes of more or less artistic design. The problem is a very simple one: merely start on your summer outing and go from Philadelphia to Erie, passing through every one of the cities but once and without going over any road twice. That is all there is to it. The cities are numbered so as to enable solvers to describe their routes by a sequence of figures. In this trip the usual practice of getting there by the 'shortest route possible' will be dispensed with. Just get there without minding the cyclometer, and get an answer by giving the sequence of towns passed through.

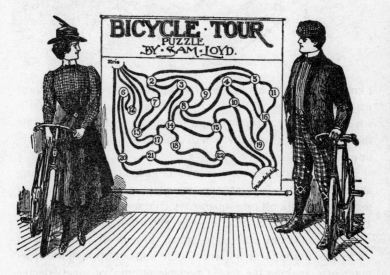

MILITARY TACTICS BY SAM LOYD

I knew the veteran hero General Winfield Scott as a skillful chess player, and now recall the fact of building a curious chess puzzle, which I intended to present to him, if occasion occurred, to illustrate the military tactics of a division of soldiers passing through a public park.

It does not require a knowledge of the game, as it is a puzzle, pure and simple; but to facilitate explanation, I have taken the liberty of marking the park off into squares, which resemble a checker board. The problem, however, is quite pretty: Show how a military division should enter at one outer gate, march through all of the squares under the triumphal arch in the middle, and out through the other outer gate, making the fewest possible number of ninety-degree turns.

Mark an 8 × 8 diagram of sixty-four squares upon a piece of paper and then essay with a pencil to pass over every square beginning and ending at the gates shown, and it is safe to say you will make several attempts before you get the shortest possible answer, which is so pretty that you will know when you have guessed it.

MILKMAN'S PUZZLE

There are practical problems in all trades, so it is safe to say that no one is an adept at his business unless he has picked up a few wrinkles which pertain to his calling. Honest John says that what he 'don't know about milk is scarcely worth mentioning', but he was nearly flabbergasted once when he had nothing but two ten gallon cans full of milk, and two customers with a five and a four quart measure wanted two quarts put into each measure.

It is a juggling trick pure and simple, devoid of trick or device, but it calls for much cleverness to get two exact quarts of milk into those measures employing no receptacles of any kind except the two measures and the two full cans. You can try the problem with the fullest assurance that it is a legitimate proposition and not a silly catch.

Note: 4 quarts = 1 gallon

Here's a problem which has been puzzling Clancy ever since he got on the force. He has made a diagram of the situation and asks for the assistance of our clever puzzlists. He patrols seven blocks of the eighth ward, beginning and ending his nightly tour from the point he is indicating at the corner of Avenue A and Second Street. His orders are to patrol an uneven number of blocks on each street and avenue, so, as shown by the route, he goes either one, three, five or seven blocks before he turns.

He knows all the servant girls in the houses he passes and some of them he says are right smart and pert, but before he selects a wife he would like to extend his route so as to discover a dark eyed beauty named Maggie Murphy, who he thinks lives in one of the houses off of his beat. You see he only passes those white houses and he wishes to find a route which complies to the regulations about only going an odd number of blocks on each avenue and street but will take him past the greatest possible number of houses.

Now, see if you can aid Clancy in the search for Maggie Murphy's home.

The sketch shows a migratory couple, who, having had their worldly belongings landed by contract into their cozy little six-room flat, have been wrestling for several hours with a puzzle. They have five large articles, the bedstead, table, sofa, ice box and bureau, which are so bulky that no two can be placed in any one room at the same time on account of the close packing of the other small articles, which minor belongings, however, need not be mentioned, as pertaining to the problem. It so happens, however, that the ice box and the bedstead were placed by the furniture wreckers in the wrong rooms, and the man and his good wife have been struggling for several hours to transpose them.

The man has marked out a diagram of his flat on the table, with the connecting doors as shown, and has placed five articles on the squares to represent the pieces which are to be moved. It is only necessary to mention that the whisky flask represents the bedstead and the scrubbing brush may be taken for the ice box, and that you are to transpose the positions of these two articles by moving one piece at a time in a sequence of plays in which the flat-iron, pepper box and mouse trap may be used to advantage.

Solve the puzzle by the use of small pieces of paper for counters placed on the diagram of the flat. In how few moves can you transpose the position of the whisky flask and the scrubbing brush?

Start from that heart in the center, and go three steps in a straight line in any one of the eight directions, north, south, east or west, or on the bias, as the ladies say, northeast, northwest, southeast or southwest. When you have gone three steps in a straight line, you will reach a square with a number on it, which indicates the second day's journey, as many steps as it tells, in a straight line in any one of the eight directions. From this new point when reached, march on again according to the number indicated, and continue on, following the requirements of the numbers reached, until you come upon a square with a number which will carry you just one step beyond the border, when you are supposed to be out of the woods and can holler all you want, as you will have solved the puzzle.

We call attention to Alice's trip through Wonderland and her remarkable experiences with the Cheshire cat which had such a way of vanishing away into thin air, so that nothing but its irresistible smile remained. When Alice first saw her feline friend she desired to find out what species of animal it was, and as they always ask questions in Wonderland by writing, she wrote out her query. But as they generally read things backward, or up and down in Wonderland, she wrote it as shown in the puzzle.

This permits readers to commence and end where they please, just as they should in Wonderland; but, as Lewis Carroll forgot to give the answer to his conundrum of why a desk was like a crow, he also forgot the main question in this riddle, which is simply to tell how many ways there are to read the question: 'Was it a cat I saw?'

OUTWITTING THE WEIGHING MACHINE

This puzzle is so named because old weighing machines worked on the principle of requiring one coin each time the needle rested at the zero mark. The method below allows several weights to be ascertained for just one coin.

Some school children had discovered that by getting on a weighing machine in couples, and then exchanging places, one at a time, they could get the correct weight of a whole party on the payment of but one cent. They found that in couples they weighed 129 pounds, 125 pounds, 124 pounds, 123 pounds, 122 pounds, 121 pounds, 120 pounds, 118 pounds, 116 pounds and 114 pounds. What was the weight of each one of the five little girls if taken separately?

The old Dutch game of Kugelspiel, from which the modern ten pin alley was derived, used to be played with thirteen pins placed in a row, so that only one or two pins could be knocked out at one shot. The bowlers stood so close to the pins that it did not call for much skill to hit any single pin, or two adjacent ones, which the player desired to knock down. At first it would look as if it made no difference whether one or two pins got knocked down, for the players bowled alternately, one ball at a time, and the point of the game was to see who could knock down the last pin.

It is assumed that they played with such skill that any desired pin could be hit at will, for, according to the old rules, a player loses if he scores a single miss. Supposing, therefore, that a player can hit any single pin or any two adjacent ones he wishes and that they play alternately, one ball at a time, who can solve the problem that now confronts Rip Van Winkle?

The little man of the mountain with whom he is playing has just rolled a ball and knocked out pin No. 2. Rip has the choice of twenty-two different plays: any one of the twelve single pins, or any one of the ten middle spots which will bring down two pins. Which is his best shot to win the game? It is assumed that the game is continued to the end, with the best possible play on both sides.

A STUDY IN EGGS

Prof. Burbanks, who developed the seedless orange and coreless apple, and proved that figs might grow on thistles and that leopards can change their spots by lying down on some other spots, has been playing all sorts of pranks with his domestic fowls. He has produced a brand of nestless chickens who are trained to fill up a crate of eggs without the useless intermediary nests, thereby saving the labor of packing and counting.

Each hen keeps account of her own eggs by making it a rule never to lay more than two eggs in line in any possible direction, up and down, right and left, or on the diagonals. This is a very pretty puzzle, which restricts, or sort of unionizes the work of the hens, and betrays a higher intelligence than is developed by the goose, who cannot be taught to perform the feat.

Can you tell how many eggs it is possible to place in this 6 × 6 crate without having more than two eggs in a row? We have placed the first two, so you must place no more on that diagonal.

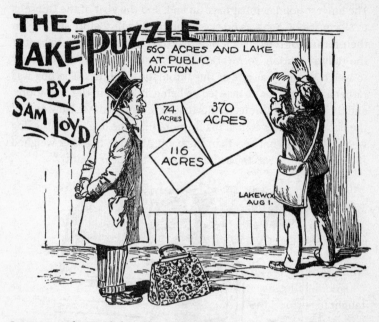

I went to Lakewood the other day to attend an auction sale of some land, but did not make any purchases on account of a peculiar problem which developed regarding what the buyer would get for his money. It was advertised as shown in the posters on the fence as 560 acres, including a lake. The three plots show up the 560 acres without the lake, but as the lake was included in the sale, I, as well as other would-be purchasers, wished to know whether the lake area was really deducted from the land.

The auctioneer guaranteed 560 acres 'more or less', which was not satisfactory to the purchasers, so we left him arguing with some Katy Dids, and shouting to the bullfrogs in the lake, which in reality was a swamp.

The question which I ask our puzzlists who revel in just such questions, is to determine just how many acres there would be in that triangular lake, surrounded as shown by square plots of 370, 116 and 74 acres.

BABY'S WEIGHT

The longest holiday must have an end, and the visit of the Dobsons to Slocombe-on-Sea was no exception to the rule. Before starting on their return journey they found that they had some time to wait at the railway station, so Mr. Dobson thought it a good opportunity to weigh the baby at one of the automatic machines. The dog was rather a nuisance, as he insisted on being included in the operations, and these are the curious results that were obtained. Mr. Dobson and the baby together weighed 162 lb. more than the dog, while the dog weighed 70 per cent less than the baby. All three together weighed 180 lb. Now, what was the actual weight of that dear infant?

THE WAY TO BERLIN

Look at the accompanying chart and see if you can discover the best way from London to Berlin. The lines represent stages from town to town, and it is necessary to get from London to Berlin in an even number of stages. You will find no difficulty in getting there in 3, 5, 7, or 11 stages, but these are odd numbers and will not do. The reason they are odd is that they all omit the sea pas-

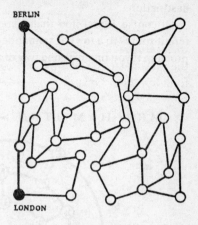

sage, a very necessary stage. If you get to your destination in an even number of stages, it will be because you have crossed the North Sea. Which line represents the stage of crossing the North Sea?

A BANK HOLIDAY PUZZLE

Two friends were spending their bank holiday on a cycling trip. Stopping for a rest at a village inn, they consulted a route map, which is represented in our illustration in a simplified form, for the puzzle is interesting enough without all the original com-

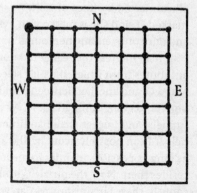

plexities. They started from the town in the top left-hand corner. It will be seen that there are forty-two such towns, all connected by straight roads. Now they discovered that there are exactly eighty-four different routes by which they may reach their destination, always travelling either due south or due east. The puzzle is to discover which town is their destination.

Of course, if you find that there are more than eighty-four different routes to a town it cannot be the right one. It is quite an easy problem if you hit on a good way of attacking it.

MRS. HAMILTON'S HOLIDAY TOUR

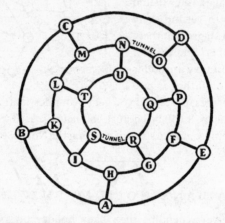

The illustration represents a plan, very much simplified for puzzle purposes, for a tour that my friend Mrs. Hamilton proposed to make in the early summer. It will be seen that there are twenty towns, all connected by lines of railways. Mrs. Hamilton lives at the town marked H, and she wants to visit every one of the other towns once, and once only, ending her tour at home.

It may interest the reader to know that there are just sixty different routes from which she may select. But there is a tunnel between N and O, and another between R and S, and the good lady very much objects to going through these. As she put it to me, 'I never did like tunnels, and I never shall like tunnels, and I never go through tunnels if I can possibly avoid it.' She also wants to delay her visit to D as long as possible, in order to meet the convenience of a friend who resides there. Now, the puzzle is to show Mrs. Hamilton her very best route in these circumstances. Can you help her?

THE NOBLE DEMOISELLE

Seated one night in the hall of the castle, Sir Hugh desired the company to fill their cups and listen while he told the tale of his adventure as a youth in rescuing from captivity a noble demoiselle who was languishing in the dungeon of the castle belonging to his father's greatest enemy. The story was a thrilling one, and when he related the final escape from all the dangers and horrors of the great Death's-head Dungeon with the fair but unconscious maiden in his arms, all exclaimed, "Twas marvellous valiant!' But Sir Hugh said, 'I would never have turned from my purpose, not even to save my body from the bernicles.'

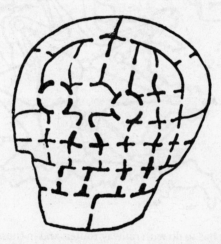

Sir Hugh then produced a plan of the thirty-five cells in the dungeon and asked his companions to discover the particular cell that the demoiselle occupied. He said that if you started at one of the outside cells and passed through every doorway once, and once only, you were bound to end at the cell that was sought. Can you find the cell? Unless you start at the correct outside cell it is impossible to pass through all the doorways once and once only. Try tracing out the route with your pencil.

This puzzle has to do with railway routes, and in these days of much travelling should prove useful. The map of England shows twenty-four towns, connected by a system of railways. A resident at the town marked A at the top of the map proposes to visit every one of the towns once and only once, and to finish up his tour at Z. This would be easy enough if he were able to cut across country by road, as well as by rail, but he is not. How does he perform the feat? Take your pencil and, starting from A, pass from town to town, making a dot in the towns you have visited, and see if you can end at Z.

NELSON'S COLUMN

During a Nelson celebration I was standing in Trafalgar Square with a friend of puzzling proclivities. He had for some time been gazing at the column in an abstracted way, and seemed quite unconscious of the casual remarks that I addressed to him.

'What are you dreaming about?' I said at last.

' Two feet —' he murmured.

'Somebody's Trilbys?' I inquired.

'Five times round —'

'Two feet, five times round! What on earth are you saying?'

'Wait a minute,' he said, beginning to figure something out on the back of an envelope. I now detected that he was in the throes of producing a new problem of some sort, for I well knew his methods of working at these things.

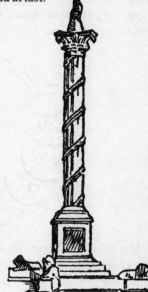

'Here you are!' he suddenly exclaimed. 'That's it! A very interesting little puzzle. The height of the shaft of the Nelson Column being 200 feet and its circumference 16 feet 8 inches, it is wreathed in a spiral garland which passes round it exactly five times. What is the length of the garland? It looks rather difficult, but is really remarkably easy.'

He was right. The puzzle is quite easy if properly attacked. Of course the height and circumference are not correct, but chosen for the purposes of the puzzle. The artist has also intentionally drawn the cylindrical shaft of the column of equal circumference throughout. If it were tapering, the puzzle would be less easy.

THE NUMBER-CHECKS PUZZLE

Where a large number of workmen are employed on a building it is customary to provide every man with a little disc bearing his number. These are hung on a board by the men as they arrive, and serve as a check on punctuality. Now, I once noticed a foreman remove a number of these checks from his board and place them on a split-ring which he carried in his pocket. This at once gave me the idea for a good puzzle.

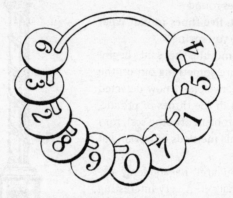

It will be seen from the illustration that there are ten of these checks on a ring, numbered 1 to 9 and 0. The puzzle is to divide them into three groups without taking any off the ring, so that the first group multiplied by the second makes the third group. For example, we can divide them into the three groups 2 – 8 9 0 7 – 1 5 4 6 3, by bringing the 6 and the 3 round to the 4, but unfortunately the first two when multiplied together do not make the third. Can you separate them correctly? Of course, you may have as many of the checks as you like in any group.

THE MILLER'S PUZZLE

The Miller took the company aside and showed them nine sacks of flour that were standing as depicted in the sketch. 'Now, hearken, all and some,' said he, 'while that I do set ye the riddle of the nine sacks of flour. And mark ye, my lords and masters, that there be single sacks on the outside, pairs next unto them, and three together in the middle thereof. By Saint Benedict, it doth so happen that if we do but multiply the pair, 28, by the single one, 7, the answer is 196, which is of a truth the number shown by the sacks in the middle. Yet it be not true that the other pair, 34, when so multiplied by its neighbour, 5, will also make 196. Wherefore I do beg you, gentle sirs, so to place anew the nine sacks with as little trouble as possible that each pair when thus multiplied by its single neighbour shall make the number in the middle.'

As the Miller has stipulated in effect that as few bags as possible shall be moved, there is only one answer to this puzzle, which everybody should be able to solve.

THE RIDDLE OF THE TILED HEARTH

It seems that it was Friar Andrew who first managed to 'rede the riddle of the Tiled Hearth'. Yet it was a simple enough little puzzle. The square hearth, where they burnt their Yule logs and round which they had such merry carousings, was floored with sixteen large ornamental tiles. When these became cracked and burnt with the heat of the great fire, it was decided to put down new tiles, which had to be selected from four different patterns (the Cross, the Fleur-de-lys, the Lion, and the Star); but plain tiles were also available.

The Abbot proposed that they should be laid as shown in our sketch, without any plain tiles at all; but Brother Richard broke in:

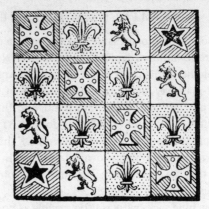

'Let these sixteen tiles be so placed that no tile shall be in line with another of the same design' (he meant, of course, not in line horizontally, vertically, or diagonally) 'and in such manner that as few plain tiles as possible be required.' When the monks handed in their plans it was found that only Friar Andrew had hit upon the correct answer, even Friar Richard himself being wrong. All had used too many plain tiles.

THE SPIDER AND THE FLY

Inside a rectangular room, measuring 30 feet in length and 12 feet in width and height, a spider is at a point on the middle of one of the end walls, 1 foot from the ceiling, as at A; and a fly is on the opposite wall, 1 foot from the floor in the centre, as shown at B. What is the shortest distance that the spider must crawl in order to reach the fly, which remains stationary? Of course the spider never drops or uses its web, but crawls fairly.

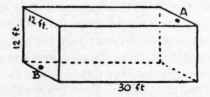

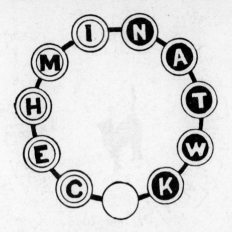

In the illustration we have eleven discs in a circle. On five of the discs we place white counters with black letters – as shown – and on five other discs the black counters with white letters. The bottom disc is left vacant. Starting thus, it is required to get the counters into order so that they spell the word 'Twickenham' in a clockwise direction, leaving the vacant disc in the original position. The black counters move in the direction that a clock-hand revolves, and the white counters go the opposite way. A counter may jump over one of the opposite colour if the vacant disc is next beyond. Thus, if your first move is with K, then C can jump over K. If then K moves towards E, you may next jump W over C, and so on. The puzzle may be solved in twenty-six moves. Remember: a counter cannot jump over one of its own colour.

THE MOUSE-TRAP PUZZLE

This is a modern version, with a difference, of an old puzzle of the same name. Number twenty-one cards, 1, 2, 3, etc., up to 21, and place them in a circle in the particular order shown in the illustration. These cards represent mice. You start from any card, calling that card 'one', and count, 'one, two, three', etc. in a clockwise direction, and when your count agrees with the number on the card, you have made a 'catch', and you remove the card. Then start at the next card, calling that 'one', and try again to make another 'catch'. And so on. Supposing you start at 18, calling that card 'one', your first 'catch' will be 19. Remove 19 and your next 'catch' is 10. Remove 10 and your next 'catch' is 1. Remove the 1, and if you count up to 21 (you must never go beyond), you cannot make another 'catch'.

Now, the ideal is to 'catch' all the twenty-one mice, but this is not here possible, and if it were it would merely require twenty-one different trials, at the most, to succeed. But the reader may make any two cards change places before he begins. Thus, you can change the 6 with the 2, or the 7 with the 11, or any other pair. This can be done in several ways so as to enable you to 'catch' all the twenty-one mice, if you then start at the right place. You may never pass over a 'catch'; you must always remove the card and start afresh.

THE SIXTEEN SHEEP

Here is a new puzzle with matches and counters or coins. In the illustration the matches represent hurdles and the counters sheep. The sixteen hurdles on the outside, and the sheep, must be regarded as immovable; the puzzle has to do entirely with the nine hurdles on the inside. It will be seen that at present these nine hurdles enclose four groups of 8, 3, 3, and 2 sheep. The farmer requires to readjust some of the hurdles so as to enclose 6, 6, and 4 sheep. Can you do it by only replacing two hurdles? When you have succeeded, then try to do it by replacing three hurdles; then four, five, six and seven in succession. Of course, the hurdles must be legitimately laid on the dotted lines, and no such tricks are allowed as leaving unconnected ends of hurdles, or two hurdles placed side by side, or merely making hurdles change places. In fact, the conditions are so simple that any farm labourer will understand directly.

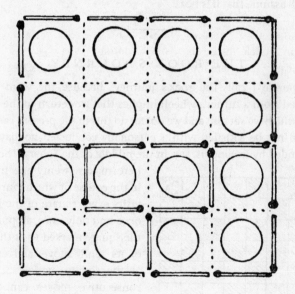

THE ROOK'S TOUR

The puzzle is to move the single rook over the whole board, so that it shall visit every square of the board once, and only once, and end its tour on the square from which it starts. You have to do this in as few moves as possible, and unless you are very careful you will take just one move too many. Of course, a square is regarded equally as 'visited' whether you merely

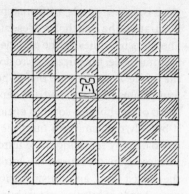

pass over it or make it a stopping-place, and we will not quibble over the point whether the original square is actually visited twice. We will assume that it is not.

THE ROOK'S JOURNEY

This puzzle I call 'The rook's journey', because the word 'tour' (derived from a turner's wheel) implies that we return to the point from which we set out, and we do not do this in the present case. We should not be satisfied with a personally conducted holiday tour that ended by leaving us, say, in the middle of the Sahara. The rook

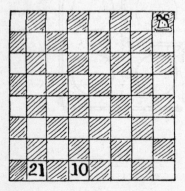

here makes twenty-one moves, in the course of which journey it visits every square of the board once and only once, stopping at the square marked 10 at the end of its tenth move, and ending at the square marked 21. Two consecutive moves cannot be made in the same direction – that is to say, you must make a turn after every move.

ANCIENT CHINESE PUZZLE

This next puzzle is supposed to be Chinese, many hundreds of years old, and never fails to interest. White to play and mate, moving each of the three pieces once, and once only.

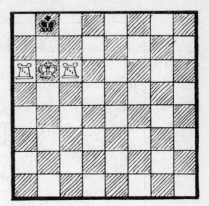

DOMINOES IN PROGRESSION

It will be seen that I have played six dominoes, in the illustration, in accordance with the ordinary rules of the game, 4 against 4, 1 against 1, and so on, and yet the sum of the spots on the successive dominoes, 4, 5, 6, 7, 8, 9, are in arithmetical progression; that is, the numbers taken in order have a common difference of 1. In how many different ways may we play six dominoes, from an ordinary box of twenty-eight, so that the numbers on them may lie in arithmetical progression? We must always play from left to right, and numbers in decreasing arithmetical progression (such as 9, 8, 7, 6, 5, 4) are not admissible.

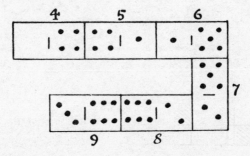

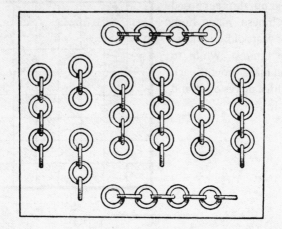

Dudeney writes: This is a puzzle based on a pretty little idea first dealt with by the late Mr. Sam Loyd. A man had nine pieces of chain, as shown in the illustration. He wanted to join these fifty links into one endless chain. It will cost a penny to open any link and twopence to weld a link together again, but he could buy a new endless chain of the same character and quality for 2s. 2d. What was the cheapest course for him to adopt? Unless the reader is cunning he may find himself a good way out in his answer.

CHAPTER 2

The World of Words

'Wrote to Tenniel on the subject of an idea which I first entered in my memorandum book, Jan 8th, of printing a little book of original puzzles etc. which I think of calling *Alice's Puzzle-Book*.' So Lewis Carroll wrote in his diary for the entry of 1 March 1875. By 1885, the idea had evolved into: 'A collection of Games and Puzzles of my devising, with fairy pictured by Miss E. G. Thomson. This might also contain my *Memoria Technica* for dates, etc., my "cipher-writing", scheme for Letter-registration, etc. etc.' In 1893, one of his novels announced a forthcoming tome entitled *Original Games and Puzzles*. Alas, the book never materialized, but we are still able to value Carroll's contributions to the world of puzzles.

THE PUPPET MASTER

Carroll was born Charles Lutwidge Dodgson in Daresbury, a tiny village near Warrington, Cheshire, on 27 January 1832. His life is full of contrasts – in particular, although he became a mathematics lecturer he is most famous for his use of words, writing the children's fantasy novel *Alice's Adventures in Wonderland*,

Lewis Carroll

its sequel *Through the Looking-Glass*, and the poems *The Hunting of the Snark* and 'Jabberwocky'.

Dodgson began studying mathematics at his father's alma mater, Christ Church, Oxford, in January 1851. It was a difficult time for him, as his mother died two days into his studies, and his work became erratic and patchy. Nevertheless, his talent at mathematics was recognized, and after graduating with first-class honours he took up a lectureship in 1855, a job he was to stay in until 1881.

He didn't like academia or even mathematics particularly, and was prone to making mistakes. In the company of adults his personality was dull, but he loved entertaining children. He delighted his brothers and sisters with magic shows and puppet plays, yet his day job in abstract mathematics couldn't have been further from such amusements.

However, 1856 was a good year, with several outlets providing for more creative work. In February, Dodgson submitted poems for a short-lived publication called *The Train*. To differentiate this work from his academic output, he needed a pen name – but what alias was he to use? He offered a number of alternatives to the editor, Edmund Yates, including 'Dares' (a shortened version of his birthplace), 'Edgar U. C. Westhill', 'Edgar Cuthwellis' (both anagrams of Charles Lutwidge) and 'Lewis Carroll' (a Latinized variation of Lutwidge Charles). Yates plumped for Lewis Carroll, and that was the name under which Dodgson's poem 'Solitude' appeared the following month. Around that time, his Oxford chum Reginald Southey persuaded Carroll to buy his first camera, which led to a long and successful sideline as a photographer.

AN ACROSTIC FOR ALICE

In April that same year, Carroll was photographing Oxford's cathedral when he met Henry Liddell, a new dean of Christ Church, and his family. One of his daughters, Alice, was almost four years old at the time. Carroll became a close friend of the family, and was soon taking some of the Liddell children out on regular trips. On a boating expedition on the river Isis in 1862, in the company of his friend Robinson Duckworth and Lorina,

Edith and Alice Liddell, Carroll told one of his invented stories, which delighted Alice so much that she begged him to put it down on paper. It wasn't until late into 1864 that a handwritten manuscript (*Alice's Adventures Under Ground*) was delivered to her.

If Carroll took his time to do things, he was certainly tenacious and full of ideas. He harangued his publisher Alexander Macmillan (co-founder of what is now the Macmillan Group) with endless demands on how his books should look: he wanted books with various different coloured bindings, text printed in gold type, and parcels of books to be tied in a particular way (illustrated with a 'helpful' diagram). Nevertheless, Macmillan liked what he saw when Carroll presented him with an unfinished manuscript in 1863, and so with the new title *Alice's Adventures in Wonderland* his first major work was published, in 1865.

Lest anyone be in any doubt of the true identity of the book's protagonist, at the end of the sequel *Through the Looking-Glass, and What Alice Found There* is an untitled poem. It hides an acrostic – the name Alice Pleasance Liddell is formed by the first letter of each line.

> *A boat beneath a sunny sky,*
> *Lingering onward dreamily*
> *In an evening of July –*
>
> *Children three that nestle near,*
> *Eager eye and willing ear,*
> *Pleased a simple tale to hear –*
>
> *Long has paled that sunny sky:*
> *Echoes fade and memories die:*
> *Autumn frosts have slain July.*

Still she haunts me, phantomwise,
Alice moving under skies
Never seen by waking eyes.

Children yet, the tale to hear,
Eager eye and willing ear,
Lovingly shall nestle near.

In a Wonderland they lie,
Dreaming as the days go by,
Dreaming as the summers die:

Ever drifting down the stream –
Lingering in the golden dream –
Life, what is it but a dream?

Wonderland was a runaway success, and brought Carroll unexpected fame and fortune. There is a story, sadly probably untrue, that Queen Victoria read *Adventures in Wonderland* and requested the author to send her another book of his making. Carroll is said to have sent her *An Elementary Treatise on Determinants and Their Application to Simultaneous Linear Equations and Algebraical Geometry, For the Use of Beginners.*

THE FATHER OF INVENTION

Carroll published on a panorama of different topics. He was constantly inventing and scheming, always looking for a better way to do things. Irritated by the lack of good material for performing in toy puppet theatres, he wrote new scripts of his own. Irked by the unfairness of tennis, where it is technically possible for the player who won fewer points to win the overall match, he released a pamphlet entitled *Lawn Tennis Tournaments: The True Method of Assigning Prizes, with a Proof of the Fallacy of the Present Method*.

He published pamphlets on how to memorize dates, how to censor Shakespeare (to avoid offending young girls), a system for calculating postage rates and a list of common errors in spelling. He came up with ideas for putting pegs on chess pieces to form a travelling chess set, proposed a form of sticky tape with glue on both sides, and developed an early version of Scrabble: 'December 19, 1880: The idea occurred to me that a game might be made of letters, to be moved about on a chessboard till they form words.'

Other things on his mind included a plan for controlling the traffic at Covent Garden, and electoral reform: 'June 3, 1884: Concocted a new "Proportional Representation" scheme, far the best I have yet devised. The chief novelty in it is giving to each candidate the power of transferring to any other candidate, the votes given for him.'

PILLOW PUZZLES

Although Carroll never got round to completing his aforementioned puzzle book, his playfulness with words – and further evidence of his sheer cheek – is evident in his writing. Several of his letters to friends, young and old, consisted of amusing twists and tricks. One was written backwards, not only in mirror-writing but with the words listed in the reverse order. Another was written as a rebus puzzle, with small pictures taking the place of some of the words.

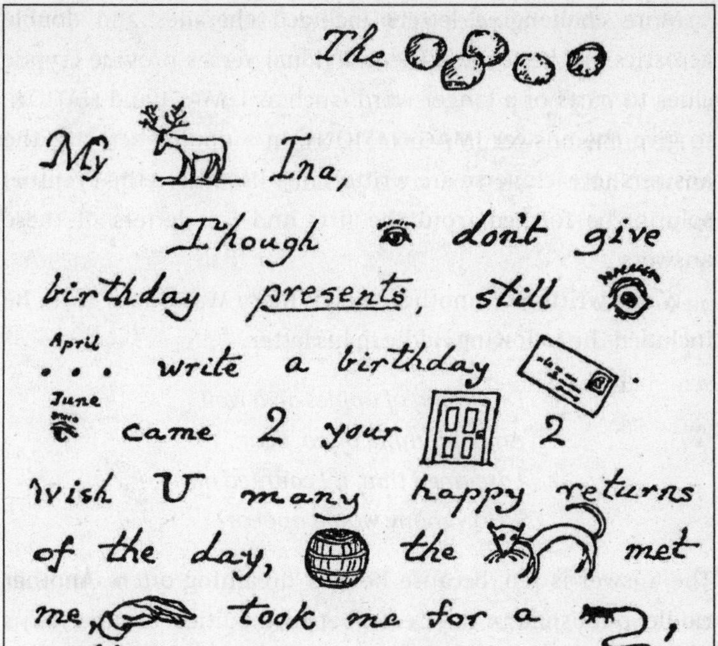

Carroll's rebus letter

More challenging letters included charades and double acrostics. In the former, the individual verses provide cryptic clues to parts of a longer word (such as I, MAGI and NATION, to give the answer IMAGINATION). In a double acrostic, the answers to each verse are written in a list where the eventual solution is formed from the first and last letters of these answers.

When writing to another friend, Mary Watson, in 1870, he included the following riddle in his letter:

> *Dreaming of apples on a wall,*
> *And dreaming often, dear,*
> *I dreamed that, if I counted all,*
> *– How many would appear?*

The answer is ten, because he was 'dreaming *often*'. Another riddle, published in the December 1870 edition of *Aunt Judy's Magazine*, was similarly bold:

> *A stick I found that weighed two pound:*
> *I sawed it up one day*
> *In pieces eight of equal weight!*
> *How much did each piece weigh?*

The accurate answer is 'Just less than 4 ounces' because some matter is lost in the form of sawdust.

His most famous riddle is posed by the Mad Hatter in *Alice's Adventures in Wonderland*: 'Why is a raven like a writing-desk?' No answer is given, because Carroll himself did not then have one, though that didn't stop many people guessing what it might be. One of the best offerings, noted by Sam Loyd, was 'Poe wrote on both' – a reference to writer Edgar Allan Poe and his poem 'The Raven'. In the preface to a later edition, Carroll offered his own solution: 'Because it can provide a few notes, tho they are *very* flat; and it is never put with the wrong end in front!'

Since the Middle Ages, anagrams have been a source of amusement and propaganda – in 1610, Louis XIII of France hired Thomas Billon to be his own official royal anagram maker. In a similar vein, Carroll wrote to the press submitting anagrams of the famous names of the day: for Florence Nightingale he came up with FLIT ON, CHEERING ANGEL, and the politicians William Ewart Gladstone and [Benjamin] Disraeli became WILD AGITATOR! MEANS WELL and I LEAD, SIR. Carroll suffered from insomnia, and often created anagrams and other puzzles during his vain attempts to get to sleep. He later published 72 mathematical puzzles, created entirely in his head during these sleepless hours, in a book called *Pillow Problems*.

LITERARY LADDERS

You have probably already encountered Carroll's most famous word puzzle without realizing its source. It first appeared in *Vanity Fair* in 1879, after he wrote to the magazine explaining the rules thus: 'Two words are proposed, of the same length; and the Puzzle consists in linking these together by interposing other words, each of which shall differ from the next word in one letter only … As an example, the word HEAD may be changed into TAIL by interposing the words HEAL, TEAL, TELL, TALL. I call the two given words a Doublet, the interposed words, Links, and the entire series a Chain … It is, perhaps, needless to state that it is *de rigeur* that the links should be English words, such as might be used in good society.'

Carroll's game of Doublets – usually called a word ladder these days – was run in the magazine for four months, although the simplicity of the idea was somewhat marred by the list of strict rules imposed by Carroll on what types of word were allowed. Irked by the laxity in some of the entries sent in by readers, Carroll penned a poem of admonishment to the competition entrants, filled with words such as SPICK, AIN, STEAN and SHENT which Carroll deemed illegal by his rules. It is, without doubt, the most enduring of the many logic, mathematical, board and word games he devised.

Lewis Carroll died a bachelor from bronchial influenza at his sister's house in Guildford, Surrey on 14 January 1898. Despite never producing any mathematical work of great note (his diary entry for 1 January 1855 states 'tried a little mathematics unsuccessfully'), many of his puzzles in physics, chess, logic, probability, codes, algebra, geometry and arithmetic are still reprinted in puzzle compendiums such as this one. Although he was an all-rounder, arguably it is for his wordplay and sense of fun that he is most loved today. *Alice's Puzzle-Book* never saw the light of day, but Carroll's life and work in anagrams and charades, rebuses and riddles, provide an intriguing snapshot into the puzzles of his day.

The Puzzles

―――

FORE WORDS

Limber up your linguistics with this quick quiz.

1. Read forward, I am an outdoor game; read backward, I am to whip. What am I?

2. Which other letter could join this group, and under what circumstances could there be another letter?

B, C, D, G, P, T, _?

3. Concealed in each sentence that follows is the name of a fruit made up of consecutive letters. For example, 'When the doorbell rang, Fid*o ran ge*ntly downstairs' contains ORANGE.

   (a) On the island of Capri, cotton clothes are recommended.

   (b) She had to type a children's Christmas story by noon.

   (c) The same long-winded tale cropped up almost every evening.

   (d) The floodlit match commenced at eight o'clock sharp.

   (e) The tribesmen tried to rob an Anatolian peasant.

   (f) The starving wolf ignored the farmer and made for the poultry run.

4. Which word should fill all the blanks?

   1 _, 2 _, 3 _, 4, 5 _, 6 _, 7 _, MORE

5. Find this ten-letter word by simply replacing the blanks with the letters, N, O, S, Y, using each one twice:

   _ _ _ _ _ _ M _ U _

6. Drop the letters into each column (in some order) to reveal a phrase.

```
B  E  A  G     H     A  E
D  E  A  N  G  E  R  A  O  E
E  E  E  O  H  G  R  A  T  F  D  M
R  X  P  T  R  T  S  E  V  T  L  Y  Y
```

7. Although this appears to be a list of related pairs, all these words are …?

NOTE	SONG
CASH	CHEQUE
OPEN	CLOSED
HYMN	PRAYER
TEXT	PICTURE
DAY	YEAR
WORD	PHRASE
WORK	PLAY

8. What phrase is this? It has four words, of 3, 3, 2, 4 letters.

FO R T UN E

9. Which five-letter word, when the last four letters have been removed, sounds the same? And which five-letter word, when the first four letters have been removed, sounds the same?

10. Start with a particular eight-letter word. If you delete the second and third letters, you're left with a sort of hole often found in a wall. If instead you delete the first and third letters, you're left with a hole found in fabric. And if you were to delete the first and second letters, what remained may one day explore black holes. What is the eight-letter word you started with, which is also a type of hole?

11. Which word do these letters represent? There is a logical sequence.

12. Find the nine-letter word that is spelled out using one silent letter from each of the words below. The first word gives you the first letter, and so on.

HAUTBOY
AISLE
TABLEAUX
BUSINESS
HANDSOME
TWITCHED
FORECASTLE
MNEMONIC
PRAYER

13. What word can be written so that it looks the same forwards, backwards and upside down?

14. What connects all these words:

    BUY, BRING, CATCH, FIGHT, SEEK, TEACH, THINK, WORK?

15. Choose one letter from each line in order to spell out a similar word:

YELLOW

PURPLE

BLACK

GREEN

GREY

RED

16. Which day of the week (in English) can be anagrammed into another common English word? What is the new word that is formed?

17. A man with the same name as the leader of the Apostles (who was an accomplished wind instrument player) went to a shop and, after much deliberation, selected two gallons of the family Piperaceae of the order Piperales that had been preserved in brine or vinegar. How is that story normally told?

18. A lost explorer might utter this phrase. It is also an anagram of which quartet of related words?

TUT! THAT'S NOWHERE – SOS!

19. What sequence goes: First rate, well done!, fool, alluvial deposit, reflected sound, dance, ball game, hostelry, Asian country, Romeo's lover, mass unit, Peru's capital, bug, 11th month, film award, father, Canadian City, Juliet's lover, mountain range, another dance, unvarying, winner, alcoholic drink, Roentgen discovery, type of bet and North Natal native?

20. Which girl's name is this?   *I*

DOUBLE CROSSING

Transfer one letter from one word to the other so that two words of similar meaning are created. For example, if the words were DIED and ANTE then you could take the N over to the left to form the correct couple DINED and ATE.

1.	PEST	CARES
2.	GROVE	ROUT
3.	SHRED	BAN
4.	LICE	RELINE
5.	SALVE	SAVAGE
6.	WHILED	SPURN
7.	OUR	START
8.	FLAT	PUMP
9.	CURT	CAVE
10.	LOPES	SHILLS

RHYME AND REASON

If 'Sprain forearm' is TWIST WRIST, and 'Express elevator' is SWIFT LIFT, find rhyming couplets for the following clues:

1. Not enough (3, 3)
2. Huge hog (3, 3)
3. What a gastronome eats (4, 4)
4. Agree business terms (4, 4)
5. Peak viewing period (5, 4)
6. First woman's clothes? (4, 6)
7. Immobile lorry (5, 5)
8. Cardiograph (5, 5)
9. Extra seating for a visitor (5, 5)
10. Butter, margarine or jam? (5, 6)
11. Extinct animal (6, 5)
12. Where Goldilocks sat (5, 6)
13. Slender projectile (6, 5)
14. Ethical dispute (5, 7)
15. Win back admiration (6, 6)
16. A fall from the top (6, 7)
17. Lovesick cat (7, 6)
18. Tennis equipment cover (7, 6)
19. Scare a strongman (8, 5)
20. Cheese grater (7, 8)
21. Education (7, 9)
22. Realtor's job (8, 7)

23. Horrible pair (8, 7)
24. Afflicted hen (8, 7)
25. Brief encounter (8, 7)
26. Food poisoning panic (8, 8)
27. Educator's facial parts (8, 8)
28. Mends riding trousers (8, 8)

29. 'Hi!' (8, 8)
30. Best part of the sunset (8, 9)
31. Cause of divorce? (9, 8)
32. Faulty instruction (9, 9)
33. The White House (10, 9)
34. Float motorboat (6, 6)

SYNONYM CROSSWORDS

Complete the mini-crosswords so that each one contains several words of the same meaning. The theme is different for each puzzle.

Synonyms 1

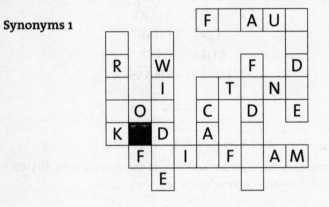

Synonyms 2

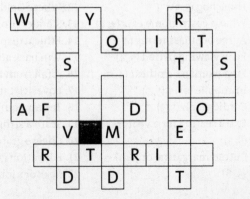

Synonyms 3

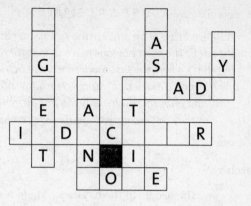

Synonyms 4

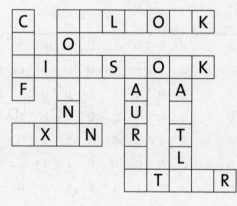

Synonyms 5

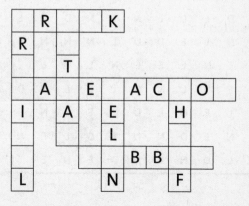

SEARCH ME

A 1968 edition of an advertising newspaper in Oklahoma might not be the most obvious place to look for historic puzzles, but that's where the first modern wordsearch – created by one Norman Gibat – was printed. The game quickly caught on, and publishers were only too happy to make more as they were so easy to create using computers.

Search 1

Can you find the needle in the haystack? There is only way of reading the word NEEDLE in a straight line in one of eight directions. Where is it?

E	D	E	N	E	D	L	D	N	E	N	E	L	L	N
L	L	E	D	L	E	E	D	D	D	L	N	E	E	D
N	N	D	L	N	E	L	L	D	N	L	D	E	L	E
E	D	E	D	L	E	D	D	E	N	E	D	E	D	N
E	N	E	E	E	D	N	N	E	E	D	D	E	L	N
N	N	E	L	N	D	N	N	L	E	L	E	D	N	D
E	L	E	D	E	L	L	E	L	D	N	L	D	L	L
L	L	E	L	L	N	N	N	E	E	E	L	E	N	L
D	D	L	L	L	N	L	N	D	D	L	E	D	E	E
E	N	L	E	D	D	L	N	N	N	D	N	D	L	E
N	E	N	E	E	E	N	L	L	L	E	E	L	E	E
D	E	D	L	N	D	L	E	E	N	D	N	L	E	E
D	L	E	D	E	D	D	E	E	N	E	D	N	D	L
E	N	L	D	N	N	E	D	L	E	N	E	D	E	E
D	L	D	N	E	N	D	E	N	E	E	E	N	D	N

Search 2

This wordsearch has the EX factor. Find all the listed words in the puzzle. Words may run horizontally, vertically or diagonally, and may be in back-to-front order.

D	M	I	A	L	C	X	E	X	C	E	R	P	T	P	E	S
A	S	E	E	S	N	A	P	X	E	T	E	E	I	E	X	E
C	E	X	E	X	C	U	S	E	D	E	X	X	E	R	E	L
I	X	P	Y	L	T	C	A	X	E	E	T	T	X	O	R	A
T	P	U	Y	P	O	R	T	X	E	M	R	R	A	L	T	H
O	E	L	L	E	E	X	U	L	T	E	D	A	C	P	E	X
X	N	S	E	X	A	M	E	D	T	R	N	C	B	X	D	E
E	S	E	S	O	P	X	E	X	E	T	A	T	P	E	X	P
S	E	E	T	X	T	N	T	X	S	X	I	R	T	O	P	E
D	N	X	E	U	I	C	T	D	T	E	E	O	D	X	X	T
E	I	A	T	A	C	O	N	I	E	S	X	E	L	H	E	D
E	M	M	L	I	R	E	S	I	S	X	R	P	A	P	E	N
C	A	P	E	T	T	O	X	L	T	M	P	U	L	M	X	L
X	X	L	S	X	P	C	C	E	E	X	S	U	U	O	A	E
E	E	E	E	X	P	O	U	N	D	T	E	H	N	A	D	X
H	X	T	E	X	P	E	R	T	S	E	X	E	P	G	E	E
T	P	R	O	T	I	B	I	H	X	E	E	X	P	L	E	E

EXACTLY	EXHALES	EXPLAIN	EXPUNGE
EXAMINE	EXHAUST	EXPLODE	EXTENDS
EXAMPLE	EXHIBIT	EXPLOIT	EXTINCT
EXCEEDS	EXHUMED	EXPLORE	EXTORTS
EXCERPT	EXODERM	EXPOSES	EXTRACT
EXCLAIM	EXOTICA	EXPOSIT	EXTREME
EXCUSED	EXPANSE	EXPOUND	EXTROPY
EXECUTE	EXPENSE	EXPRESS	EXTRUDE
EXERTED	EXPERTS	EXPULSE	EXULTED

Search 3

The key words are given in anagram form – appropriately enough, because they can all precede MIXED to form a new phrase.

```
K   N   I   R   D   O   U   B   L   E   S   R   A   S
B   A   G   N   I   M   R   A   F   P   E   C   N   B
Y   M   O   N   O   C   E   W   B   B   A   Y   N   R
S   D   T   I   U   R   F   G   M   J   O   R   F   E
G   E   F   L   A   N   G   U   A   G   E   O   T   H
N   C   R   B   D   C   N   L   P   I   U   U   A   Y
I   I   G   L   M   K   O   K   A   R   R   R   B   T
L   M   N   E   C   O   F   M   S   T   O   R   A   I
E   A   I   S   H   Q   T   O   P   H   S   B   A   S
E   L   H   S   O   C   M   I   P   A   I   Y   E   M
F   O   T   I   R   E   N   A   V   L   N   C   R   X
N   U   A   N   U   D   T   U   I   E   I   Y   E   C
N   B   B   G   S   E   J   T   B   P   S   Q   U   D
A   I   D   E   M   O   Y   T   S   G   R   I   L   L
```

LABITIY	EODSBUL	GUNAAELG
BGA	KIDRN	GREIMAAR
AGBINTH	NOCOEYM	MEAID
BINSLEGS	FMRGANI	PRAEMOHT
UNCHB	FELNSGEI	IOVETSM
HSROUC	OESMFUOR	UEBNMR
OAPCYMN	IRUTF	TNUS
SACRTLY	IRGLL	ARPTY
ELCDAIM	SRHBE	SESPCI

84 · The Riddles of the Sphinx

Search 4

To the science lab, now. How many commonly named chemicals can you find, given their first letters and their chemical formulae?

D	R	Y	I	C	E	D	M	E	A	P	A	E	E	A	A
A	E	Z	E	E	R	F	I	T	N	A	O	L	M	D	Z
A	M	M	O	N	I	A	L	C	Z	I	B	T	Z	I	H
Q	L	M	F	A	A	B	K	M	A	R	E	B	A	S	L
E	G	U	O	P	S	L	O	V	A	C	A	F	O	S	R
N	D	S	O	O	P	E	F	M	I	K	I	D	F	E	H
O	I	P	L	R	I	A	M	Q	I	T	A	R	V	A	E
T	C	Y	S	P	R	C	A	N	A	W	A	L	T	T	C
S	A	G	G	N	I	H	G	U	A	L	I	M	I	I	Q
M	Y	Y	O	Z	N	S	N	T	X	S	C	H	I	U	C
I	R	N	L	U	O	R	E	T	K	A	P	O	A	N	D
R	E	K	D	D	A	R	S	C	A	A	R	R	H	V	C
B	T	R	A	G	E	N	I	V	R	L	T	O	N	O	V
T	T	S	U	R	U	U	A	G	B	Z	C	N	B	S	L
R	A	S	K	V	Q	E	P	S	O	M	S	A	L	T	S
C	B	S	T	A	B	L	E	S	A	L	T	H	Q	N	D

A__	C_2H_5OH	D__I__	CO_2	Q__	SiO_2
A__	NH_3	E__S__	$MgSO_4.7H_2O$	Q__	Hg
A__	CH_2OHCH_2OH	F__G__	FeS_2	R__	Fe_2O_3
A__	$C_9H_8O_4$	G__	C	S__W__	H_2CO_3
B__S__	$NaHCO_3$	G__	$CaSO_4$	S__	$C_{12}H_{22}O_{11}$
B__A__	H_2SO_4	L__G__	N_2O	T__S__	$NaCl$
B__	$NaClO$	L__	CaO	T__	$Mg_3(Si_4O_{10})(OH)_2$
B__	$Na_2B_4O_7.10H_2O$	M__	$CaCO_3$	V__	CH_3COOH
B__	S	M__O__M__	$Mg(OH)_2$	V__C	$C_6H_8O_6$
C__	$C_8H_{10}N_4O_2$	P__	K_2CO_3		
C__A__	$C_6H_8O_7$	P__	C_3H_8		

Search 5

Pairs of words that make up phrases of the form '— and —' have been hidden in these two separate puzzles. For example, if the phrase is FISH and CHIPS, you'll find the word FISH in the left-hand puzzle and CHIPS on the right. Can you find all forty pairs? Sorry, but no word list is supplied this time!

B	S	W	P	T	R	G	G	P	E	U	H	I	G	H
I	E	N	A	K	H	E	N	N	U	G	R	K	H	N
T	W	D	C	T	Y	D	I	N	O	C	A	B	E	O
A	H	A	T	I	T	G	K	O	S	B	B	T	O	P
Y	L	R	R	K	H	L	A	T	A	L	R	E	N	U
B	D	E	A	T	M	E	E	R	F	C	C	E	B	R
Y	K	O	O	N	S	A	R	A	E	A	L	N	A	E
B	R	O	B	R	K	R	B	E	T	S	E	I	C	D
T	T	T	N	T	A	A	I	H	E	H	A	W	K	N
N	P	S	N	A	K	E	S	F	C	S	N	C	B	A
R	O	S	L	U	B	O	W	S	S	A	A	A	H	H
K	E	P	S	H	O	R	T	A	I	R	L	C	R	K
B	H	S	O	N	G	C	U	A	U	L	R	R	O	W
A	D	T	H	S	B	L	N	B	T	H	K	O	I	K
B	L	A	I	R	T	I	P	S	O	R	H	P	H	I

```
K T N L A S T S O S N S I M K
I L P O L I S H M R S D E S R
D A N C E M T W E E C E A O E
N O T E N P O T G D C H U U J
E F I L E L S B A D I B A L B
Y L D I E E A D W A N A M I B
D B D R W T K I O L O T D D N
I T R O T G N I R E T N E N E
P O E E O S T N R E I T N U F
R I R E A B F A A M I C D O C
E Y N E W K A R D H R Y O S W
G R Y I S S F C W A H T R O F
G E F I O U I A N I B U T C E
S L L I A N O N S S A U C E R
R E T T U B Y M T T N E N I D
```

Search 6

Here you have to find pairs of words which can be combined to make the items below. For example, if we've listed the drink CUBA LIBRE as a clue, the words you actually have to find in the grid are RUM and COLA, its two main constituents. When you've finished, the unused letters will spell out two more words that can be similarly combined.

S	E	L	B	A	T	E	G	E	V	P	B	K	F
R	S	O	D	I	U	M	A	R	O	R	R	L	R
O	E	S	R	O	H	L	M	T	E	O	N	O	E
T	E	D	I	R	B	E	A	S	T	E	E	Y	N
A	T	I	N	U	A	T	I	A	R	G	G	M	C
R	A	K	M	T	O	R	N	D	E	R	Y	O	H
E	S	E	H	E	E	I	H	F	A	E	X	O	L
M	N	M	S	T	M	R	C	S	D	E	O	R	O
U	A	A	O	O	U	Y	R	A	I	N	L	G	R
N	L	G	N	K	E	O	A	I	B	L	S	O	I
T	I	E	L	K	E	T	M	L	E	B	G	F	N
N	D	A	N	W	A	T	E	R	C	R	A	N	E
L	H	O	H	Y	D	R	O	G	E	N	U	G	E
C	D	G	O	D	L	L	U	B	N	V	C	H	E

BRINE
BROWN
BUBBLE AND SQUEAK
CEMENT
COMMON SALT
DRY MARTINI

HEN'S EGG
FRACTION
FRANGLAIS
MARRIAGE
MULE
PEWTER

PIT BULL
RAGOUT
SMOG
STAIR
WATER

BEFORE AND AFTER

For each line, find the two letters that can be prefixed and suffixed to the given letters to complete a nine-letter word:

1

2

3

4

5

ARS MAGNA

Each of these remarkable anagrams provides a clue to its eventual answer. For example, if we gave you 'Lies – let's recount' (8, 7), the best solution is 'Election results'. How many can you solve?

1. They see (3, 4)
2. A cent tip (8)
3. Life's aim? (8)
4. Stopped? No (9)
5. Minus lace (9)
6. Nine thumps (10)
7. Spice in 'em (5, 4)
8. Dirty room (9)
9. Exit on cue (9)
10. Lithe acts (9)
11. Seen as mist (10)
12. Our men earn it (12)
13. Got as a clue (10)
14. Tender names (11)
15. Swen or Inga (10)
16. Ah, not a smile? (3, 4, 4)
17. On any screen (4, 7)
18. It eggs us on (10)
19. Hated for ill (5, 6)
20. I'm dot in place (7, 5)
21. It is to an end (11)
22. Voices rant on (12)
23. Restore plush (12)
24. Adept him or her (13)
25. Built to stay free (6, 2, 7)
26. Cash lost in 'em (4, 8)
27. No city dust here (3, 11)
28. Often sheds tears (15)
29. One old fort now (5, 2, 6)
30. Often a fun dream (4, 3, 7)
31. Change car's image (6, 9)
32. Smart curing utensils (8, 11)
33. What a foreign stone pile! (3, 7, 5, 2, 4)
34. A novel by a Scottish writer (7, 2, 3, 6, 5)
35. Those radio men once learnt it (3, 13, 5, 4)
36. A pistol in an actor's rebel hands; a fine man is shot (3, 13, 2, 9, 7, 7)

JIG SQUARE

Your aim is to construct a valid word square to form a total of eight English words, four across and four down. This is done by interlocking the fifteen jigsaw pieces into the frame. Clues to all eight words are given here in random order: *song, piece of stone, knife, curve, like, little dog, decorative ball, musical instrument.*

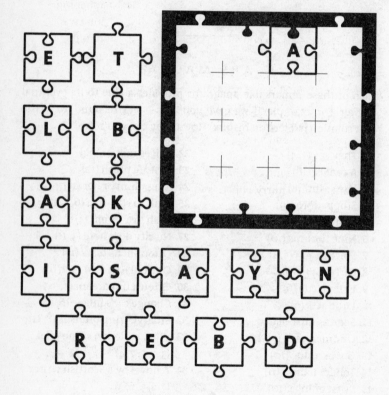

LOST IN TRANSLATION

Well-known sayings have been put through a number of computer translation programs before being translated back into English. Can you guess what the original sentences were?

1. Ha ha during the final, to laughter more for much time.
2. Increases of the job in order to fill up profit the hours.
3. A time that one has insect chomp, wary the next happening.
4. Precipitations of imbeciles inside where the good don't walk.
5. A phase for him, an enormous branch office for humanity.
6. A gulp doesn't manufacture the warm season.
7. Exclude the connecting bar and it damages the little one.
8. The value of grand text is vision.
9. I do not have anything to explain – I excluded my technical.
10. The inner part weak person has gained never the good Mrs.
11. Can old one friend have it is it forgotten and never obtained the head?
12. The need is the nut of newness.
13. Connect in the hurry, which is sorrowfulness at the spare time.
14. Invisible, insane.

HALFWAY HOUSE

More verbal quickies

1. Read forward, I am a coarse, cotton material; read backward, I am dug for metals. What am I?

2. Complete:

_____ cheque
_____ page
_____ verse
look _____
point _____
total _____

3. Find a ten-letter word in which the letters R, S, T and U appear successively and in alphabetical order.

4. What letter should be entered here so that the longest possible word can be read around the circle?

5. These words have a special property. What is it?

bathtub, manservant, pussycat, taxicab

6. There is something from which you can take its whole and yet some remains. What is it?

7. Complete the final line:

March 4th
April 1st
July 3rd
October 6th
June 3rd
December 1st
February 6th
September ...

8. Complete the blanks in this sentence: KATHERINE EDGE went to the party accompanied by HER TEENAGE KID. Meanwhile, TRISTAN HAGUE decided to take ___ _____ ____?

9. This is the first sentence from the book *Gadsby* by E. V. Wright. What is so unusual about it?

If Youth, throughout all history, had had a champion to stand up for it, to show a doubling world that a child can think, and possibly do it practically, you wouldn't constantly run across folks today who claim that "a child don't know anything".

10. Eleven of these words can precede the same word to form new words. Shade these in – what is formed?

writ	sore	hear	kit	chris
bat	wig	flat	ant	mit
of	plank	rot	bit	forgot

11. Yreka, a small town in California, used to be famous for its local bread outlet. Can you see why?

12. What royal word in the plural becomes singular when you add one letter?

13. Suggest a word that could continue this sequence:

NUMBER

BOARD

WORLD

DAY

COLUMNIST

SENSE

?

14. Here are some proverbs in a long-winded format. Can you translate them into the more familiar version?

(a) Tailor your apparel in conformity with the dispositions of the material at your disposal.

(b) Receptacles absolutely devoid of contents occasion a super-abundance of sonority.

(c) A nincompoop and his numismatic accumulations are expeditiously divorced.

(d) Plumage of a gorgeous character creates superb ornithological vertebrates.

15. Starting with one of the letters in one of the circles, move to the next circle in a clockwise fashion, choosing a different letter each time round. You should find a nine-letter word when you have finished, using up all the available letters. It may sound easy at first but wait till you try it out for yourself!

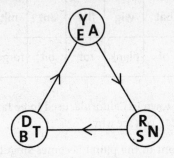

16. Find a nine-letter English word that contains only one vowel and one syllable.

17. SEVENTEEN has nine letters but, in figures, has only two digits. In English, what is the lowest whole number that contains the same quantity of letters and digits?

18. Which accountancy job is unusual because it contains three pairs of identical letters?

19. What connects the Italian banker COSIMO DE MEDICI, the opera singer DAME KIRI TE KANAWA, the tennis player GORAN IVANIŠEVIČ, the WWII officer ISOROKU YAMAMOTO and A MEXICAN-AMERICAN?

20. Read forward, I am heavy; read backward, I am not. What am I?

DITLOIDS

This type of word equation puzzle was devised in 1975 by Morgan Worthy, and subsequently popularized in GAMES *magazine by Will Shortz in 1981. Shortz recalls: 'Some anonymous person had retyped the puzzle from* GAMES *(word for word, except for my byline), photocopied it, and passed it along. This page was then re-photocopied ad infinitum, like a chain letter, and circulated around the country.' Until recently, such puzzles had no particularly snappy name until the* Daily Express *columnist William Hartston proposed the title 'Ditloid' after the title of the Russian story: 1 DITLOID = 1 Day in the Life of Ivan Denisovich.*

If 366 DIALY = 366 Days in a Leap Year, identify these common statistics and phrases:

1 FO the CN

1 F in the G

2 H on a BC

2 SUP is an E

3 BM, SHTR!

3 C in a F

3 S and YO

3 S on the B of an I

4 PC on MR

4 Y between OG

5 FO in a G

5 W in the A

6 P in an IHT

6 P on the S of D

7 W of the AW

7 Y of BL for B a M

8 M for S to RE

8 P of B in an AA

9 CL

9 M to H a B

10 P in a S in B

11 P in a CT

12 L of H

13 S on the AF

14 L in a S

15 M of F per P, A to AW

16 T and WDYG?

17 S in a H

18 H on a GC

19 GS for the VP of the US

20 YS by RVW

21 K of the D

22 Y in a CP

23 P of C in a HC

24 C in SG

25 Y of M for a SA

26 L of the A

27 B in the NT

28 D in a S

29 D in F in a LY

30 DHS, A, J and N

32 DF at which WF

36 BK on a P

46 C in a HC

50 W to LYL, A to PS

54 C in a P with the J

57 HV

60 D in EA of an ET

66 B in the KJB

76 TL the BP

78 C in a TP

88 C in the S

94 L of a BC in F

99 B of B on the W

116 Y in the HYW

147 MB in S

200 P for PG in M

206 B in the HB

212 DF at which WB

221 BBSA of SH

235 I of U in the AB

451 DF at which BB

500 S in a R

666 N of the B in the B of R

969 YL by M

1000 W that a P is W

1296 SI in a SY

1600 PA, A of the WH

2001 ASO

10000 D of YM

20000 LU the S

86400 S in a D

WORD TARGET

How many words of four letters or more can you form from these nine? Each letter can be used only once per word, but every word must contain the central H. Plurals and proper names are allowed.

WORD TRACKER

In each case find a 12-letter word, moving from one letter to the next until all the letters have been used. In puzzles 1 to 4, horizontal and vertical moves are required. In puzzles 5 to 8, diagonal moves are also allowed.

Word tracker 1

Y	I	S	N
L	D	E	O
B	A	R	C

Word tracker 2

V	I	G	R
A	E	F	O
B	L	N	U

Word tracker 3

O	H	W	A
U	S	E	R
G	N	I	M

Word tracker 4

D	E	X	S
I	A	T	U
B	M	R	O

Word tracker 5

Y	O	G	L
C	H	E	R
I	X	P	A

Word tracker 6

A	L	W	O
N	T	K	R
G	I	E	M

Word tracker 7

Y	T	O	R
U	N	I	M
S	B	A	L

Word tracker 8

T	C	I	H
S	E	G	P
N	O	A	R

CRYPTANALYSIS

We'll meet cryptic crosswords later in the book, but as an aperitif here are some famous clues that have raised a chuckle over the years. You don't need to know anything about crosswords to attempt them, just try to think in a lateral manner. For example, 'Powered flight' (9) gives ESCALATOR. The first two clues are classics by the first compiler of the Times *crossword, Adrian Bell.*

Find the answers to the following cryptic definitions:

1. Die of cold (3, 4)
2. The cylinder is jammed (5, 4)
3. Lost your shirt? Play the stock market (6)
4. Sailor producing two sets of cards (4, 4)
5. Prepare to win the lot (3, 3)
6. First day cover (3, 4)
7. Brave doctor (8, 3)
8. All points bulletin (4)
9. Pot of ale (4, 5)
10. Modern art (3)
11. He represents one, and I another (7)
12. Painting with rollers (8)
13. They tend to bring up unrelated issues (6, 7)
14. A stiff examination (4, 6)
15. When depressed, one gives no impression of character (5, 3)
16. Charge of the Light Brigade (11, 4)
17. Novel device for making mocassins (4, 2, 3, 8)
18. GGES (9, 4)
19. o14? (6, 5)
20. STUVW (4)
21. HIJKLMNO (5)
22. O (8, 6)
23. Ca (4, 3)
24. (1, 6, 3, 1, 4)

STAIRCASES

In these puzzles we're putting words on the rack and stretching them to breaking point! Beginning with a one-letter word and working downwards, answer the clues so that each word is an anagram of the previous word plus an extra letter. For example, if the previous answer was TRIES and the next clue says 'Line pattern (6)', the solution would be STRIPE [TRIES + P].

Staircase 1

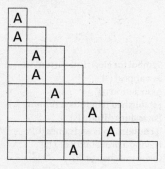

Best grade (1)
Since (2)
Took an exam (3)
Food grain seeds (4)
Switzerland hasn't one (5)
Near a rib (6)
Impassive (7)
Edith Piaf, for instance (8)

Staircase 2

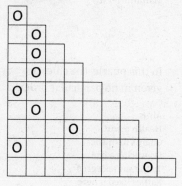

Universal donor blood group (1)
In the direction of (2)
Nonsense (3)
Moved quickly (4)
Worth 25 points in darts (5)
Caused the enemy to flee (6)
Scenic routes (7)
Stranger (8)
He aims to spot typos (9)

Staircase 3

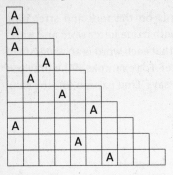

Indefinite article (1)
Astatine's chemical symbol (2)
Consumed (3)
Green tinged with blue (4)
More modern (5)
The selling of goods (6)
Solo performance (7)
Bound by contract (8)
Placed restrictions on (9)
Quite drunk (10)

Staircase 4

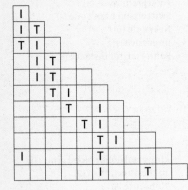

Symbol for electrical current (1)
Sex appeal (2)
Association (3)
Established religious ceremony (4)
Potassium nitrate (5)
It contains rods and cones (6)
Having a probability of 1 (7)
Chemical change (8)
The act of incinerating (9)
Grandness (10)
Manumitter (11)

Staircase 5

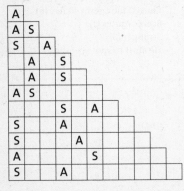

In this puzzle, the clues are given in no particular order.

Aim
Health resort
Chants to music
Skewering a fish
To the same degree
Raffles liked it here
Analyze syntactically
Artaxerxes I, for instance
Making signals with flags
1st letter of the Roman alphabet
Plant with seeds in a closed ovary

ACROSTICS AND ASSOCIATES

A selection of traditional word conundrums

1. Each of the words described contains four letters. When these are placed one below the other, the initial and final letters spell the name of an inventor.

> Pulled apart
> Leader
> Prefix for 'All'
> Quantity of matter
> In the year (Latin)
> Avoid.

2. My first is in RAT, but not in MOUSE,
   My second is in MANSION, but not in HOUSE,
   My third is in LADY, but not in MAN,
   My fourth is in BILL, but not in DAN,
   My fifth is in NOTICE, and also in MENTION,
   The whole is the name of a wonderful invention.

3. My first is in PECKISH but isn't in RICE,
   My second's in STACCATO but isn't in TWICE,
   My third is in GIANT but is far from SIGHT,
   My fourth is in ALMOND and also in BLIGHT,
   My fifth is in CHINA and also in GAME,
   What is this creature's name?

4. I am a word of seven letters:
   Without my 1, 5, 7, I am a garment;
   Without my 2, 4, 5, 7, I am a poet;
   Without my 1, 4, 7, I am a character;
   Without my 4, 5, I am a preface;
   Without my 5, 7, I am an inquiry;
   My whole is a difficult matter.

5. I am a word of six letters:
   Without my 5, 6, I am a scheme;
   Without my 1, 6, I am a narrow path;
   Without my 5, I am a vegetable organism;
   Without my 4, 5, I am to lay out in plots;
   Without my 1, 2, 5, I am an insect;
   My whole is a heavenly body.

6. Alone, I am nothing.
   With B, I am purchased.
   With F, I am struggled.
   With N, I am nothing again
   With S, I am looked for.

7. My first represents company,
   My second avoids company,
   My third convenes company,
   My whole perplexes company.

8. My first is in WELL, but not in ILL,
   My second is in PAY, but not in BILL,
   My third is in FAST, and also in SLOW,
   My fourth is in HIGH, but not in LOW,
   My fifth is in WIN, but not in LOSE,
   My sixth is in STOCKING, but not in SHOES,
   My seventh is in RIGHT, and also in WRONG,
   My eighth is in CHANT, but not in SONG,
   My ninth is in ONLY, but not in MERE,
   My tenth is in LISTEN, but not in HEAR,
   The whole is the name of a patriot true,
   Who gave glorious service to the Red, White and Blue.

3 × 3 TRACEWORDS

Trace out words of three letters or more by moving horizontally, vertically or diagonally to adjacent letters. Each letter may be used only once for any one word. Plurals and well-known proper names are allowed. The targets for the first two puzzles require only basic English words. The second pair use more demanding vocabulary in the answers.

Traceword 1

Good: 40 words
Very Good: 54 words
Excellent: 65 words

Traceword 2

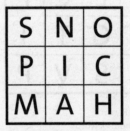

Good: 35 words
Very Good: 48 words
Excellent: 60 words

Traceword 3

Good: 18 words
Very Good: 25 words
Excellent: 30 words

Traceword 4

Good: 27 words
Very Good: 38 words
Excellent: 50 words

4 × 4 TRACEWORDS

The rules are the same as the previous puzzles, but now your answers must contain at least four letters.

Traceword 5

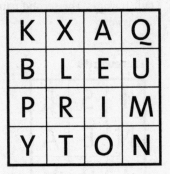

W	N	A	B
K	E	C	F
U	G	T	I
R	S	V	P

Good: 18 words
Very Good: 25 words
Excellent: 30 words

Traceword 6

K	X	A	Q
B	L	E	U
P	R	I	M
Y	T	O	N

Good: 45 words
Very Good: 60 words
Excellent: 75 words

WORD LADDERS

This section includes many of Lewis Carroll's original word ladder puzzles. Due to the variation in vocabulary between Carroll's day and modern times, it may be possible to solve some puzzles in fewer steps than indicated.

In these puzzles, change the word at the top of the ladder into the destination word at the bottom. At each stage, change one letter at a time, forming a valid English word at all times. For example, JACK to KING could be achieved in five steps: JACK, TACK, TICK, KICK, KINK and KING. For the longer puzzles, clues have been provided for words that may be unfamiliar. However, you don't have to follow the trails so indicated – any valid ladder will do.

Word ladder 1

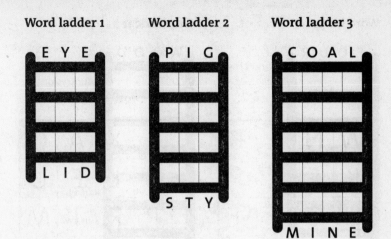

E Y E

L I D

Word ladder 2

P I G

S T Y

Word ladder 3

C O A L

M I N E

Word ladder 4

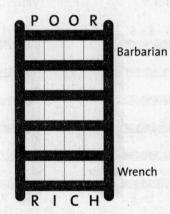

N O S E

C H I N

Word ladder 5

P O O R

Barbarian

Wrench

R I C H

Word ladder 6

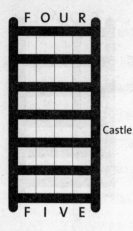

F O U R

Castle

F I V E

Word ladder 7

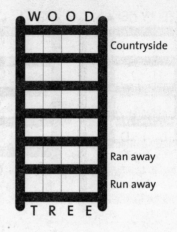

W O O D

Countryside

Ran away

Run away

T R E E

Word ladder 8

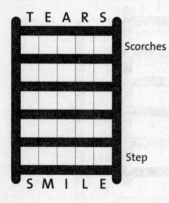

T E A R S

Scorches

Step

S M I L E

Word ladder 9

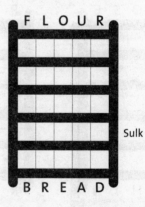

F L O U R

Sulk

B R E A D

Word ladder 10

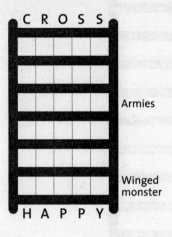

C R O S S

Armies

Winged monster

H A P P Y

Word ladder 11

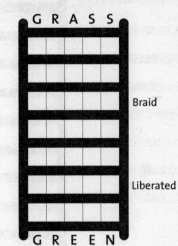

G R A S S

Braid

Liberated

G R E E N

Word ladder 12

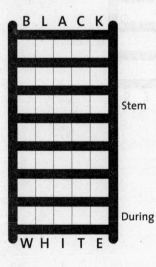

B L A C K

Stem

During

W H I T E

Word ladder 13

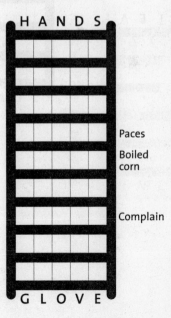

H A N D S

Paces

Boiled corn

Complain

G L O V E

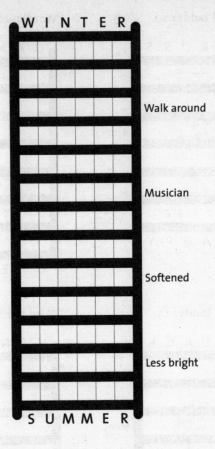

WINTER

Walk around

Musician

Softened

Less bright

SUMMER

KANGAROO WORDS

Each word contains the letters of a word with a similar meaning somewhere in its letters, in the correct order. For example, JOVIALITY contains the word JOY. Try to find the hidden synonym in each of the following words:

1. Rotund
2. Observe
3. Prosecute
4. Deceased
5. Recline
6. Catacomb
7. Salvage
8. Instructor
9. Precipitation
10. Municipality
11. Appropriate
12. Perimeter
13. Encourage
14. Matches
15. Regulates

16. Splotches
17. Respite
18. Calumnies
19. Rapscallion
20. Before
21. Transgression
22. Indolent
23. Deliberate
24. Supervisor
25. Fabrication
26. Because
27. Unsightly
28. Umpteenth
29. Destruction
30. Container (2 answers)

RIDDLE-ME-REE

It would be remiss of us to leave the world of words without a round of riddles. They range from the quickfire to the poetic.

1. What can be half full, three-quarters full or full, but never empty?

2. What do you throw out when you want to use it, but take in when you don't want to use it?

3. What is put on a table, cut, but never eaten?

4. What gets harder to catch the faster you run?

5. What is it that when you take away the whole, you still have some left over?

6. If you have it, you want to share it, but if you share it, you don't have it. What is it?

7. What part of your body disappears when you stand up?

8. What goes around the world and yet stays in a corner?

9. I am a place where yesterday always follows tomorrow. What am I?

10. I banish darkness from your house for hours, yet add a letter and I illuminate the whole sky for only a second. What am I?

11. I can be cracked, I can be made.
I can be told, I can be played.
What am I?

12. I'm part of the bird that's not in the sky,
I can swim in the ocean and yet remain dry.
What am I?

13. I know a word of three letters thee,
Add two, and fewer there will be.
What am I?

14. Walking beneath me as you pass through,
Or a small land with an Everglade view,
I'm useful to have where landmarks are shown,
Notes by the seven with concordant tone.
One in a million will let you see
A vital secret when you have me.

15. I run over fields and woods all day.
Under the bed at night, I sit all alone.
My tongue hangs out, up to the rear.
I am awaiting to be filled in the morning.
What am I?

16. As a whole, I am both safe and secure.
   Behead me, and I become a place for a meeting.
   Behead me again, and I become the partner of ready.
   Restore me, and I become the domain of beasts.
   What am I?

17. With thieves, I consort,
   With the vilest in short
   I'm quite at ease in depravity;
   Yet all divines use me,
   And savants can't lose me
   For I am the center of gravity.
   What am I?

18. Two sisters are we, one dark and one fair.
   In twin towers dwelling, we're quite the pair.
   One from the land, and one from the sea.
   Tell us truly, who are we?

19. Pronounced as one letter,
   And written with three,
   Two letters there are,
   And two only in me.
   I'm double, I'm single,
   I'm black, blue and grey,
   I'm read from both ends,
   And the same either way.

20. In a marble hall white as milk,
   Lined with skin as soft as silk.
   Within a fountain crystal-clear,
   A golden apple doth appear.
   No doors there are to this stronghold,
   Yet thieves break in to steal its gold.
   What is it?

21. Whoever makes it, tells it not.
   Whoever takes it, knows it not.
   Whoever knows it, wants it not.
   What is it?

22. When I am filled I can point the way;
    When I am empty nothing moves me.
    I have two skins, one without and one within.
    What am I?

23. People are hired to get rid of me,
    I'm often hiding under your bed,
    In time I'll always return you see,
    Bite me and you're surely dead.
    What am I?

24. You can have me but cannot hold me;
    Gain me and quickly lose me.
    If treated with care I can be great,
    And if betrayed I will break.
    What am I?

25. To five a fourth of five append,
    One-third of one take then;
    Let fifty follow, and to end
    Affix two-thirds of ten.
    Two-thirds of this will yield sweet sounds,
    The whole with perfume sweet abounds.

HARSH WORDS

A final tricky batch of verbal vexations. Have a care –
some of the solutions require a lateral mindset.

1. The missing letters in each row have something in common:

di__r__d

e_c_rp__nt

gos____r

hi_t__in_

___pl_

te_t___nt

2. In terms of its letters, what record can the following word claim to have?

DERMATOGLYPHICS

3. What unusual property connects the following words: august, job, lima, natal, nice, polish, rainier, reading?

4. Starting with one of the letters in one of the circles move to the next circle in a clockwise fashion, choosing a letter as you go on. You should find a nine-letter word when you have finished, using up all the available letters.

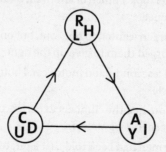

5. If you took all the English words, spelled them backwards then listed them in alphabetical order, what would be the final entry?

6. Which three consecutive letters of the standard English alphabet can complete this word?

hazar___s

7. A spy has received this message but it appears to be in pieces. Can you reassemble it?

EVACUATION BROWN NIGHT ARNOLD MONDAY TROUBLE PATROL YOURS, FOR HARBOR QUICKLY – RECKONS VICTORY CAN WEDNESDAY, DO JERSEY. OR ZACK. LOW UNDERWAY. XAVIER! IN SOME KEEP GERRARD'S.

8. Read forward, I am a living creature; read backward, I am a thin plate. What am I?

9. What phrase is this? It has four words of 4, 4, 2, 3 letters.

ENTURY

10. Concealed in each sentence that follows is the name of a four-footed beast consisting of consecutive letters. For example, 'The six*th or se*venth shot failed to hit the target' contains 'horse'. Now try these:

(a) Having lost his hundredth yen, Asimoto left Tokyo without uttering a single word.

(b) The colonel took a pinch of snuff, then carried on as if nothing had happened.

(c) The tribesmen wanted to hold out, but one of them, a Moslem, urged them to give up the fight.

(d) Instead of a second-hand motor car, I bought a brand-new motor-cycle.

(e) Never before had the climbers experienced such a moist climate or such a snowstorm.

(f) The fishermen had been told that a pirate ship had been sighted ten km off shore.

11. How could you 'spell out' the word DEFLATE using one press of three consecutive keys on a keyboard?

12. Which three numbers have been jumbled up here?

HIT OFF ENTIRETY

13. Place the letters of the following words into the appropriately numbered area so that, when you have finished, a 6 × 6 word square is formed. The same six words read both across and down.

1. SOLO
2. VIOLET
3. SERENE
4. TRIOLET
5. REVELS
6. VIE
7. EVEN

14. I am a male. Add a letter and I become female. Add another letter and I become male again. Add three more letters and I return to being female. Find all four words.

15. I'm thinking of two five-letter words. Each word is an anagram, homophone and synonym of the other – that is, they use the same letters, sound alike and mean the same thing. What are the words?

16. Find the twelve-letter word which, when written in a zigzag from top left to bottom right, completes the six English words reading across:

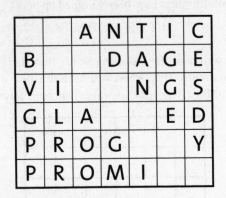

		A	N	T	I	C
	B		D	A	G	E
	V	I		N	G	S
	G	L	A		E	D
	P	R	O	G		Y
	P	R	O	M	I	

17. In which English word does the letter I appear seven times? One other vowel appears in the word.

18. The 'average' letter of the word ACE is C, because it is the average of the 1st, 3rd and 5th letters of the alphabet. Which seven-letter word also has an average of the letter C?

19. Which English word:
    – has five consecutive consonants,
    – is recognized as one of the most frequently misspelt, and
    – is almost always preceded by three, five or seven?

20. What 12-letter word is represented by the rebus below?

CHAPTER 3

Codes and Ciphers

'The magic words are squeamish ossifrage' may sound like non-sense, but in fact it's one of the most remarkable sentences of the 1970s. It opened up a new world of interest for mathematicians, puzzlists, businessmen and governments.

The ability to keep messages secret can save lives, keep our personal matters private and, for some, rack up huge profits. In the USA, some codes are so powerful in espionage that they are categorized as weapons of war, and export controls are placed on them. Codes are not something that went away after the end of World War II – they have widespread applications in today's electronic world, from DVDs to computer passwords, money transactions to wireless Internet connections.

ALL GREEK TO ME

The word 'cryptography' is derived from the Greek for 'hidden writing', and is the catch-all term for the science of keeping messages secret. Before the modern era, cryptography was all about keeping the message hidden in the first place – if a message could not be found at all, how could any information be gleaned from it? A range of ingenious methods were devised in the ancient world. One was to shave a messenger's hair, tattoo the text onto his head, wait for the hair to grow back and send the messenger to the recipient, who could read the message after a swift and severe haircut. A technique used by the Greeks attempted to hide the method of finding the message, rather than the text itself. When a strip of apparently random letters was wound around a cylinder called a scytale (pronounced 'sit-ahl-ee'), the message could be read along the length of the cylinder. Unless you had a scytale of the correct diameter, the message would not appear.

Not all codes hide the messages in a format we are accustomed to. The English essayist Francis Bacon devised a cipher that required the use of two similar typefaces. It was thus not the letters of the message that were important, but the sequence in which the typefaces were employed. Suppose the two typefaces are called type 1 and type 2. If the first five letters of the coded message are all printed in typeface 1 (i.e. 11111), this translates to the plaintext letter A. If, instead, the final letter was type 2 (i.e. 11112), this decodes to B. Continuing in this vein, we can build up an entire alphabet in which each letter is represented by a unique sequence of typefaces: 11121 = C, 11122 = D, 11211 = E, and so on up to 21222 = Z (with I/J and U/V each sharing the same code). Each group of five letters in the printed text is analysed to reveal the hidden message.

Coded messages can be hidden in the format of a document too. For example, an innocuous-looking double space before a word could mean 'take the first letter of the next word', with all such letters forming a hidden message. A similar technique was used to humorous effect in 2006 when Justice Peter Smith, presiding over a claimed case of breach of copyright concerning the novel *The Da Vinci Code*, sprinkled a number of italicized letters through his final judgement which themselves formed a coded message. Spies have also devised codes where key letters appear on the creases when the paper is folded in a certain way. The writer Edgar Allan Poe was a great fan of codes and invited people to send him encrypted messages, the vast majority of which he managed to crack.

Although the words 'cipher' and 'code' are often used interchangeably, there is a subtle but distinct difference between them. A code replaces the message you want to convey with some other token or visual symbol. For example, in the early days of telegraphic communications, to save time many phrases were replaced with a five-letter codeword such as LIOUY ('Why do you not answer my question?') or BYOXO ('Are you dishonouring our agreement?'). Similarly, spies have used codebooks to encode their messages. Codes are difficult to break unless you can find the codebook, work out a message's context from other information or obtain insider assistance.

However, codes cannot be used in all circumstances. Codebooks allow only a limited number of messages to be sent. It would be far better if you could send any message you liked by scrambling the letters in such a way that the intended recipient could unscramble them later. If a codebook were stolen, though, then any previously intercepted messages would become instantly readable to the enemy. Scrambled letter-based messages are known as ciphers, and although they are very flexible and offer security (to varying degrees), most ciphers have inherent vulnerabilities.

One of the earliest uses of a cipher system is credited to Julius Caesar. According to the historian Suetonius, 'if he had anything confidential to say, he wrote it in cipher [so] that not a word could be made out. If anyone wishes to decipher these, and get at their meaning, he must substitute the fourth letter of the alphabet, namely D, for A, and so with the others.' So, for example, the word QUICK would become TXLFN. This system is now called a Caesar shift cipher. Julius Caesar opted to use a three-letter shift in his messages, but any offset can be chosen, so as to keep interlopers guessing. Julius Caesar's nephew Augustus is believed to have used the same system, but with a shift of one letter.

The Caesar cipher is not particularly difficult to break. With only 25 different possibilities to try out, in the English alphabet at least, you would have to test only the first few letters of the message to work out the correct offset to apply to the whole text. However, this was not a major concern of Caesar as few of his enemies could read, never mind crack ciphers. Simple though it may be, a 13-letter Caesar shift called ROT13 (for 'rotate 13 places') is still used on Internet newsgroups as a way of hiding information in certain portions of messages (an answer to a puzzle, or a joke's punchline, for example).

A rather more sophisticated technique uses what is called a substitution cipher. Here each letter of a message is replaced with another letter throughout, but unlike the Caesar cipher the substitution scheme uses an alphabet in which the order of the letters has been completely rearranged rather than just shifted. While much more difficult to crack, the substitution cipher is susceptible to a method of attack called frequency analysis. Suppose we know that the message that has been enciphered was written in English. Since the most common letter in English is E, we have a reasonably simple method for finding potential candidates for E in the code – if there are more Q's in the code than any other letter, it's quite likely that Q in the code represents E in the original message. Likewise, if there are only one or two R's in the enciphered message, it is likely that R represents a rare letter such as J, Q, X or Z. Once a few letters have been guessed, other letters and words in the message can be deduced, which in turn opens up other words to guesses. Eventually, the entire message can be deciphered by hand without much difficulty, provided that the text is sufficiently long.

This was the downfall of Mary, Queen of Scots in 1586. She was imprisoned in Chartley Hall, Staffordshire, but through an intermediary managed to exchange messages with co-conspirator Anthony Babington. Their messages, which were enciphered using twenty-three letter substitutions together with thirty-six special symbols for common words or phrases, contained details of a plot to overthrow Mary's cousin and reigning queen, Elizabeth I, and were concealed, ready for transfer, in the hollowed-out stopper of a beer barrel. The messages were easily intercepted by Elizabeth's chief minister, Sir Francis Walsingham, because the intermediary, George Gifford, was a double agent. Each letter was first decoded by Walsingham's spy school and then passed on intact without any action being taken. That was until a letter written by Mary on 17 July 1586 was found to contain enough detailed information to seal her fate. The evidence was so clear-cut that the judges at her trial, held at Fotheringhay Castle, felt compelled to recommend the death penalty, and Elizabeth concurred by signing the death warrant. Mary was beheaded on 8 February 1587.

THE UNBREAKABLE CIPHER
THAT BROKE

However much the cipher alphabet is scrambled, it is still very simple to use frequency analysis to break it. The problem hinges on the use of just one alphabet – if the entire message is written in the same cipher, frequency analysis is straightforward. But what if several different alphabets were to be used? In 1586, a diplomat called Blaise de Vigenère presented the idea of a poly-alphabetic code to Henry III of France. As often happens in the world of secrets, the idea had already been hit upon by others, but it is the name of Vigenère that has stuck to this cipher.

The simplest Vigenère cipher uses a codeword which is known to the sender and recipient – let's say it's CHIEF. We convert this word into five different offsets: 2, 7, 8, 4 and 5 (using A = 0, B = 1, C = 2, D = 3 etc.). If we want to encipher the word DANGER, the first letter D is offset by 2 letters in the alphabet to obtain F, the A advances by 7 letters to H, the N is advanced by 8 letters, and so on throughout the word. For the sixth letter, we go back to the start and use an offset of 2. In this way, DANGER is enciphered into FHVKJT. Essentially, we are using five different Caesar shift ciphers in a cyclical order: 2, 7, 8, 4, 5, 2, 7, 8, 4, 5, 2, 7, …

This so-called polyalphabetic cipher was much lauded at the time, and stood up to well over two centuries of scrutiny. During the American Civil War the system was used by the Confederacy, but their messages often contained the same phrases, providing Union cryptographers with an easy 'crib' with which to decipher them. The French called a more advanced version of Vigenère's system *le chiffre indéchiffrable* ('the unbreakable cipher'). The eccentric English scientist Charles Babbage, who once baked himself in a hot oven for a few minutes to see what would happen to him, developed a method to crack Vigenère ciphers in 1854 – some 268 years after the 'unbreakable' cipher was originally devised.

Babbage found himself in hot water when a dentist from Bristol, John Hall Brock Thwaites, claimed to have devised a brand new cipher, which he submitted to the *Journal of the Society of the Arts*. Babbage demonstrated that Thwaites's 'invention' was the Vigenère cipher in another guise. Incensed by Babbage's accusation, Thwaites presented Babbage with a passage of his enciphered text and challenged him to decrypt it. After first trying to back out, Babbage took it on and discovered that the mystery text was from an Alfred Tennyson poem that had been encrypted with the keyword EMILY, the name of Tennyson's wife. Babbage saw that, for sufficiently long passages of text, a polyalphabetic cipher was not immune to frequency analysis, nor did it stop short words or common letter groups such as ING from recurring in the code. The Polish codebreaker Friedrich Kasiski was the first to publicize these weaknesses of the Vigenère cipher, in 1863.

SHORT-WAVE SPIES

The key problem with the Vigenère cipher was the repetition of the codeword. But what if the keyword were as long as the message itself – giving a unique Caesar cipher offset for every single letter? That would be impossible to crack. DJBBDCILNA, for example, could stand for ATTACKCITY, but equally it could represent LOVESOPHIE or DONALDDUCK – or indeed anything else. Without knowing which ten numerical offsets have been applied to the original message, you could 'deduce' any ten-letter phrase from DJBBDCILNA. Because the code is as long as the message itself, words and common letter groups will appear completely different in different parts of the cipher.

This unbreakable system is called a one-time pad, after the small pads of paper provided to spies for encrypting messages. Each sheet in a pad contained a long string of letters or numbers which provided the key to decrypting a message. After being used once, the sheet was burnt to prevent discovery; the pads were sometimes printed on 'flash paper', making them highly flammable. The pads were small so that they could be easily hidden – spies were found to have concealed them in objects such as a bar of soap and a walnut shell. One-time pads are a simple, unbreakable code as long as the sequence of code numbers used is truly random, and each number sequence is used for one message only.

One-time pad codes are everywhere, yet few people are aware of their existence. In fact, transmitting codes via short-wave radio began sometime in the 1940s. If you tune a standard full-band radio to certain frequencies, you will hear – usually on the hour or at regular times around the clock – coded messages being sent through the aether. A common form of broadcast code consists of a short tone or piece of music followed by groups of numbers spoken by a mechanical voice. Radio enthusiasts who listen in to these broadcasts have given these voices cosy nicknames such as the Russian Man, Swedish Rhapsody and Bulgarian Betty. One, known as the

Lincolnshire Poacher and believed to be operated from an RAF base in Cyprus on behalf of MI6, quirkily starts with bursts of an English folk song called 'The Lincolnshire Poacher', followed by a mechanical female voice.

It may well be that secret services such as MI6, the CIA and Mossad are behind some of these 'numbers stations'. Some of them are known to be decoys or hoaxes, but given their global prevalence it would be remarkable if they were all the work of amateur radio pranksters. We can only conclude that enciphered messages are being sent to operatives around the world – but that doesn't necessarily mean that they are all sent by spooks to spooks. Large corporations use codes to transmit commercially sensitive information using spy-like techniques, and even fishing fleets, for example, are sent enciphered messages telling them where to find valuable shoals of fish.

STATION X

In World War II the benefits of a cipher with little inherent repetition was well known to the Germans, who used a highly sophisticated system based on machines called Enigma. It had been used commercially in the 1920s but came into its own during the war.

The standard Enigma machine consisted of a keyboard connected to a set of three rotors, each one containing a set of wires which connected with wires in adjacent rotors. When a key was depressed, an electrical signal was sent through the wires in the rotors and back again. The signal finally lit up one of an array of lights labelled with the letters of the

An Enigma machine

alphabet situated in front of the keyboard which displayed the enciphered output.

The genius of the machine lay in its use of the rotors. Each time a key was pressed, the first rotor would click around one position – rather like the way a car's mileometer works. This tiny change altered the path the signal followed through the set of rotors so that, if the same key were pressed a second time, a different letter would light up. The rotors cycled through

16,900 different permutations, making messages very difficult to crack, especially as the Germans limited their messages to 250 characters, giving almost the same security as a one-time pad. There was worse still – on the front of the machine was a series of sockets where different pairs of connections could be plugged together, increasing the number of permutations. Furthermore, different rotors could be chosen and their order could be varied, and no message began with the rotors in the same place. The initial settings for each day's communications were set out in special codebooks. The German Navy was provided with codebooks printed with water-soluble ink, so that they could be destroyed to avoid them falling into enemy hands, or would be lost if the ship sank.

All this meant that on the standard Enigma machine somewhere in the region of 100,000,000,000,000,000,000,000,000 different permutations were available. However, a code is unbreakable only if it has no flaws and its operating procedures are followed to the letter. Fortunately for the Allies, Enigma was exploitable on both fronts. In 1939, a secret base known as Station X was set up in a manor house at Bletchley Park, in Buckinghamshire. It was staffed with linguists, chess champions and crossword experts as well as mathematicians and codebreaking specialists. They also included Geoffrey Tandy, a former curator at the Natural History Museum, among their number. He had explained at his interview that he was an expert in cryptogams (a type of primitive plant), which the recruiting officer had mistaken for 'cryptograms'!

The Bletchley Park team set about cracking the Enigma code, based on German communications intercepted by listening posts. One weakness of the Enigma machine was a component called the reflector, which took the initial electronic signal after

Bletchley Park

it had passed through the three rotors, turned it round via a U-shaped connection and sent it back through the rotors on a different path. This meant two things: the Germans could decrypt their messages by the reverse process that was used for encryption, but it also introduced a key flaw – no letter could encode to itself. If you pressed T on the keyboard, the resulting code letter would be anything but T. While this doesn't seem to reduce the possibilities very much, it was just enough to give the codebreakers a hook: if you received the message UHZ, you knew that it couldn't represent THE because the H couldn't represent itself.

Human failings were the other chink in Enigma's armour. Operators were frequently clumsy, and sometimes messages were resent if the recipient had a poor signal strength. Some messages were predictable in their content, especially weather reports which contained the same terms and abbreviations time and again. By deducing the content of the weather report, the day's code settings could be worked out, and these were used to attack more important messages from the same day.

The German operators could also be inherently lazy, such as sending a test message by hitting the 'T' key repeatedly – and when the British received a message without a single T in it, they guessed that this was what had happened. Also, the initial positions of the rotors were chosen by the operators, who would often select meaningful triplets of letters instead of a purely random setting. The letters, often their or their girlfriend's initials, became known as 'cillies' when one regular operator kept using the sequence CIL.

In 1941, more staff were urgently required to cope with the workload. One of the recruitment tactics was a letter planted in the *Daily Telegraph* on 3 December: 'I challenge your correspondent who claims to have solved the crossword of the previous week in six minutes to make good his claim by solving one of your prize crossword puzzles in double that time.' The challenge was extended to all-comers, and £100 for a charity (the Eccentric Club Minesweepers' Fund) put up in prize money. Twenty-five solvers took up the gauntlet, and a competition run under exam conditions took place in the *Telegraph*'s newsroom the following month. The winner, one Mr Hawes of Dagenham, completed the partially cryptic puzzle in 7 minutes 57.5 seconds. Four others beat the 12-minute deadline and another was only one clue away from finishing. All six were later contacted by the War Office and recruited to Bletchley Park.

Station X was helped by vital information about the Enigma machine's workings from the Polish, and financial assistance and resources from the Americans. By 1945 the Bletchley Park staff were able to decode almost all communications within 48 hours. A much stronger, more complicated German cipher machine, Lorenz, was also cracked by building Colossus, one of the very first digital computers, which exploited techniques discovered by Alan Turing. Both Winston Churchill and Dwight Eisenhower recognized that the codebreaking effort was decisive in bringing the war to a decisive conclusion years earlier than might have been possible. But after the war the staff were honour-bound to keep quiet, and on the orders of Churchill the larger codebreaking machines were smashed into pieces 'no bigger than a man's hand'. It was not until the 1970s that details began to emerge of this heroic effort.

ALICE AND BOB

With the advancement of communications technology to the point where swathes of information can be transferred in the blink of an eye, the ability to maintain the integrity and secrecy of data is more important than ever. This is now possible, thanks to prime numbers.

Here's a puzzle. Suppose that Alice wants to send Bob a message in the mail, and to receive a reply back from Bob. She puts the message inside an indestructible box and posts it to Bob (sending a box through the mail is an analogy for enciphering and transmitting). But Eve, who works at the post office, can eavesdrop on their 'conversation' simply by opening the box. To prevent this from happening, Alice and Bob buy a padlock that comes with two keys. Alice puts the message in the box and locks it with the padlock. Alice sends it to Bob, who can open the box using his copy of the key. The process is reversed for sending the reply. Unless Eve manages to get a copy of the key, Alice and Bob's messages can't be read.

The main disadvantage of this system is that Alice and Bob need to physically meet beforehand so that each can take a copy of the key. However, there is an ingenious practical solution. When Alice is ready to send her message, she puts it in the box, locks it with her padlock and sends the whole thing to Bob. Bob then puts his own padlock on the box and returns it to Alice. She unlocks her padlock and returns the box – now with only Bob's lock on it – to Bob, who can now unlock the box using his key and read the message. In this way Alice and Bob never exchange keys. This is a much more flexible method because Alice and Bob don't need to meet, and there's no need to send the key through the mail, where Eve could intercept and copy it. Unfortunately, though sound in physical terms, it doesn't work in cryptography. Because Alice was the first person to encipher her message, she needs to be the last person to decipher it for the message to make sense. However, in this example it's Bob who's taking the final step to reveal the message. It's a little like putting your shoes and socks on – the practical order must be: socks on, shoes on, shoes off, socks off.

In 1976, Whitfield Diffie and Martin Hellman published a revolutionary new idea that would work cryptographically – what if Alice and Bob use two different methods, one to encipher the message and a different one to decipher it? As before, Alice and Bob purchase their own padlock. Each lock has a key which they keep to themselves. Bob sends Alice his open padlock through the mail, and she uses it to lock the box by clicking it shut. The padlocked box containing Alice's message is sent to Bob, who uses his 'unlock' key to open it and read the note. If Alice also sends one of her open padlocks, Bob can use it to lock the box containing his reply and send it back to Alice, who can unlock it because she has the key for that lock. In this way, Alice and Bob never exchange keys – only padlocks. This is a much more flexible method because Alice and Bob didn't need to meet, and there's no need to send the key through the mail, where Eve could intercept and copy it. Furthermore, it works cryptographically because the first person to encipher the message is also the last person to decipher it.

Mathematically, this works on a principle called a trapdoor function, which is easiest explained by an example. Suppose you were asked to find the result of multiplying 2,399 by 443. Finding the answer, 1,062,757, isn't much of a challenge, especially if you have a calculator handy. But if instead you were asked to find the two prime numbers which, when multiplied together, give 1,062,757, you would find yourself struggling for at least a few minutes, and probably quite a bit longer. Finding which two prime numbers are the factors of a larger, so-called composite number is easy for a computer, but if the numbers involved are extremely large, then even with all the computing power in the world it could take many lifetimes to find the answer. This is the essence of a trapdoor function: something that is trivial in one direction but inherently difficult to perform in the other – just like falling through a trapdoor.

The real genius of the Diffie–Hellman system is that much of the information can be made public. In effect, instead of Alice sending a padlock to Bob privately, Alice can make the design of her padlock known to the public, available to whoever wants to send her a message. Bob makes a padlock to Alice's publicly available description, puts his message in the box, clicks the padlock shut and sends the whole thing to Alice. She can then use her exclusive special key to open the padlock. In maths terms, the composite number – two prime numbers multiplied together – is a code number used to scramble Bob's message, i.e. click the padlock shut. This is an easy process which anyone can do. However, only Alice knows how to open the padlock. Her knowledge of which two prime numbers are part of her padlock design allows her, and only her, to unlock the padlock.

Although Diffie and Hellman knew that their method was theoretically possible, it took a trio of researchers at the Massachusetts Institute of Technology to find the prime number algorithm required to put it into practice. The method was called RSA, for the surnames of Ronald Rivest, Adi Shamir and Leonard Adleman. When RSA was first announced in Martin Gardner's *Scientific American* column of August 1977, it was hailed as 'a new kind of cipher that would take millions of years to break'. A challenge was set with an encoded piece of text and a public key, a large composite number. Factorizing the public key into its two parts would yield the hidden message.

In fact, using advanced modern computers and the combined resources of six hundred volunteers, breaking the cipher took only until 26 April 1994. The message was discovered to be 'The magic words are squeamish ossifrage' (ossifrage being a species of vulture). Although the code had been cracked, the theory that it was a difficult thing to do had been proved. As it happened, Gardner's challenge used a size of prime number that, in the modern era, is considered to be too small, and today much, much larger primes (billions and billions of times larger) are used instead. Using these stronger code numbers, messages encoded in RSA cannot be deciphered even if you had all the computers in the world at your disposal for the age of the known Universe.

It later turned out that a variant of RSA had already been discovered by a British mathematician, Clifford Cocks, working at the UK government's central cryptography service, GCHQ, in 1973. The information was classified and put to one side – partly because no one quite knew what to do with the technique, but also because the computing power then available was not sufficient to make the method practical. Further advances have allowed senders of messages to encrypt the design of their key within the message, not only adding extra security but also providing a definitive way of verifying the identity of the claimed sender and that the content of the message has not been tampered with. This system is so secure that in some countries it has the same legal status as a handwritten signature.

Code puzzles are an insight into the same techniques that have been used over the past thousand years. Frequency analysis, the essential tool for cracking a cryptogram puzzle, is the very same method that has been employed by some of the brightest minds of all time. While it can be difficult to justify the purpose of a wordsearch or spot-the-difference puzzle, other than the honing of observational powers, the puzzles that follow are simplified examples of some of the greatest challenges of all time.

The Puzzles

A TYPEWRITER CRYPTOGRAM

This puzzle by Henry Dudeney serves as an introduction to the puzzles ahead.

A man told us that a business friend of his had invented a simple but very easily worked cipher for use in his secret correspondence. He had simply taken a typewriter and changed the key letters into utter disorder, so that when you struck the A it printed, say, M, when you struck B the result was R, and so on throughout. However, the strange jumble of letters got on his typist's nerves so much that she refused to continue with it. His friend therefore had to do the cryptic correspondence himself.

The following is a sentence written on the typewriter and we were asked if we could translate it. Of course, it is one of the simplest forms of cryptogram, and will not give the reader much trouble.

P gk ntyyz et ngz kz ezhpne pn g hmybmie bttd.

DOUBLE VISION

Identify the two messages in this grid:

CRYPTOGRAMS

A cryptogram takes the form of a message or quotation in which the letters have been scrambled by a random encoding sequence. For example, the letter A might have been replaced by the letter Q throughout. By using frequency analysis and your powers of deduction, can you decode the messages back into English?

In some of the puzzles, you also have to find the person to whom the quotation is attributed. The letter code used is different for each puzzle. The letter key at the bottom of each puzzle can be used to help you work out what each letter decodes to. Not all 26 letters are used in any one puzzle.

Cryptogram 1

Q	U	G		V	Q	W	B	Z		V	W		Y	M	B	:		P	R		Q	U	G	
																:			N					

H	G	S	P	R	R	P	R	S		Q	U	G		E	R	P	L	G	B	V	G		A	M	V
				N	N		N								N										

X	B	G	M	Q	G	O	.		Q	U	P	V		U	M	V		D	M	O	G		M
							.																

F	W	Q		W	Y		N	G	W	N	F	G		L	G	B	Z		M	R	S	B	Z
L											L									N			

M	R	O		U	M	V		H	G	G	R		A	P	O	G	F	Z					
	N										N						L						

B	G	S	M	B	O	G	O		M	V		M		H	M	O		D	W	L	G	.	
																						.	

A	B	C	D	E	F	G	H	I			L	M	N	O	P		R	S	T	U	V	W		Y
					F								R											

This long quotation should be an easy start. In the key at the bottom, we have eliminated those letters that are not used anywhere in the quote. Two letters have been given as clues.

> *Tip* Almost without exception, a single letter must represent A or I.
> The most frequently used letters, in order, are E, T, A, O, I, N, S, H, R and D.

Cryptogram 2

Here, the author's name appears at the end of the puzzle.

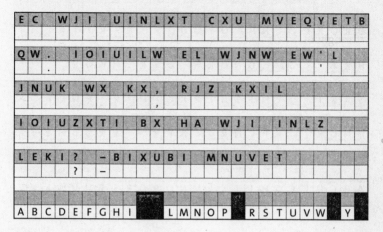

Cryptogram 3

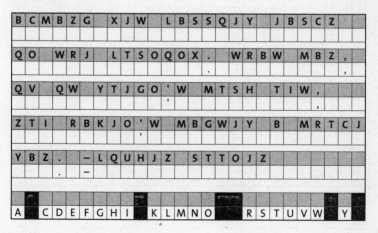

Cryptogram 4

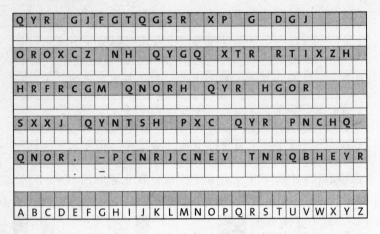

Q	Y	R		G	J	F	G	T	Q	G	S	R		X	P		G		D	G	J			

O	R	O	X	C	Z		N	H		Q	Y	G	Q		X	T	R		R	T	I	X	Z	H

H	R	F	R	C	G	M		Q	N	O	R	H		Q	Y	R		H	G	O	R			

S	X	X	J		Q	Y	N	T	S	H		P	X	C		Q	Y	R		P	N	C	H	Q

Q	N	O	R	.		-	P	C	N	R	J	C	N	E	Y		T	N	R	Q	B	H	E	Y	R
				.		-																			

A	B	C	D	E	F	G	H	I	J	K	L	M	N	O	P	Q	R	S	T	U	V	W	X	Y	Z

Cryptogram 5

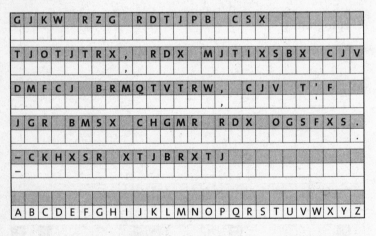

G	J	K	W		R	Z	G		R	D	T	J	P	B		C	S	X					

T	J	O	T	J	T	R	X	,		R	D	X		M	J	T	I	X	S	B	X		C	J	V
								,																	

D	M	F	C	J		B	R	M	Q	T	V	T	R	W	,		C	J	V		T	'	F
														,							'	

J	G	R		B	M	S	X		C	H	G	M	R		R	D	X		O	G	S	F	X	S	.
																								.

-	C	K	H	X	S	R		X	T	J	B	R	X	T	J							
-																						

A	B	C	D	E	F	G	H	I	J	K	L	M	N	O	P	Q	R	S	T	U	V	W	X	Y	Z

Tip Try to weed out the differences between vowels and consonants. Vowels tend to be repeated during a word, and aren't seen as often at the start and end of long words.

Cryptogram 6

W		B	V	J		M	I	Y	T	W	K	D		V	S	M	Y	D	P		J	I	N	D	S

M	I	Y		Q	V	K	W	J	T		W	J	K	D	J	E	D	P			

P	A	J	V	C	W	E	D	,		N	R	E		I	J	S	A		V		M	W	D	J	P
								,																	

W	J		Q	R	C	V	J		M	I	Y	C		B	I	R	S	P		Q	V	K	D

W	J	K	D	J	E	D	P		E	Q	D		J	I	N	D	S		L	Y	W	H	D	.
																								.

A	B	C	D	E	F	G	H	I	J	K	L	M	N	O	P	Q	R	S	T	U	V	W	X	Y	Z

Cryptogram 7

D	Z	R	I		T	A	O		B	A		L	I	H	A		E	A	O	C	H		T	A	O

N	C	R		Y	O	H	H	L	I	B		T	A	O	C		X	N	H	R		L	I	H	A

H	Z	R		Z	N	I	P	K		A	X		H	D	R	J	W	R		Y	R	A	Y	J	R

D	Z	A		D	R	C	R	I	'	H		K	S	N	C	H		R	I	A	O	B	Z		
									'																

H	A		B	R	H		A	O	H		A	X		Q	O	C	T		P	O	H	T	.		
																							.		

A	B	C	D	E	F	G	H	I	J	K	L	M	N	O	P	Q	R	S	T	U	V	W	X	Y	Z

Tip Look carefully at similar words. For example, if a quotation contains PWT and PW, could those letters stand for AND and AN? Or for ITS and IT?

Cryptogram 8

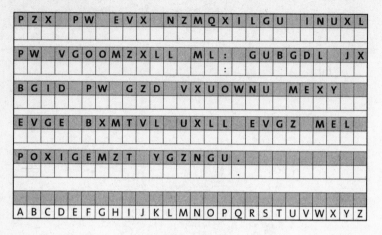

P	Z	X		P	W		E	V	X		N	Z	M	Q	X	I	L	G	U		I	N	U	X	L

P	W		V	G	O	O	M	Z	X	L	L		M	L	:		G	U	B	G	D	L		J	X

B	G	I	D		P	W		G	Z	D		V	X	U	O	W	N	U		M	E	X	Y

E	V	G	E		B	X	M	T	V	L		U	X	L	L		E	V	G	Z		M	E	L

P	O	X	I	G	E	M	Z	T		Y	G	Z	N	G	U	.

A	B	C	D	E	F	G	H	I	J	K	L	M	N	O	P	Q	R	S	T	U	V	W	X	Y	Z

Cryptogram 9

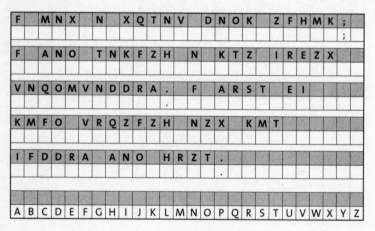

F		M	N	X		N		X	Q	T	N	V		D	N	O	K		Z	F	H	M	K	;

F		A	N	O		T	N	K	F	Z	H		N		K	T	Z		I	R	E	Z	X

V	N	Q	O	M	V	N	D	D	R	A	.		F		A	R	S	T		E	I

K	M	F	O		V	R	Q	Z	F	Z	H		N	Z	X		K	M	T

I	F	D	D	R	A		A	N	O		H	R	Z	T	.

A	B	C	D	E	F	G	H	I	J	K	L	M	N	O	P	Q	R	S	T	U	V	W	X	Y	Z

Cryptogram 10

P	H	T	E	D	O	K	F	V		B	Q	J	J		I	K	S	K	F		O	L	X	K

O	A	K		E	J	L	P	K		H	C		Y	H	H	X	V	.		N	H	D
																		.				

P	L	I	'	O		V	O	L	I	M		H	I		L		C	J	H	E	E	N
			'																			

M	Q	V	X		O	H		F	K	L	P	A		L		A	Q	W	A		V	A	K	J	C

A	B	C	D	E	F	G	H	I	J	K	L	M	N	O	P	Q	R	S	T	U	V	W	X	Y	Z

Cryptogram 11

E	H		C	U	V	T	O	R	V		T	V	L	'	M		A	S	S		K	E	A
														'									

U	S	H	R	S	T	M	E	N	L		E	L		V		W	E	U	U	N	U	,
																					,	

K	N	J		T	N	W	S		K	E	A		K	V	E	U		E	A

V	R	J	V	Z	A		A	N		L	S	V	M	R	Z		T	N	W	Y	S	C	?
																						?	

A	B	C	D	E	F	G	H	I	J	K	L	M	N	O	P	Q	R	S	T	U	V	W	X	Y	Z

A CRYPTIC WORD

Here is a well-known English word. Can you read it?

E10100010001000UNI100ATXN

A LITTLE ADVICE

Properly read, this number contains advice to a person who has forgotten his luncheon:

102840

What is it?

DATE WITH DESTINY

The following innocent-looking letter was intercepted by an alert detective. It contained a message which might have caused disastrous consequences, had it not been discovered. Can you find the key and decode the message? (Phyllis Fraser and Edith Young, 1947)

July Fifth, 1944

Dear Will,

Can you take me to Bert's with you on Sat? Webster's car is broken and won't run. The man at Herman's repair shop stayed and worked again. He was at work for two days. Result: nil.

I won't see you now until Fri. Hope Ed's better.

Chuck

ALTERNATELY

Insert letters in place of the asterisks in the following eight sentences. When all the words are rightly completed, select a word from each sentence. These extracted words together form an old adage. (Arthur Hirschberg, 1920)

1. H*I*U*E*S*A*O*T*I*B*S*N*S*
2. D*N*T*L*L*E*
3. I*E*W*A*T*E*R*B*E*I*
4. H*H*S*G*O*H*A*O*H*S*H*U*D*R*
5. I*N*W*H*T*H*T*S*I*H*
6. A*O*D*R*E*D*E*R*W*L*
7. G*T*T*E*O*O*T*E*L*S
8. T*E*I*G*O*E*C*O*N*F*O*D

NEXT!

Decipher the following code arrangement of an old proverb:

DZQKX SN ADC, DZQKX SN QHRD,

LZJDR Z LZM GDZKSGX, VDZKSGX, ZMC VHRD.

Similarly, which famous sentence is expressed in the following code:

XIBU IBUI HPE XSPVHIU?

(Arthur Hirschberg, 1920)

WORDS OF WAR

This message was sent in code by a scout to an officer at headquarters. Can you decode it? (Arthur Hirschberg, 1920)

S	O	P	O	B	O	R	N	E	N	E
A	I	D	M	S	P	E	D	S	E	E
G	S	N	B	E	L	A	I	S	M	H
N	O	A	S	N	A	G	N	I	Y	T

Codewords are cipher-based crosswords where each letter has been replaced by a number from 1 to 26. Every letter of the alphabet can be found somewhere in each puzzle. To get you started, a few of the letters may be given. This, together with deducing the most frequent letters, will help you to complete the entire crossword.

Codeword 1

1	19	13	4	■	4	25	7	7	23	7	14	13
9	■	12	■	6	■	10	■	26	■	18	■	4
19	15	14	10	20	22	2	■	15	19	6	13	7
21	■	6	■	17	■	8	■	7	■	17	■	25
11	6	16	■	4	12	19	17	9	19	20	5	■
19	■	■	■	7	■	4	■	■	■	10	■	8
15	10	2	7	5	22	■	7	9	17	26	17	14
24	■	19	■	■	■	16	■	19	■	■	■	19
■	2	7	20	13	25	7	19	14	■	19	14	15
8	■	13	■	7	■	22	■	22	■	15	■	7
19	15	4	10	14	■	13	7	20	13	6	19	9
20	■	14	■	3	■	7	■	26	■	4	■	7
16	7	10	2	7	4	14	22	■	5	7	8	4

1 F	2	3	4	5 D	6	7	8	9	10	11	12	13
14 R	15 C	16	17	18	19	20	21	22	23	24	25	26

A B C̶ D̶ E̶ F̶ G H I J K L M N O P Q R̶ S T U V W X Y Z

Codeword 2

22	20	5	24	24	5	20	25		22	23	5	20
25		3		25		1		12		3		5
2	4	14	16	3		25	26	5	20	15	25	13
15				9		3		8		24		9
20	4	19	16	15	2	5		15	18	4	11	
16		16				11		20		2		10
7	4	5	7	2	6		9	5	21	4	18	25
4		7		15		5				22		13
	7	3	5	14		18	4	14	16	22	4	7
15		15		18		22		15				3
18	4	2	15	4	26	4		9	4	24	17	25
15		2		3		15		1		16		16
22	4	4	7		23	2	5	20	6	23	16	22

1	2	3	4	5	6	7	8	9	10	11	12	13
14	15 I	16	17	18 B	19	20	21	22	23	24 C	25	26

A B̸ C̸ D E F G H I̸ J K L M N O P Q R S T U V W X Y Z

Tip It can be easy to go wrong in these puzzles, so cross out letters you've already deduced on the alphabet list provided.

Codeword 3

18	22	11	8	24	1	12	21	■	24	10	18	6
14	■	18	■	10	■	3	■	18	■	6	■	8
12	7	7	16	6	■	20	16	6	9	12	1	17
1	■	2	■	8	■	16	■	7	■	12	■	18
22	19	24	10	8	10	24	1	18	■	23	18	4
■	■	18	■	■	■	8	■	21	■	■	■	8
24	8	25	1	21	15	■	11	18	5	18	6	22
13	■	■	■	18	■	26	■	■	■	9	■	■
16	24	8	■	10	17	18	16	24	1	3	17	8
8	■	4	■	2	■	6	■	20	■	1	■	21
18	9	18	5	1	21	15	■	19	1	8	17	22
2	■	7	■	21	■	12	■	17	■	21	■	12
19	8	20	1	■	16	21	22	8	6	20	12	25

1 I	2	3	4	5	6	7	8	9	10	11	12	13
14	15	16	17	18	19 Y	20	21	22	23	24	25	26

A B C D E F G H J̷ J K L M N O P Q̲ R S T U V W X Y̷ Z

Tip Remember the Greek wine RETSINA – it contains the seven most common letters in English text.

Codeword 4

18	20	14	20	23	20	1	20		20	17	16	20
22		19		22		16		26		16		7
12	23	4	26	26	4	23		14	22	15	26	7
4		21		4		15		22		25		22
	8	20	7	7		26	21	22	22	5	4	23
13				7		7				4		21
4	10	4	13	4	21		7	8	15	21	9	4
21		12				11		14				19
9	10	15	18	24	26	4		22	24	20	10	
4		7		22		24		22		23		13
6	10	15	25	5		14	15	24	2	22	21	4
16		22		4		19		4		26		23
10	19	21	3		9	23	4	4	21	4	23	19

1	2	3	4	5	6	7 T	8	9	10	11	12	13
14	15	16	17	18	19	20	21	22	23	24	25	26 S

A B C D E F G H I J̶ K L M N O P Q R̶ S̶ T̶ U V W X Y Z

Tip Keep a look-out for interesting patterns of numbers. For example, if 23 is always followed by 14, could 23 = Q and 14 = U?

Codeword 5

2	15	25	13	15	26		19	18	11	6	17	16
	4		6		8		13		3		18	
24	10	5	11		24	12	5	8	17	17	15	21
	17				10		16		17			
11	6	6	16	8	15				3	19	8	14
	20		3		17		19		19		2	
20	15	2	10	17	8	21	6	12	5	8	24	7
	17		15		3		2		14		25	
15	10	19	13				22	21	3	4	15	2
			6		14		15				19	
3	14	1	5	10	3	2	10		23	8	10	15
	5		24		9		10		8		6	
19	6	13	15	17	15		8	7	25	5	17	15

1	2	3	4	5	6 O	7	8	9	10	11	12	13
14	15	16 G	17	18	19	20	21	22	23	24	25	26

A B C D E F Ø H I J K L M N Ø P Q R S T U V W X Y Z

> *Tip* If a number is repeated many times in the same word, it is more likely to be a vowel than a consonant.

HARDLY THE BARD

Insert in the proper places three A's, three E's, six I's, nine O's, 4 U's and one Y, and a couplet from Shakespeare will appear. (Arthur Hirschberg, 1920)

S T R F L S L V T H T N Y R W L L
T H G H Y D N T H N G H T H N K S N L L

THE 'CAN INN ALE' CODE

Here is a real code that was used during the American Civil War. It was sent on November 25, 1862 from Abraham Lincoln to Commander Burnside in Virginia. Lincoln was growing impatient with the slow progress of his army of the Potomac, so he sent a message to Burnside to arrange a meeting on the steamer *Baltimore*.

The staff of the Union Telegraph devised a simple but deceptive code to broker the possibility of meeting. Can you crack it?

Washington, D.C.,

November 25, 1862.

BURNSIDE, Falmouth, Virginia:

Can Inn Ale me withe 2 oar our Ann pas Ann me flesh ends N. V. Corn Inn out with U cud Inn heaven day nest Wed roe Moor Tom darkey hat Greek Why Hawk of Abbot Inn B chewed I if. — Bates

---

WHAT A TEASE

In order to read the following sentence properly, the same letter must be inserted fourteen times:

A L H O U G H H E W O O S I E R E D ,
H E Y O L D H E O F O L D A L E .

149 · Codes and Ciphers

RIGHT THIS WAY

Can you find the hidden message?

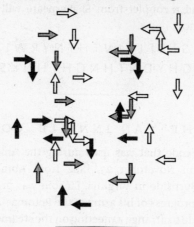

MISSING WORDS

Complete with words. What can you locate down column shown?

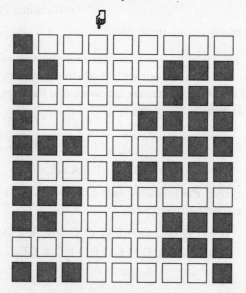

COLLECTED CODES – PART 1

In each case, find the code which reveals the message in English. Simple codes are followed by more complicated ones.

1. YTEIR AVETI NIFNI REHEL ATSMO TSUCR ONREH REHTI WTONN ACEGA

2. NSTME TAGAI HOLDI LDYOU DYWOU FULBO EAUTI HADAB IDYOU IFISA

3. STHEREN WARED ANONES ASOM OBLINDY WASP CTHOSEN LTHATA SWILLD ENOTX PSEEM

4. CFUUFS UIF EFWJM ZPV LOPX UIBO UIF EFWJM ZPV EPO'U

5. UP USBWFM IPQFGVMMZ JT B CFUUFS UIJOH UIBO UP BSSJWF

6. BAPR ZBER HAGB GUR OERNPU QRNE SEVRAQF BAPR ZBER

7. UNPREDICTABLY: GKFJITQOKGSOTS SJVGCFOXOYKM – FGOGSKJJFHSKM OGSKJJINVSOIG JKCFOTOSOIGKM

8. ZXXRWVMGH DROO SZKKVM RM GSV YVHG IVTFOZGVW UZNRORVH

A FAIR COP

'What do you get if you multiply XX by itself?' my niece Cecilia asked me.

'CCCC,' I replied. 'Twenty times twenty is four hundred.'

'Aha!' said Cecilia. 'You're jumping to conclusions, Uncle Timothy. XX isn't 20; it's a code of my own, in which each digit is represented by a letter. And XX multiplied by itself is MMCC.'

'I see,' I said, rather stuffily. It was a 'fair cop'.

'Try again,' said Cecilia. 'Divide XX by C and square the quotient. What does it come to in my notation?'

CRYPTARITHMS

Here you need to use your numeric code-breaking skills. These puzzles are known to be hundreds of years old, but it wasn't until Maurice Vatriquant coined the term 'crypt-arithmetic' in 1931 that they got a name. In 1955, the puzzle maker J. A. H. Hunter suggested the alternative name of 'alphametic' (alphabetic arithmetic) for cryptarithms that use recognizable words.

Each letter represents a different digit (from 0 to 9) throughout the puzzle. Given the encoded version in letters, you must deduce what digit each letter represents so that a valid mathematical equation is formed. For example, if the puzzle were TAURUS + PISCES = SCORPIO, the answer would be 859,091 + 46,1371 = 1,320,462, where S = 1, O = 2, C = 3, P = 4, and so on.

Since each digit is represented by one letter only, a maximum of ten different letters can be used in one puzzle. In most cases only one solution is possible. You can therefore use a range of logical techniques and case-by-case analysis to reduce the possibilities to a unique answer.

Cryptarithm 1

This puzzle is not in true Roman numerals (6 + 6 + 6 + 6 = 24) but, treating them as code letters, what addition sum does it represent?

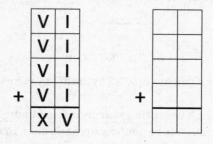

Cryptarithm 2

Here's a puzzle for those of you fluent in Spanish (2 + 2 + 3 =7).

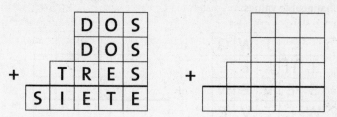

Cryptarithm 3

A French cryptarithm.

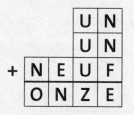

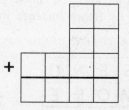

Cryptarithm 4

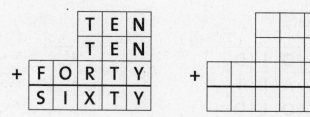

Cryptarithm 5

This puzzle has two possible answers – the letters O and N have interchangeable values.

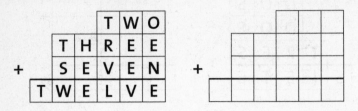

Cryptarithm 6

This is possibly the most famous puzzle of its type. It was originally published by Henry Dudeney in the July 1924 issue of *Strand* magazine.

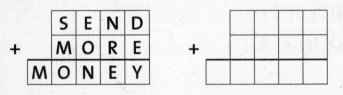

Cryptarithm 7

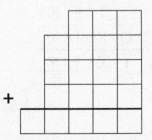

Cryptarithm 8

```
      F I F T Y
+   S T A T E S   +
  A M E R I C A
```

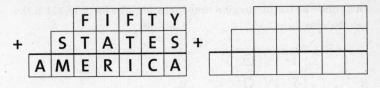

Cryptarithm 9

```
    S A T U R N
    U R A N U S
  N E P T U N E
+     P L U T O   +
  P L A N E T S
```

Cryptarithm 10

This was devised in honour of Martin Gardner's retirement from his long-running column in *Scientific American*.

```
    M A R T I N
+ G A R D N E R   +
  R E T I R E S
```

Cryptarithm 11

```
    L E T T E R S
+ A L P H A B E T
  S C R A B B L E
```

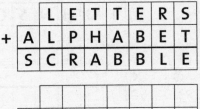

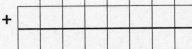

155 · Codes and Ciphers

Cryptarithm 12

This time, the calculation is a multiplication. The EE in THREE is the key to this puzzle.

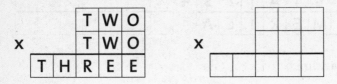

Cryptarithm 13

This is the first 'crypt-arithmetic' provided by Minos, the penname of Maurice Vatriquant, in the May 1931 issue of *Sphinx*, a Belgian magazine of recreational mathematics.

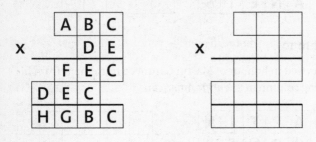

Cryptarithm 14

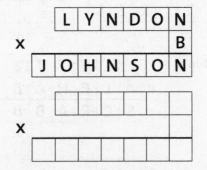

LETTER-FIGURE PUZZLE

Every letter in the system of equations below represents a different digit. AC, BC, etc. are two-digit numbers. Can you find the values in figures of all the letters?

$$A \times B = B$$
$$B \times C = AC$$
$$C \times D = BC$$
$$D \times E = CH$$
$$E \times F = DK$$
$$F \times H = CJ$$
$$H \times J = KJ$$
$$J \times K = E$$
$$K \times L = L$$
$$A \times L = L$$

Henry Dudeney, to whom this puzzle was sent, notes that 'It is not difficult, if properly attacked.'

ON THE TIP OF YOUR TONGUE

What words of advice for those in the world of espionage can be read here?

Awe lisp eyes shoe had prow take dares eke rates.

CON-SEQUENTIAL

You've intercepted these words from a suspected gang of thieves. What's going on?

PUTT	HEM	ONE
YOU	TOFF	RON
TWIN	DOWN	OW

DRIVEN DOTTY

Remember how to do dot-to-dot? Trace a path from letter to letter. You'll notice that we've already joined up the first word, WHAT. When you've finished, tell us what the answer to the riddle is.

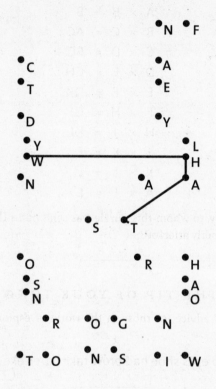

SENSE OF DIRECTION

Which two-word phrase is encoded here? In fact, it is two codes in one.

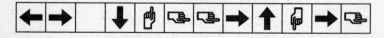

KEY WORD

I typed a well-known English word into my laptop. I pressed all the right keys, yet this mess appeared on the screen:

4NS*6RTSOAN352E

What word did I type, and can you work out why this happened?

KEY CODE

What is the key to solving this long sequence of curious numbers?

4 23 51   36 26 33 11   5 25   19 20
22 23 9   32 33 51 46 22 24 14 28

ALL KEYED UP

Two puzzles for the price of one. Use the diagram to decode the encrypted message below. Then see if you can provide a suitable answer for the puzzle that will then become apparent.

UD 'RTOWQEURWE' UA BIR RGW

IBKT KIBFWAR QIES YAUBF

KWRRWEA DEIN RGW RIO EIQ,

RGWB RGW IRGWEA NYAR VW...?

ANACROSTICS

Elizabeth S. Kingsley is credited with inventing the first anacrostic puzzle, under the name 'Double-crostic', for the Saturday Review *in 1934. Since then, various different terms for the puzzle have appeared. Sometimes, the compilers go one step further and use clues that are related to the quotation.*

Anacrostics are so called because they are a combination of anagram and acrostic. Their construction is ingenious as there are three ways to attack the puzzle. The aim of each puzzle is to complete the encoded quotation.

The first step is to try to answer as many of the word clues as you can. Each box should contain one letter. The number in that box shows you where that letter should be entered into the main quotation grid. After that, see if you can complete any of the words in the quotation. Any extra letters gleaned can be transferred back into the clues via the cross-reference given in the quotation grid (e.g. if you deduce that 42 D contains an 'S', then you can also put an S in the box labelled 42 in clue D).

Finally, keep an eye out on the initial letters of all the clue answers. These, when read in order from top down, will reveal the person to whom the quotation is attributed.

Anacrostic 1

1 J	2 H	3 A		4 H	5 E	6 G		7 G	8 F	9 E	10 C	11 J	12 A	13 B	
14 B	15 A	16 I		17 J	18 C	19 H	20 B		21 I	22 J	23 E		24 I	25 A	26 B
27 E	28 H	29 I	30 J	31 D	32 G	33 E	34 E	35 F		36 H	37 F	38 G	39 H		40 J
41 A	42 H	43 D		44 C	45 H	46 I	47 F		48 F	49 E	50 J	51 J	52 F	53 G
54 G	55 I	56 B		57 I	58 J	59 J	60 F		61 G	62 H	63 C	64 I	65 E	66 E	67 A	68 B	69 G
70 E	71 E	72 F	73 F		74 C	75 B	76 I	77 G	78 A	?

A. | 41 | 25 | 3 | 12 | 67 | 15 | 78 |

B. | 14 | 68 | 13 | 20 | 26 | 56 | 75 |

C. | 74 | 63 | 18 | 10 | 44 |

D. | 31 | 66 | 43 |

E. | 49 | 70 | 27 | 23 | 9 | 65 | 71 | 33 | 34 | 5 |

F. | 60 | 47 | 73 | 52 | 8 | 72 | 37 | 35 | 48 |

G. | 69 | 6 | 54 | 77 | 38 | 7 | 32 | 61 | 53 |

H. | 39 | 28 | 4 | 62 | 45 | 2 | 42 | 36 | 19 |

I. | 21 | 24 | 76 | 64 | 16 | 29 | 57 | 46 | 55 |

J. | 1 | 11 | 50 | 30 | 17 | 58 | 59 | 40 | 22 | 51 |

CLUES

A. Pungent red pepper
B. Text added to the end
C. Cries like a lion
D. Fled
E. Can be placed in water
F. Your cilia
G. Type of draw in chess
H. Nocturnal person
I. Government investigator
J. Viniculture

Anacrostic 2

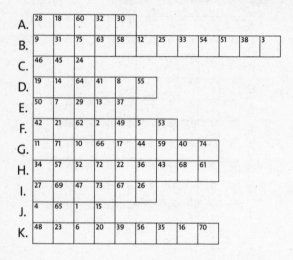

1 J	2 F	3 B		4 J	5 F	6 K	7 E	8 D	9 B	10 G		11 G	12 B	13 E	14 D	
15 J	16 K	17 G	18 A	19 D	20 K	21 F	22 H	23 K	24 C	25 B	26 I		27	28 A		
29 E	30 A	31 B	32 A		33 B	34 H	35 K		36 H	37 E	38 B	39 K	40 G	41 D		
42 F	43 H	44 G		45 C	46 C	47 I	48 K		49 F	50 E		51 B	52 H		53 F	54 B	55 D
56 K	57 H	58 B	59 G	60 A	61 H	62 F		63 B	64 D	65 J	,	66 G	67 I		68 H	69 I
70 K	71 G	72 H		73 I	74 G	75 B										

A. | 28 | 18 | 60 | 32 | 30 |

B. | 9 | 31 | 75 | 63 | 58 | 12 | 25 | 33 | 54 | 51 | 38 | 3 |

C. | 46 | 45 | 24 |

D. | 19 | 14 | 64 | 41 | 8 | 55 |

E. | 50 | 7 | 29 | 13 | 37 |

F. | 42 | 21 | 62 | 2 | 49 | 5 | 53 |

G. | 11 | 71 | 10 | 66 | 17 | 44 | 59 | 40 | 74 |

H. | 34 | 57 | 52 | 72 | 22 | 36 | 43 | 68 | 61 |

I. | 27 | 69 | 47 | 73 | 67 | 26 |

J. | 4 | 65 | 1 | 15 |

K. | 48 | 23 | 6 | 20 | 39 | 56 | 35 | 16 | 70 |

CLUES

A. Metalworker
B. Maze-like
C. Veneration
D. Greek goddess of the Moon
E. Naked boys on Renaissance art
F. Curdled milk dessert
G. To which
H. Holiday after a wedding
I. Type of computer printer
J. Ballerina's short skirt
K. Compensation

Anacrostic 3

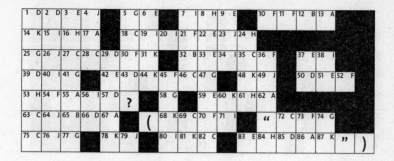

CLUES

A. Erase from memory
B. Everything
C. Sufficiently interesting
D. 315 degrees
E. Type of hand in bridge
F. Municipal pound employee
G. Green, transparent beryl
H. Haitian magic
I. Atrocious cruelty
J. Crisp, smooth lustrous fabric
K. Outgrowths

Anacrostic 4

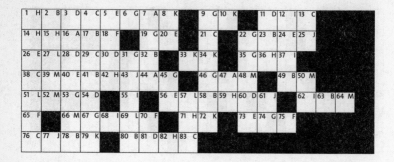

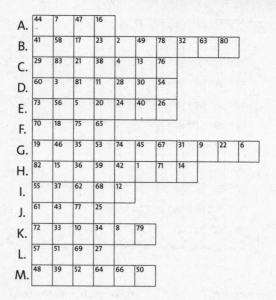

CLUES

A. Head of a college
B. Burial
C. Viral disease in children
D. Commemoration
E. Duo
F. Small ostrich-like bird
G. Zoological study of fish
H. A ray of light at night
I. Overflowing
J. Highway
K. Hardened caramelized sugar
L. Wild mountain goat
M. Ribbon-like strip of pasta

Anacrostic 5

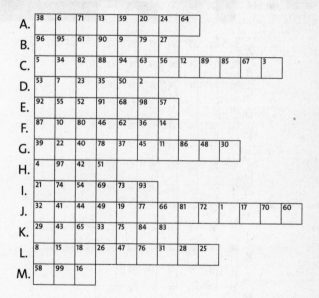

1 J	2 D		3 C	4 H	5 C	6 A	7 D	8 L	9 B	10 F	11 G		12 C	13 A	14 F	15 L	16 M
17 J	18 L		19 J	20 A		21 I	22 G	23 D	24 A	25 L		26 L	27 B	28 L		29 K	30 G
31 L	32 J	33 K	34 C	35 D	36 F	37 G	38 A	39 G		40 G	41 J	42 H		43 K			
44 J	45 G	46 F	47 L		48 G	49 J	50 D		51 H	52 E		53 D	54 I	55 E	56 C	57 E	58 M
59 A	60 J		61 B	62 F	63 C	64 A	65 K			66 J	67 C		68 E	69 I	70 J	71 A
72 J	73 I		74 I	75 K		76 L	77 J	78 G	79 B	,	80 F		81 J	82 C	83 K	84 K
85 C	86 G		87 F	88 C	89 C		90 B	91 E		92 E	93 I		94 C	95 B	96 B	97 H	98 E	99 M

A. 38 6 71 13 59 20 24 64

B. 96 95 61 90 9 79 27

C. 5 34 82 88 94 63 56 12 89 85 67 3

D. 53 7 23 35 50 2

E. 92 55 52 91 68 98 57

F. 87 10 80 46 62 36 14

G. 39 22 40 78 37 45 11 86 48 30

H. 4 97 42 51

I. 21 74 54 69 73 93

J. 32 41 44 49 19 77 66 81 72 1 17 70 60

K. 29 43 65 33 75 84 83

L. 8 15 18 26 47 76 31 28 25

M. 58 99 16

CLUES

A. Exterior of an ovum
B. Nocturnal American mammals
C. Ceremonial induction
D. Friendly
E. Conceals the sound
F. Long-term prospects
G. Suitable for driving

H. Edible starchy tuberous root
I. Fussy
J. Medicine for treating allergies
K. Around Wednesday?
L. Confused
M. This is it!

Anacrostic 6

1 J	2 D		3 A	4 L	5 M	6 G	7	8 E	9 C	10 J	11 D	12 J	13 J
14 N	15 A	16 H	17 F	18 J	19 G	20 M		21 C	22 D	23 E	24 N	25 B	26 K	27 H
28 B	29 E	30 A	31 I		32 L	33 E	34 G	35 M	36 B		37 A		38 C	39 A	40 M
41 K	42 G	43 H	44 A		45 M	46 L	47 G		48 C	49 A	50 N		51 D	52 B	53 A	54 L	55 K
56 E	57 B	58 G	,	59 K		60 H	61 E	62 F	63 M	64 K	65 L	-	66 H	67 N	68 G	69 K	70 B
71 J	72 C	73 N		74 F	75 C	76 F		77 M	78 I		79 H	80 J	81 M	,	82 A
83 I	84 E	85 B	86 D		87 F	88 E	89 D	90 A	91 J		92 G	93 J	94 A
95 H	96 K	97 B	98 C		99 K	100 L	101 D		102 K	103 J

A. | 94 | 53 | 82 | 90 | 37 | 30 | 49 | 3 | 39 | 44 | 15 |

B. | 97 | 52 | 85 | 70 | 28 | 25 | 36 | 57 |

C. | 98 | 9 | 21 | 38 | 72 | 48 | 75 |

D. | 89 | 2 | 101 | 86 | 22 | 51 | 11 |

E. | 84 | 29 | 88 | 33 | 23 | 61 | 56 | 8 |

F. | 76 | 17 | 74 | 87 | 62 |

G. | 19 | 34 | 47 | 68 | 58 | 6 | 92 | 42 |

H. | 27 | 60 | 16 | 66 | 95 | 43 | 79 |

I. | 31 | 83 | 78 | 7 |

J. | 71 | 12 | 18 | 93 | 91 | 13 | 1 | 80 | 103 | 10 |

K. | 96 | 55 | 35 | 41 | 102 | 64 | 26 | 69 | 59 | 99 |

L. | 4 | 100 | 65 | 54 | 46 | 32 |

M. | 63 | 81 | 20 | 77 | 5 | 40 | 45 |

N. | 14 | 24 | 67 | 73 | 50 |

CLUES

A. Flashy

B. Pacific fish with spiny fins

C. The situation, in brief

D. Optic cleanser

E. Denial of all authority

F. Sketched

G. Position of the last cricketer?

H. Ground one's teeth

I. Teased out information

J. Farthest down

K. Spectator at the scene

L. Beat

M. Side-on

N. Turns at an angle

MONOCHROME CODE

These circles hide a well-known saying. What is it?

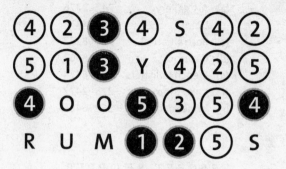

SCENE AND HERD

The following message was intercepted as it passed between two enemy agents. It transpired that it contained a contact's nationality and where he should have been met. See if you can find both pieces of information.

> She must see why the pea green shoes are easy on the eye. Oh, and tea time lengthens the queue you should join, aye? The golf tee she can owe me.

PHONEY

In some countries, companies can advertise their phone number using a word mnemonic such as 0800 FLOWERS for a florist. Here, FLOWERS represents the telephone number 356-9377, using the usual telephone keypad code:

Can you guess the mnemonics used by the following companies given their local phone number?

(a)	Art gallery	742–2776
(b)	Dairy	964–4878
(c)	Portrait artist	226–8277
(d)	Casino	367–8863
(e)	French polishers	827–6474
(f)	Cake shop	325–2477
(g)	Wine merchant	252–6465

SECRET SHOPPER

This shopping list has been typed out for the buyer, but a fault on the typewriter has occurred. Identify the four foodstuffs being requested.

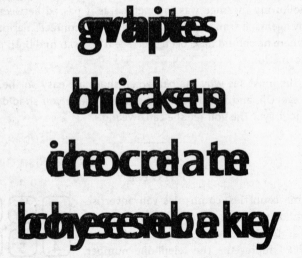

COLLECTED CODES – PART 2

1. What piece of useful information is encoded by FOR TOOTH, I'VE ATE NIGH – NATO?

2. If QUIETER TYPEWRITER represents 1783534 5603248534, which letter is encoded by the digit 9?

3. In 1979, which British band released an album entitled 5317704?

4. Which two messages are found here? TNHEEIRTEHSENROOTN IEMTEHLIINKGENTOHRETPHREEOSTEHNETR

A NOVEL CODE·

Which well-known literary code can be found using these letters and the stencil provided?

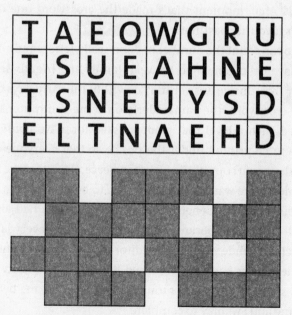

CHAPTER 4
Cruciverbalism

HOME COOKING, CHINESE STYLE (5,4,4)

Crosswords are all about a meeting of minds: your brain versus the compiler's. If you can see past the deception and find the correct solution – in this case BIRD'S NEST SOUP – then you're on just the same wavelength as another human being. Perhaps it's this 'Aha!' moment that's made the crossword one of the world's favourite pastimes.

Who can count the number of phone calls, letters and e-mails that have been generated between family and friends searching for that elusive answer to 17 down? In the early days of the *Times* crossword, the camaraderie on some commuter trains reached such a level that readers asked for a 'No conferring' notice to be printed under the puzzle so that everyone could solve their own copy of the puzzle in peace. Nevertheless, it was conceded there was much satisfaction to be gained from hearing your fellow passengers discussing a clue you had already solved. Crosswords became part of the rhythm of everyday life: reader Joan Zunde wrote to the editor of *The Times*, reminiscing how her father had once returned home from his daily commute, sighing: 'Ah, it was a tough one today, took me between Barming and Swanley to complete.'

FUN AT CHRISTMAS

In 1913, Arthur Wynne, a Liverpudlian who ended up working at the New York *World* newspaper, was searching for something different to add to his festive puzzle page. The newspaper's FUN supplement had used many word squares and other verbal puzzles before. He came up with a new kind of puzzle – words had to be entered into a grid, and clues for each word were listed under the headings 'Horizontal' and 'Vertical'.

Wynne's first effort wasn't particularly good – several of the clues weren't accurate, others were downright obscure, and one word appeared twice in the grid (a no-no by today's standards). Nevertheless, on 21 December 1913 this first 'Word-cross' puzzle was foisted on the unwitting American public. Words had been intersected before – in Latin and even Egyptian hieroglyphs – but this was the first time that this had been done specifically in puzzle form. When the *World* tried dropping the puzzle, the paper received so many complaints that it was reinstated.

In 1924, two young entrepreneurs, Dick Simon and Max Schuster, opened their new office. Not for them the nine-to-five grind, they were 'Simon & Schuster – Publishers' according to the sign on their door. Cruelly, some wag had scrawled 'Of what?' underneath. The culprit had a point – they needed something to sell. Thankfully, salvation came in the form of Simon's Aunt Wixie, who happened to mention that she would like a book full of those crossword puzzles that appeared in her newspaper.

Simon and Schuster approached the *World* and a deal was struck. With the help of three newspaper staff, a compilation of fifty puzzles was to be published. The *World*'s columnist in

Arthur Wynne's very first FUN crossword
(the solution is on page 184)

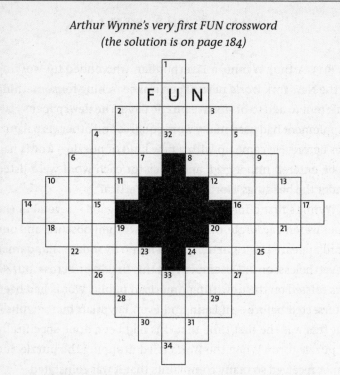

2–3. What bargain hunters enjoy.
4–5. A written acknowledgment.
6–7. Such and nothing more.
10–11. A bird.
14–15. Opposed to less.
18–19. What this puzzle is.
22–23. An animal of prey.
26–27. The close of a day.
28–29. To elude.
30–31. The plural of is.
8–9. To cultivate.
12–13. A bar of wood or iron.
16–17. What artists learn to do.
20–21. Fastened.
24–25. Found on the seashore.
10–18. The fibre of the gomuti palm.

6–22. What we all should be.
4–26. A day dream.
2–11. A talon.
19–28. A pigeon.
F–7. Part of your head.
23–30. A river in Russia.
1–32. To govern.
33–34. An aromatic plant.
N–8. A fist.
24–31. To agree with.
3–12. Part of a ship.
20–29. One.
5–27. Exchanging.
9–25. To sink in mud.*
13–21. A boy.

*Wynne meant to say 'Stuck in mud'

residence, Franklin P. Adams ('F.P.A.'), was horrified at this news. Despite being a paid-up member of the crossword fan club, he was certain that the young men would lose what little money they had on the venture. Another publisher was similarly wary, so much so that he advised them to publish the volume under a pseudonym.

And so, under the moniker of the Plaza Publishing Company (named after the local telephone exchange), the first 3,600 crossword books were released into the wild under the title *The Cross Word Puzzle Book: An anthology of fifty cross word puzzles selected as the best of the thousands that have been submitted to the New York World published here exclusively for the first time.* Columnist F.P.A. gave it a plug in his column on publication day: 'Hooray! Hooray! Hooray! The cross word puzzle book is out today.' A pencil was attached to each copy of the book to make it as easy as possible for the purchaser to become hooked.

A small ad for the book was placed in the *World.* 'Attention cross word puzzle fans! The first book of cross word puzzles – $1.35. Your money back if not 100% satisfied!' A subsequent advert took the hype to another level, making it out to be the Next Big Thing: '1921 – Coué [a French psychologist and publishing phenomenon], 1922 – Mah Jong, 1923 – Bananas,* 1924 – THE CROSSWORD-PUZZLE BOOK.' Despite very slow initial sales and its very high price tag, the book slowly began to grip the public's attention. In the first three months of publication 40,000 copies were sold, rising to 400,000 by the end of the year.

---

*There was a sudden banana craze in 1923 leading to a supply shortage; the song 'Yes, We Have No Bananas' was written in that year.

CRAZY DAYS

A craze was now firmly in place. Dictionaries became intensely sought after – public libraries rationed each visitor to five minutes of looking-up time, and librarians often blanked out the crossword puzzle in newspapers to stop people from hogging them. Train companies provided dictionaries for the benefit of passengers, and boats stocked up on crosswords (with solutions) and copious reference books for passengers in search of a solution mid-voyage.

As may be expected, the reaction of the clergy to this 'time wasting' was not positive, although a forward-thinking Reverend George McElveen of Pittsburgh did provide a crossword for his congregation to solve before mass, the answers containing the themes of his sermon for that week.

Even the fashion industry got in on the act. Sales of chequered fabrics rose substantially, and black and white squares became a trendy colour combination. If you see on eBay pieces of American jewellery from 1924/25 with black and white square patterns, the chances are they were inspired by crosswords. One far-out designer even offered a wrist-mounted dictionary, albeit with rather fewer words in it than the *Oxford English Dictionary*.

In Britain, the crossword took almost as long to fully take hold. *Pearson's* magazine had given the puzzle a try-out in 1922, and in 1924 some of Arthur Wynne's puzzles were syndicated to British papers such as the *Sunday Express*. But it was perhaps on 30 July 1925, when the *Daily Telegraph* began its own daily puzzle, that the British public began to take notice. The *Manchester Guardian* followed suit in 1929.

The early attempts of the Britons to replicate the American fad were somewhat amateurish. The grids were ugly: sometimes in several unconnected pieces, or unsymmetrical, with more black squares and awkward interlocking. Clearly, the British compilers had great difficulty in achieving a credible level of intermesh. Over the next five years or so, the task became simpler as it became acceptable to interlock only the alternate letters of the solutions, allowing compilers far more freedom in the words they could incorporate. The clues were straightforward, but even in the very earliest crosswords, some hint of wordplay and clever definitions was evident.

THE TIMES, THEY ARE A-CHANGING

The Times was disparaging. Under the headline AN ENSLAVED AMERICA, it reported that 'all America has succumbed to the crossword puzzle' and calculated that the craze was costing American productivity the equivalent of five million man-hours a day – far more than was lost through industrial disputes. However, eventually *The Times* relented and began publishing a crossword once a week.

Then the requests started coming in. A Lieutenant-Commander in the Royal Navy, A. C. Powell, led the charge: 'Sir, I am interested to see that you are including a cross-word puzzle in your Weekly Edition. Would it not be an additional attraction to your many readers – of whom I am pleased to be one – if the same cross-word puzzle were reproduced on one day of the week in your daily edition?' The letters of support for this idea far outnumbered the nay-sayers – as Mrs Blanche Hulton put it: 'To many persons these clever puzzles are an enjoyment second only to the best programmes of the B.B.C.'

'So many readers,' the paper subsequently announced, 'have written to express the desire that the cross-word puzzle, which is now a feature of the Weekly Edition, should be reproduced in the daily issue of *The Times* that effect will be given to this suggestion from tomorrow.' The idea took hold with the readership, and the editors announced that the puzzle would run daily from 1 February 1930. Soon the British were to be caught up in a crossword fever of their own. London Zoo refused to answer any more questions about EMUs and GNUs, such were their prevalence in crossword solution grids.

ÉMINENCE GRISE

The public's interest was piqued. Who were the mysterious figures who scribed these puzzles? In the case of *The Times* it was Adrian Bell, a young farmer whose journalist father had passed on the enquiry, and who had been given a mere ten days' notice to acquire the art of compiling crosswords and produce his first six. Luckily, he was more than up to the challenge and contributed over five thousand puzzles to *The Times* in the following years. He declared that cruciverbalism – the setting (and solving) of crosswords – was 'the ideal job for a chap with a vacant mind sitting on a tractor harrowing clods, or cycling'.

During World War II, when paper was scarce, the *Times* crossword continued to appear, with puzzles mostly written and edited by Ronald Carton. When the editorial office started shortening the clues to save paper, he protested that 'the clues of the crossword are written, and always have been written, with the greatest economy of words. That is what makes them bright and pungent. To cut down what is already succinct is to impair the general quality of the work.'

Many aspects of British crosswords were established by Edward Powys Mathers, whose puzzles appeared under the pseudonym Torquemada. He helped to evolve grid patterns from the American originals, and increased the use of cryptic indications. His series of Feelers puzzles in the *Saturday Westminster* magazine may be considered the first true crosswords that used complete sets of cryptic clues. As innovative as they were, his clues were often fiercely difficult, bordering on unfair. In one puzzle where the theme was to identify people's names in the style of a game of Knock Knock, one clue ran: '— who? — pants, I make-a you another pair', the answer (which must be said out loud in your best cod Italian accent) is EURIPIDES.

Another compiler was 'Afrit' – A. F. Ritchie, the headmaster of Wells Cathedral School. He summed up what he felt was fair play in cryptic crosswords thus: 'I need not mean what I say, but I must say what I mean.' In other words, if a sentence is worded ambiguously and you choose to grab hold of the wrong end of the stick, that's your tough luck. Afrit's rule is still regarded by modern compilers as a golden rule by which all cryptic clues should be judged. In 1966, Derrick Somerset Macnutt, known as Ximenes, published an important book on the standards of fair play that modern solvers should expect. To this day, compilers who play by his rules are called Ximeneans. Together, Mathers, Ritchie and Macnutt established what the modern, solid cryptic crossword should be about. Not everyone agrees with them, but their ground rules certainly helped to avoid the situation getting out of hand.

The personality mix of today's crossword compilers is not a huge leap from the early pioneers. There is still a healthy mix of boffins, classical music buffs, civil servants, retired school-masters and clergymen. Many are retired and compile puzzles as a useful, if not lucrative, hobby. Of the few that make a living from compiling, their output is near legendary. Roger Squires, by far the record holder for being the most prolific, had his 66,666th crossword, containing his two-millionth clue, published in May 2007 – more than twice as much as his nearest rival, while in 2004 Ruth Crisp retired from a lifetime of compiling aged 87. Many others have compiled several thousand puzzles.

CONSTRUCTION WORKERS

Compilers are frequently amused, or bemused, by the most common question thrown at them: 'Which do you do first, the grid or the clues?' It seems logical to assume that the words are fitted together first, rather than the compiler writing 32 brilliant clues then somehow finding a way for the answers to fit together in a symmetrical pattern – and this is indeed the case. Once the words have been chosen, each clue is composed. An editor checks over the puzzle and rewords any unsound clues. An official reference source is used to check the veracity of the definitions used in the puzzle, and it may be tested by some expert solvers before publication.

Publishers of dictionaries have been keen to use crosswords as a way of selling their wares. An early edition of *Chambers* features the following blurb on its front cover: 'Torquemada of the *Observer* writes "All my solvers know well enough by this time that the main dictionary I use, and the only small one is *Chambers's Twentieth Century Dictionary*. It is far the best English dictionary of its size and I have worn six copies to tatters."' Another edition splashes on its cover: '£500 won by using *Chambers's Twentieth Century Dictionary*', the result of one purchaser scooping the jackpot in a crossword-based lottery where many of the clues had multiple valid answers. Here's an example clue from such a puzzle: 'To have to wait in — in the dentist's office is infuriating'; the solver had to guess whether to insert VAIN or PAIN into the grid.

Crossword compiling has changed in recent years with the increase in computing power and the arrival of dedicated software. This is particularly helpful for compilers of American crosswords, where the fierce amount of interlocking – every single letter is part of both an across and a down clue – often caused headaches for the pre-digital compilers. To this day, many compilers prefer to use some combination of pen, pencil, eraser, dictionary and squared paper. As *Times* setter Mike Laws explains, 'My necessaries for work consist of a pint of beer, one tatty dictionary, and a kind of box on the wall which provides meaningless background noise to cover potential distractions.' His theory is that if he can't compile a crossword in a pub, how can he expect his solvers to solve it?

Given their predilection for hiding behind pseudonyms, which are often in-jokes based on their real name or classical references, it is perhaps not surprising that compilers are not exactly household names. However, many people already mentioned have famous links. Songstress Carly Simon is the daughter of Dick Simon (of Simon & Schuster), former MP and war correspondent Martin Bell is the son of Adrian Bell (the first *Times* compiler), and Paul McCartney's cousin Bert Danher compiled the Thursday crossword of the *Daily Telegraph* for 25 years.

BLACK (AND WHITE) HUMOUR

For some, the fun to be had with crosswords is too much to resist, although it's not always intentional. The wit and caricaturist Sir Max Beerbohm offered a crossword of his own making to *The Times*, admitting that the majority of the clues were complete nonsense. A few clues were genuine (such as 'A Victorian statesman lurking in a side lair' – answer: DISRAELI) to entice unfortunate solvers into vain attempts to solve the puzzle. In 1978, the *Daily Telegraph* printed an April Fool's Day crossword where 1 across was BACKWARDLY and all the other answers had to be entered into the grid in reverse. *The Times* made an inadvertent joke on 1 April 1986 when they accidentally printed the wrong grid beside the clues. While many complaints were received, some readers were able to complete the puzzle on grids of their own making – a few even cheekily suggesting that they enjoyed the extra challenge and could they do it more often.

The next time you do a crossword, look carefully. Occasionally, compilers like to make things difficult for themselves. It's possible that the constructor has put an extra something into the puzzle to make things more interesting. The compiler Don Manley (who goes by the handles Pasquale, Quixote and Duck – all famous Donalds) put one such message in the *Daily Telegraph*'s puzzle for 30 October 2004: reading the 'unchecked' letters around the perimeter of the grid revealed FOR CHAVE MANLEY'S CENTENARY, commemorating the hundredth anniversary of his father's birth. *The Times*'s 75th anniversary puzzle in 2005 contained a surprise in the across answers, the surnames of all their crossword editors to date (sometimes split across two clues): CARTON, we(AKEN/ HEAD)sea, GRANT, a(GREE/R)earwards, corn(LAWS) and (BROWN/E)levation. Hidden features such as these, known as Ninas,* are more prevalent in quick crosswords because they are far easier to compile.

An ingenious puzzle by American compiler Jeremiah Farrell was published on the day of the 1996 US Presidential election. The clue for 39 and 43 across is 'Lead story in tomorrow's newspaper!' Many solvers were baffled until they realized that the entire puzzle worked regardless of whether you entered BOB DOLE ELECTED or CLINTON ELECTED. This feat was achieved by making many of the clues ambiguous, for example 39 down's 'Black Halloween animal' could be BAT or CAT. These hidden messages can backfire: one reader of *The Times* wrote in to offer his condolences to the compiler who had positioned the solutions DESOLATE/MOTHER and AUNT/DECEASED symmetrically in the grid; thankfully, no such double tragedy had befallen the compiler.

Crosswords have carried many different types of messages. Several couples have said 'I do' following a proposal hidden by special arrangement. In wartime, propaganda messages have been hidden in puzzles. One lady, Anetta Duel, passed away aged 99 but was able to scribble her final will beside the *Daily Telegraph* crossword. Because Duel had signed her statement and *Telegraph* crossword editor Val Gilbert was able to date

*So called because the American cartoonist Al Hirschfeld hid the name of his daughter, Nina, in his drawings.

the crossword conclusively, the will was legally admitted as evidence of her final wishes.

RECORD-BREAKERS

The challenge of crosswords has taken both compilers and solvers to extremes. Competitive crossword solving is common among aficionados, with annual championships held in the UK and the USA. In the early days of the *Times* crossword, one correspondent recounted a story of how the Provost of Eton School timed his eggs by the time it took him to do the puzzle ... and he didn't like hard-boiled eggs! Like many such stories this one is apocryphal, but it didn't stop another reader from trying to emulate this feat: 'I started [boiling the egg] at 8.00 and it is now 15.05 and the egg has burst.' However, egg-timing speed has been achieved: in 1970, Roy Dean solved the cryptic *Times* crossword in 3 minutes 45 seconds.

The devotion to crosswords can be remarkable. One *Times* reader wrote in 1933 that he'd solved all 1,272 puzzles published so far, while in 1966 a lady from Fiji took the record for the longest-ever solving time when she announced that she'd finally finished the puzzle published on 4 April 1932!

The longest word believed to have ever appeared in a crossword is LLANFAIRPWLLGWYNGYLLGOGERYCHWYRNDROBWLL-LLANTISILIOGOGOGOCH, the famous village in Anglesey, Wales. Many newspapers have printed puzzles up to 45 × 45 in size, often at Christmas or for special anniversaries. In one such puzzle set by Brian Greer for *The Times*, the solution to 185 across was Winnie the Pooh's lament I AM A BEAR OF VERY LITTLE BRAIN AND LONG WORDS BOTHER ME. Sadly, it seems that no one has ever completed the 6,334-clue puzzle set by Robert Stilgenbauer in the 1940s.

The Mount Everest of word puzzles is surely the *Listener* crossword, which originally appeared in a BBC publication of that name but since 1991 has appeared each week in *The Times*. Not content with using vocabulary more difficult than in a standard cryptic, the setters make use of clues that can contain unnecessary words or letters (which often spell a message), themed answers in the grid and special treatments in the way your answers must be entered. Previous puzzles have made use of Latin, Russian, chess, Shakespearean quotations, hexadecimal numbers, musical scores, codes and even plumbing.

While the audience for *Listener* puzzles is not large – responses range from a few hundred down to less than ten – some solvers are so dedicated that they compete to complete an entire year's puzzles correctly. An annual dinner is held for the small handful of solvers who manage this feat. The game is intended to be a solitary pursuit; though (discounting solutions openly submitted as a group) could it be that some people cheat by undeclared collaboration? As the magazine's response to the entries from an early *Listener* puzzle confirms: 'We can hardly be expected to commiserate with the eighteen competitors from Stirling who all sent in solutions which, fortunately, contained an identical, rather stupid mistake.'

WRITE ON

Will the crossword outlast sudoku? The answer is surely 'yes', although compilers are begrudging – even hostile – to the new kid on the block. Crossword fan and writer Colin Dexter, who named his famous characters Inspector Morse and Sgt Lewis after two famous compilers, finds that 'their final impersonal answers are inevitably unmemorable – and indeed unmemorizable', unlike the ability of crossword fans to quote their favourite clues. With many newspapers printing three or four sudokus every day, often in more prominent positions than the lowly crossword, perhaps we can understand his point.

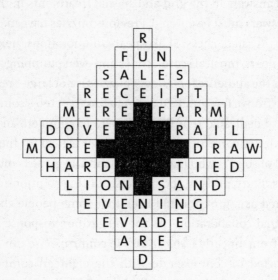

The Puzzles

WORD SQUARES

We begin with the simplest crossword possible. The word square dates back to Roman times – one example found in the ruins of Herculaneum reads SATOR AREPO TENET OPERA ROTAS in both directions. It even forms a tenuous message, usually translated as: 'Arepo the sower leads the plough with his hand'. The following puzzles are called 'double word squares' as they form different words across and down.

Word square 1

1	2	3	4
5			
6			
7			

ACROSS
1. Meat from between the ribs and rump
5. Cruel, wicked and inhuman person
6. Wearisome
7. Canvas shelter

DOWN
1. Misplaced
2. Leer at
3. Main constituent of steel
4. Semiaquatic salamander

Word square 2

1	2	3	4
5			
6			
7			

ACROSS
1. Tube of a tobacco pipe
5. A small inlet
6. It is enclosed by a perimeter
7. Repair

DOWN
1. Swindle
2. Ruptured
3. Level
4. Fermented honey and water

Word square 3

1	2	3	4
5			
6			
7			

ACROSS
1. Turn sharply
5. Domicile
6. Wading bird with long, down-curved bill
7. Saucy

DOWN
1. Vessel carrying passengers or freight
2. Where earrings can be worn
3. Independent ruler or chieftain
4. Course of 270 degrees

Word square 4

1	2	3	4
5			
6			
7			

ACROSS
1. Hydrated magnesium silicate powder
5. Succulent African plant
6. Compact mass of earth
7. Uncouth, ill-bred person

DOWN
1. Diplomacy
2. A friendly nation
3. Expression
4. Relinquish control

Word square 5

1	2	3	4	5
6				
7				
8				
9				

ACROSS
1. Let in
6. Lying face downward
7. One's ancestors
8. Picture within a picture
9. Wary

DOWN
1. May comes after it
2. Stingless male bee
3. Large northern deer, also an elk
4. Bury
5. Fractious

Word square 6

1	2	3	4	5
6				
7				
8				
9				

ACROSS
1. Quiet!
6. Shaped and dried dough
7. Anaemic-looking
8. Spirited horse
9. Full of fun

DOWN
1. Involuntary muscular contraction
2. Overly eager speed
3. Official doorkeeper
4. Bullock
5. Easy to reach

Word square 7

1	2	3	4	5
6				
7				
8				
9				

ACROSS
1. Unction
6. Barrier to contain the flow of water
7. Projecting bay window
8. Leaf of grass
9. Gumption

DOWN
1. Slovens
2. The European blackbird
3. Characteristic of birds
4. A bassoon has two of them
5. Noisy, riotous fight

Word square 8

1	2	3	4	5
6				
7				
8				
9				

ACROSS
1. Hoard
6. Girl's name
7. Out of bed
8. Dance involving a rhythmical step
9. Dirty and disorderly

DOWN
1. Involuntary, muscular contraction
2. Gustatory sensation
3. Cars
4. Loses weight
5. A malicious, fierce-tempered woman

Word square 9

1	2	3	4	5	6
7					
8					
9					
10					
11					

ACROSS

1. An unquestionable truth
7. Engaged in military operations
8. One of the three bones in the ear
9. Bread makers
10. Strongly opposed
11. Male infant sponsored at baptism

DOWN

1. Boring person
2. Book formed by folding papers three times
3. Put at risk
4. Those using drones and chanters
5. Very
6. Decrease in size, extent or range

Word square 10

1	2	3	4	5	6
7					
8					
9					
10					
11					

ACROSS

1. Sweet white grape
7. Small recess opening off a larger room
8. Lines on which musical notes are written
9. Marked by absence of sound
10. Come out into view
11. Moved with sudden speed

DOWN

1. Brought together into a group or crowd
2. The last syllable of a word
3. Electronic pulse counter
4. Secret or hidden
5. Take revenge for a perceived wrong
6. Tried out

LETTER FITS

Place each of the listed words and phrases into the grid exactly once to form a completed crossword.

Letter fit 1

4 LETTERS	6 LETTERS	REFEREE	TO AND FRO
CLEF	HEROIC	TEAR GAS	
GIRO	INTENT		9 LETTERS
SOYA	RETAIL	8 LETTERS	CHARACTER
TSAR	SILICA	AIGRETTE	RARE EARTH
		AIRBORNE	
5 LETTERS	7 LETTERS	AMENABLE	15 LETTERS
ALIBI	ARTLESS	DEADLINE	SPLIT INFINITIVE
ETHER	BRIGAND	STARGAZE	TERRITORIAL ARMY
EXTRA	ENDORSE	SURVEYOR	
GRAPH	EVACUEE	TIRAMISU	

Letter fit 2

All the words listed are used in Spanish.

3 LETTERS
AJA
AXE
CHA
CHE
ECO
FEA
OSA
URA

4 LETTERS
AFER
CIJA
CORA

CUNA
DALA
EIRA
OCAL
ROPA

5 LETTERS
ADAZA
ASCIA
ATEJE
CEAJA
CIANI
ERROR

6 LETTERS
BAZAAR
CALANA
CUADRA
LACTEO

7 LETTERS
AZACAYA
CHACATE
CHANCLA
ENRIADA
LLABANA

8 LETTERS
ESCUADRA
LEMANAJE

9 LETTERS
ANACORETA
ENRANCIAR

10 LETTERS
FORMULARIO
GARABATADA

Letter fit 3

In this puzzle, every word contains an O, which may make things a little trickier.

4 LETTERS
HOPE
IRON
KNOW
ONCE
OXEN
POOL
ROSE
TOSS

6 LETTERS
BRONZE
COPIED
EMPLOY
GALLON
HOPPED
LONGER
LOSERS
LOSING
MOVIES
OBJECT

OCCUPY
PISTOL
PROFIT
REGION
STOLEN
WAGONS

7 LETTERS
BIOLOGY
BOTTLES
EMPEROR

EQUATOR
NOISIER
NOTICED
OCTOPUS
OPINION
PORTION
PRODUCT
PROGRAM
REMOVAL
SHALLOW
YOGHURT

BLACKOUT

All the black squares have been removed from these crossword grids and replaced with letters. Can you black out all the surplus letters to reveal the correctly filled crossword grid pattern?

O	F	F	E	R	S	V	H	I	L	L	S	I	D	E
R	E	H	A	X	T	W	A	F	O	J	A	R	R	X
R	A	N	G	F	A	T	T	R	A	C	T	I	O	N
G	T	M	L	Z	R	V	F	O	V	E	U	V	W	B
T	H	R	E	A	T	N	S	T	E	E	R	I	N	G
G	E	R	N	Y	E	T	C	O	S	E	D	R	E	D
P	R	O	C	E	D	U	R	E	G	W	A	N	D	Y
B	T	K	U	I	R	B	E	N	G	R	Y	I	O	T
P	R	I	P	E	D	H	A	R	V	E	S	T	E	D
Y	E	M	B	I	A	E	M	I	I	B	R	R	A	W
A	C	C	O	U	N	T	S	C	O	T	H	E	R	S
F	O	V	A	R	S	T	R	O	L	B	U	N	A	L
E	V	E	R	Y	W	H	E	R	E	S	N	I	C	E
U	E	P	D	R	E	A	V	E	N	O	T	S	H	O
P	R	E	S	E	R	V	E	B	T	O	S	S	E	D

SPLIT DECISION

Reveal a completed crossword by deleting one of the two letters in each divided square.

SMALLEST AND HARDEST

They're small, but deadly. Can you complete these pint-sized puzzles?

Small and hard 1

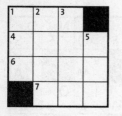

ACROSS
1. Dandy, swell
4. Of a similar nature
6. A branching stand
7. A wile, trick

DOWN
1. Adipose tissue
2. Gumbo
3. Buttress, gate pillar
5. Fabric knotted into meshes

Small and hard 2

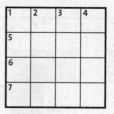

ACROSS
1. Informal Italian greeting
5. Prefix: 'all'
6. Thomas —, German novelist
7. In a frenzy

DOWN
1. Envelope of comet head
2. Muslim potentate, leader
3. Latin: 'in the year'
4. Porcine sound

Small and hard 3

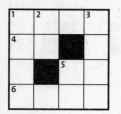

ACROSS
1. Protection, patronage
4. Until
5. Group of Chinese dialects
6. Escape slowly

DOWN
1. Latin abbrev.: 'and others' (2, 2)
2. Japanese board game
3. Arabic open-air market
5. The Evergreen State (abbrev.)

Small and hard 4

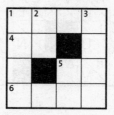

ACROSS
1. Dweeb
4. Adult castrated bull
5. Indefinite article
6. Demented

DOWN
1. Common sense
2. Former partner
3. Unpleasantly cool and humid
5. Sinusoidally varying electric current

Quick crossword 1

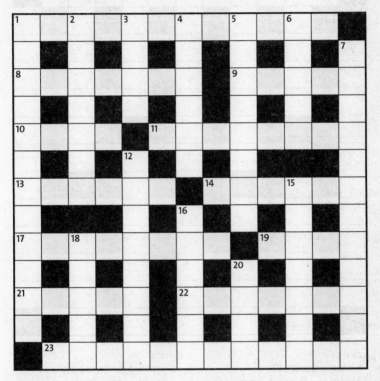

ACROSS

1. E.g. Colonel Bogey (8, 4)
8. Like a gap when bored? (7)
9. Date approximately (5)
10. Overlook (4)
11. Torch used in night processions (8)
13. Football team (6)
14. Seismic vibration (6)
17. He beat Mark Antony (8)
19. Fleur-de-lis (4)
21. Grock or Grimaldi, for instance (5)
22. Printing pattern (7)
23. Irregular weather (5, 7)

DOWN

1. Traditional village folk performance (7, 5)
2. Western TV series from the 1960s (7)
3. Call for a cab (4)
4. Argue over petty things (6)
5. Type of maple tree (8)
6. Care for a shark? (5)
7. New year, new prices (7, 5)
12. 1952 Olympics venue (8)
15. Act of God (7)
16. Veg that are good for the heart? (6)
18. Band of musicians (5)
20. American-style lottery game (4)

Quick crossword 2

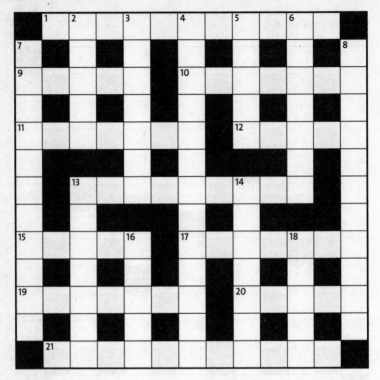

ACROSS

1. Most urgent (3, 8)
9. With one extremity towards the observer (3, 2)
10. Retired professors (7)
11. Back seat of a vintage car (7)
12. Child (5)
13. Fatty type of spread? (6-3)
15. Waist measurement (5)
17. Shade empty spaces, prevent escape (5, 2)
19. Galileo's surname (7)
20. Boat that's 21 across (5)
21. With a low centre of gravity (6, 5)

DOWN

2. Mr Nash, American writer of epigrams (5)
3. Small-minded person? (7)
4. Balanced (2, 11)
5. Thin, like an oboe (5)
6. Church apse containing the bishop's throne (7)
7. Where to shed ones bags (4-7)
8. Sane (5-6)
13. Cultivated sour cherry (7)
14. Cells with soft walls (7)
16. The Planets composer (5)
18. Former name of Mariinsky, Russian ballet school (5)

Quick crossword 3

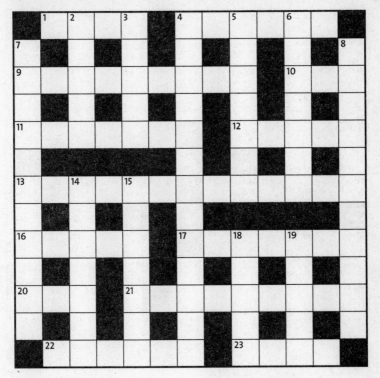

ACROSS

1. The Flintstones' pet (4)
4. Calvin's pet tiger (6)
9. Protestant Irishman (9)
10. — -Wan Kenobi, Jedi Knight (3)
11. E.g. Charles Lindbergh (7)
12. Kim —, Vertigo actress (5)
13. He was fond of racing pigeons (4, 9)
16. Immoralities (5)
17. Waldo's myopic uncle (2, 5)
20. Stimpy's cartoon friend (3)
21. With care and persistence (9)
22. He appears, with Snowy, on some Euros (6)
23. Sandwich condiment (4)

DOWN

2. Native of modern-day Mesopotamia (5)
3. Should (5)
4. TV's most famous 'Asst. rod watcher, class 3' (5, 1, 7)
5. Source of great riches (7)
6. Underwent development (7)
7. They fight like cat and mouse (3, 3, 5)
8. Character with a trivial job? (6, 5)
14. Dry red Italian table wine from Tuscany (7)
15. Aloof or far away (7)
18. Woman, either way (5)
19. Friend of 8 down (5)

Quick crossword 4

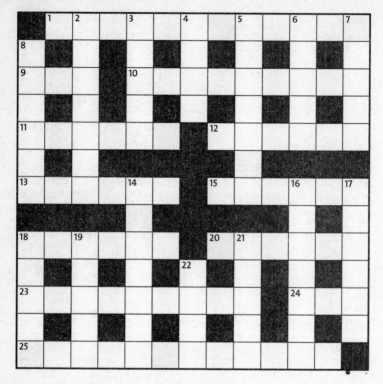

The clues in italics relate to the theme at 1 across.

ACROSS

1. *Theme, a well-known code* (4, 8)
9. Female pronoun (3)
10. Pardon, please return! (4, 5)
11. *Mountain range* (6)
12. Ornamental French style (6)
13. *American* (6)
15. Pour out liquid (6)
18. *Winner* (6)
20. *Famous Capulet* (6)
23. Sudden reduction in food intake (5, 4)
24. Smallest whole number (3)
25. A sheep's backbone and loins (6, 2, 4)

DOWN

2. Be in accord (5, 2)
3. *Doled out on Feb 29th* (5)
4. *Peru's capital* (4)
5. Prevent with guillotine? (4, 3)
6. *Well done!* (5)
7. *Ballroom dance* (5)
8. *Scotch Scotch?* (6)
14. Marking a new era (7)
16. *Consistent clothing* (7)
17. The king of Persia's wife (6)
18. Moral weaknesses (5)
19. Spinach beet (5)
21. Up to that time (5)
22. *2.2 pounds* (4)

Quick crossword 5

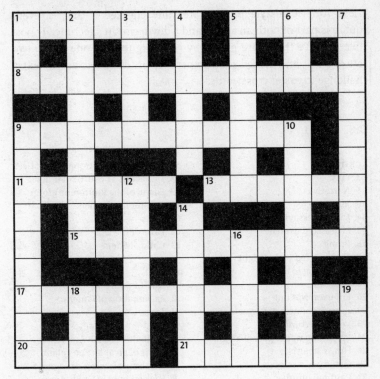

The clues in italics have a common theme

ACROSS

1/5. *I'm dot in place* (7, 5)
8. *Adept: him or her?* (13)
9. *Name for ship* (1, 1, 1, 8)
11. *In duet* (6)
13. *'Rotter!'* (6)
15. Every so often (3, 3, 5)
17. *Apers in motion* (13)
20. Long tales (5)
21. *Spend it* (7)

DOWN

1. Homer's first note? (3)
2. *Rich saint* (9)
3. Florida resort (5)
4. Banking brothers (6)
5. *Moot rep* (7)
6. Here in France (3)
7. *Hint: hotel* (3, 6)
9. *I sew of hue* (9)
10. Serving to bring to mind (9)
12. British triple jumper (7)
14. *So, nude!* (6)
16. Early computer game company (5)
18. 21st Greek letter (3)
19. Sign of assent (3)

U.S.-STYLE CROSSWORDS

These American-style puzzles are fully checked – that is, every square is part of both an across and a down clue. It's technically possible to solve the entire puzzle by referring to only one of the two sets of clues, and indeed some expert solvers do this to add an extra challenge to easier crosswords.

U.S.-style 1

ACROSS

1. Filly
5. Narratives
10. Puncture
14. Famous essayist
15. Like an old woman
16. Prong
17. Transported with delight
18. Pertaining to the hair
19. Mad talk
20. Emerson was one
22. Roman goddess of vegetation
23. Very dull company
24. Projecting upper part of a hill
26. Hunts stealthily
29. Quality of a scrooge
33. Cardinal number
34. Weeping easily
35. Gobbled
36. Figure of Cupid
37. Minor Anglo-Saxon noble
38. Trampled
39. Lapdog
40. Small nails
41. Tuscan province in Italy
42. Gulps down
44. Prison official
45. Grain cereal
46. Mark with stripes
47. Mountain peak
50. Disturbed unwarrantably
54. Went horseback
55. To bear patiently; to tolerate

57. To flow slowly through interstices
58. Declare in a positive manner
59. Island of the Philippine group
60. Greater in numbers
61. Cysts
62. Parts of the legs
63. Child of Shem

DOWN

1. Lake or pool
2. Exclamation of lament
3. Tears
4. Food
5. Animals of South America
6. Seeds of an apiaceous plant
7. Rhythmical swing, or cadence
8. Highest note in Guido's scale
9. East Indian unit of weight
10. Scattered
11. Headdress (poetic)
12. Woman's name
13. Stakes
21. To couple; join
22. Rabbit
24. Edible seeds
25. Unusual
26. Stages in a flight of stairs
27. Cast; hurl
28. Fragrance
29. Meadows
30. Supplied with ear-like appendages
31. Rock

32. Type of automobile
34. Becomes fluid or semifluid
37. Jog
38. Tending to bore; irksome
40. Utter raucously or inconsiderately
41. Auction
43. Unsuccessful contestants
44. Australian horses
46. Deity in Teutonic mythology

47. Crop of a bird
48. Wander
49. Paradise
50. Girl in opera *La Bohème*
51. Instrument of a handicraftsman
52. A book of the Old Testament
53. Consider
55. Stupid fellow
56. An exclamation of contempt

U.S.-style 2

ACROSS

1. Boast
5. Dry
9. Drive down with gentle strokes
13. Tree of the myrtle family
14. Took an oath
15. Mental image
16. God of love
17. Nautical flag
18. Titles of respect
19. Remove from office
21. Enlivens
23. File
25. Paradise
26. Put in mind
30. Large water jugs
33. Silly
34. Bellows
36. Secreted
38. Entrance to a garden
39. An end
40. Passport endorsement
41. Playing card
42. Mountain nymph
43. Last
44. Clan
46. Indian tribe
48. Performs
50. To have courage
51. Sowed again
55. Papal representative
59. Melody
60. A city in Florida
62. Murderous frenzy
63. Factory
64. Mountain range
65. Ratio; proportion
66. Insects
67. Gas
68. Rude shelter

DOWN

1. Born and raised
2. Unusual
3. At the pinnacle
4. Petroleum product
5. Reverential fear
6. Roster
7. Goddess of peace
8. Scoffers
9. Medicated decoction
10. Mine entrance
11. Only
12. Go by
14. Incur expense
20. Trigonometrical term
22. Cries, as a cat or sea gull
24. Weird
26. Latvian seaport
27. Decree
28. Mother
29. Spanish titles
31. Combining form: the
32. Strong white fiber
35. Helped
37. Proofreader's term
39. Slave legally emancipate
40. Condiments
42. Musical instrument
43. Discharge a gun
45. Standards of perfection
47. Disease of horses
49. A river in France
51. Reincarnation of Vishnu
52. Island near England
53. Sand or mud deposited by running water
54. Part of the base of a pedestal
56. East Indian nurse
57. Carry or transport
58. Pieced out
61. Males

U.S.-style 3

ACROSS

1. To be driven swiftly, as a ship before a gale
5. Narrow strip of some flexible material
10. Charity
14. Mass of pollen-bearing scales of the pine
15. To bring about; to effect
16. A cleansing agent
17. Artifices
18. City in Cattaraugus County, New York
19. The right to hold court (Anglo-Saxon law)
20. Disclosed to view again
22. Regarded with favor
23. Metal-bearing masses
24. Greek god equivalent to the Roman Cupid
26. Imparts a granulated surface to
29. Crying like a goat or calf
33. Utters reproaches
34. To becloud
35. To plague or pester constantly
36. Pointed instruments for piercing
37. Men
38. Watery portions of animal fluid
39. River in Wales
40. A Spanish title of respect
41. Shatter by explosion
42. The European shrew
44. Shuts
45. Baked dishes
46. Seize
47. Panama seaport
50. A game at cards
54. Scent
55. The Jewish Feast of Lot
57. Biblical name (Joshua 19:43)
58. Roster
59. Irregularly notched as if gnawed
60. Peruse
61. Emmets
62. Dividing walls
63. Puts in place

DOWN

1. Disfigure
2. Hard central portion in some fruits
3. To
4. Strips of belongings; plunders
5. Scotch cakes
6. Emergency jurors
7. Regretted
8. Son of Abijah, a king of Judah
9. Indite
10. Give support to in an undertaking
11. Appearance of the countenance
12. To produce, frame, or fashion
13. Proceeded with celerity
21. Sea birds of prey
22. Clay-like earth
24. Officer of a Presbyterian church
25. Gold coins of Portugal and Brazil
26. Arrange in order, steps, or degrees
27. Colder; chillier; said of weather
28. Suffered illness
29. Beneath
30. Embodying forms of a conception
31. To care for tenderly or sedulously
32. Small biting flies
34. Any causes of ruin
37. A sheet of standing water
38. Slavers
40. Part of the leg
41. Chatter; babble
43. Amusements
44. A peninsula in southern Russia
46. Grain to be, or that has been, ground
47. Genus of African trees
48. Norse deity
49. Gone out of one's possession
50. Craw

51. On a vessel's sheltered side
52. Hollow-horned ruminant
53. Extremities
55. Footlike part
56. Suffix: act; being

GENERAL KNOWLEDGE CROSSWORDS

General knowledge 1

ACROSS

1. For which 1979 Vietnam War epic did Francis Ford Coppola win an Academy Award? (10, 3)
8. Which ancient city of Crete was home to the Minotaur's labyrinth in Greek mythology? (7)
9. What term describes a test screening of a film designed to gauge audience reaction? (7)
11. Which tropical member of the gourd family is often used for cleaning the skin? (6)
13. Lasting a period of 365 days? (8)
15. What word describes long lines of hair found on the necks of many animals, especially horses, lions and wolves? (5)
16. Offenbach composed the operetta — in the Underworld in 1858 (7)
18. What type of church was first founded by the Englishmen Smyth and Helwys in Amsterdam in 1609? (7)
19. Which type of flesh-eating demon takes on the form of a beautiful woman? (5)
21. In psychology, what type of therapy uses a stimulus (such as electric shocks) to dissuade someone from a bad habit? (8)
23. In printing, what term describes a slanted form of lettering? (6)
25. What type of military settlement is stationed far from the main camp? (7)

26. What form of gliding dance, a forerunner of the foxtrot, is set to music with two beats in the bar? (3-4)
28. Which famous Belgian detective dies in the 1975 murder mystery novel *Curtain*? (7, 6)

DOWN

2. In English, which part of speech can be either personal, demonstrative, interrogative or indefinite? (7)
3. What mathematical function is the ratio of the adjacent side to the hypotenuse in a right-angled triangle? (abbrev.) (3)
4. Which computer language derives its name from the abbreviation for List Processing? (4)
5. In *Monty Python's Flying Circus*, what was the collective name for the strange-talking women portrayed by the cast? (10)
6. What title is given to certain chiefs in North Africa and also all those descending from Mohammed? (5)
7. Anything portending evil can be said to be what? (7)
8. Which mountain, situated in Tanzania, is the highest in Africa? (11)
10. What trophy is competed for in the annual matches between women tennis players of the USA and Britain? (8, 3)

12. Which Greek slave from Phrygia wrote fables in the 6th century BC? (5)

14. In economics, what type of merger brings together firms from the same level in the production chain? (10)

17. What word for 'a striking effect' derives from the French word *éclater*, meaning 'to shine'? (5)

18. Which word is more commonly used to mean 'respire' when pertaining to humans? (7)

20. What is the name given to someone who has a Negro parent and a Caucasian parent? (7)

22. What school of philosophy was founded in Athens by Zeno in 300 BC? (5)

24. In organ music, what mechanism is used to prevent a given row of pipes from sounding? (4)

27. What is the French word for 'yes'? (3)

General knowledge 2

ACROSS

1. Which type of Chinese-style plate design was popularized in England by Mintons Ltd in 1783? (6, 7)

8. This word means 'to reduce one's reserves' (7)

9. What, in the English language, is a statement used to express a generally accepted observation about everyday life? (7)

11. What is the name of a type of knitted pullover with a distinctive collar? (1-5)

13. Which American missile contains a television camera which it uses to follow its target? (8)

15. A physicist might call it light amplification by stimulated emission of radiation. How is it more commonly known? (5)

16. In the field of insurance, what name is given to a regular amount of money paid to insure against possible larger losses? (7)

18. What Italian dish is made from envelopes of pasta stuffed with meat or cheese, usually served in a sauce? (7)

19. The best possible (5)

21. What geometric term is defined as 'to draw a figure as large as possible inside another figure'? (8)

23. What architectural term means 'to decorate with raised stone or wood work'? (6)

25. What type of gas, commonly found near oil deposits, consists of a mixture of gases such as butane and propane? (7)

26. What title was given to an empress of Russia? (7)

28. What medical condition, formerly called mongolism, is caused by the presence of three copies of chromosome 21? (5, 8)

DOWN

2. Which word means 'to print' and 'to influence the mind'? (7)

3. Which general commanded the Confederacy during the American Civil War? (3)

4. Which small bird has the scientific name Troglodytes troglodytes? (4)

5. In what order is a lexicon usually arranged? (10)

6. Which demonstrative pronoun is the plural of 'that'? (5)

7. Which radioactive metallic element has the chemical symbol Re? (7)

8. In economics, what term describes the reduction of the home currency's exchange rate in the international money markets? (11)

10. What dessert is made from hot meringue filled with cold ice cream? (5, 6)

12. To which Leningrad ballet company did Rudolf Nureyev belong? (5)

14. Which birds, similar to ibises, are distinguished by their flat beaks? (10)

17. What term describes a phrase particular to a given language that is a grammatical exception to normal reasoning – e.g. 'a flight of stairs' doesn't fly? (5)

18. Which Italian dish is made from rice cooked with saffron, stock, meat, vegetables and/or cheese? (7)

20. What psychological condition is identified by an overuse of the word 'I'? (7)

22. What word means 'to repeat a radio or television broadcast' and 'to repeat a race'? (5)

24. In computing, what word describes a small picture intended to represent a particular action, such as saving a file? (4)

27. What mainly consists of 78% nitrogen, 21% oxygen? (3)

General knowledge 3

ACROSS

8. What flower is a variation of the buttercup, with smaller petals? (8)

9. What word, also used as a suffix, describes an irrational fear of a particular situation, place or object? (6)

10. What is the common name for the hyoid bone at the front of the neck, so called because of a legend in Genesis, Chapter 3? (5, 5)

11. What name is given a person who comes from regions of northern Finland, Norway or Sweden? (4)

12. What name can be given to an emergency or state of panic? (6)

14. What is the practice of giving employment to those related to you, rather than on the basis of individual merit? (8)

15. Which form of government was employed in Italy in 1922–43? (7)

17. What classical architectural features rest on a base and are surmounted by capitals? (7)

20. What word, also meaning 'concerning the head', is the name of an index concerned with various head measurements? (8)

22. Which Egyptian city was a capital of ancient Egypt and is the site of present-day Luxor and Al-Karnak? (6)

24. In astronomy, what is a large body of gas, held together by gravity, that emits radiation, usually including visible light? (4)

25. What is another word for 'to shorten'? (10)

27. Which alloy is primarily made from copper and tin? (6)

28. What word connects a county of New York City, a borough of London, and the main Confederate capital during the American Civil War? (8)

DOWN

1. What name is given to someone involved in the buying and selling of goods, in particular those who use bartering? (6)

2. Which of the three sporting activities in a triathlon do contestants perform first? (4)

3. Which by-product of sugar, also called treacle, was taxed in the USA by the British Parliament in the 18th century? (8)

4. What term describes a soldier's pay, or the payment received by a parish minister in Scotland? (7)

5. What word describes the maintenance of a building or the costs involved? (6)

6. Which salad vegetable comes from the second largest of the Dodecanese Islands? (3, 7)

7. In music, the — normal is a standard set in the 1887 Vienna Conference to fix the pitch of the A above middle C (8)

13. Which powder, prepared from toluene, is 550 times sweeter than sugar in its purest state? (10)

16. Which part of a camera is a hole variable in size to alter the amount of light that falls onto the film? (8)

18. What word means 'to overstretch' and 'the extent of involvement of an organization with the surrounding population'? (8)

19. What punctured five of the *Titanic*'s sixteen waterproof compartments, causing it to sink, on 14 April 1912? (7)

21. St Peter is closely associated with the Biblical story of the — and fishes (6)

23. What word, derived from Latin, means 'to still be standing or existing'? (6)

26. What is the name for a part of a verse consisting of an unstressed syllable followed by a stressed one? (4)

General knowledge quickie

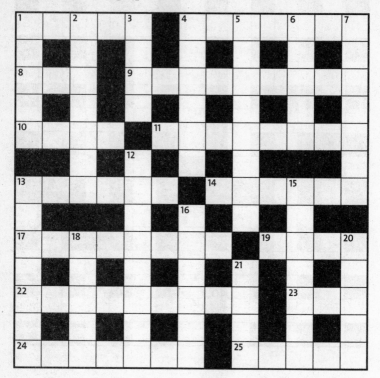

ACROSS

1. [2] = Written essay (5)
4. [55] = Green beryl (7)
8. Everything (3)
9. Opposite of 11 (4, 5)
10. [13] = Shoe tie (4)
11. [70] = Blonde colour (8)
13. Get support for paint? (6)
14. Fast ball game (6)
17. Once more (3, 5)
19. Lift manufacturer (4)
22. London theatre (3, 3, 3)
23. Spelling contest (3)
24. [3] = Polishing cloth (7)
25. [35] = Unfertilized lobster roe found in reef? (5)

DOWN

1. [30] = Mollusc gem (5)
2. Pedestrian crossing (7)
3. [40] = Cockney curry? (4)
4. Without difficulty (6)
5. Hostilities (8)
6. Glenn Miller's real forename (5)
7. Quandary (7)
12. Hookah, water pipe for smoking (8)
13. [15] = It's very clear! (7)
15. Russian revolution (7)
16. [25] = With grey hair (6)
18. 8th Greek letter (5)
20. [11] = Knife sharpener (5)
21. Electrifying band? (2-2)

A primer for cryptic clues

Many people are wary of cryptic crosswords, and that's quite understandable given that they are almost always published without any kind of rules. However, when the principles are explained, you should find that cryptic puzzles provide a challenge of your vocabulary and logic and will often appeal to your sense of humour.

In non-cryptic ('quick') crosswords, the clues for each word are given in the form of a synonym or, very occasionally, a clearly indicated anagram. In cryptic crosswords, there are *two* parts to the clue: the definition (just as in a quick crossword) and the cryptic clue. Both parts point to the very same answer. So let's be clear – not only are you given the clue that you'd normally be given in a quick crossword, but you're also given an *entirely separate* way of obtaining the answer. Free extra information!

So with two ways into each clue, shouldn't cryptic crosswords be a cinch? Well no, because of two key factors: you don't know where in the clue is the dividing line between the definition and the cryptic part, and you don't know which way round the definition and the cryptic part are – it could be cryptic/definition or definition/cryptic.

In addition, a well-composed cryptic clue – when read as a whole – will appear to form a valid and coherent phrase or sentence. This quality, the 'surface' in technical parlance, can make it much more difficult to analyse the clue into its constituent parts.

Here's an example: *Gleeful worker adheres to special holiday – the 6th and 7th off.* The 'surface' here seems to be talking about an employee who has been given two days off work. This is not what we're looking for – we must avoid being sucked in by this trap. Here, the definition (*Gleeful*) is given at the start, the rest forms the cryptic part. In crosswords, a 'worker' is often a BEE or, as in this case, an ANT. A special holiday is a JUBILEE, but *6th and 7th off* is telling us to remove the sixth and seventh letters, leaving JUBIL. So the answer is JUBILANT, meaning *'Gleeful'*, which is formed when ANT *adheres to* the end of JUBILEE without EE.

Don't worry if that seems complicated. Almost all crosswords contain easier clues than that to get you started, and then the cross-checking letters (those in both an across and a down answer) help with the more difficult material.

Types of clue

Although there is no official manual of the techniques a crossword compiler may use, the main devices you will encounter are as follows:

- **Double definition** The cryptic part is simply another definition. Example: *Yearn for quite a while* (4) = LONG, which is clued by both *Yearn* and *for quite a while*.

- **Subtraction** Some letters have to be removed from another word clued by the cryptic part. Example: *Crime evident when churchman loses his head* (5) = ARSON, a crime, formed by taking the *head* off PARSON.

- **Reversal** One element of the clue is written in reverse order. In an across or down clue, this might be clued as 'looks back' or 'goes up' respectively. Example: *Drat! The celebrity's returned* (4) = RATS, the reverse of STAR (*celebrity*).

- **Homophones** The answer sounds like another word that is clued. Example: *South American country is cold, it's said* (5) = CHILE, which sounds like 'chilly' (*cold*). Homophones are often indicated by 'it's said' or 'we hear'.

- **Container** One part of the clue lies inside another. Example: *Mound of German wine received poorly* (7) = HILLOCK, meaning a small hill or mound, which is formed from ILL (*poorly*) *received* by – i.e. placed inside the letters of – HOCK (*German wine*).

- **Hidden word** The answer appears within the clue itself, often spanning two or more words. Example: *Cutter reveals rhubarb eradication* (6) = BARBER, a hair cutter, which is *revealed* in 'rhubarb eradication'. These clues are quite easy, as the answer is in plain sight, and crosswords usually contain only one or two such clues.

- **Anagram** Good anagram clues are indicated by a word which implies some kind of mixture (as a noun) or the act of rearrangement (as a verb), in addition to the required letters. Example: *He gets receipt in mix-up* (9) = RECIPIENT (defined by *He gets*), the letters of which are a *mix-up* of *receipt in*.

- **Combination** Often, a clue will use two or more of the elements listed above to make up one cryptic definition. Example: *Laugh – Royal Marine's not quite full or dangerous* (7) = HARMFUL, put together from HA (*laugh*) plus RM (*Royal Marine*) and FUL (*not quite full*). Here the word *or* marks the division between the cryptic part and the definition.

Occasionally, you will also encounter:

- **Initial letters** The first letters of some of the clue words form the answer. Example: *At first, eggs add sustenance to everyone's religious holiday* (6) = EASTER, the first letters of *eggs add sustenance to everyone's religious*. If the wording of a clue looks a little strained or unnatural, it might be of this kind.

- **Moving letters** One or more letters should be moved to a different location. Example (for a down clue): *Point of weapon went down to obtain fruit* (5) = PEARS, with the S of SPEAR moving *down* to the end of the clue. *To obtain* is a linking phrase indicating that the cryptic part yields the definition.

- **Cryptic definition** The whole clue is a punning definition of the answer, often ending with a question mark to signal the joke. Example: *A stiff examination?* (10) = POSTMORTEM. Watch out for these as they do not conform to the standard definition/cryptic pattern.

- **& lit (and literally so)** The entire clue acts as both a cryptic part and a definition. Example: *Terribly angered!* (7) = ENRAGED, which is the letters of *angered* in a terrible state (i.e. an anagram), and to be enraged is to be *terribly angered*.

Common abbreviations

Many clues use standard abbreviations as part of the cryptic build-up. If, for example, a clue begins 'Doctor is removed ...', it may be asking you to remove the letters DR (Dr = Doctor) from something. In general, compilers use common abbreviations found in dictionaries, although, mainly as hangovers from an earlier period of clue-writing, some quite obscure devices crop up occasionally even though they are rare in contemporary usage. Some abbreviations come up time and again, and the following brief bluffer's guide will prime the cryptic beginner with enough knowledge to get by. Readers not conversant with culture in the UK, where most cryptic crosswords are compiled, will also find it of use.

Bible	'Books' often refers to OT or NT (Old or New Testament).
Chess	B (bishop), K (king), N (knight), P (pawn), Q (queen), R (rook or castle).
Cricket	Frequently referred to in British crosswords. 'Side' could imply IN or OUT. There are six balls (deliveries) in an OVER.
Directions	N, E, S, W – sometimes clued by 'point' (as in compass point), 'quarter' or even as card players (e.g. 'bridge partners' might be WE). Also, L (left) and R (right).
Doctor	DR, MD, MO (medical officer).
Education	BA (degree or bachelor), MA (master).
Family trees	B (born), D (daughter or died), S (son).
Foreign languages	'The French' = 'the French for "the"' = LE, LA or LES. Similarly for German DIE, DER or DAS, and Spanish EL.
Geography	As seen on maps: CH (church), H (hospital), L (lake), P (parking), R (river), RY (railway – watch out for this as it is often clued as just 'lines', tenuously justified by 'lines' = 'railway lines'). US zip codes and state abbreviations are used – watch out for Georgia, which is GA, not GE.

Music	F (forte = loud), P (piano = soft, quiet), PP (pianissimo = very quiet). 'Note' could mean any of A, B, C, D, E, F or G and sometimes DO, RE, ME, etc.
Numbers	Roman numerals: I = 1, V = 5, X = 10, L = 50, C = 100, D = 500, M = 1000. 'One' can mean the letter I (9th letter of the alphabet) or, sometimes, A. A number may indicate a cross-reference to another clue (e.g. '13 is odd' could mean 'make an anagram from clue 13's answer').
O	The letter O can be clued as 'ring', 'circle', 'nothing', 'love' and many others.
Politics	Depends on the country. In the UK, left-wing abbreviations imply LAB (Labour) or RED, and similarly right-wing connotations give CON (Conservative) or TORY.
Sailor	AB (able-bodied seaman), RN (Royal Navy), TAR (a jolly jack tar).
Science	I (electrical current), T (time). Chemical symbols are common, including AG (silver), AU (gold), PB (lead) and SN (tin). 'Gold' can also be OR (in French).
Sizes	S (small), L (large), M (medium), OS (oversized, very big).
Soldier	GI, RE (Royal Engineer, 'sapper'), TA (Territorial Army).
Time	D (day), H (hour), M (minute or month), S (second), Y (year).
U	Rarely used these days except in crosswords, U (upper class) can be indicated by 'posh' or 'fashionable'.
Various	Some others that crop up frequently include CHE (revolutionary, as in Che Guevara), DO (party), IC (in charge), IN (fashionable), RED (communist).

CRYPTIC CROSSWORDS

The first couple of puzzles have a few letters filled in to get you started.

Cryptic crossword 1

ACROSS

2. One studying with pips in view? (5)
5. Those attending match note tea-break (4)
7. One on the board occupied by chairman? (4)
8. In being given weapons our appearance was protectively coated (8)
9. Guess how much it will be to achieve tie with teams (8)
11. Fullness of wine, as opposed to spirit? (4)
12. Inferior status of one's intellect? (13)
15. Gets to the head of work in a backstreet (4)
17. Mob unfortunately perished after the East incorporated it (8)
19. Like half-sister to Edward helped out (8)
21. Go very fast and it may create a hold-up in the middle (4)
22. Don't go for support (4)
23. We may spend every other letter slipped in gradually (5)

DOWN

1. Tank-top: why, it's a crime! (7)
2. Stop filming the joint (3)
3. After a tipple, a play (5)
4. Artist's colour putting a finish to uncontrolled anger (7)
5. Was conversant, we hear, with an antelope (3)
6. Tyre pattern to press with one's foot (5)
10. Said to be wrong about the East, they nevertheless come to mind (5)
11. Foretold how I – me, too – got excluded from 17 (5)
13. Reps, etc., going about with spirit (7)
14. Parts of compasses require a boy to furnish them (7)
16. Film crew found here at start of attack (5)
18. Waits for one to be in bed somehow with start of sickness (5)
20. Is vacillating, yet such are the initials of Hedera (3)
21. A layer of oysters at the bottom of the sea (3)

Cryptic crossword 2

ACROSS

1. Cut top off hedge and fasten it metallically (5)
4. Parts of tennis match not up to scratch as one starts (4, 3)
8. Supporter sat back with convulsive movement, quite dreamlike (9)
9. Thanks to the right, it's black (3)
10. Break tin and be impolite so to thrust oneself in (7)
12. Part of foot one will move very slowly (4)
14. One left Pict free and easy inside what is ideal (7)
17. Money put up when one dined around the North (4)
18. Upbringing owes much to nurse: true, it is adapted (7)
20. Sign of coolness pleasant if not begun (3)
21. It put deal out saying it's trite (9)
23. Figures look like anaesthetics (7)
24. King George to dine on what is super (5)

DOWN

1. Iron Great Fire melted down with the opposite effect (13)
2. In New York it follows Virginia for self-appreciation (6)
3. Swaps Unionist Conservative leaders within as one calumniates (8)
4. One doesn't stand as candidate – and will do so if successful (3)
5. To sail against the wind is something that has point (4)
6. Go up and hold pint spilled when suddenly taking it (6)
7. Meanwhile, what is money used as donation-wise? (3, 3, 7)
11. The Spanish take a bit of fish like a fairy (5)
13. Is making its mark, frightening one right inside (8)
15. Blood's course one might be able to master (6)
16. Time to come when Ute fur is ruffled (6)
19. When surrounding pulpit-top, East spells the end of church (4)
22. Girl going topless is a foolish person (3)

Cryptic crossword 3

ACROSS

1. Tom is to blame, in a way, for this organic change (10)
6. Some snipe from Lewis, probably (4)
9. We are pleased to be in it! (4, 6)
10. King of wrasse to leave a mark, maybe (4)
12. An affluent society such as the Israelites found in Goshen? (4, 2, 6)
15. This erect tube explains what those who prefer cigarettes may not be able to do! (5-4)
17. Lachrymose old announcer? (5)
18. The best part of the literature syllabus (5)
19. The players are apparently inflamed with passion for short whiskers! (9)
20. One who trades in braces and is not to be trusted? (6-6)
24. A point for 14 down to attend to, perhaps (4)
25. Required as a condition to put deals another way? (10)
26. Still one might be described as a human beast! (4)
27. Doesn't sit up, but withdraws? (6, 4)

DOWN

1. They're very silly people, swots! (4)
2. Made a conquest to approve of? (4)
3. See what we need water for and where we may get it from! (4, 3, 5)
4. Was first about in the morning, though unable to make satisfactory progress (5)
5. If she fled, this city might be (9)
7. Mr Polly became one to get away from Fishbourne (10)
8. Not what politicians assume little girls appear at their best in! (5, 5)
11. Mallets made of ebony for voracious six-footers? (5-7)
13. Sway, possibly, though not rock (10)
14. She'll deal with the hands if they should get rough! (10)
16. A member of the team dismissed the wrong way round? (6, 3)
21. Execute canto in a different arrangement (3, 2)
22. Hapsburg claimant, an abstainer in spectacles! (4)
23. A study Nasser has shown considerable interest in (4)

Cryptic crossword 4

ACROSS

1. This column backs one up (6)
4. Room in the garden? (5, 3)
9. He took Miss Lou in (9)
11. Nothing on the local tax is just talk (5)
12. What Britannia took from Neptune (7)
13. Madame got waxy about people (7)
14. Useful references for place hunters (7, 3, 5)
17. Will acts so intentionally (4, 2, 2, 7)
19. Double antithesis to strong drink (4, 3)
21. Give one a right to be called names? (7)
23. More mature (5)
24. Crying 'It's tennis with a difference!' (9)
25. There is argument about this in Court circles (8)
26. Royal builder of ships for Liberty (6)

DOWN

1. Half a tick by the sound of it (7)
2. This month one wicket (9)
3. Aroused fear: arrests, fine (5)
5. The usual journalistic hustle? (8, 5)
6. Above bad temper, one might think (5, 4)
7. Stately part of a tomahawk (5)
8. Pressure is of course applied to this in foot-pounds (7)
10. This questionable job with suspects is anyone's for the asking (13)
15. How a little bird told the tale (9)
16. Are the trunks in the loft part of these? (4, 5)
17. Somehow, pod drew such moisture (7)
18. A choosy person, formerly Hanoverian (7)
20. It first brought to notice the gravity of the world's position (5)
22. Opera about Ascot (5)

Cryptic crossword 5

ACROSS

1. Declining offers here in Amsterdam? (5, 7)
8. Gunners who shoot (7)
9. What is his Lordship doing up on the bench? (7)
11. See, it controls this area (7)
12. Four in the Test? That's of no importance (7)
13. Box body, in part (5)
14. Regulation one found in the Artillery (9)
16. Needed by gymnasts putting lines round the pole (9)
19. Douse the glim and there's no smoke from this form of tobacco (5)
21. Old settler at 1 across – who finishes the frame, say? (7)
23. Twist perhaps to gain a quarter – or take the top bunk? (7)
24. But the accountant's may relate to outgoings (7)
25. Crazy to turn it into foreign currency (7)
26. Anti-tank obstacles – the seeds of war? (7, 5)

DOWN

1. One's bored perhaps. Do this and go to bed (7)
2. What's my line? Touch and go (7)
3. That infernal place, York, noted for curing madness (9)
4. Like the vendor when this price isn't reached (5)
5. Thomas Good on watch (7)
6. The view is, there's nothing to tie up (7)
7. The Rhine at one point seems so fragrant! (3, 2, 7)
10. Mission Impossible? No, thanks to Medea (6, 6)
15. Defeat by depriving of sweets? (9)
17. Dishonest dancer (7)
18. Journalist at the last gasp in current revolution (7)
19. Observe quiet time for the percolation effect (7)
20. Open at lunch, maybe (7)
22. How bread's gone up! (5)

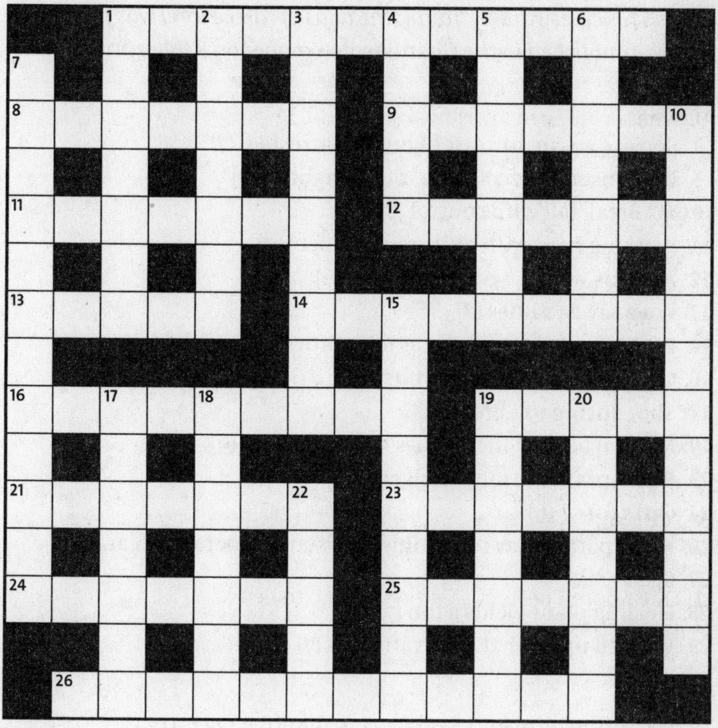

Cryptic crossword 6

*This crossword by Taupi (the alias of Albie Fiore) was first
published in the* Guardian *newspaper on 8 July 2003.*

ACROSS

1. Society gossip to 5? He should be arrested! (7)
5. No nonsense – 20's pitch is the brightest (7)
10/27. Break fall with control (8)
11. Working hard with officer in Cabinet (10)
12. At 19, as 18 said, you cannot be 5 (6)
13. 1 of 2 say 24's lines (8)
14. Burning without flames as John Brown's body did (9)
16. Chicago's said to be nervous (5)
17. Shot during 19's break (5)
19. Maiden bowled in matches here? Unlikely (9)
23. Puts up with family headgear (8)
24. Girl's for 5? (6)
26. Fool's paradise as retreating lines start to march in fear (10)
27. See 10 (4)
28. Healing plant yields a ton (7)
29. Washed up is what Old Trafford is (7)

DOWN

2. UK prime ministers said by 18 to describe 19 (3, 4)
3. What some Asians call a thick stick? (5)
4. Allowance made for Conservative with sexual deviation (7)
6. No life can be recorded (2, 4)
7. 'Delicate' – meaning it's with intravenous injection (9)
8. Sworn when a 5 went wrong (7)
9. Up to you to record right-winger's current departure (13)
15. Watchful man died first (9)
18. First of championship's players accepting line call? (7)
20. Clip showing male animals (7)
21. Vegetable inspiring holy thought (7)
22. Pinner has gardens bordered by south-east's river (6)
25. Rubber ball's so round (5)

In skeleton crosswords the clues are given without word lengths. It's up to you to complete the grid, which has reflectional symmetry about the horizontal and vertical axes. For example, if you decide that the top-left square should be black, then all three other corners should also be black. In this first example, a few black squares and clue numbers have been added to start you off.

Skeleton 1

ACROSS

1. Where a greaser keeps his food
5. Nearly all the best policy
8. Main colour
9. Is what he sells the result of handicraft?
11. Stick to it just where you are
13. The enterprise includes a mixed revue
16. An article on me is the subject for discussion
17. Try a short street as a rendezvous
18. Withdraw
19. The weight of no cue
21. Fall from grace of a number on part of a church
23. Above all it makes me super
27. There's wine aboard for the games
28. Totting up with some noise
29. Peer perhaps, but not peep
30. Percolated
31. The story of a couple of letters shows some innate cleverness

DOWN

1. No dark residences for keepers
2. Heron river
3. Bit of cheese!
4. Powdered stud
5. One who has something coming to him
6. Polish cloth, but not necessarily from Warsaw!
7. x 4
10. This mountain gives the girl a breather
12. Angry at being stung?
14. Put on the wrong way round, which gets you down! (2 words)
15. The sort of custom which makes us grow old
20. So one is in a loop
22. I am in a position to show some balance
24. Accustomed
25. Disorderly flight of the hero utterly
26. Liquor ingredient mainly bad abroad

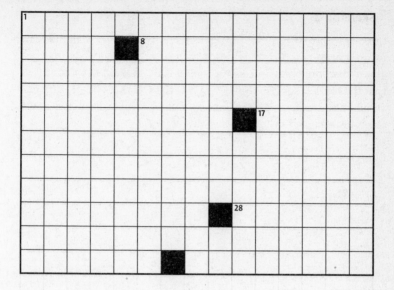

In case you make a mess of your first attempt at a skeleton cross-word, here's a duplicate grid:

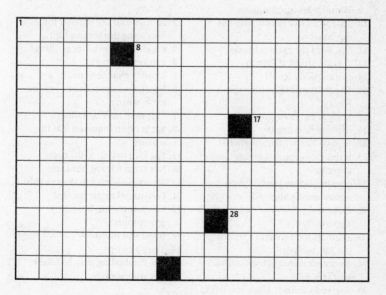

Skeleton 2

ACROSS

3. Here's your very good health!
9. Warmth-promoting game
10. This attractive personality has our heart
11. Not all of the grass is inside
12. Unauthorised, if French
14. Not so ruddy fencer?
16. The military rank which spoils Henry
18. She's a deal changed!
19. Alphabetical finger
20. Female North African official?
23. It indicates encouragement and approval
25. May be plighted and subsequently blighted
28. Outstanding, yet not clever apparently
29. Animals seen around a French garden, perhaps
30. Dances featured at the Cotton Workers' Ball?
31. Say, keen, are our Allies you'll find

DOWN

1. Stone found in a jeweller's shop always
2. Sounds as if the butcher might find some use for this bird
3. Building material for nothing?
4. Pointer's warmth!
5. Mouldy change of heart
6. No; these criminals need not be extra strong
7. This man may be a diner
8. Rot is often found on it at the seaside
13. The bird begins to die back
15. Not French leave, but Latin
17. An accolade may make you this!
21. Consumed in the tea tent
22. Steep, certainly, but not precipitous
23. Bundle of mischief?
24. Mary's troops
26. The foreboding may be on me
27. Fricative sound

Skeleton 3

ACROSS

1. 549 meet Austen heroine – that's the difficulty
5. Does he both take the eggs and cook them?
9. Bus tour (anag., 2 words)
10. Minimum
12. Nobly ahead of time?
14. Number in a sheep to start with
16. Not a suitable place for high livers
17. A drink of fine gusto
18. State of the meandering Rio Gage
21. Dive-bomber
23. Canned, perhaps, but not tinned
26. Travel talk on a platform maybe
27. Comparatively fat provision merchant, by the sound of it
28. Would this solve a monster problem?

DOWN

1. It's laid up!
2. Hot stuff in a cool avalanche
3. Very windy curb market?
4. The course of a doctor in a little island
5. A prodder
6. Really a tent (anag.)
7. Usually duplicated in approbation
8. Just a stone to polish off a letter
11. There's something distinctive amid the clatter
13. An arm of the sea, but not the Fleet Air Arm
15. Listener
19. Happen to be one in charge of a dog
20. What's left when a greedy eater loses his inner man
21. Self-satisfied spot!
22. Unfasten
24. The G-unit is no longer with us
25. XXX

This section features some of the work of Derrick Somerset Macnutt, otherwise known as Ximenes. Although some of his clues may now seem a little stilted or oblique, there is still much to admire in these puzzles. Be warned, however, that in these highly interlocking grids it is seen as 'fair play' for the compiler to use much more esoteric vocabulary. Equally, it is not frowned upon for the solver to make use of dictionaries where required.

All but the first of this final selection of crosswords have specific instructions.

Advanced 1

ACROSS

1. This fish, mum, is bad (8)
7. Twigs used in U.S. for making temporary abodes (4)
10. I helped to make Cleopatra loose: later, the bloody Queen reproached herself about me (6)
11. Breadwinner out of work? The puir, clumsy fush (6)
12. I was handed over to Uncle Jock – savagely tawsed (6)
14. Come back, love, and dress – the precious lump (6)
15. What's becoming to a don when one's put on (4)
18. Treat stupid recipe thus – and eggs, for omelettes (7)
19. Semi-paralysing ailment, one hears, the twitch (12)
21. Like Corinthians, 'e wants to shoot one in (12)
23. Dance for all, free – forward, reverse, forward (7)
25. I shall be hearing before about you (4)
26. The C.I.C.'s a gent, the reverse of a reformer (6)
28. Type of fern with an unusual stripe (6)
30. Rough-haired Scotch terriers do it (6)
31. Divisions remaining among Government employees (6)
32. To make keen – yes, keen (4)
33. Engineers obliterate a vessel – it's ill-advised (8)

DOWN

1. Balance about one penny: that helped investors (7)
2. Small rodent by eating it makes a hole (6)
3. Wrecked – gold in sea, no distance from port (9)
4. Get awa' wi' a gee-gee that has foals? (4)
5. I'm in leg-business – get chirpy taking in wolf (10)
6. Spring here! Je monte à cheval (5)
7. Separate – that sounds prudent (8)
8. Small fish, thought to have no tail (3)
9. Late Jan. – early Feb.: rise of wasting disease (5)

13. Hides questionably: it's O.K. to have a caress in (10)
16. Misguided use of data that were given by Ximenes (9)
17. Biblical critic, formerly baffled, vexed at heart (8)
20. Black stuff, suitable for a funeral (7)
22. Banters, as in leg-pulls (6)
23. Thquabbleth are plentiful in Glasgow (5)
24. Linnet, apt to vex by wepetition (5)
27. A thousand feet take part in a lively dance (4)
29. This was quite enough wine to turn the head (3)

Advanced 2: Printer's devilry

Each clue is a passage from which the printer has removed a hidden answer, closing the gap, taking liberties sometimes with punctuation and spacing, but not disturbing the order of the remaining letters. Thus, in the sentence *Now that it's so much warmer, can't I let the boiler go out?*, MERCANTILE is hidden: the printer might offer as a clue: *Now that it's so much wart, the boil: ergo, out!* Each passage, when complete, makes sense.

ACROSS

1. They who beat through TNT – they to be recalled (9)
11. The man who was cruel with a girl, as he'd slaves (4)
12. Metal is poured, that in a mould, in casting (8)
13. On TV the mike is one of the announcers (4)
14. Author of words sung with an orgie, din (1866) (8)
15. When one's tending any, Ben's always in the Wash (6)
16. Police caught her in: did hidings: now in bag (5)
17. She looked a perfect skimp – trimmed bombazine (7)
20. This is nice. Grew? O! Hundred kilos off! Nancy's much more! (7)
24. Coarse aroma of rapers – in nostrils it stinks (7)
25. 'What's in Africa?' ses Rab (bit cut up and white). 'Sauce! We'll stick to S.A., lad!' (7)
27. What did you drink in Virgin I., Aby? The pot of ullage, rale flat! (5)
30. If you called a Sir 'maid', you'd be right (6)
31. Won't a matron, knowing the rotter who cuts duty? (8)
32. Some climbers who forge axes came to grief (4)

33. When I've hypnotised the girl, she'll be my Sally (8)
34. Where is it that rivers of gold floor a do? (4)
35. To the keen, rugby county matches may not appeal (9)

DOWN

2. It may not help a traveller to have a mast (8)
3. If left with a baby, you'd call it, if anyone came, to classing (8)
4. I've had my say: now I tours! (5)
5. If I'm to play Borodin – tense practice (7)
6. Some pal try, or model even – hundred guineas! (7)
7. If you've a cat, Arnold – O! 'e's no good! (6)
8. Shog!, as the stallite said to the stripper … (4)
9. … and Adam's 'ight more than ale – long! (4)
10. Insular? Hosts of foreigners: hosts will behave (9)
15. Ground's hard, so, wise man, bet for big stakes (9)
18. Leaving his lady, boy with a flick-knife (8)
19. Would a jester call an Irish tow sérac, Asian? (8)
21. The product of hives, as a tribute to a Queen (7)

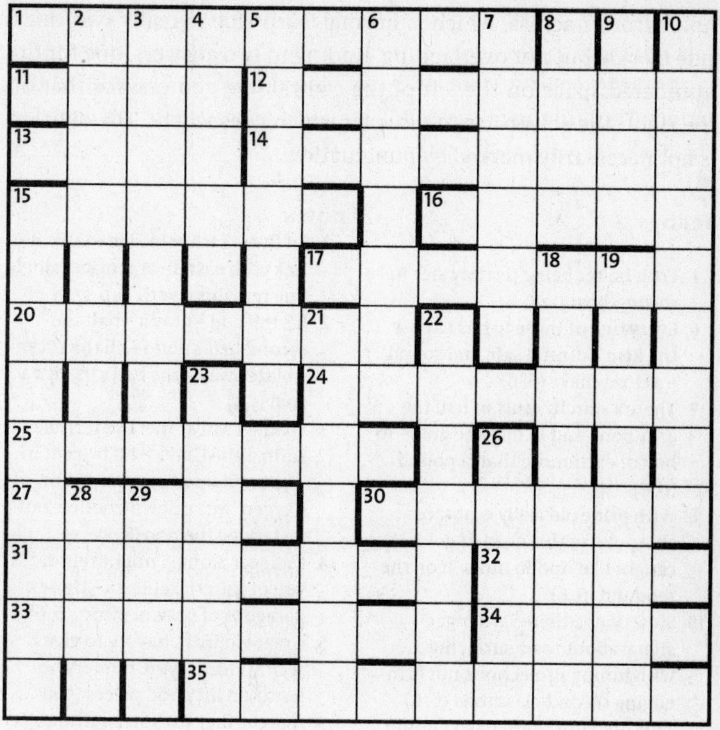

22. Repeat message, at least: 'twill be forgotten (7)
23. That's a tricky piece, thinner: can't play! (6)
26. Get Bacon on 'Sense'; you'll all see the play (5)
28. I haven't got a bed: I envy the rich (4)
29. I ward off cold with woolly bootee: sandal past (4)

Advanced 3: Right and left

Apart from 1 across, which is normal, each clue is really two clues, side by side but not overlapping, leading to two answers, one for the numbered space on the left of the central line and one for that on the right: the solver has to discover which goes where. The division is not necessarily marked by punctuation.

ACROSS

1. Fruit bolter being terribly sick in rowing-boat (12)
6. Every one of these fish is to pass the Rear Admiral safe and sound – a close shave (6, 6)
7. There's starchy stuff in half the arm-bone and in half the guts – in half of each more than a pound (6, 6)
8. With pride old Nelly embraces an Apollo with a head of gold, caught like Apollo himself on the rebound (6, 6)
10. Slow down: there's a danger signal about road-surfacing with lumpy projections not firm edging second-class road (6, 6)
12. This predatory bird hasn't quite got the dash to catch carp, or scarlet-backed carp-like fish (6, 6)
16. Mum, a mercenary Venus, needs to be got up in the old, old way, i.e. long curls innumerable (6, 6)
17. A thing which stands for Britain, with what's British in it, to provoke a shy creature around America (6, 6)
18. Preserve one bed for each: this fertiliser is not quite at full strength (6, 6)
19. A dark blue cloth – something unique I got in jumble-sale – a short yard, with a margin to spare (6, 6)

DOWN

1. Jet flyer crashes bridge – G. W. R. link with east disorganised: single line remains – verb. sap. (7, 7)
2. It's the Cup – grand – half the second half's gone – all the tricks – blaze away – the ball's in – it's a goal (5, 5)
3. Spanker's near me: I've terrible Latin, little Greek – I'll be kept in – not well up in courses about oxygen: we're downtrodden, but na tanned the noo (8, 8)
4. I stagger along: I might remind you of the cricket tests – those paragons of patient effort (6, 6)
5. Great violinist, having to give a recital among you, renders no less than fifty odd pieces (5, 5)
9. A night-flier with strength subject to diminution can hardly fly at all – pulls up, being about to fit sails (8, 8)
11. Saintly man in France has his prime interrupted by the Nine wild and eery busting the clerical domicile (7, 7)
13. She'll advise you, for example, up the river to go slowly and take it easy with little work (6, 6)
14. An Admiral, born to be on the water, that's to say a fatherly man where there are ships (5, 5)
15. The organ stops: part of the woodwind has perished and rings sharper: some of the cellos elope (5, 5)

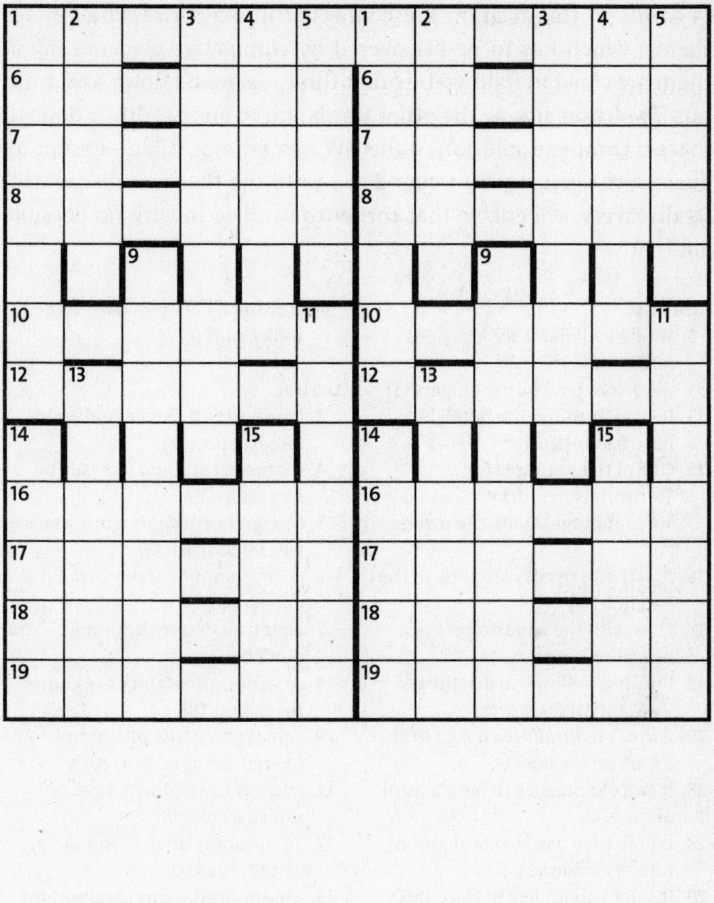

Advanced 4: Spot the theme

13 words in the diagram are connected into a series by a certain theme, which has to be discovered by cumulative evidence. 10 of them are clued in italics. The other three, 1 across, 1 down and 3, are not clued, nor, among the other words, are 10 and 14: this is done to make a complete solution of the NW corner impossible – except by guesswork against very long odds – until the theme is discovered: its discovery will enable that corner to be filled in with no possible alternatives.

ACROSS

5. *Where you might see jazz fiend about nude* (7)
11. A warmer for a butter-fingers (4)
13. It's cooler round the hotel: let's have haddock (6)
15. One of the premises for Territorials in mucky surroundings? Quite the reverse (5)
16. A bachelor needs company in the Bahamas (5)
18. Flow with the wind, to produce fish when contrary (7)
19. Bunting, yellow – to disembark – no start of disease (7)
20. *Parrot's regurgitated a ring from what's on the floor* (7)
26. It's an old practice to have a meal of fungi (7)
28. Where they used to sport among serene meadows (5)
29. It's right about five to wake up (5)
30. The old seer gives a tip about us (6)
32. Run away back out of the way, with knobs on (6)
33. One doctor's a prophet of inevitable doom (4)
34. Musical Parisienne to make mari go astray (4)
35. *It's drab. Hush – what's outside may be gayer* (7, two words)
36. It's after time – ten: have some milky stuff (5)

DOWN

2. One bird that can't rise rises in Swedish port (4)
4. It's mean – it could so easily be nicest (6)
5. Mongrel with short name that's a wee bit Scottish (4)
6. *Fix the amount of pay in R.A.F. (altered)* (6)
7. First fruits: have the orange – you don't have to (5)
8. At deuce, after faults, ace comes in: endless (8)
9. *Some signs of discontent in menial metal-workers* (6)
11. Leather, or spoil with love, an unusual child (8)
12. To the point when fallow lacks carted crops (5)
15. Misappropriations need suit for redress (8)
17. Vital parts of engine incompetent taxi-men lose (8)
20. *Endless stiff ascent. Inn? Not quite: try sledge* (6)
21. *Show sounds like what its sponsors eagerly await* (5)
22. *A ferment, unorganized – in a frenzy mentally* (6)

23. I no longer tend hearths: heat is got otherwise (6)
24. *It's the devil with scrap: it may be dutiable* (6)
25. *Stop fighting to rub ointment, perhaps, on tendon* (6)
27. Indecently disrobe society girl, 'orrid witch (5)
30. A sloop makes an appeal to those who sail (4)
31. Name of girl, and of boy, seem very odd (4)

Advanced 5: Playfair

For instructions see page 244.

ACROSS

1. Nightcap Scot comes home to looks very potent (6)
6. *These stays are available in tasteful crape* (6)
11. I appear to be praying – and so are my backers (9)
12. Heavyweight rugger man, almost a legend (7)
13. Big bell: two could be used in the percussion (3)
14. Prayer, Latin, employed in university service (5)
15. Sort of rice I'll have to get out of the old pan (5)
17. Sentence on Jock, caught in returning plastered (7)
18. Prepare an outdoor floor-show – teaser welcome! (6)
20. Nature worship – no, this is a perverted form (6)
22. Anagram of treason for top right-hand corner (7)
26. Torment – there's often a wait before you get it (5)
28. Senator was anti-League: guy, that's swell! (5)
29. Glory, no bus to catch (3)
30. 5s form part of the topic in question (7)

31. Midday raider, one hears, in Arctic projects (9)
32. *Slays sounding likely to have names on backs* (6)
33. Sinister old trail for each to follow of old (6)

DOWN

1. Obviously born to plunder, beat and hector (11)
2. Rising of the French seen in Parisian festival (5)
3. Composer, essentially English, gripped by cricket (5)
4. *Sucking up – gosh! – after beaks turn up* (6)
5. Polled, a small number abstaining (4)
6. Most superbly dressed in two undergarments (7)
7. Cerda in serious trouble in the wood (5)
8. Reverse of in the clear, I am – it's the sack (6)
9. Young things with manes are potentially tonsile (7)
10. Negative French master taking shell, grey, old – type that can't chew its food (11)
16. Youngsters whose iron aim is troublous (7)
17. Doom that no one talks of – clan wiped out (7)
19. Original skirt embraced by boyfriend (6)
21. *Fearsome female, but one able to be amused* (6)
23. Ruminant to be seen in oriental country (5)
24. Active in forbidding Arab encampment (5)
25. Journeys which, when over, sound like the edge (5)
27. Here's the photo: mine's like yours (4)

Playfair instructions

Answers to clues in italics are to appear in the grid in code; the other clues are ordinary and their answers should be entered in the usual way. The encoding system is a 'Playfair' code-square. As shown in the example below, this consists of a keyword (in which no letter recurs) followed by the remaining letters of the alphabet in order. I does duty for both I and J.

B	A	N	K	R
U	P	T	C	I
E	S	D	F	G
H	L	M	O	Q
V	W	X	Y	Z

Suppose that one of the clues in italics has the answer BREVETED. To encode, we split it into pairs of letters thus: BR EV ET ED. If the letters of a pair occur in same row, as is the case for BR, we take the letters to the right of each, so BR becomes AB (use the first letter if there is no letter to the right). If the letters appear in the same column, as with EV, we encode into the letters below each, so EV becomes HB (use the top letter if there is no letter below). When the letters in a pair appear from different rows *and* columns, treat them as opposite corners of a rectangle. In this manner, ET becomes DU (not UD). Therefore, BR EV ET ED is encoded into AB HB DU SF, and that should be entered into the grid.

Clearly, it is simplest to begin with the ordinary clues. Most of the encoded words can be found from interlocking words, from which the code-square used can be deduced. The remaining squares of the diagram can then be completed.

CHAPTER 5

Gatherings for Gardner

Imagine looking up at the night sky, knowing that somewhere up there is an asteroid named after you. Imagine that every couple of years, hundreds of people from around the world come to a party held in your honour. Imagine gazing proudly at six shelves of books, every single one of which you've written. Imagine that you've had more influence on the understanding of modern mathematics than anyone else. Imagine that your name is Martin Gardner.

DIVIDE AND CONQUER

For some, the world of mathematics is an inherently alienating experience. Mention a key word such as 'algebra', 'quadratic' or 'hyperbolic' in polite company and they recoil in horror. Memories of unhappy schooldays solving $y = mx + c$, chasing acute angles around an isosceles triangle, or finding the lowest common multiple come flooding back. When these people try to understand a solution to a mathematical puzzle, they ask for it to be described 'the easy way', perhaps with the aid of a diagram or model, leaving out all those x's and y's. In truth, algebra *is* the easy way – that's why it was developed, yet it is seen by some non-mathematicians as an obstacle to insight rather than a powerful problem-solving tool.

A shame, then, that many members of the public are sadly unaware of the fascinating areas of interesting mathematics that surround us – the stuff they didn't teach you at school, though they insisted that the cosine rule might one day save your life, or at least bump you up a grade. Take, for instance, the Fibonacci series, first brought to wide attention by Leonardo of Pisa in 1202. It consists of the infinite list of numbers 1, 1, 2, 3, 5, 8, 13, 21, 34, 55, 89, ..., where each number is the sum of the previous two terms (so the next number would be 55 + 89 = 144).

As you continue the series to infinity, the ratio of two successive terms gets closer to a constant number, 1.61803..., which is equal to half the sum of one and the square root of five – or, if you're not frightened by symbols, ½(1 + √5). This number is so aesthetically pleasing that it has been given a special name, the golden ratio, and the length/breadth ratio of many familiar items, from books to paintings, credit cards to widescreen televisions, is often very close to this value. It has been conjectured that landmarks such as Egypt's pyramids and the Parthenon in Athens were built with the golden ratio in mind.

We can go further – the spiral grooves seen in the seedhead of a sunflower are often Fibonacci numbers (e.g. 34 clockwise, 55 anticlockwise), allowing the maximum number of seeds to be packed onto the flower's head. The amount of rotation between one leaf and the next around the stem of a plant is a fraction made from two Fibonacci numbers (e.g. 1/2, 1/3 or 2/5 of a circle) so that the leaves receive the best distribution of sunlight. Our sense of aesthetics inherently tells us when something 'looks right', which is often when it adheres to the golden ratio, yet few of us study such phenomena as part of our education.

Is maths simply less interesting to the average punter because in our everyday lives most of us encounter ten numerals, a few arithmetic symbols and little else? Which fact do you find sexier: that PRESBYTERIANS is an anagram of BRITNEY SPEARS, or that 6 is the first perfect number because it is the sum of its proper positive divisors? But that's pretty irrelevant. Mathematics is involved in virtually every job, problem or task you could name. Our advancement as a species would have hit a ceiling without the research done by those men and women with nothing more than a blackboard, notepad or laptop for company. Not for nothing has mathematics been dubbed the Queen of the Sciences.

But no matter how important or relevant a topic might be, one still has to sell it as fun and interesting. The world-famous British physicist Professor Stephen Hawking was once warned by an editor that his potential readership would halve for every equation he included in his book *A Brief History of Time*. With this in mind, he included just one: $E = mc^2$, and rued how much more successful his book would have been without it! How, then, can we get the interesting stuff in front of the average intelligent adult without boring or confusing them, but without coyly avoiding equations and graphs either?

Martin Gardner

MATHEMATICAL GAMES

Enter our hero, Martin Gardner, stage left. After a career in the US Navy and attending college at the University of Chicago, Gardner honed his early journalistic experience to become a full-time self-employed author. His first book, *Mathematics, Magic, and Mystery*, was written in 1955 when the Oklahoma-born Gardner had turned 41 years of age. Ostensibly a magic book – covering tricks with cards, dice, rubber bands, coins and numbers – it showed the reader how mathematical magic can appeal to the heart as well as the mind. With Gardner's explanations of *why*, not just *how*, one could learn to love magic thanks to the clever underlying mathematical principles that make the tricks work almost by themselves.

The book was the result of a contact Gardner had made with Jekuthiel Ginsburg of New York, who edited a magazine called *Scripta Mathematica* devoted to the history of mathematics. Gardner explains: 'I did a series of pieces, one on card tricks and one on dice tricks … and so on, and I put those together and that became a book. Dover published it and I was paid a total of $500 for it. No royalties, but later it got translated into French and German, and fortunately for me, and unfortunately for Dover, they forgot to put into the clause anything about foreign sales. So I got all the royalties on foreign sales and made far more on the German edition then I did on the English one.' Although it was published over fifty years ago, *Mathematics, Magic, and Mystery* has never been out of print.

The following year, Gerry Piel – publisher of the popular science magazine *Scientific American* – offered Gardner the column for which he was to become most famous. It was a big deal for Gardner, in terms of advancing his career and earning a decent wage for the first time. Piel's offer of work came about when *The World of Mathematics* by James Newman, a four-volume collection of essays suitable for the layman, did good business for Simon & Schuster (who, as we've already seen, popularized the modern crossword). Piel sensed that there was a public appetite for more. Writing under the banner of 'Mathematical Games', Gardner set about explaining various mathematical concepts in a coherent manner that was understandable to anyone willing to take the time to read his column. 'I have always followed [the writing style of] Bertrand Russell,' says Gardner. 'He said that whenever he thought of a simpler word to substitute for a more complicated word, he would use the simpler word. That's a piece of advice that I've tried to follow.'

Throughout his 25-year tenure at *Scientific American*, Martin Gardner covered many topics that were revolutionary at the time but have now worked their way into public use, one way or another. The Soma Cube puzzle became a bestseller, polyominoes are used in the computer game Tetris, and fractals can be seen in design and art. The advancement of computers in the 1970s and 1980s prompted Gardner to write about John Conway's Game of Life – an early computer simulation model – and the four-colour theorem. This is a rule that any political map can be coloured in using four colours, and was proved only by exhaustive computer analysis of 1,936 different situations. Gardner even wrote two columns about the number zero.

Gardner retired from writing his column in 1981, and the rumour is that the magazine's circulation dropped significantly as a result. 'I do indeed miss writing the *Scientific American* column,' he said later. 'I had reached a point where I could no longer keep up the column and write the books I hoped to write as long as I had my wits about me. Also, I felt it was time for younger writers to take over the column.' He was replaced by Douglas Hofstadter, who called his column 'Metamagical Themas', an anagram of 'Mathematical Games'.

PUZZLE PARTY

Gardner's columns from the magazine have been published as fifteen standalone books. Their readership is wide and varied, from businessmen wishing to 'keep their mathematical hand in' to bright teenagers seeking to stretch themselves a little further than their own school lessons. Thanks to a career of over fifty years, Gardner's audience also spans quite a timeframe, and many eminent research scientists, authors, magicians and puzzlists have grown up with their young imaginations nurtured by his output, as he acknowledges: 'One of the lasting benefits of having done the column was getting to know, as personal friends, so many mathematicians, real mathematicians, far more knowledgeable than I, and whose work I could only dimly appreciate … Another continuing pleasure is getting letters from mathematicians telling me it was my column that aroused their interest in math when they were in high school and led them to decide on math as a career.'

Martin Gardner's fans became sufficient in number that puzzle collector Tom Rodgers spotted the opportunity to organize a get-together in his honour. The invitation-only symposium, which takes place roughly every couple of years, consists of Gardner fans socializing and exchanging research papers on topics of their choosing which are distributed to all as a takeaway gift. Creators of three-dimensional puzzles bring along their newest wood and metalwork sculptures to torment the other delegates, and in respect to Gardner's magical background, various conjuring performances are also to be seen.

Gardner's interests are much wider than the mathematics that made him famous. To an extent, his columns and book royalties paid the mortgage, but he could have become an authority in any of various fields. He majored in philosophy, and takes great delight in debunking paranormalists and those with other non-scientific beliefs. Speaking to the Mathematical Association of America in 2006, he said: 'My main interests are philosophy and religion, with special emphasis on the philosophy of science ... I'm glad I majored in philosophy, though had I known I would be writing some day a column on math, I would have taken some math courses. As it was, I took not a single math course. If you look over my *Scientific American* columns you will see that they get progressively more sophisticated as I began reading math books and learning more about the subject. There is no better way to learn anything than to write about it!' However, he also admits that 'There are big gaps in my knowledge, one of the largest of which is classical music. I have a poor ear. My tastes run to Dixieland jazz and melodies I am able to hum and play on a musical saw (one of my minor self-amusements). I know nothing about sports other than baseball. I have never played a game of golf or seen a horse race. I never watch football or basketball. I think boxing should be outlawed as too primitive and cruel.'

RECREATIONAL FACILITIES

Much of Gardner's material was submitted to him by mathematicians wanting to reach out to a lay audience, but where have all the other number puzzles and games come from? In the trade, this field of study is somewhat lightheartedly referred to as 'recreational mathematics'. Its name seems to imply that this is the stuff that professors might tackle on a slow day, during a coffee break, or when there's no other research to do – and to some extent that's true. Is there a way to define what subset of mathematics is of the recreational type?

Professor David Singmaster, a leading expert in the field, says that 'An obvious definition is that recreational mathematics is the mathematics that is fun, but almost any mathematician will say that he enjoys his work, even if he is studying eigenvalues of elliptic differential operators, so this definition would encompass almost all mathematics.' Singmaster offers two test criteria: first, that recreational mathematics should be fun and easily understood by the layman, even if the solution may be out of their reach. Second, it should explain a mathematical principle to the reader, as if it were a teaching tool.

By these criteria, recreational mathematics encompasses a whole swathe of material, including mathematical puzzles dating back some four thousand years to the ancient Egyptians, and the growth of the subject matter, thus defined, has accelerated ever since. From the late nineteenth century onwards, key developments such as matchstick puzzles, chess magazines, magic manuals, optical illusions, the Towers of Hanoi, riddle books and sliding block puzzles attained widespread popularity. Newspapers printed number puzzles of various kinds. In Britain, it was the done thing for Victorian ladies to keep their numerical minds nimble, and several mathematical publications were aimed at them.

The playfulness of recreational mathematics often has a justifiable practicality in the same way that we benefit from CD players, faster computers and pens that can write upside down thanks to spin-off technology originally developed for space missions. The study of gambling games by the Frenchman Blaise Pascal formed the foundations of the actuarial and insurance industries. The Babylonians attempted to solve complicated equations of the form $Ax^3 + Bx^2 + Cx + D = 0$, even though they had no use for them whatsoever, and the Greeks did exercises in geometry just for kicks. A field of study called graph theory is now used by your car's satellite navigation system to find the quickest route from A to B. Even the Chinese

Rings, one of those annoying metal puzzles that seems to have no purpose other than to test your sanity, can be solved using a principle called a Gray code which is now used to ensure that your digital TV signal has no blips in it.

Perhaps when mathematicians put out press releases announcing the discovery of the maximum number of possible sudokus, solving the latest Rubik puzzle, or how to cook the perfect burger, they know they're firmly in recreational mathematics territory. Yet they still know that there's an appreciable chance that their work will have an application in mainstream mathematics somewhere down the line – even in hundreds of years' time.

The puzzles that follow include some of Martin Gardner's favourites. They vary from the type of standard textbook exercises that have been used as teaching aids since 1800 BC to practical examples of cutting-edge mathematics. Although it's been an uphill struggle at times, the public perception of maths has changed thanks to people like Martin Gardner, a fact that will always be reflected in his legacy of 70 books, and in the asteroid (2587) Gardner somewhere above us now.

The Puzzles

EASY AS 1, 2, 3, ...

We start with a quick quiz to get your numerical thinking into first gear.

1. What is one-half of two-thirds of three-quarters of four-fifths of five-sixths of 12?

2. An eel is 20 inches in length. If the tail were twice as long as it is, the head and tail together would be as long as the body. If the head and tail are equal in length, how long is the body?

3. If you turn this number upside down or reflect it left-to-right you get 11 either way, but the original number is not 11. What is it?

4. In which numbered parking space has the car been left?

5. Which two numbers add up to 25, and give the greatest possible product when they are multiplied together?

6. What should the next letter in this sequence be?

OTATF, FHAT, THAFS, OHATE, SF, TT, S, E, F, T, O, H, ?

7. In the calculation 43 + 57 = 207, every digit is precisely one away from its true value. What is the correct sum?

8. What is the length of the side of a square if its area (in square inches) is equal to twice its perimeter (in inches?)

9. Write 24 with three equal digits, none of which is 8. There are two solutions to this problem.

10. How can Guy Fawkes use these scales three times so that 100 g of gunpowder can be split into piles of 82 g and 18 g? He only has 2 g and 5 g weights.

11. By placing posts 2 feet apart around his garden, a gardener found that he was in need of 200 more. If, however, they were placed at intervals of 3 feet, there would have been a surplus of 25 posts. How many posts had he?

12. Hans lives in a house with the reverse number of Gretel. The difference between the house numbers ends in 2. What are their house numbers?

13. If you saw a piece of gold jewellery with this hallmark, how many carats of purity would the gold be?

14. If Caesar ordered 40 extra-large togas and 50 large togas, how many medium-sized togas did he order?

15. In Mr Reid's exotic animal collection, all but four of the creatures are lizards, all but four are snakes, and all but four are frogs. How many creatures are there in total?

16. Two fish start side-by-side. They swim for 6 metres, make a right turn, then swim for 8 metres. What is the largest distance apart they could be now?

17. Which three whole numbers must A, B and C be given that they are all different?

$$\frac{1}{A}+\frac{1}{B}+\frac{1}{C}=1$$

18. A river is 760 feet wide. One-fifth of the bridge stands on one bank of the river and one-sixth over the other side. How long is the bridge?

19. Paula loves making families of snowmen. Today she made snowmen in three different sizes – a small snowman requires 8 kg of snow, a medium snowman needs 17 kg, and it takes 23 kg to make a large snowman. If there was 132 kg of snow available, how many snowmen of each size did Paula make?

20. A psychic predicts that she will live for 99 years. Two-thirds of her past life is equal to four-fifths of her future existence. How old is she?

PYRAMIDS OF PERPLEXITY

For these first puzzles, each block is equal to the sum of the two numbers beneath it. Your task is to find all the missing numbers to complete the pyramid. The final puzzles provide a number of twists on a similar theme.

Pyramid 1

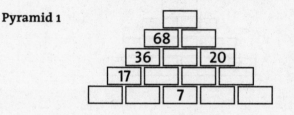

Pyramid 2

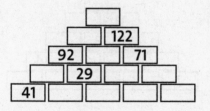

Pyramid 3
Here, the key is to find the number between 14 and 11.

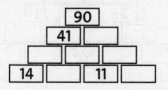

Pyramid 4

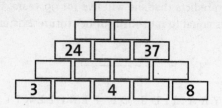

Pyramid 5

Find the two missing numbers on the bottom row.

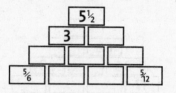

Pyramid 6

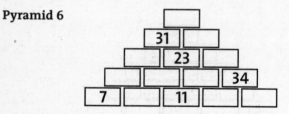

Pyramid 7

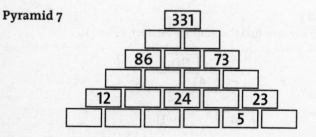

Pyramid 8

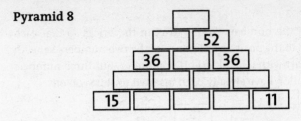

Pyramid 9

Given that X + Y = 11, what will be top number be?

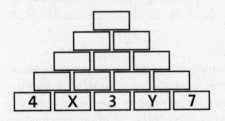

Pyramid 10

Enter each of the numbers from 1 to 10 in the bricks so that each block is equal to the positive difference of the two numbers beneath it. For example, if the top block is 8, the blocks in the second row must be 1 and 9.

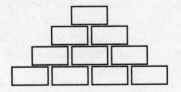

Pyramid 11

Enter each of the numbers from 1 to 15 in the bricks so that each block is equal to the positive difference of the two numbers beneath it. You can start with a blank grid if you prefer, but three numbers from our solution have already been inserted to start you off.

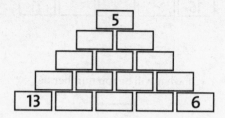

Pyramid 12

Each block in this pyramid is the total of the two blocks below it. Find all the numbers, given that only the *digits* from 1 to 6 inclusive are used, and there are no negative numbers or fractions. The bottom five numbers must satisfy the conditions specified.

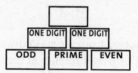

Pyramid 13

Each box represents a different positive whole number. A, B and C contain the sum of the two numbers below them. A must be as large as possible. B is prime. C consists only of straight lines when spelled out (e.g. 9 = NINE). D, E and F all contain exactly five letters when spelled out. Find all six numbers.

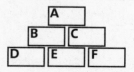

Pyramid 14

Each block in the upper four rows is equal to the highest whole number that divides exactly into the two numbers beneath it. For example, if the blocks in the second row were 6 and 9, the top block would be 3 because 6 and 9 are both multiples of 3. Complete the pyramid.

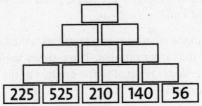

| 225 | 525 | 210 | 140 | 56 |

Pyramid 15

Each block is equal to the sum of the two numbers beneath it. Can you reconstruct the original triangle of numbers given the initial letters of the numbers involved? For example, E might be EIGHT, ELEVEN, EIGHTEEN, EIGHTY, etc.

NUMBER CRUNCHING

In this quiz, some school algebra might help you out.
The questions range from simple trifles to brain aches.

1. A certain number is increased by 3, and the result is then divided by 2. The result is twice the original number. What is the number?

2. If a two-digit number is tripled, and the number's original digits are added to this result, you obtain the original number but with the digits reversed. What was the original quantity? (*Hint:* start by expressing the number as 10A + B, where A and B are its digits.)

3. What number leaves a remainder of 1 when divided by 2, 3, 4, 5 or 6, and no remainder when divided by 7?

4. Find the values of the digits X, Y and Z, given that only X is prime, Y is even, Z is odd, and X + Y + Z = 15.

5. If one less than the smaller of two numbers is doubled, it will give one more than the larger number. Three times the smaller added to four times the larger is equal to the product of the two numbers. What are the numbers?

6. The hypotenuse of a right-angled triangle is 26 units long. The sum of the other two sides is 34 units. How long are each of the two sides?

7. A number is divided into four parts, so that the first is one less than the second; the third is as much as the first and second combined; and the fourth as much as the sum of the first, second and third. What is the number, and what are the parts?

8. Divide 48 into two parts in such manner that if one is divided by 6, and the other by 3, the sum of the quotients will be 9.

9. Divide the number 100 into four parts (call them A, B, C and D) such that adding 4 to A, subtracting 4 from B, dividing C by 4 or multiplying D by 4 gives the same result.

10. I'm thinking of two whole numbers. The difference between their squares is a cube, and the difference between their cubes is a square. What are the numbers?

11. Which three consecutive numbers are these? The sum of the squares of the two smallest numbers equals the square of the largest number. There are two solutions to this problem.

12. Find two consecutive numbers, such that 1/7 of the smaller is 1 less than 1/6 of the larger.

13. Without using a calculator, find the value of this expression:

$$\frac{67^2 - 33^2}{51^2 - 49^2}$$

14. What four-digit number will produce a number with the same four digits but in reverse order when:
(a) multiplied by 4? (b) multiplied by 9?

15. Arrange the nine digits 1 through 9 so that the first three shall be 1/3 of the last three; and the central three equal to the difference between the first three and the last three.

16. Two whole numbers result in the product of 1,000,000 when multiplied together. Neither number contains a zero. What are the two numbers? What valid answer can you offer if you could choose any two positive numbers, but your choices had to use the least number of different digits?

17. Use the digits from 1 to 9, inclusive, once each, in the form ABCD/EFGHI so that the fraction thus formed equals ½. Now repeat this for all the 1/x fractions from one-third down to one-ninth.

MAGIC SQUARES AND FRIENDS

All these puzzles rely on your ability to make the sums add up in many different directions at once. Forward planning, insight and a little guesswork are all useful.

Magic 1

A magic square has the special property that all the numbers in each row, column and both main diagonals add up to the same number. With this in mind, complete this magic square so that it contains nine consecutive numbers.

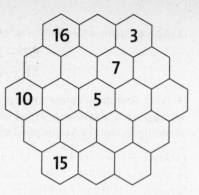

Magic 2

Complete the hexagon so that it contains the numbers from 1 to 19 inclusive in its nineteen cells. In all directions, every straight line of three, four or five connected hexagons totals 38. We've started you off.

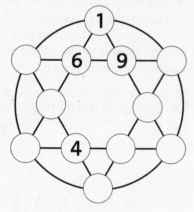

Magic 3

Put the numbers from 1 to 12 in the circles so that each line adds up to 26. In addition, the six numbers that lie on the outside circle total 26. We have placed four numbers for you.

Magic 4

Complete this magic square, where each row, column and main diagonal adds up to the same total.

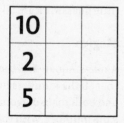

Magic 5

In Victorian times, these were the nine smallest values of postage stamp available: ½d, 1d, 1½d, 2d, 2½d, 3d, 3½d, 4d and 5d. Place these stamps in the nine squares so that each row, column and main diagonal adds up to the same amount. You will need to use exactly ten stamps – that is, one denomination is used twice, the others once each. Eight squares contain one stamp, the ninth contains two stamps. (Lewis Carroll)

Magic 6

Here we have a system of fortifications. It will be seen that there are ten forts, connected by lines of outworks, and the numbers represent the strength of the small garrisons. The General wants to arrange the armies so that there shall be 100 men in every one of the five lines of four forts. Can you show how it can be done? The garrisons must be moved bodily – that is to say, you are not allowed to break them up into other numbers. It is quite an entertaining little puzzle with counters, and not very difficult. (Henry Dudeney)

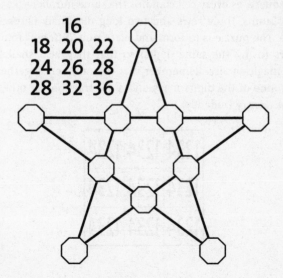

Magic 7

Can you form a magic square with all the columns, rows and two long diagonals adding up alike, with the numbers 1 to 25 inclusive, placing only the odd numbers on the shaded squares in our diagram, and the even numbers on the other squares? We have placed some of the numbers to get you started. (Henry Dudeney)

	22	1	10	
24				20
5				21
6				2
	16	25	4	

Magic 8

In this square, as every cell contains the same number – 1,234 – the three columns, three rows and two long diagonals naturally add up alike. The puzzle is to form and place nine different four-figure numbers (using the same digits) so that they also shall form a perfect magic square. Remember that the numbers together must contain nine of the digits 1, 2, 3 and 4. No fractions or other tricks are used. (Henry Dudeney)

1234	1234	1234
1234	1234	1234
1234	1234	1234

MONEY, MONEY, MONEY

In this section, we test your business acumen
with some money matters.

1. The receipts of a car dealer were £21,000, after having sold a certain number of cars at a uniform price. Had he sold one more car and received £100 less per car, he would have received the same sum. How many cars were sold, and what was the price of each?

2. Steve went to the greyhound races with £64. On each of the six races, he bet half the money that he had on the even-money dog. Half the dogs he backed won. Ignoring betting duty, how much did he end up with?

3. These four people owe each other money, as illustrated. What is the simplest way for them to settle up?

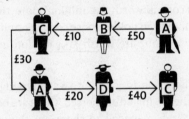

4. In a round robin soccer tournament, 13 teams play everyone else once. Winning a match earns £100. Tied matches earn £50 for each team. How much prize money will be given out during this tournament?

5. If the greengrocer makes the same profit on either of these deals, how much profit does he make?

6. King John was thinking: 'If I paid my courtiers four groats each, I'd have 18 groats left in my bank account. But if they demanded payment of seven groats each instead, I'd be overdrawn by 21 groats.' How many groats does King John have?

7. A US game show contestant receives a car worth $30,000. However, he is taxed at 20 per cent on all prizes and receipts. How much could the TV company pay the winner in cash so that in effect he receives the car tax free?

8. The popular Internet gadget website sprocketheadz.com offers £9 gift vouchers to its existing female customers and £6 to its existing male customers. While half of the men took up this offer, only one-third of the women did the same. If the website has 500 eligible customers, what was the total value of the vouchers issued during the promotion?

9. If stonkingrich.com is worth $15 million more than filthylucre.com, $7 million more than goldengoose.com, $12 million more than quids-in.com, and all four are worth $154 million in total, what is each site worth?

10. Sarah has to share a lottery win of £8,268 among the members of her lottery syndicate. Including herself, there are between 80 and 150 members. If Sarah managed to share out the winnings fairly using whole pounds only, how much did each person in the syndicate receive? (*Hint*: You can work it out logically rather than trying lots of different values.)

11. Egor was to be paid 100 groats plus a shiny new buckle if he worked for Lord Xerxes for one year. However, Egor had to leave after only seven months so he received fair payment of 20 groats plus the buckle. How much is the buckle worth?

12. The employees of Square Deal Co. are paid a basic monthly salary plus a bonus equal to the square of their age in dollars. In a certain month, Paul and Peter earned $1,411 and $1,075 respectively. If Peter is six years younger than Paul, find out their ages and their basic salary.

13. When cashing a cheque, a bank clerk makes an error and swaps the pounds and pence figures. If you were to spend £1.18 of the money you received, you would have exactly double the value of the cheque. What was the amount on the cheque? (*Hint*: let L be the number of pounds and D be the number of pence. How can you write the above as an equation?)

14. I have a certain amount of money in my wallet. The number of pence is three times the number of whole pounds plus one. Alternatively, if you were to swap the pounds and pence figures, the result would be three times as much as you started with plus one penny. How much money is in my wallet?

SOVEREIGN LAND

Here is a piece of land marked off with 36 circular plots, on each of which is deposited a bag containing as many sovereigns as indicated by the figures in the diagram. I am allowed to pick up as many bags of gold as I like, provided I do not take two lying on the same line. What is the greatest amount of money I can secure?

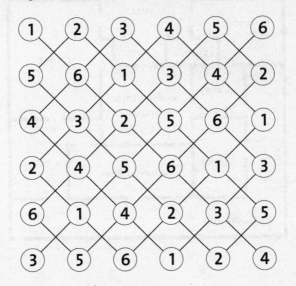

TWODOOR'S TOWN HOUSE

This puzzle is concerned with a branch of mathematics called topology, which deals with the way things are connected together rather than their actual form or how far apart they are. For example, a diagram of a train network is a simplified topological representation of how the routes connect rather than a faithful map of their positions.

Henry Twodoor, the eccentric millionaire, had a personal motto: 'Never use one door when you can use two.' Accordingly, he had an architect design a house so that he could go from any one room to any other by passing through just two doors. After living there for some time, he called the architect and complained that there were too many doors. The architect had a good look and decided that there were two doors that could be blocked up so that Henry could still go from any one room to any other by passing through just two doors. What were the two doors? (Albie Fiore)

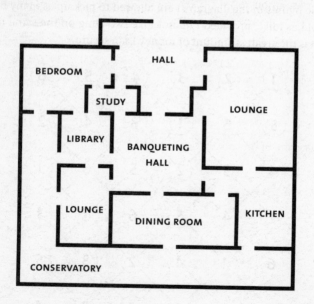

HALFWAY HOUSE

It's once again time to test you with some quickfire questions.

1. Which of these is the fairest sport, and why: bowls, darts, golf, snooker, table tennis, tennis?

2. Which number provides the next few terms of this series?

$$E, O, E, R, E, X, N, ...$$

3. The greatest number you can make using only three 1's is 111. The greatest number you can make using only three 2's is 222. The greatest number you can make using only three 3's is ... ?

4. Use the same digit eight times with '+' signs to produce the total 1,000.

5. This blue cheese has a rectangle cut out of it. You need to use one cut to slice the cheese into two pieces of equal volume. Can you find two different solutions?

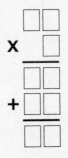

6. If you rotate the number 6 by 180 degrees, it becomes 9 (a 50 per cent increase). What's the largest increase possible by rotating a number by 90 degrees?

7. In the calculation 2,910 − 1,497 = 2,106, every digit is precisely one away from its true value. What is the correct sum?

8. Make sense of this calculation:

$$5 = 13 \ 3^B$$

9. Use the digits 1 to 9 once each to complete a valid two-stage calculation:

10. Sofia has drawn an outline figure which has an area of 1 sq cm and a perimeter of 4 cm. On what enlargement factor should she photocopy her drawing such that the area (in sq cm) and perimeter (in cm) are numerically equal?

11. Find the 100th term of the logical series which begins as follows:

$$81, 73, 52, 42, 34, 22, 18, 10, \ldots?$$

12. How many 4 ft by 1 ft planks could you cut from a rectangular sheet of plywood measuring 6 ft by 10 ft?

13. What is clever about the arrangement below, formed from the numbers 1 to 32 inclusive?

4	32	17	19	30	6	3	13
21	18	31	5	11	25	24	12
28	7	29	20	16	9	27	22
8	1	15	10	26	23	2	14

14. In what sense is this ordering of the numbers from 1 to 10 palindromic (i.e. reads the same from left to right as right to left)?

$$1 \quad 4 \quad 3 \quad 5 \quad 10 \quad 2 \quad 6 \quad 9 \quad 8 \quad 7$$

15. It is possible to use the digits from 1 to 9 once each so that they add up to 1. Complete the sum:

$$\frac{9}{1\square} + \frac{\square}{\square 4} + \frac{\square}{68} = 1$$

CROSSNUMBERS

These numerical crossword puzzles are not for the faint-hearted.
Each one executes its own ingenious twist on the theme.

Crossnumber 1

Complete this number crossword, and find the values for a, b and c.
(P. Kendall and G. Thomas)

ACROSS
1. $ab^2c - bc - c$
5. $\frac{1}{2}bc$
6. $bc + 1$
7. $b^2 - bc$
9. $b - 2$
10. $4b^3 - 2$

DOWN
1. $3ab^2$
2. c^3
3. $\frac{1}{2}(b^2 + c)$
4. $(4b^2 - 1) \times b$
8. $(2b - 1) \times a$
9. $b - 1$

Crossnumber 2

Note that one number begins
with a zero. (P. Kendall and
G. Thomas)

ACROSS
1. The second three form a number
   equal to three times the first three
   plus three.
6. To multiply by two put the first
   two digits at the end.
8. A square palindrome.
9. The sum of the digits is three.
10. The first and second, third and
    fourth, and fifth and sixth digits
    add up to the same total.
11. A multiple of the sum of its digits.
12. Cube of a prime plus square of
    another prime.

DOWN
1. A fourth power.
2. A power of two.
3. Reverse power of three.
4. Contains a digit twice which does
   not appear elsewhere.
5. 7 down in the scale of 7.
7. See 5 down.

Crossnumber 3

This number crossword by Henry Dudeney seems impossible, but there are several possible approaches. One entry is a bit of a cheat because it begins with a zero. As this is an early crossword, some clues (e.g. 4 across) refer to entries that are only one digit long.

ACROSS

1. A square number.
4. A square number.
5. A square number.
8. The digits sum to 35.
11. Square root of 39 across.
13. A square number.
14. A square number.
15. Square of 36 across.
17. Square of half 11 across.
18. Three similar figures.
19. Product of 4 across and 33 across.
21. A square number.
22. Five times 5 across.
23. All digits alike except the central one.
25. Square of 2 down.
27. See 20 down.
28. A fourth power.
29. Sum of 18 across and 31 across.
31. A triangular number.
33. One more than 4 times 36 across.
34. Digits sum to 18 and the three middle numbers are 3.
36. An odd number.
37. All digits even, except one, and their sum is 29.
39. A fourth power.
40. A cube number.
41. Twice a square.

DOWN

1. Reads both ways alike.
2. Square root of 28 across.
3. Sum of 17 across and 21 across.
4. Digits sum to 19.
5. Digits sum to 26.
6. Sum of 14 across and 33 across.
7. A cube number.
9. A cube number.
10. A square number.
12. Digits sum to 30.
14. All similar figures.
16. Sum of digits is 2 down.
18. All similar digits except the first, which is 1.
20. Sum of 17 across and 27 across.
21. Multiple of 19.
22. A square number.
24. A square number.
26. Square of 18 across.
28. A fourth power of 4 across.
29. Twice 15 across.
30. A triangular number.
32. Digits sum to 20 and end with 8.
34. Six times 21 across.
35. A cube number.
37. A square number.
38. A cube number.

TIME AND MOTION

How quickly can you polish off this set of puzzles based on time, speed and distance?

1. It takes 4 minutes and 17 seconds for Mary to make an ice cream sundae. Working at the same rate, how long would she need to fulfill her daily order of 60 sundaes?

2. Two brothers enter an air rifle competition. Daniel shot 5 pellets in 10 seconds, while in another event Dennis shot 10 pellets in 20 seconds. Which brother is quicker at reloading their rifle?

3. Mr Tabako drives his Honda Superspeed car around a one-mile circular track at 30 mph. At what speed must he travel on his second lap in order to average 60 mph for the two laps? (Paul Varley)

4. February 2000 had five Tuesdays. When is the next year that will repeat that feat?

5. Big John has been driving his 10-wheeler since 8 a.m. John will have his mid-morning snack in 20 minutes' time, when his driving time will be three times the time from now until 11 a.m. What time is it now?

6. Two running partners follow the same route at the same time at the same pace. However, one measures their pace in terms of minutes taken for one mile, whereas the other uses kilometres per hour. Curiously, both statistics turn out to give the same number. How fast were they going? You may assume that 8 kilometres = 5 miles.

7. In the USA, the date 4 June 1991 would be written 6/4/91, but in the UK it is written as 4/6/91. Both dates are potentially valid without knowing which system is being employed. How many dates in a year are ambiguous this way?

8. One hour ago, it was as long after 1 p.m. as it was before 1 a.m. What time is it now?

9. On petri dish A there are currently 5,000 bacteria, which between them produce another 250 bacteria per hour. On petri dish B there are currently 12,000 bacteria, but of these 100 bacteria per hour die. When will both dishes have an identical bacteria population?

10. Clayton climbs an escalator at the constant rate of 10 steps per minute. The escalator's 60 steps, of which 24 can be seen at any one time, take two minutes to perform one complete cycle. (a) How long will it take Clayton to travel the length of the escalator? (b) How fast would Clayton have to walk up that escalator but going the *wrong* way if he's to touch all 60 steps during his journey?

11. In a grassy field with no other food, 11 goats could last for seven days before they run out of grub. Ten goats could last for eight days. How long could three goats survive before going hungry?

12. A security guard is working a long night shift. At ten past one in the morning he makes his first patrol. He patrols another four times at 70-minute intervals. He can then rest for a few hours before the patrol just after ten o'clock. He completes two more patrols with 70-minute gaps before clocking off at lunchtime. What superstition does he have?

13. Find a connection between these times: 9:57, 8:23, 1:32, 11:25, 9:13 and 2:48.

14. A radio signal travelling at 300 km per second is reflected back and forth between two satellites which start 10,000 km apart. How far will the signal travel before the satellites collide?

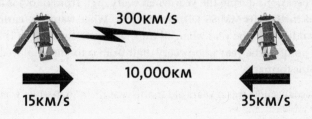

300KM/S

10,000KM

15KM/S   35KM/S

15. At the weekend, Mary usually cuts her grass lawn in 4 hours. However, today she has Mungo to help her. If, with Mungo's constant help, the job now took 2 hours 24 minutes, how long would it take Mungo to mow the lawn on his own?

16. Working on their own, Groucho and Chico could build a given brick wall in 3 and 4 days respectively. On his own, Zeppo could knock it down in 12 days. How long will it take them to build the wall if Groucho and Chico are building and Zeppo is demolishing, all at the same time?

17. A man's age at his death was one-twenty-ninth of the year of his birth. How old was he in the year 1900? (Henry Dudeney)

18. Boadicea died 129 years after Cleopatra was born. Their united ages (that is, the combined years of their complete lives) were one hundred years. Cleopatra died in 30 BC. When was Boadicea born? (Henry Dudeney – writing in 1930)

19. 'Here's an arithmetical puzzle,' wrote Lewis Carroll, 'which I invented two days ago, which you can give to Helen, to console her for not coming to dine.' Three men, A, B and C, are to run a race of a quarter of a mile. Whenever A runs against B, he loses 10 yards in every 100: whenever B runs against C, he gains 10 yards in every 100. In the second heat, how much head-start should be given to runner A, and runner C be handicapped, so that, if the race were run again with the same performances, it would be a dead heat?

20. Jenny has a clock which displays the date and time. There are some occasions during the year when every digit from 0 to 9 is displayed in the HH:MM:SS DD/MM format. What were the earliest time and date in the year when all the digits were seen? What is the latest point in the year when every digit from 0 to 9 is displayed in the same format?

21. If a man said 'I was n years old in the year n^2' in 1971, when was he born?

22. Starting at rest, a speedboat has to race across 216 nautical miles of ocean. If it proceeds at a constant 3 knots per hour, how long will it take?

23. Two people are chatting on the Paris to Berlin express train as the ticket inspector checks their tickets. The younger one says to the other, 'If you add together the individual numbers of the year I was born, you get my age.' The other replies, 'Funnily enough, the same applies to me.' The ticket inspector, who is an able mathematician, then states with absolute certainty, 'In that case, I must wish you both a happy birthday.' What day of what month of what year did this take place? (Albie Fiore)

MATCHSTICK PUZZLES

Matchstick puzzles continue to provide popular entertainment in pubs and bars throughout the world. For the following challenges, a few rules need to be assumed. When a puzzle says 'Move three matches', you must move exactly three matches from one part of the puzzle to another – you can't throw them away. 'Leave three squares' means that you must leave the puzzle in such a way that it is possible to see three different geometric squares, of any size, without any odd or orphan matches remaining.

Matchsticks 1
Starting with a 2 × 2 array of squares:

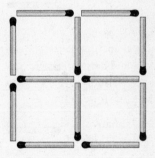

(a) Move three matches and leave three squares.

(b) Move four matches and leave two squares.

(c) Move four matches and leave three squares.

(d) Move four matches and leave ten squares.

(e) Remove two matches and leave two squares.

Matchsticks 2

Starting with a 3 × 3 array of squares:

(a) Remove four matches and leave five squares.
(b) Remove six matches and leave five squares.
(c) Remove six matches and leave three squares.
(d) Remove eight matches and leave four squares.
(e) Remove eight matches and leave three squares.
(f) Remove eight matches and leave two squares.

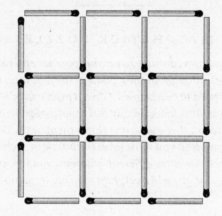

Matchsticks 3

Move four matches to leave just two squares.

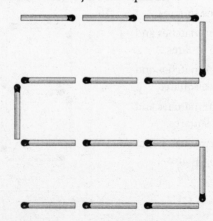

Matchsticks 4

Move two matches so that six triangles
of any size remain.

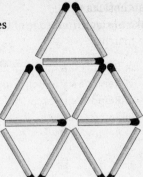

Matchsticks 5

Remove three matches to leave
seven triangles.

Matchsticks 6

How can you arrange six matches so that you form:

    (a) Four equilateral triangles?
    (b) One large square?
    (c) Three equal squares?

Matchsticks 7

Make a bridge from edge of the lake to the central island using only two matches.

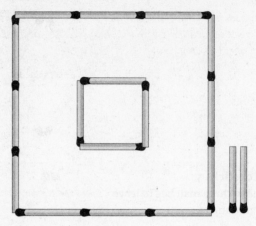

Matchsticks 8

Add three more matches to make two areas that are equal in shape and size.

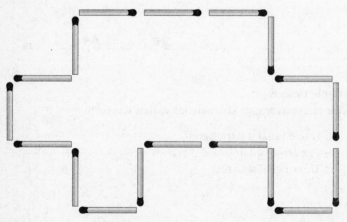

COMBINATION SALAD

This selection of problems involves permutations, combinations and related mathematics that enable one to solve complicated problems simply, avoiding the need to consider many individual cases separately. Given the wide-scale use of these principles in all sorts of games, from lucky lotteries to skilful poker, they're worth getting to grips with.

1. If there are 25 stations on a railway line, what is the maximum number of different fares required in order that there is a ticket price set for every possible journey from any one station to any other?

2. Ernie the electrician can't see very well in his dingy garage. He has 19 fuses of 3 amp rating, 23 fuses of 5 amp rating and 28 fuses of 13 amp rating mixed up in a small dish. Since the writing on the fuses is too small to see in the poor lighting, how many fuses does he need to take from the dish in order to be sure of having five fuses each of all three ratings?

3. One of seven guests of a restaurant dined there each day; a second guest dined there every second day; a third every third day, and so on to the seventh, who ate there once every seventh day. After how many days would all seven guests appear at the same time?

4. Following the logic of the arrows at all times, how many routes are there from Start to Finish? You might find it useful to calculate the number of routes leading to each square, then add these up along the route.

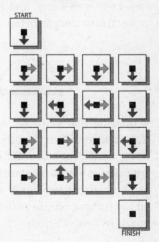

5. Suppose you wrote down all the whole numbers from 1 to 1,000,000. What is the total of all the digits you have written down? How can you do it using mental arithmetic only?

$$1 + 2 + 3 + 4 + 5 + 6 + 7 + 8 + \ldots + 1 + 0 + 0 + 0 + 0 + 0 + 0$$

6. In tenpin bowling, you get two attempts to knock down the ten pins. Theoretically, how many different situations are possible after you have bowled the first ball?

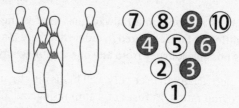

7. Two dining clubs were formed. The first had 15 members, who agreed to dine four at a time until all possible combinations had been used. The second club consisted of 21 members and dined in groups of three at a time, until all possible combinations had been used. Which group served more dinners, and how many more?

8. Suppose that you can step over one stone or jump over two stones. There are three ways you could cross a row of three stones: step–step–step, step–jump, and jump–step. How many ways could you cross (a) four stones; (b) ten stones?

9. Imagine that you have some wooden cubes. You also have six tins each containing a different colour of paint. You paint a cube using a different colour for each of the six faces. How many different cubes can be painted using the same set of six different colours? Remember that two cubes are different only when it is not possible, by turning one, to make it correspond to the other. (Based on a puzzle by Lewis Carroll)

OUT OF THIS WORLD

*Don't get your head in a spin with these brainteasers
on planetary motion.*

Out of this world 1

Planets A and B are in orbit around the same sun. Planet A takes 10 years to make one complete orbit, while Planet B takes 9 years. Currently, Planet B is 60 degrees further into its orbit than Planet A. How long will it be before B lies on a line connecting Planet A and the sun?

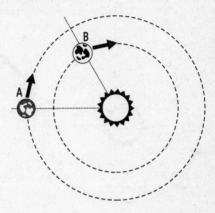

Out of this world 2

Both planets are orbiting clockwise around this sun. Planet C takes 3 years to orbit, planet D takes 5 years. At the moment, the middles of C, D and the sun all lie on the same line. How long will it be before this happens again?

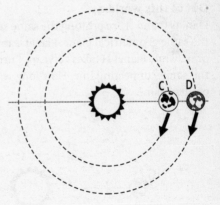

Out of this world 3

Two planets are each orbiting their own sun. There is one point where the planets could collide. Planet E, which takes 8 years to orbit its sun, is 135 degrees past that point. Planet F, which takes 10 years to orbit its sun, is only 36 degrees past the collision point. Will they collide, and, if so, how long will it be before it happens?

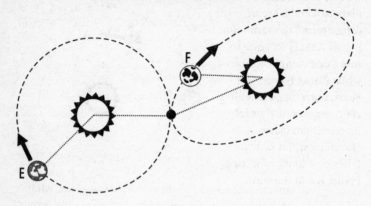

Out of this world 4

Planets G and H are orbiting the same sun, but their orbits are not in the same geometrical plane. Planet G takes 28 years to complete one orbit, while Planet H takes 20 years. Currently, all three bodies are on the same connecting line. How long will it be before this situation occurs again?

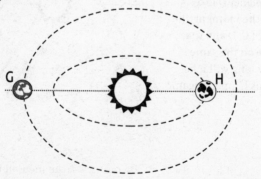

CHANCE WOULD BE A FINE THING

*The areas of probability and statistics can be the most
befuddling of all. You can work out the likelihood of something
to be 75 per cent, but unless you perform an experiment
hundreds of times, how can you be sure you're right?
Paradoxes abound here, so mind your step.*

1. A stick is broken into two pieces, at random. What is the average length of the shorter piece?

2. Two of these cups hide a marble. What is the probability that the marbles are in adjacent cups?

3. In most card games, the lowest card is the 2 and the highest is the Ace, and the suits have a particular order of importance. If you drew three cards at random from a well-shuffled deck of 52 cards, what is the probability that they will be drawn in order of increasing importance?

4. A spy looks through his binoculars and peers at the Pentagon building. What is the probability that three of its sides will be visible to him?

5. 100 balls are dropped into the top of this structure. On average, how many will fall into the buckets?

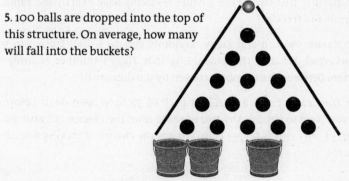

6. I'm thinking of four numbers. The mode is 1, the median is 2 and the mean is 3. What are the numbers?

7. In a survey of 100 people, 24 people drink both tea and coffee while 7 people drink neither. If twice as many people drink coffee as drink tea, how many drink tea?

8. 800 women are surveyed in the street. Three per cent of them are wearing one earring. Of the other 97 per cent, half are wearing two earrings, half are wearing none. How many earrings all together are being worn by these 800 women?

9. Mrs Tabako has fifty natural pearls, fifty cultured pearls and two Ming jars. If she uses all the pearls, how should she distribute them in the two jars in such a way that when Mr Tabako enters the room and picks one pearl out of either jar at random, he will have the best possible chance of picking a cultured pearl? (Doc Hume)

10. An incomplete set of playing cards contains an equal number of hearts, diamonds, and clubs. The entire spade suit is now added. However, the odds of choosing two random cards of the same suit remain the same. How many cards are there in the original set? (Albie Fiore)

11. On the little-known Scottish island of Ruddinora, the latest census has just been published. Not only do they know that there are 1,002 people on the island, but they also know that nobody on the island has more than 1,000 freckles on their skin. What is the probability that two of the island's residents have exactly the same number of freckles?

12. Xavier, Yasmin and Ziggy randomly choose a digit from 1 to 5 (inclusive). What is the probability that Ziggy's number is somewhere between the numbers chosen by the other two?

13. Four cards from a standard pack of 52 have been dealt below. If you were to choose any two of these four, the chance of getting a pair of red cards is 50 per cent. What is the chance of picking a black pair?

14. In the pub betting game Crown and Anchor, one player acts as a bookie while the others place their bets on one of the six symbols on the three identical dice. Higher odds are paid out for doubles and triples. (a) What is the chance that all three dice show different symbols uppermost after the roll? (b) The bookmaker pays you off at evens, 2 to 1 and 3 to 1 if one, two or all three dice show the symbol you have backed, respectively. As there are six symbols and three dice, the even money payoff is fair and the higher odds for a double or three of a kind are clearly a bonus. So, is the game fair?

15. In the game Clock Patience, you deal out a shuffled pack of 52 cards into 13 piles as shown. You turn over one of the middle cards.

If it is (e.g.) a seven, you take the next card from the 7 o'clock position. If it is a Jack or Queen, you take it from the 11 or 12 o'clock position. A King means you take the next card from the middle. What is the probability that you will win the game – i.e. turn over all 52 cards without running out of cards?

16. A bag contains one counter, known to be either white or black. A white counter is put in, the bag shaken, and a counter drawn out, which proves to be white. What is now the chance of drawing a white counter?

17. Be warned: the answer to this will surprise you! What is the probability, in per cent, that a randomly chosen whole number will contain the digit '3'?

The end is in sight, but not until you've made it past these tricky number conundrums that we've kept in our back pocket until now.

1. Four Egyptians are standing so that the distance between any pair of Egyptians is exactly the same. They can all see one another, so how are they positioned?

2. In a knock-out singles tennis tournament, 54 players will play. Excluding byes, how many matches will be played during the contest?

3. Which 12-letter mathematical word is missing?

> Less than five
> Minus one
> Multiplied by ten
> Equals two
> _____ one hundred

4. This is called the 'Eban series'. Can you see why? Now supply the next term.

$$2, 4, 6, 30, 32, 34, 36, 40, 42, 44, 46, \ldots$$

5. The difference between two numbers is 4, and the difference between their squares is 48. What are the numbers?

6. There is a way of expressing the number 1 using all the digits from 0 to 9 exactly once. We've started it off, can you complete it?

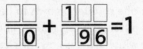

7. Two numbers consist of the same two digits reversed. The smaller number is one less than one-half the larger number. What are the numbers?

8. Use four different five-letter numbers (in English usage) to make this calculation correct:

$$(\underline{\hspace{1.5cm}} \div \underline{\hspace{1.5cm}}) + \underline{\hspace{1.5cm}} = \underline{\hspace{1.5cm}}$$

9. Substitute for the stars all the ten digits in each row, so that a little multiplication is arranged. The 0 does not appear at the beginning or end of either number. Can the reader find an answer? (Henry Dudeney)

$$\begin{array}{r} * \; * \; * \; * \; * \; * \; * \; * \; * \; * \\ \times 2 \\ \hline * \; * \; * \; * \; * \; * \; * \; * \; * \; * \end{array}$$

10. Rotate two lines in both rows for this to make sense:

IF IOIOIOIOIII70,

THEN IOIOIIIO.

11. What is the smallest whole number such that when it is multiplied by 7 the result is a string of 4's? (*Hint*: Rearrange.)

$$7 \times \underline{} = 4\dots4$$

12. In the calculation 1,663 × 3 = 21,379, every digit is precisely one away from its true value. What is the correct calculation?

13. The sum of any three consecutive letters (such as D, E and F) equals 16, no matter which three you choose. Find the value of F.

14. A rabbit has a number of baby carrots in his cage. Each day he eats one quarter of the carrots. After four days he has eaten 350 carrots. How many were there to start with?

15. Without using a calculating device, determine which of these numbers is the larger:

$$10^{\frac{1}{5}} \quad 4^{\frac{1}{3}}$$

See if you can put what you've learnt to the test with this final batch of long numerical brainteasers.

1. I can fit in all but six of my CDs into my CD rack. By buying an additional rack, adding 50 per cent to my capacity, I can fit in all my CDs and have room for eight more. How many CDs do I own?

2. A label on my new 2 kg box of cereal reads: 'Contains 98 per cent cereal, by total packet weight.' After I pour some cereal into a bowl for my breakfast, the box now contains 95 per cent cereal by weight. How much cereal did I have for breakfast?

3. Mrs Smith has ten boxes of coins, but one of the boxes is full of fakes which are all 1 g lighter than the real deal. However, there are no markings on the boxes or the coins by which to tell them apart. If Mrs Smith knows that real coins weigh 50 g, what is the least number of weighings that she will need to perform on her accurate weighing machine to determine which box contains the fakes? (This puzzle made an appearance on an episode of the TV detective series *Columbo*.)

4. Farmer Giles planted 129 vegetables. He planted three times as many potatoes as onions; half as many radishes as onions and potatoes combined; half as many tomatoes as potatoes and radishes combined; and half as many beets as radishes and tomatoes combined. How many of each kind did he plant?

5. Mrs Wilkinson bought a bunch of ice lollies to pacify her triplets. Tom took all the lollies and ate half of them, plus another half a lolly for good luck, before passing them on to his brother. Dick similarly ate half of them plus another half lolly before giving the remainder to Harriet. She, too, ate half the total lollies remaining and another half a lolly, after which there was nothing left. Given that no lollies were dropped or melted along the way, how many lollies did Mrs Wilkinson originally buy?

6. Colin the Clown is on balloon duty today. Visitors to the carnival are invited to buy one of his novelty balloons for a very reasonable price. There are six shapes of balloon, each one costing a different amount (namely 1, 2, 3, 5, 7 and 10 pence). Jamie's mother wishes to buy some for her son and his friends. Unfortunately she has forgotten which shapes were required. However, she does know that she needs four each of three of the shapes, and five each of the other three shapes. Given that she was able to buy what she needed using only 20 pence coins, what balloons were bought?

7. When my Aunt Enid goes away for the weekend (Saturday and Sunday), she always carries her vitamin pills with her – two vitamin B and two vitamin C tablets. Unfortunately, her pillbox has broken and all four tablets have fallen out. Furthermore, both kinds of tablet look, taste and weigh exactly the same. How can she use these same four tablets and still ensure that she receives the required dose – one vitamin B and one vitamin C tablet – on each of the two days?

8. At a sports camp, there are 94 children learning how to play different team sports. Some children are playing basketball, others netball and the rest hockey. Basketball games are played between two teams of 5 players, netball games between two teams of 7 players and hockey games between two teams of 11 players. At any given time, all the children at the camp are playing games and at least one game of each sport is taking place. How many children are playing each sport?

9. When standing for secretary of the local pigeon fanciers' club, John beat Albert, Brian and Charlie by 18, 27 and 41 votes respectively. If the total number of votes cast for all four men was 142, how many votes were received by each candidate?

10. Most chess players have heard of the knight's tour, where the knight visits all 64 squares of the chessboard. There are several different ways this can be done. Is it possible to devise a route so that the knight starts in one corner and finishes up in the opposite corner?

11. No matter how Simon shares out the sweets in his jar between the other office workers (of which there are between 2 and 10 inclusive), there's always exactly one sweet left for Simon. How many sweets are there in the jar?

12. Sally and Peter are standing in a cattle field at the same time. Sally can see the same number of bulls and cows in the field. However, Peter doesn't agree. He can see twice as many cows as there are bulls. Can you explain the difference of opinion and deduce how many bulls and cows are in the field?

13. Denise and Daniel know that there are 49 silver coins and 51 copper coins down the back of their sofa. (Their father really needs to get some trousers with zipped pockets.) They also have 100 copper coins in their piggy bank. They decide to play a game. In turn, each child plunges their hand down the sofa and retrieves two coins at random. If they are of two different colours, they keep the copper coin but the silver coin must be returned into the sofa. If they are of the same colour, they keep them both but one of the copper coins from the piggy bank is returned to the sofa. What colour will the last coin in the sofa be?

CHAPTER 6

Truth Will Out

You wouldn't expect books entitled *Theory of Formal Systems* and *First Order Logic* to race to the top of the sales charts. Nevertheless, over a 25-year career the author of these titles – Raymond M. Smullyan – has gone on to enchant millions of readers with his puzzle books set in unique worlds where nothing can be taken for granted.

THE MOTLEY FOOL

Smullyan, born in New York in 1919, encountered his first important logical argument at the age of six. In his first popular mathematics book, *What is the Name of This Book?*, he tells how his 16-year-old brother, Emile, warned him, 'Well, Raymond, today is April Fool's Day, and I will fool you as you have never been fooled before.' Smullyan, who was bedridden that day, waited … and waited … and waited. No trick came. The poor child couldn't go to sleep, fearing the worst for the supposed incoming prank, but no prank came. 'Emile,' snapped their mother, 'will you please fool the child?'

Raymond didn't know what to make of it. He argued

with Emile about whether he had been fooled or not. He was expecting to be fooled, but no fool came, so he was fooled, right? Or maybe not. Smullyan didn't know what the answer was, but Emile's tortuous trick sowed the seed of a career in logic. As his interest in magic and mathematical puzzles grew, Smullyan pursued an academic career in studying so-called formal systems. These are logical playgrounds consisting of two elements: a set of given truths called axioms (such as 'o represents nothing', 'all positive numbers are multiples of 1'), and a set of rules from which new results can be deduced (such as '1 plus 1 equals 2'). The basic rules of arithmetic form the best-known formal system, but there is no theoretical reason why we could not start from scratch and devise a brand new playground with different givens and rules.

$$1 + 1 = \ldots$$

WE'LL TELL YOU LATER

Between 1910 and 1913, Alfred North Whitehead and Bertrand Russell published a landmark work on formal systems, one of the most important books of the twentieth century. Sad to say, it is almost unreadable. Full of complicated mathematical symbols, the three-volume *Principia Mathematica* attempted to set down the known mathematical world as a logical argument. It took Whitehead and Russell 379 pages before they could state a vital conclusion: 'From this proposition it will follow, when arithmetical addition has been defined, that $1 + 1 = 2$.' In fact, it wasn't until addition was defined on page 86 of the second volume that we could all rest easy in our beds knowing that 1 plus 1 really did equal 2. This landmark result was annotated by the sly comment: 'The above proposition is occasionally useful.'

With our basic arithmetical world 'proved' by Whitehead and Russell, you would imagine that mathematicians were happy. Not a bit of it. What bothered the academics most, sometimes to the point of madness, were the propositions that could not be proved or refuted. Take the Goldbach Conjecture, which has been maddening the best brains since 1742. It simply states that 'Every even whole number greater than 2 (i.e. 4, 6, 8, 10, …) can be written as the sum of two prime numbers'. The first few terms are easy to prove: $4 = 2 + 2$, $6 = 3 + 3$, $8 = 3 + 5$ and $10 = 3 + 7$ or $5 + 5$. With computing power constantly increasing, mathematicians have been able to establish that the conjecture is true for higher and higher numbers. By April 2007 they had checked all numbers up to 18 digits in length without finding a counterexample. But this doesn't necessarily mean that, just around the corner, the very next number won't fail the conjecture's test. Without a conclusive proof that covers all the even numbers to infinity, there's always a chance – however slim – that a counterexample might be found.

In 1931, Kurt Gödel proved two 'Incompleteness Theorems' that seriously upset the mathematical apple cart. He stated that it doesn't matter which axioms or rules of deduction you begin with, as long as they are non-trivial then your mathematical world will always contain propositions such as the Goldbach Conjecture which cannot be proved, even though exhaustive trial and error suggests that they are almost certainly true. A consequence of this is that the system described in *Principia Mathematica* has inherent inconsistencies, and so will any other mathematical world you care to invent. In his *History of Mathematics*, Carl Boyer sagely notes the wider-reaching consequences of incompleteness: 'It appears to foredoom hope of mathematical certitude through use of the obvious methods. Perhaps doomed also, as a result, is the ideal of science – to devise a set of axioms from which all phenomena of the external world can be deduced.'

Gödel was an eccentric character who was convinced that his enemies were trying to kill him with poison gas or by tampering with his food. As a result, he'd keep the windows open in winter and refuse to eat any food except what was cooked by his wife. Unfortunately his wife was several years older than him, and in 1978, after she had become unable to look after herself, Gödel died of malnutrition. Although he may not be as famous as the friend who coached him through his American citizenship exam – one Mr Albert Einstein – his name lives on in the logical laws that bear his name. The world of mathematics can never be perfect, but at least thanks to Gödel we can stop worrying about it.

LIES, DAMNED LIES

Smullyan was fascinated by Gödel's Theorems, and in 1957 published a paper about them in the *Journal of Symbolic Logic* which set out a contemporary understanding of their ramifications. Put simply, Gödel's Theorems are the mathematical equivalent of someone coming up to you in the street and saying, 'I am lying'. If that person were lying, then they are telling the truth and therefore can't be lying. If they are telling the truth, then 'I am lying' isn't correct and a contradiction is reached. This paradox was first discussed by the Greek philosopher Eubulides of Miletus in AD 330, and the problem was still causing headaches – and worse – sixty years later. The Alexandrian poet Philetas of Cos worried about the Liar Paradox so much that he died of insomnia. His epitaph reads 'Philetas of Cos am I, 'Twas The Liar who made me die, And the bad nights caused thereby.' Gödel's Theorems use a variation of the Liar Paradox by stating that 'Gödel's Theorems cannot be proved to be true' and so reach a similar contradiction.

Noticing this parallel between high-end mathematics and everyday situations, Smullyan smuggled Gödel's Theorems and other logical concepts into his series of puzzle books, which had titles such as *This Book Needs No Title*, *The Lady or the Tiger?*, *To Mock a Mockingbird* and Forever Undecided. To help ease the reader into his logical world, he cleverly borrows themes from stories such as *Dracula*, *Alice in Wonderland* and *Scheherazade* so that the characters may be familiar even if the material is not.

The secret to cracking puzzles of truth-tellers and liars is to attack on several fronts. There could be enough information for you to reach a logical conclusion in the usual detective fashion. You may be able to work through the various possibilities and prove that there is only one case that does not lead to a contradiction. But what makes the very best puzzles is often an extra nugget of information that you have to deduce for yourself.

One of the most popular problems in this field crops up so regularly in management seminars, chain letters, puzzle books and pub conversation that it's worth looking at in detail. There is a forked pathway, one path leading to freedom and the other to certain death. In front of each path is a guardian, who will respond to questions, but only those that have a yes/no answer. One guardian always tells the truth and the other always tells lies, but you do not know which is which. The challenge is this: to find out which path leads to freedom by asking one guardian just one question. Most questions that might first occur to you to ask, such as 'Is the path behind you safe?' or 'Are you telling the truth?', would lead either to two 'Yes' or two 'No' answers from the guardians, leaving you none the wiser.

The answer lies in noticing that although you don't know who is the liar, the guardians do. Therefore it's possible to construct a question which uses their knowledge to identify who is telling lies and therefore which path is safe. A suitable question would be: 'If I asked the other guardian to point to the path that leads to freedom, would he point to the left path?' Because the question involves both guardians, it doesn't matter which guardian we ask – the effect of the liar guardian will be included somewhere along the line. In response to the above question, either guardian would say 'No' if the left path is safe and 'Yes' if the right path is safe, and so we can happily avoid certain death.

Truth-teller and liar puzzles first became popular in the 1930s, but received a technological boost in the 1950s and 1960s thanks ultimately to the benefits of the miniaturized logic devices made possible by the advent of transistors, which in turn made possible the modern electronic computer. Computer science became an acceptable academic subject to be taught in universities, and as a result students and teachers set logic puzzles to test each other's wits. Some logic puzzles have had recent revivals thanks to distribution on the Internet, newsgroups, websites and in email circulars. During the 1990s, a river-crossing puzzle involving members of the Irish rock band U2 became all the rage, possibly because it was said to be an interview question posed to job applicants hoping to join Microsoft. Despite this contemporary context, this kind of puzzle dates back to the early ninth century, and the now infamous Fox, Geese and Corn puzzle is depicted in medieval drawings.

A PROBLEM IN BLACK AND WHITE

The exact origins of another regularly circulated logic problem, usually known as Who Owns the Zebra? (page 302), are unclear – it's often claimed that Albert Einstein wrote it as a boy, but with no known version earlier than 1962, this seems highly unlikely. The format is very similar to most logic problems found in today's magazines. A number of statements are given as fact, and the reader must process them and fill out a results table. The correspondences are unique and exclusive – so, for example, if we are told that 'The Englishman lives in the red house' then we can assume that the Englishman doesn't live in any of the other houses, and also that the red house does not provide a home for any of the other people mentioned in the puzzle.

The solution to this puzzle is on page 305. Although it is possible to solve it by logical deduction alone, the process is so complicated that few solvers would find it much fun. During the 1970s and 1980s, magazines dedicated to logic and mathematical puzzles were launched, and as part of that development someone had a bright idea. What if a grid were printed alongside the puzzle that gave a complete set of correspondences between all the variables? For example, if 'Coffee is drunk in the green house' then we can make a positive connection for 'Coffee' and 'Green house' and put a

WHO OWNS THE ZEBRA?

There are five painted houses in a row.

The Englishman lives in the red house.

The Spaniard owns the dog.

Coffee is drunk in the green house.

The Ukrainian drinks tea.

The green house is immediately to your right of the ivory house.

The Old Gold smoker owns snails.

Kools are smoked in the yellow house.

Milk is drunk in the middle house.

The Norwegian lives in the leftmost house.

The man who smokes Chesterfields lives in a house next to the man with the fox.

Kools are smoked in a house next to the house where the horse is kept.

The Lucky Strike smoker drinks orange juice.

The Japanese smokes Parliaments.

The Norwegian lives next to the blue house.

Now, who drinks water? Who owns the zebra?

HOUSE	PAINT	NATIONALITY	DRINK	SMOKE	PET
1					
2					
3					
4					
5					

tick in the box that connects them. Similarly, 'The man who smokes Chesterfields lives in a house next to the man with the fox' allows us to deduce that there is no connection between 'Chesterfields' and 'Fox' and we can put a cross in that box.

SPEED DATING

So, how do you use these grids? In this simpler example, the grid provides all the boxes needed to make connections between three different attributes – the men, their dates and the location they went to:

	DATE			LOCATION		
	Susan	Tina	Ursula	Shopping	Film	Restaurant
Alfred						
Bernie						
Charles						
Shopping						
Film						
Restaurant						

Here are the clues to accompany the grid:

Tina went to see a film, but not with Charles.
Bernie didn't date Susan, and neither did he go to the movies.
Charles never goes to restaurants with a date.
Which man went shopping with his date?

If we put these clues into the grid, it now looks like this:

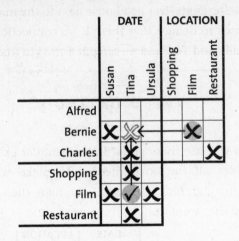

Because Tina went to see a film, we know that Tina didn't go anywhere else, and neither did any of the other dates see a film. (Each time we obtain a tick, we can cross off the other possibilities in the same row and column within that 3 × 3 box.) From here, we can now deduce more information. We have a tick for 'Tina' and 'Film', but we have a cross for 'Bernie' and 'Film'. We can thus deduce that Bernie did not date Tina – if he had, he must have gone to see a film, which we know is not true. Diagrammatically, we can state that where an empty intersection lies between a tick and a cross, the intersection must contain a cross. This newly deduced cross allows us to complete the top-left section of the diagram:

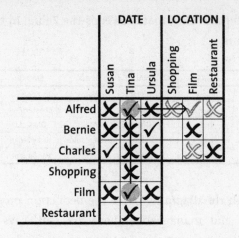

	DATE			LOCATION		
	Susan	Tina	Ursula	Shopping	Film	Restaurant
Alfred	✗	✓	✗	✗	✓	✗
Bernie	✗	✗	✓		✗	
Charles	✓	✗	✗	✗	✗	✗
Shopping		✗	
Film	✗	✓	✗
Restaurant		✗	

If Tina went to see a film, and Alfred dated Tina, then it follows that Alfred also went to see a film. This allows us to put one tick and three crosses into the right-hand side of the diagram. It swiftly follows that Bernie must have gone to the restaurant and Charles went shopping.

And so the process is complete. The techniques are quite simple when you understand how the diagram helps you: examine the empty squares that lie at intersections; move known information (positive or negative) around the diagram; and finally remember that – in this example – each box of 3 × 3 squares must have exactly one tick in each row and each column.

SO, ABOUT THAT ZEBRA ...

It's possible to draw up a similar table to solve the Zebra problem, but you'll need a 25 × 25 diagram to solve it. If you do attempt it, you'll find the solution to be that the Norwegian drinks water and the Japanese keeps the Zebra. In table form, the answer is:

HOUSE	PAINT	NATIONALITY	DRINK	SMOKE	PET
1	Yellow	Norwegian	Water	Kools	Fox
2	Blue	Ukranian	Tea	Chesterfield	Horse
3	Red	Englishman	Milk	Old Gold	Snails
4	Ivory	Spaniard	Orange Juice	Lucky Strike	Dog
5	Green	Japanese	Coffee	Parliament	Zebra

Although the diagrams make the deduction process much more fun and manageable, there are still ways in which the compilers can get you to think much harder about the situation. For example, one clue might say 'Ernie took his date out later in the working week than Bert'. Although this does give you some information (Ernie couldn't have been on a date on Monday; likewise for Bert on Friday) you'll certainly have to revisit the clue later when you have more definite information about Bert or Ernie's amorous activities. Harder puzzles involve additional diagrams – such as table plans and timetables – to turn what could have been a simple box-ticking exercise into a fully fledged mental workout.

Logic puzzles may not be as widely known as crosswords and sudoku, but there is a lot to commend them. They don't require you to have had an exemplary education. Young and old can understand them equally. And once the rules are understood, anyone in the world can attempt them on a level playing field. For these reasons, it is the purest form of puzzling you can do.

The Puzzles

———

LOGIC WARM-UPS

The varied teasers that follow should get the logical parts of your brain in gear for what lies ahead. Beware of the occasional puzzle that has a lateral – but entirely fair and logical – twist to it.

1. While sitting in the barber's chair having my hair cut, I noticed that the word BARBERS, which was painted on the shop window behind me, appeared the right way round in the mirror. How did it appear to people outside the shop?

2. Six letters have all been delivered to the wrong household. What is the maximum number of swaps it will take before each household has the letter that was originally addressed to them?

3. What letter combination completes this sequence?

HC, OP, TP, TOAK, S, F, FH, FOAK, SF, ??

4. A light bulb is connected to a circuit containing three or four switches (as appropriate). For each of these four cases, find the simplest way of expressing the required switch combinations so that the bulb will be lit.

(a) The bulb is off if switches A and B are on; *or* switches B and C are on; *or* switch B is off.

(b) The bulb is off if at least switch B is on; *or* A is in the same state as C; *or* exactly one switch is on.

(c) The bulb is off if switches A and B are on; *or* switches A, B and C are off; *or* C and (A or B) is on.

(d) The bulb is off if fewer than two switches are on; *or* (B and D) are on; *or* A is in the opposite state to D; *or* (A and D) are on but B is off.

5. Six spies each think of a codename for themselves. Each spy needs to know all six codenames. How many coded messages do they need to exchange to achieve this? When two spies exchange messages, they include all the codenames that they know.

6. Midway through a transatlantic airmail flight, one bag of mail fell out of the back of the plane. At the very same time, one of the rubber landing wheels fell off the plane, falling vertically. Would the mail bag or the landing wheel hit the ground first?

7. Jason works in a printing shop that makes calendars. He's fed up with the typesetting alterations required for the days in each month. One day he notices that there are only a certain number of different layouts that he'll ever need for the standard Gregorian calendar. How many are there?

8. While in a sprint you overtake the runner in second place just before crossing the finishing line. What was your final race position?

9. Given that this series begins at zero, find the hidden logic and explain why the series can't be continued:

0, 1, 8, 10, 19, 90.

10. Answer all four questions correctly:

(1) The first question with 'A' as the correct answer is:
(A) 2, (B) 3, (C) 4

(2) Which answer appears the most?
(A) C, (B) B, (C) A

(3) The answer to question 1 is:
(A) B, (B) A, (C) C

(4) Which answer appears the least?
(A) A, (B) C, (C) B

11. In the '100 game', two players take turns to subtract any number between 1 and 7 inclusive from a running score which starts at 100. The winner is the player who brings the score to zero. If you were playing this game, would you go first or second, and in either case what number would you choose to subtract first?

12. From a pack of 52 playing cards, what is the maximum number of cards you could have without containing a combination of five cards that would make up a full house? (In poker, a full house consists of a pair and a three of a kind.)

13. I bet you a beer that if you buy me two beers I'll buy you three beers in return. Do you want to take the bet?

14. In some old tape-driven answering machines, the manufacturers saved money by leaving out the rewind mechanism for the tape that contained your outgoing message. How was that possible, given that this message was played over and over again to callers without any rewinding?

15. There is a duck standing in every corner of a certain room. Each duck is looking at a different duck somewhere in the room. How many ducks can say they are looking at another duck?

16. Which digit completes the final number in this ongoing series?

24, 81, 63, 26, 41, 28, 25, 65, 1_

17. A golfer was three shots over par at the end of the first day's play of a championship. His score on the second day was ten shots better than on the first day. What was his score at the end of day two?

18. There are three buttons, A, B and C, on a door entry keypad. To open the door, each button needs to be pressed exactly once. If A is pressed first, then B is second. If A is second, then B is pressed third. If B is not pressed first, then C is second. What is the correct order to gain entry?

19. Which letter comes next in this series? The answer is neither I nor X.

I, X, X, X, I, X, I, I, I, I, I, I, I, I, I, _

20. Robyn sees her grandfather's son's wife's sister's daughter's only cousin in the bathroom each morning. Who is it, and what can you deduce about them?

21. Complete this analogy:

Q is to B

as U is to N

as P is to D

as M is to _

22. Warning: this is difficult! You are at a party with nine other people. When you leave, everyone writes down how many people they've met at the party. The answers you receive say '1', '2', '3', etc. up to '9'. In other words, everyone else has met a different number of people. How many people have you actually met at the party?

IQ ASSAULT COURSE

This section contains some of the more interesting examples you might find in an IQ test or a general aptitude exam. All kinds of principles are involved here – mirrors, numbers, directions, electronics, sequences, time ... the list goes on. Many are easy, some are rather trickier – it's up to you to work out what's what.

1. Which number is unreadable?

461375808

77345663

37047734

378163771

5376616

45188075

77183045

2. Which digit should complete this number?

−17436 ?

3. Princess Irena was preparing for a royal garden party. How much more coffee will she be able to serve from pot B than from pot A?

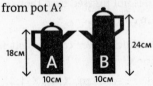

4. This is a tricky one: move one 1 and one 0 to make this statement valid:

10110010=9.5

5. Following the arrows at all times, how many different routes run from A to B?

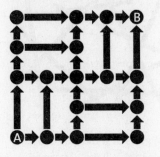

6. Which box would logically contain a 7 to complete the series?

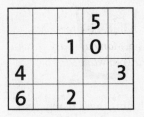

7. How many 3 × 1 planks (like the example shown) can you cut from the larger sheet? The order of the colours on the planks doesn't matter.

8. Which arrow is the odd one out?

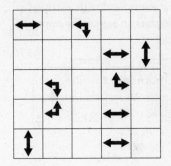

9. Given that the larger weight is heavier than the smaller one, which two pendulums will swing at roughly the same rate?

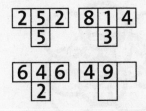

10. Supply the two missing digits:

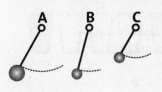

11. Which letter in this line-up is the odd one out and why?

HEINZSOX

12. Which of these playing cards must you turn over to be certain that every card with a striped back has an ace on the opposite side?

13. Assuming that no other equipment is available, how many glasses must be moved so that only the 2nd and 4th glasses are full of water?

14. Which two rings are different to the rest?

15. Which line is the odd one out? (*Hint*: pair them up.)

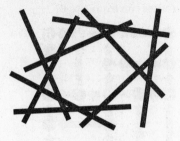

16. A glass of water has two ice cubes in it. What will happen to the level of the water in the glass when the ice cubes have completely melted?

17. Including the starting position, how many squares on this miniature chessboard can the knight visit (using his usual L-shaped move) without visiting a square twice?

18. Lions and Christians is a game played in the same way as Noughts and Crosses except that the aim is to lose – that is, force your opponent to complete a three-in-a-row. What move should 'noughts' make next?

19. Place three more X's in this grid so that each row, column and main diagonal contains exactly two X's.

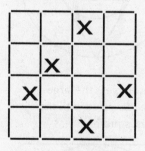

20. What would the next number be?

3, 8, 15, 22, 32, 42, 51, 58, 70, 79, 88, ___

21. If you completed the diagram continuing its logic, which spoke would have no label at all?

22. Which of these five diagrams is the odd one out?

23. Should the top square be shaded or black?

24. What should the missing clock say?

25. Which three hexagons need to be repainted (white, shaded or black) so that no adjacent spaces are the same colour?

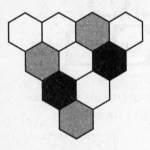

26. Complete the centre clock:

27. Complete the final clock:

28. How large is the area of the large circle compared with the small circle?

29. How large is the largest square compared with the smallest square?

30. What is the logic used here?

A=11   N=10
C=4   P=6
E=12   X=12
F=10   Y=9

31. Order the liquids in these layered cocktails from least to most dense:

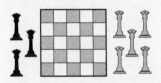

32. Place three black queens and five white queens on this chessboard so that no queen of any colour is attacking one of the opposite colour:

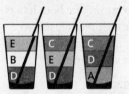

33. A crime has been committed. Given that precisely one of these three people is telling the truth, who is guilty?

34. Place six letters in this grid so that it is possible to trace out PLAIN, COAL, LINGO and CHAIN by travelling horizontally, vertically or diagonally to adjacent letters.

35. Place seven letters in this grid so that it is possible to trace out PARQUET, QUARTS, ORATE and STRAP by travelling horizontally, vertically or diagonally to adjacent letters.

36. Place seven letters in this grid so that it is possible to trace out ARMS, MARKETS and PASTURE by travelling horizontally, vertically or diagonally to adjacent letters.

37. Theoretically, what could be calculated by (Force × Speed of light squared) divided by (Voltage × Current × Acceleration)?

$$? = \frac{Fc^2}{VIa}$$

38. In which direction should the final hexagon's arrow point?

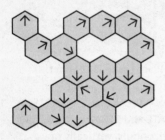

39. Here, each square tile is touching two other tiles. How many identical square tiles would you need in total if each one touched exactly four other tiles along an edge?

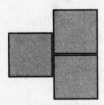

40. A clock has fallen on the floor, and there are no distinguishing marks to tell you which way up it should be. However, given that both hands are pointing precisely to two adjacent minute marks, can you work out what time it is?

See the introduction to this chapter for a tutorial in logic puzzles.

FILM FUN

The local multi-screen cinema is showing four different films this evening. Can you match each screen number with the time at which each film starts and the type of film being shown?

CLUES

1. The science fiction film starts either ten minutes before or ten minutes after the film on screen 1 (which doesn't start at 7.00 pm).

2. The film that starts at 7.30 pm is showing on either screen 2 or screen 4.

3. The film that begins at 7.10 pm is showing at a screen with a higher number than that on which the comedy will feature.

4. The film that starts at 7.20 pm is showing on a screen with a number either one higher or one lower than that showing the action movie (which starts ten minutes after the film showing on screen 3).

	START TIME				FILM TYPE			
	7.00pm	7.10pm	7.20pm	7.30pm	Action	Comedy	Musical	Sci-fi
Screen 1								
Screen 2								
Screen 3								
Screen 4								
Action								
Comedy								
Musical								
Sci-fi								

FLYING VISITS

The CEO of Multigrand is on a promotional tour and has a busy schedule this week. He'll be visiting five clients, each in a different European city. Can you match each city destination with the departure day and time of the flight on which he is booked to travel?

CLUES

1. The flight that leaves at eight o'clock departs more than one day later in the week than that to Madrid, which leaves at thirty minutes past the hour.
2. The flight to Rome leaves half an hour earlier in the day than Wednesday's scheduled flight.
3. Tuesday's flight (which isn't to Brussels) leaves exactly on the hour.
4. The flight that departs at seven o'clock leaves the day before the one to Vienna.
5. The Copenhagen flight leaves the day before the one that departs at half past six.

	DAY					TIME				
	Monday	Tuesday	Wednesday	Thursday	Friday	6.30am	7.00am	7.30am	8.00am	8.30am
Brussels										
Copenhagen										
Madrid										
Rome										
Vienna										
6.30am										
7.00am										
7.30am										
8.00am										
8.30am										

GAME GIRLS

Discover the sport of each of the men in this puzzle, as well as the name of his girlfriend and the number of times she has watched him play.

CLUES

1. Jed's girlfriend has watched two more games than Jilly, who isn't going out with the man who plays tennis.
2. Milly never watches tennis. Ned never plays football.
3. Tilly has seen fewer games than the woman who watches her boyfriend playing tennis.
4. Ted's girlfriend has seen him playing rugby more times than Lily has watched her boyfriend indulging in his favourite sport.
5. Jilly isn't Ned's girlfriend.

	SPORT				GIRLFRIEND				No. OF TIMES			
	Football	Hockey	Rugby	Tennis	Jilly	Lily	Milly	Tilly	6	7	9	10
Ed												
Jed												
Ned												
Ted												
6 times												
7 times												
9 times												
10 times												
Jilly												
Lily												
Milly												
Tilly												

COPY-CATS

For their end of term exam, four art students are each copying a painting by a different artist. Can you match each student to his or her home city, the number of years for which he or she has been studying, and the name of the painter being copied?

CLUES

1. Danny has been a student for either one or three years and comes from a city whose name starts with a later letter of the alphabet than the home city of the student copying a Martine painting.
2. Ricky is from Northton. The artist from Easton has been a student for longer than Louisa.
3. The artist from Weston has been a student for either two or four years. Eliza hasn't been a student for exactly three years.
4. The man who is copying a painting by Deloire has been studying for longer than the person from Southton.
5. The artist who is copying a painting by Rouleau hasn't been a student for the shortest period of time.

	CITY				YEARS				PAINTER			
	Easton	Northton	Southton	Weston	1	2	3	4	Deloire	Martine	Rouleau	Van Loda
Danny												
Eliza												
Louisa												
Ricky												
Deloire												
Martine												
Rouleau												
Van Loda												
1 year												
2 years												
3 years												
4 years												

PRESENT TIME

Dawn has four relatives who all have birthdays next month. She has bought a different present for each, wrapping the gifts in papers with different patterns. Can you unwrap the mystery of who celebrates her birthday on each of the listed days, which present she will receive and in which patterned wrapping paper?

CLUES

1. The gift wrapped in bells can be opened on the 17th.
2. The silk scarf was chosen as a gift for the woman whose birthday falls either four days before or four days after that of Dawn's sister.
3. The gloves are either for Dawn's mother (whose birthday isn't on the 21st) or for the woman (not Dawn's mother) who has a birthday on the 12th.
4. The perfume was bought for someone whose birthday falls either four days before or four days after that of the woman whose gift is wrapped in plain paper.
5. Dawn's grandmother celebrates a birthday either five days before or five days after that of the woman who will receive the CD.
6. The present wrapped in star-patterned paper (not for her niece) isn't for the woman whose birthday is on the 12th of the month.

	RELATIVE				PRESENT				WRAPPING			
	Grandma	Mother	Niece	Sister	CD	Gloves	Perfume	Scarf	Bells	Floral	Plain	Stars
8th												
12th												
17th												
21st												
Bells												
Floral												
Plain												
Stars												
CD												
Gloves												
Perfume												
Scarf												

ON THE BOTTLE

Four friends recently attended a wine-tasting session at a local vintners. At the end of the evening, each friend purchased a number of bottles of his or her favourite. How many bottles did each purchase, from which country is the wine, and is it red or white?

CLUES

1. The Australian red wine was chosen either by Eric or by his friend, who bought eight bottles.

2. Bella bought either half as many or twice as many bottles as the person who chose the English wine, which was of the same colour as the wine chosen by the person who bought ten bottles.

3. The wine from Chile was chosen by the man who purchased fewer bottles than Tina.

4. Roger bought either two bottles more or two bottles fewer than the person who purchased the French wine.

5. One of Eric's friends bought six bottles of white wine.

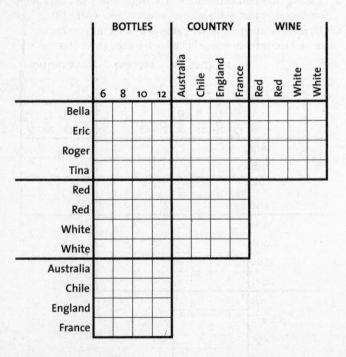

UP IN FLAMES

Four couples were invited to a barbecue and each brought along a different type of food. Can you match each couple with the food they brought and the number of their house?

CLUES

1. Laura and her husband either live at No. 12 or are the couple who brought prawns to the barbecue.

2. Boris and his wife live in a house numbered either three higher or three lower than that belonging to the couple who brought steak.

3. Leo (whose wife is Jenny's sister) lives at either No. 9 or No. 11. George and his wife live in a house with a lower number than that which belongs to the couple who brought hamburgers.

4. James and his wife live in a house with a higher number than that of the couple who brought sausages (who are the only couple whose names start with the same letter of the alphabet).

	WIFE				FOOD				HOUSE No.			
	Bette	Delia	Jenny	Laura	Hamburgers	Prawns	Sausages	Steak	9	10	11	12
Boris												
George												
James												
Leo												
No. 9												
No. 10												
No. 11												
No. 12												
Hamburgers												
Prawns												
Sausages												
Steak												

AGES AND AGES

Five pairs of brothers and sisters all attend the same school. Your homework is to match each brother with his sister and then work out their respective ages.

CLUES

1. Pam is older than her brother.
2. Rob is one year younger than Dan.
3. Rob's sister is one year younger than Jan, whose brother is one year younger than the shortest boy, who isn't Ian.
4. Ann is one year younger than Sue, whose brother is one year younger than Guy, who isn't Ann's brother.
5. Fay is younger than Ann and someone (maybe Ann, maybe not) is older than Fay's brother.

		SISTER					BROTHER'S AGE					SISTER'S AGE				
		Ann	Fay	Jan	Pam	Sue	13	14	15	17	18	11	12	13	15	16
	Bob															
	Dan																
	Guy																
	Ian																
	Rob																
SISTER'S AGE	11																
	12																
	13																
	15																
	16																
BROTHER'S AGE	13																
	14																
	15																
	17																
	18																

BOOK REVIEW

Visiting her local library yesterday, Sally was delighted to find, on the new titles trolley, four books that she wanted to read. Can you match the author of each book with its title, theme and position on the trolley?

CLUES

1. The thriller is next to and between the work entitled *Somewhere* and the one written by Gail Wright.
2. The eagerly anticipated crime novel is to the left of, but not immediately next to, *High Life*.
3. *Somewhere* (which isn't book B) isn't immediately next to *High Life*.
4. *Full Time* is not the book pictured at D.
5. *Night Falls* (which isn't written by Gail Wright) is pictured further left than the book written by Emma Taylor.
6. Carla Scribe's latest work is pictured immediately next to and left of the biography.

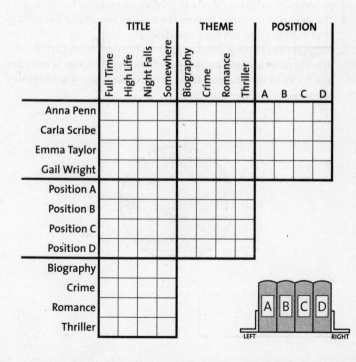

	TITLE				THEME				POSITION			
	Full Time	High Life	Night Falls	Somewhere	Biography	Crime	Romance	Thriller	A	B	C	D
Anna Penn												
Carla Scribe												
Emma Taylor												
Gail Wright												
Position A								
Position B								
Position C								
Position D								
Biography				
Crime				
Romance				
Thriller				

PANCAKE DAY

Mrs Shrove's four children are seated at the circular dining table pictured here and have just finished eating pancakes. Each child ate a different number of pancakes, from one to four, and had a different topping. From the clues and the picture can you match the position of each child in seats A to D with his or her name, the number of pancakes they ate and the topping?

CLUES

1. One of the boys ate four pancakes and is sitting one place in a clockwise direction from the child who ate only one pancake and immediately opposite the child who had lemon juice on his or her pancakes.

2. The girl who chose maple syrup is sitting one place in a clockwise direction from the child who had orange juice on his or her pancakes.

3. The child at B is either Melissa or a child who ate exactly two pancakes. The child at C had a type of syrup on his or her pancakes.

4. The child who ate only one pancake is either Jessica or a boy sitting next to Jessica (but not opposite Melissa).

5. Angus is either sitting directly opposite the person who ate one pancake more or one pancake fewer than him, or is sitting one place in a clockwise direction from the person who ate one pancake more or one pancake fewer than him.

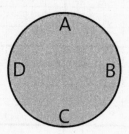

	NAME				PANCAKES				TOPPING			
	Angus	Connor	Jessica	Melissa	1	2	3	4	Golden syrup	Lemon juice	Maple syrup	Orange juice
Seat A												
Seat B												
Seat C												
Seat D												
Golden syrup												
Lemon juice												
Maple syrup												
Orange juice												
1 pancake												
2 pancakes												
3 pancakes												
4 pancakes												

SEAT	NAME	PANCAKES	TOPPING

At this point we up the stakes by taking away the main puzzle grid. Now you have to use your brain a little more to make the logical connections necessary to make progress. A couple of tips to get you started. First, if you're sure that you've extracted all the information you can from a clue, mark it as finished with. Then, for the clues that remain, keep revisiting them until you spot a link between two or three clues that enables you to make a new deduction.

IT FIGURES

Each of the thirty-six squares in the grid is to be filled with a single-digit number from 1 to 9 – each of those numbers being used four times. Use the clues to complete the square, bearing in mind that the same number must not appear in two adjacent (touching) squares either across or down. If the same number is used more than once in any row across or column down, it is stated in the relevant clue.

ACROSS

1. Two threes. Two sevens. No one.
2. Two threes. Seven is the highest number.
3. Two fives. Total thirty-three.
4. Two ones. Two twos. No eight.
5. Consecutive numbers placed in order.
6. Total thirty-three.

DOWN

1. Total twenty-one.
2. Total thirty-nine.
3. No five. No seven.
4. Consecutive numbers placed in order.
5. Two eights. No three.
6. Two ones.

RELATIVE CHANGES

Naughty Georgie has taken photos of five of his nearest and dearest relatives, then cut each into four pieces (head, body, legs and feet), reassembling them in such a way that each 'new' photo contains pieces of four old ones – thus providing some amusing combinations! How have they been reassembled?

HEAD	BODY	LEGS	FEET

CLUES

1. Georgie's uncle's head is in the same photo as his brother's legs.
2. His sister's legs (which don't end in his brother's feet) are attached to his uncle's body.
3. Georgie's aunt's feet (which don't adjoin his uncle's legs) are in the same picture as his brother's body.
4. Georgie's aunt's body is not in the same picture as his sister's feet.
5. Georgie has also cut up and used a picture of his mother – naughty boy!

FALL OUT

The first five horses and riders (one of whom was Kevin) to enter the arena at the annual gymkhana each took a fall during the first round, thus losing the opportunity of gaining the coveted Jumpers' Cup. What was the name of the unlucky rider of each horse, at what type of jump did each fall, and what was the order in which they competed?

HORSE	RIDER	JUMP	ORDER

CLUES

1. Barbara was thrown at the 5-bar gate, while the rider of Campari came off at the water jump.
2. David competed on Amity (perhaps he'll rename his horse Calamity!) immediately before the rider who was thrown at the 4-bar gate.
3. Richard, on Trotter, was fourth to enter the arena.
4. Stella entered the arena immediately before Maybelle's rider but later than the rider who was unseated at the hedge jump.
5. Nemesis may or may not be the horse that failed to jump the wall.

FIT FOR ANYTHING

On each weekday evening, one member of the family of five (which includes Isabel and Lenny) attends a different fitness group. Can you decide who attends which class, as well as the evening it is held and its location?

NAME	CLASSES	EVENINGS	LOCATION

CLUES

1. The classes at the community centre are later in the week than the aerobics classes. Neither of these takes place on a Wednesday evening.

2. Boxing classes are held on a Monday and ballet lessons are at the scout hut.

3. Brendan does not go to the community centre. The classes at the theatre take place on Tuesday evenings.

4. Sean goes to his class on Wednesday evenings.

5. Jane takes one of her two sons to jujitsu classes two evenings before Brendan takes their daughter to the church hall for her class.

6. The class at the sports centre (which may or may not be judo) is always oversubscribed.

ON THE CARDS

What is the face value and suit of each of the cards shown below? Together they total 81. All twelve cards are of different values. In the pack, the values of the cards are as per their numbers, with ace = 1, jack = 11, queen = 12 and king = 13. No card is horizontally or vertically next to another of the same colour (hearts and diamonds are red; spades and clubs are black), and there are four different suits in each horizontal row and three different suits in each vertical column.

CLUES

1. The ace is next to and to the left of the five, which is next to and below the king of spades.

2. The three of diamonds is next to and to the left of the eight, which is next to and below the queen.

3. Card F has a value three higher than that of card B, which is of the same suit as card G.

4. Card C has a value two higher than that of card K. Card L has a value one higher than that of card E.

5. The jack is of the same suit as the queen.

LEFT   RIGHT

ON LOCATION

In every circle in these two arrays is to be placed a different letter of the alphabet from A to K inclusive. Use the clues to determine their locations. Reference in the clues to 'due' means in any location along the same horizontal or vertical line.

On location 1

1. J is due west of K and due north of C.
2. G is due north of F and due east of J.
3. E is due north of A and due east of B.
4. I is due south of D and due west of A.
5. B is due north of G and due east of H.

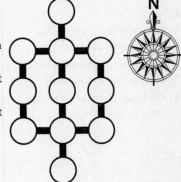

On location 2

1. F is due west of D, due north of J and due east of A.
2. H is due north of A and due west of C.
3. E is due north of I and due east of G.
4. G is due south of K and due east of B.

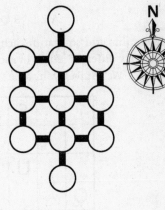

FIGURE IT OUT

Each square in this grid is to contain one of the letters from the word FIGURE such that in each row, column and long diagonal there are six different letters. Some have already been placed. Can you fill in those remaining?

There is only one correct solution to this puzzle – if you take a wrong path along the way, you won't be able to complete it!

CLUES

1. The letter in square 5 is the same as that in square 31.

2. The letter in square 6 is the same as that in square 19.

3. The letter in square 15 is the same as that in square 32.

1	2 E	3	4	5	6
7	8	9	10	11 R	12
13 I	14	15	16	17	18
19	20	21	22 G	23	24
25	26	27	28	29	30 F
31	32	33 U	34	35	36

ALL SQUARE

Complete this grid so that in each row, column and long diagonal there are six different letters in each square – i.e. each of the letters of SQUARE. We've given you some starters.

		S	A		
				S	
		U			
Q			R		
		E			

WHERE THE L?

Twelve L-shapes like the ones below have been inserted in each grid. Each L has one hole in it. There are three pieces of each of the four kinds shown below, and any piece is allowed to be rotated or flipped over before being put into the grids. No pieces of the same kind can touch, even at a corner. The pieces fit together so well that you cannot see the spaces between them, only the holes show. Can you tell where the L's are?

Where the L? 1

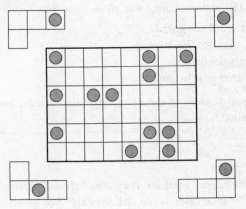

Where the L? 2

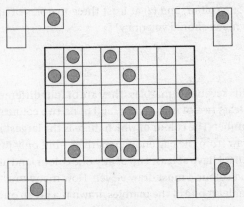

CALIBAN'S CONUNDRUMS

Hubert Phillips, otherwise known by the pseudonym 'Dogberry' or 'Caliban', was a prolific compiler of quizzes, crosswords, epigrams, poems, crime puzzles and mathematical problems – quite a remarkable range of output. Here are a handful of his best logic testers.

Caliban 1

Messrs. Fireman, Guard and Driver are (not necessarily respectively) the fireman, guard and driver of one of our fastest expresses. Who is what? When I tried to find out, I was given these four 'facts':

(1) Mr Driver is not the guard.
(2) Mr Fireman is not the driver.
(3) Mr Driver is the driver.
(4) Mr Fireman is not the guard.

It then transpired that, of the above four statements, only one is true. Who is what?

Caliban 2

A bag contains twenty marbles. They are of three different colours. There are eight blue ones, seven red ones and five green ones. You are invited to close your eyes and draw the maximum number of marbles consistent with your leaving in the bag (1) at least four marbles of any one colour, and (2) at least three marbles of any second colour. How many should you draw?

Caliban 3

A bag contains seventeen marbles. They are of four different colours: there are at least two of each colour; and of no two colours are there the same number. The colour of which there is the largest number is green. If I draw from the bag enough marbles – but only just enough – to ensure that I have at least two of any one colour, and at least one of any second colour, I must draw eleven. How many must I draw to ensure that at least one of the marbles drawn is a green one?

Caliban 4

You may recall that on Citrus Island three tribes – the Whites, the Oranges and the Lemons – have different standards of veracity. (They are otherwise indistinguishable.) Whites always tell the truth; Oranges always lie; Lemons, when asked a series of questions, tell the truth and lie alternately. A Lemon's first answer in a series may be either true or otherwise.

A visitor was somewhat confused recently when he was introduced to three natives named White, Orange and Lemon, who are – not necessarily respectively – a White, an Orange and a Lemon. There was also a fourth native, named Yellow. The visitor asked each of the first three natives (a) what his own tribe was, and (b) what was Mr Yellow's tribe. To these questions,

Mr White replied: 'I'm not a White. Mr Yellow is an Orange.'

Mr Orange replied: 'I'm not an Orange. Mr Yellow is a Lemon.'

Mr Lemon replied: 'I'm not a Lemon. Mr Yellow is a White.'

To which tribe does Mr Yellow actually belong?

Caliban 5

Messrs Spinnaker, Buoy, Luff, Gybe and Windward are yacht owners. Each has a daughter, and each has named his yacht after the daughter of one of the others.

Mr Spinnaker's yacht, the *Iris*, is named after Mr Buoy's daughter. Mr Buoy's own yacht is the *Daffodil*; Mr Windward's yacht is the *Jonquil*; Mr Gybe's, the *Anthea*. Daffodil is the daughter of the owner of the yacht which is named after Mr Luff's daughter. Mr Windward's daughter is named Lalage.

Who is Jonquil's father?

CARROLL'S SYMBOLIC LOGIC

Lewis Carroll, being a mathematician by trade, was a master at logical deduction. He devised the puzzles below as the ultimate in taking logical connections to their conclusion. Each set of clues can be combined in such a way that all the information can be used to produce a final deduction, which is the answer required. We have given the answer to the first puzzle as an example.

Example

(a) No acrobatic feats, that are not announced in the bills of a circus, are ever attempted there;

(b) No acrobatic feat is possible, if it involves turning a quadruple somersault;

(c) No impossible acrobatic feat is ever announced in a circus bill.

Answer

No acrobatic feat which involves turning a quadruple somersault is ever attempted in a circus.

---

1. (a) There are no pencils of mine in this box;
   (b) No sugar-plums of mine are cigars;
   (c) The whole of my property, that is not in this box, consists of cigars.

2. (a) No one takes in *The Times*, unless he is well-educated;
   (b) No hedge-hogs can read;
   (c) Those who cannot read are not well-educated.

3. (a) All members of the House of Commons have perfect self-command;
   (b) No M.P. who wears a coronet should ride in a donkey-race;
   (c) All members of the House of Lords wear coronets.

4. (a) Nobody who really appreciates Beethoven fails to keep silence while the *Moonlight Sonata* is being played;

(b) Guinea-pigs are hopelessly ignorant of music;

(c) No one who is hopelessly ignorant of music ever keeps silence while the *Moonlight Sonata* is being played.

5. (a) No birds, except ostriches, are 9 feet high;

(b) There are no birds in this aviary that belong to any one but me;

(c) No ostrich lives on mince-pies;

(d) I have no birds less than 9 feet high.

6. (a) A plum-pudding that is not really solid is mere porridge;

(b) Every plum-pudding served at my table has been boiled in a cloth;

(c) A plum-pudding that is mere porridge is indistinguishable from soup;

(d) No plum-puddings are really solid, except what are served at my table.

7. (a) No interesting poems are unpopular among people of real taste;

(b) No modern poetry is free from affectation;

(c) All your poems are on the subject of soap-bubbles;

(d) No affected poetry is popular among people of real taste;

(e) No ancient poem is on the subject of soap-bubbles.

8. (a) No shark ever doubts that it is well fitted out;

(b) A fish that cannot dance a minuet is contemptible;

(c) No fish is quite certain that it is well fitted out, unless it has three rows of teeth;

(d) All fishes, except sharks, are kind to children.

(e) No heavy fish can dance a minuet;

(f) A fish with three rows of teeth is not to be despised.

9. (a) All the human race, except my footmen, have a certain amount of common-sense;
(b) No one who lives on barley-sugar can be anything but a mere baby;
(c) None but a hop-scotch player knows what real happiness is;
(d) No mere baby has a grain of common sense;
(e) No engine-driver ever plays hop-scotch;
(f) No footman of mine is ignorant of what true happiness is.

10. (a) I call no day 'unlucky' when Robinson is civil to me;
(b) Wednesdays are always cloudy;
(c) When people take umbrellas, the day never turns out fine;
(d) The only days when Robinson is uncivil to me are Wednesdays;
(e) Everybody takes his umbrella with him when it is raining;
(f) My 'lucky' days always turn out fine.

11. (a) Animals are always mortally offended if I fail to notice them;
(b) The only animals that belong to me are in that field;
(c) No animal can guess a conundrum, unless it has been properly trained in a Board School;
(d) None of the animals in that field are badgers;
(e) When an animal is mortally offended, it always rushes about wildly and howls;
(f) I never notice any animal, unless it belongs to me;
(g) No animal that has been properly trained in a Board School ever rushes about wildly and howls.

12. (a) All the dated letters in this room are written on blue paper;
(b) None of them are in black ink, except those that are written in the third person;
(c) I have not filed any of them that I can read;
(d) None of them that are written on one sheet are undated;
(e) All of them that are not crossed are in black ink;
(f) All of them written by Brown begin with 'Dear Sir';
(g) All of them written on blue paper are filed;
(h) None of them written on more than one sheet are crossed;
(i) None of them that begin with 'Dear Sir' are written in the third person.

13. (a) The only animals in this house are cats;

(b) Every animal is suitable for a pet that loves to gaze at the moon;

(c) When I detest an animal, I avoid it;

(d) No animals are carnivorous, unless they prowl at night;

(e) No cat fails to kill mice;

(f) No animals ever take to me, except what are in this house;

(g) Kangaroos are not suitable for pets;

(h) None but carnivora kill mice;

(i) I detest animals that do not take to me;

(j) Animals that prowl at night always love to gaze at the moon.

CHAPTER 7

Thinking Sideways

Few book titles have entered the language as readily as Edward de Bono's *The Use of Lateral Thinking*. It's hard to imagine a time when the phrase 'lateral thinking' didn't exist, but it dates back no further than 1967, when de Bono's book was published. Born in Malta in 1933 and a Rhodes Scholar at Oxford University, de Bono became fascinated and frustrated by situations in which the brain fails to make full use of its capabilities. Showing how he himself is not immune to mental blocks despite his psychological training, he describes how he was trying to stop a loud alarm clock early one morning. Nothing he did would halt the infernal noise – pressing the buttons, smothering it, trying to dismantle it. Only after many fruitless minutes of effort did he find … the second alarm clock. De Bono had set a second clock in case he slept through the first one, and it was this one that was making all the noise.

IDEAS GENERATION

To actually define the phrase 'lateral thinking' is a tricky task, and one that de Bono himself sidesteps somewhat by defining

Edward de Bono

it in various ways. One of his snappiest is 'Vertical thinking is selective. Lateral thinking is generative.' In other words, traditional or vertical thinking involves selecting the best method from the range of obvious or previously experienced solutions available. But the lateral thinker begins by generating new possibilities, expanding the scope sideways before taking that first crucial step to completion. Puzzle author Paul Sloane describes it as 'different from conventional, logical, incremental, "vertical" thinking. It involves coming at the problem from new directions, challenging existing norms and assumptions and using imagination.'

Nearly every major invention in history has required the

use of lateral thinking – even if the term itself wasn't around. The Romans were limited in their use of mathematics because their clumsy MDCLXVI system was difficult to calculate with: how, for example, do you go about multiplying CLXII by CDLXXIV? It wasn't until the late fifth century AD that Indian mathematicians discovered the benefits of a decimal numbering system. Similarly, the development of an alphabet – rather than the pictogram-based languages of the Egyptians and Chinese – has enabled many cultures to adapt easily to more modern inventions such as typewriters and the Internet. The system of money took many centuries to develop from inscribed tokens and objects such as shark's teeth into the metal, plastic and paper trinkets we currently use. And how long will it be before they disappear altogether, to be replaced by memory chips and electronic signals? With the use of Internet banking, SWIFT transfers and pay-as-you-go mobile phone cards, perhaps we are not far away from such a revolution.

Two of the most successful British inventors used lateral thinking to come up with their greatest creations. Trevor Baylis realized that the main way to stop the spread of AIDS through Africa wasn't medicine but education. He developed a wind-up radio that could be used in communities that didn't have access to batteries or electricity. This was accomplished despite many experts telling him that his design of a highly efficient spring that released its stored energy slowly would not work, and yet it has now been incorporated into several other products. In the late 1970s, James Dyson introduced a new type of vacuum cleaner that used the effect of a cyclone to generate more suction and separate the air from the dirt more efficiently. His idea was sparked by a visit to a factory handling cereals, where a similar suction device was installed in the roof to purify the air (small particles of organic matter, when mixed with the right combination of oxygen, can be explosive). This one insight, and a lot of hard work, is estimated to have made him a billionaire.

The problem with lateral thinking in the world of puzzles is that it opens up a minefield of possible solutions. In many books on the subject, the most popular example of a lateral thinking puzzle invites the reader to connect nine dots using four straight lines without taking pen or pencil off the paper:

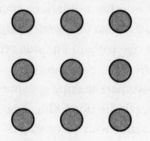

The usual solution given is this:

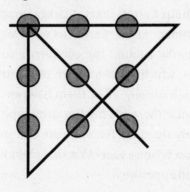

But few books seem to mention this other, highly plausible solution, which uses just three lines:

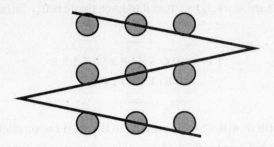

What the question meant to ask is how to connect the lines through the *centre* of each of the nine dots. Furthermore, one would also have to 'design out' other possibilities involving folding the paper or other unforeseen tricks. How, therefore, is the relationship between the puzzle designer and the puzzle doer meant to survive without one side accusing the other of cheating?

One of the newcomers making a name for himself in the world of lateral puzzles is Lloyd King, who found that he had 'a fondness for puzzles with surprising or "obvious" answers that made you want to kick yourself if you didn't solve them. I read every puzzle book I could find and especially enjoyed those by Philip Carter, Barry Clarke, Douglas St P. Barnard, Martin Gardner, Lewis Carroll, Chris Maslanka and Sam Loyd. Eventually I found the confidence to start writing my own puzzles, which are a mixture of creativity, humour and imagination. Naturally, all of them have an "Aha!" or amusing answer because those are my favourite type of puzzle and, for me, definitely the most fun to create and solve. A lot of them are visual too because I feel that this makes them much more engaging and appealing.'

Sloane expands on those 'Aha!' moments: 'You can always come up with alternative explanations for the situation in a lateral thinking puzzle. Some people find this frustrating. A good composer of these puzzles will construct them in such a way that the answer given is the most satisfying. There should be an "Aha!" experience as the puzzle is finally solved and all the pieces fall into place. Generally I don't like puzzles that involve a crummy play on words or where an animal is given a human name or where the answer is contrived or totally implausible.'

So perhaps we can regard a lateral puzzle as one whose answer is unusual and yet, when we find out what it is, we accept it as genuine but are annoyed that we didn't see it for ourselves. Such solutions are the stuff of murder mystery stories, such as the works of Agatha Christie, whose tales are renowned for their misleading set-ups and scrupulously fair solutions. She was one of the first authors to use the unreliable narrator, a storyteller who deliberately deceives the reader by the selective use of truth to give a false perception of the real events.

It's not clear from where the art form of the lateral thinking puzzle emerged. Riddles, murder mysteries and strange-but-true tales have been doing the rounds for decades, usually spread by word of mouth. One of the earliest authors to recognize a gap in the market was Paul Sloane: 'I had always enjoyed solving this type of puzzle and I had composed a few. There were some very celebrated such puzzles circulating when I was a student but I could not find a book of them so I put together a collection of all the best ones I knew. It turned into *Lateral Thinking Puzzlers*, which sold over 300,000 copies and has been translated into many languages.'

In Sloane's book and similar titles, each puzzle presents a description of an unusual scenario, and the challenge is to work out in what plausible (though possibly unlikely) circumstances that event could have come about. While some puzzles are straightforward, others are the result of a complex, almost comedic series of actions and reactions. How, then, is the solver to have any chance of deducing the answer? 'They are not designed to be read by an individual,' notes Paul Sloane. 'They work best as team games where one person knows the answer and acts as quizmaster. Other people ask questions, and the only answers allowed are "Yes", "No" or "Irrelevant". People have to check their assumptions, come at the problem from different angles, put together various clues and eventually figure out what is going on. They are ideal for children on long car journeys or at the end of lessons.'

THE EVOLUTION OF THINKING

One motive that has united writers such as de Bono, Sloane and King is they all want to promote the practical application of lateral thinking to improve our everyday lives, and in particular training or encouraging children to develop thinking skills at an early age. Lloyd King says: 'I would really like to see lateral thinking classes being introduced into the educational system as a fun way of encouraging independent thinking skills, imagination and creativity. Lateral thinking puzzles are ideal for this purpose because, by appearing impossible, implausible, bizarre or paradoxical in some way, they immediately arouse our curiosity and childlike sense of playfulness, which is the key to unlocking our creativity.'

Edward de Bono has managed to convince many countries

to integrate thinking programmes into their education policy. In Venezuela, his organization trained 106,000 teachers and persuaded the politicians to make it compulsory for schoolchildren to take part in two hours of thinking skills classes each week. Would such a move be advisable in the pressurized timetables of major Western economies? 'I think this is a great idea,' thinks Paul Sloane. 'Einstein said, "Imagination is more important than knowledge." But most of what we do in schools is pushing knowledge at children. At school for most questions there is one right answer. Children need training in imagination, ambiguity, seeing things from different viewpoints, exploring unorthodox ideas, and so on. Helping them with creative problem solving is a key part of education. And the children love doing it!'

Lateral thinking is not confined to the human species. In April 1985, the *Sunday Times* reported that a flock of sheep near the small Welsh town of Blaenau Ffestiniog had come up with a nifty idea of their own. Fancying a nibble of the lush green grass on the other side of a cattle grid, they had managed to work out that by tucking in their legs they could roll over the bars of the grid without much difficulty. So anxious were their human keepers that they were isolated from other flocks in case the practice caught on, rendering every grid entirely useless. If this sounds ludicrous, consider the humble blue tit. In Southampton in 1921, it was noticed that one of these birds was able to peck off the foil caps on milk bottles, and within the next twenty years the practice had spread countrywide. Animals are quicker than you might think at adapting to modern surroundings. In Japan, crows perch on top of traffic lights and wait for them to go red (or, more likely, wait for the traffic to stop). They then swoop down and place a nut under the front tyre of a car, then return to their perch. Once the shell is crushed by the car's weight, the crow can later retrieve the kernel.

THINKING ALLOWED

How, then, can you improve your lateral thinking skills to solve these mysteries and other problems you might face in everyday life? Here are some commonly suggested techniques:

- ***Challenge your assumptions*** Many lateral thinking puzzles exploit lazy traits of human behaviour that have become ingrained in our psyche thanks to repetition or cultural bias. For example, a popular puzzle features a doctor who, we later realize, is actually a woman, whereas many people would first visualize a man when they hear the word 'doctor'.

- ***Try random stimulation*** An excellent technique for coming up with new ideas involves opening up a dictionary at a random page. Suppose the chosen word is 'octopus' – how can an eight-legged sea creature help you solve problems? Perhaps you could consider how its tentacles can work together on one difficult problem, or do several different simple jobs at once. It can still function if it loses a leg, highlighting the benefits of redundancy. This sort of game is frequently used by advertising agencies, and may well explain why we end up with TV adverts for Irish stout featuring white horses or singing fish.

- ***Consider the opposite*** If you're trying to do a job well, why not consider what would happen if you were to deliberately make a complete hash of it? It's a funny and entertaining exercise that's particularly fun to do in groups. It breaks the ice and may eventually provide ideas for how to accomplish the original aim.

- **Be curious** Try to be more observant and question why things are the way they are. If you look hard enough, there are good reasons behind even the most innocuous of situations. In most of the larger London Underground train stations, for example, there are three escalators connecting the platforms to the booking hall, and almost always it was noticed that the set-up used was two escalators going up, and one escalator going down. Why is this? If you think about it for a moment, the answer is not too hard to find. When a train arrives, hundreds of people get off at the same time, and there is a sudden rush of people who need to go up from the platform to ground level. However, passengers arrive at the station to catch a train in a much more regular flow, so there is a more or less steady stream of people going down to the platforms. See if you can spot similar situations yourself today.

- **Use abstraction** Not everything you consider has to have a practical method or outcome. When he was sixteen, Albert Einstein dreamt of what it would be like to ride through space like a beam of light. This made him think of the possibility that the speed of the light would be constant regardless of how fast one was travelling.

The puzzles that follow have been carefully graded to ease you into de Bono's new way of thinking. So if in the past you have dismissed lateral puzzles as 'trick questions', have another go with a fresh start. You never know – you might find that you enjoy thinking sideways.

The Puzzles

CATCH QUESTION COMPILATION

Wakey, wakey! We're going to jolt your brain into action with this quickfire quiz of catch questions. Don't take it too seriously, and feel free to inflict it on your friends and family – they're guaranteed to trip up on something …

1. Who wrote Handel's *Messiah*?

2. In which direction does the Danube river flow?

3. Which languages are spoken on the uninhabited islands of the Philippines?

4. What day comes before Shrove Tuesday?

5. How far can a dog run into a forest?

6. If two's a company and three's a crowd, what are four and five?

7. Why do some people press lift buttons with their fingers and others with their thumbs?

8. How many animals of each species did Moses take onto the Ark?

9. What can be found right in the middle of Melbourne?

10. Which side of a Siamese cat has the most hair?

11. Name three perfectly edible things that you can never have for breakfast.

12. Who is featured in Vincent van Gogh's famous painting *Self-Portrait with Bandaged Ear*?

13. What shape is a complete rainbow?

14. Which ancient invention allowed people to see through solid walls?

15. Which ancient invention was the first to break the sound barrier?

16. Is there a good way to get down from a camel?

17. In which country is it legal to marry your widow's sister?

18. Removing an appendix is an appendectomy. Removing tonsils is called a tonsillectomy. Removing a growth from the head is called ... what?

19. Name a living thing that has one foot.

20. In Iraq, an Italian man cannot take a photograph of someone with a turban. Why not?

21. How many successful parachute jumps does a trainee parachutist in Britain's SAS need to make before he graduates?

22. Where do the biggest carrots grow?

23. Why is much more toilet paper purchased in England than in Scotland?

24. If a grandfather clock strikes twenty-three, what time is it?

25. Some children rake up three piles of leaves from the front of the house, and six piles from the back of the house. When they put all the piles together, how many piles of leaves will they have?

26. Would you rather a cheetah attack you or a leopard?

27. What can you hold in your right hand, but not in your left?

28. If a daddy bull drinks 25 litres of water a day, and a baby bull drinks 3 gallons of water per hour, how much would a mummy bull drink?

29. Which would you prefer to be given: an old $5 bill or a new one?

30. In a particular area of France, three out of ten people have telephone numbers that are not listed in the phone book. If you chose 100 names from the directory at random, how many would have unlisted numbers?

*This section of lateral puzzles demonstrates what a rich variety
is provided to us by our 26 letters and 10 digits.*

1. Which of these six words is the odd one out? (Lloyd King)

A TOR   D RECTOR

B SHOP   E SIGN

C RATE   F ANTIC

2. Fill in this crossword grid so that each row and column contains a common English word:

(crossword grid with letters C, A, N, R, V, A)

3. Which of the following numbers can be divided by seven?

56, 217, 348, 598, 1205

4. The name of which plant can be made from these letters without using any letter twice?

TOWAR

5. How can this statement be justified?

TAILEND = PEWTER

6. What should replace the question marks for this to make sense?

?5 × 4 = ?3
?2 × 2 = ?1
?4 × 16 = ?0

7. What is the minimum number of straight-line cuts needed to divide a pizza into eight equal slices?

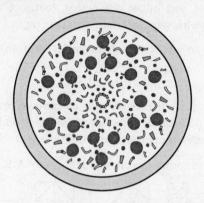

8. Which letters need to replace X and Y so that this makes sense?

$$10X = 50Y$$
$$20X = 68Y$$
$$30X = 86Y$$

9. Cross out the unnecessary letters to leave a common phrase:

ATCHEOUNMNE
MCESOSNAPRH
YRLEATTSEERS

10. These cube calendars make a nice novelty gift. How does the designer print the numbers around the faces of each cube so that every possible date (i.e. the numbers from 01 to 31) can be shown?

11. What letter should you place in the space so that a common English word is formed?

CA__TAL

12. I claim that the word 'footstool' is a palindrome (a word that reads the same backwards and forwards, such as madam or rotavator). However, you might object that 'footstool' is not quite a palindrome. In what way can I claim that I am right?

13. Find a way to justify this statement. (*Hint*: think European for both sides.)

$$10 = 509$$

14. Two-thirds of an odd number gives you an even result if the starting number is divisible by 3. Two-thirds of which odd number gives an even result even though it is not a multiple of 3?

15. Which figure comes next in this sequence – A, B, C or D? (Lloyd King)

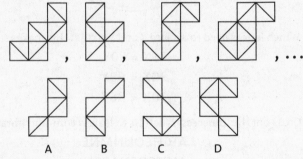

16. Rearrange these letters to form the name of a well-known country:

allpure

17. How many more building blocks need to be added so that a regular cube is formed?

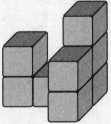

18. What is the smallest number of counters that need to be moved so that the contents of both of the hoops add up to the same total?

19. What is the smallest number of parts into which you can cut a chain if you saw across it somewhere in its middle?

20. What is the next number in this sequence? (Lloyd King)

15, 15, 6, 9, ?

21. Fill in the missing letters in the sequence: ??E, TWO, THREE, FOUR, FIVE, SIX, SEVEN, EIGHT, NINE, TEN, ????, ???EN, ?IN?. (Lloyd King)

22. How are all these letters related?

ADEHLORSTW

23. What unusual feature do these words have in common? (Lloyd King)

cling, drive, fort, motion, state

24. Which two letters of the alphabet have been cut out of this square?

25. What is the next word in this sequence (Lloyd King):

REDDEN
SEAM
BLEW
HATRED
DENSE
AMBLE
?

26. Connect a total of seven spots with eight more straight lines to make a familiar object. (Lloyd King)

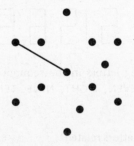

27. *Sebiro* is the Japanese word for 'business suit'. Can you see how the origin of this word has a London connection?

28. There is a somewhat unusual feature of this sentence, which will seem difficult to find at first, but once the answer is found it will be obvious – what is it?

29. Outside the castle Windlestraw, the wizard was honing his psychokinetic powers ready for the upcoming Magic Olympics. Velvet, his black cat, looked on in wonderment. 'You're bound to win, Windy!' she enthused. 'I bet there's not another wizard in the entire kingdom that can make fifteen cubes levitate.' 'Ahem!' said Windlestraw. 'If you look a little closer, Velvet, you'll see that there are, in fact, sixteen cubes.' Can you see the sixteenth cube? (Lloyd King)

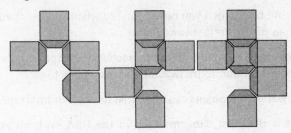

30. Can you figure out what all of these words in particular have in common? (Lloyd King)

VEIN, LOFT, SEW, ANY, TALL, SIN

31. By moving just one line segment, change this subtraction such that it is then possible to read a correct calculation:

$$182 - 882 = 695$$

32. How many changes need to be made to this arithmetical statement in order to make it correct?

$$5 - 2 \times 501 = 802$$

33. Anna absolutely loves to shop as well as to read, so when she came across two copies of her favourite novel on sale for only 90 cents each in a second-hand book shop, she just had to buy them. Can you figure out the title of this famous novel from her bill, which is shown alongside? (5, 3 and 11 letters) (Lloyd King)

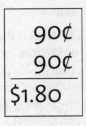

90¢
90¢
_____
$1.80

THINK ABOUT IT

Here are some more 'kick yourself' questions – a range of riddles which shouldn't be beyond you if you think about them enough.

1. In some Chinese restaurants you can find a dish called Mother and Child Reunion. Which two ingredients give this salad its name?

2. On which day of the year do the fewest people die?

3. What are black when you buy them, red when you use them, but grey when you throw them away?

4. Which 1980s computer game character was inspired by a take-away that its creator, Tohru Iwatani, had just begun to eat?

5. What is it that elephants can make that no other animal can?

6. What is the most dangerous job in the USA, with an average murder rate of over 9.3 per cent?

7. Why might someone from abroad be interested in buying £8.88 of your money from you?

8. In one of my books, the end is in the first half of the book and the preface is in the second. The foreword comes after the epilogue, but the index precedes the introduction. What book is it?

9. In the Bible, who instantaneously killed 25 per cent of the world's population?

10. A chef has 124 baking potatoes to serve his dinner guests. However, it seems that 135 people have turned up for the meal and he can't get hold of any more potatoes in time. What can he do to ensure that everyone gets a fair share and the potatoes are well presented?

11. What is the connection between can openers, scissors, computer keyboards, rulers, edging shears, guitars, peelers, fountain pens, pencil sharpeners, knives, pruning shears, bricklaying trowels, computer mice, boomerangs, golf clubs, bookmarks, tape measures, Swiss army knives, wristwatches, playing cards, chequebooks and corkscrews?

12. A man walks into a bar and asks for a beer. 'Do you want the regular beer for $2.90 or the special beer at $3.00?' enquired the bartender. 'I'll take the special,' said the man. Shortly afterwards, a second man walks into the bar and places $3 on the counter and says 'Gimme a beer, please.' The barman pours him the special beer straight away. Given that both customers were strangers to the bar, how was the bartender so sure what the second customer wanted?

13. Which fictional land was inspired by the bottom drawer of a filing cabinet?

14. Here's one to attempt if you are wearing trousers: try placing your right hand completely inside your left pocket, and your left hand in your right pocket. How can it be done?

15. A famous rock group was founded in South Dakota in 1925. All four members have since died, one of whom was assassinated. However, you can still see them today. Explain.

_____

TIGHT CORNERS

This next batch of puzzles concerns some of the curious situations that real life can throw up from time to time. Many of them are inspired by actual events.

1. A woman calls a man on her mobile phone, even though they are both in the same room and only a few steps away from each other. Why did she do this?

2. An ornithologist is given two birds that look identical. One bird is from an inner city and the other is from the countryside. Without taking any measurements or using scientific equipment, she can clearly tell them apart. How?

3. A few years ago it was suggested that the telephone number 123580 should be set up to help prevent drink-driving. Can you guess why?

4. In North America, it is not unusual to see bears climbing electricity pylons or telegraph poles. Why is this?

5. Like a few other people, my cousin Katherine has her birthday celebrations on 25 June even though it's nowhere near her real birthday. Why should that be?

6. In the seventeenth century, French sailors used petitions as a mild form of mutiny if they weren't happy with conditions on board ship. How did they list their signatures on the petition so that no one could be accused of instigating the rebellion?

7. For dinner, Frank and Pete both want to eat chicken. Neither man has any medical problems or special dietary requirements. However, Pete had to eat the beef dish offered because he wasn't allowed to eat the chicken, since that's what Frank had eaten. There were plenty of the chicken dishes to go round, so why was Pete denied his preferred dinner?

8. How was it possible for a farmer to eat two eggs every morning, even though he kept no chickens, he never bought, borrowed or stole any eggs, and nobody ever gave him any eggs?

9. A woman takes a large bundle of money and throws it on the fire. The money is real, valid legal tender and she doesn't want to burn the cash but feels she is forced to. In which real-life circumstances has this happened?

10. A US cable company broadcast a very high-profile boxing match. During one of the commercial breaks, they ran a promotion offering a free T-shirt for viewers. However, the company deliberately rigged it such that the signal was scrambled during the advert, so even the pay-per-view subscribers could not see it. Why did they do this?

11. In the 1966 Le Mans 24-hour race, the car that crossed the finishing line a close second was judged to be the winner. Why was this the case, given that there was no disqualification or appeal involved?

12. *Appleton's Cyclopedia of American Biography* (1887–89) is a comprehensive, six-volume reference work with high journalistic standards. However, up to two hundred of its biographical sketches are thought to be entirely fictitious. What practical purpose does this serve?

13. This is a countdown regularly used by particular people: 10, 9, 8, 7, 6, 4, 3, 2, 1. What sort of job would they be doing?

14. See if you can complete this piece of celebrity advice by Ian McKellen: 'When posing in a group photograph for the press, always stand on the extreme right. That way …'

15. In a cricket match, a valid delivery is bowled to the batsman on strike. He makes a good hit, which should allow him and his running partner to make two or three safe runs off the ball. However, neither batsman runs, even though they are able to do so and they only need one more run to win the match. What's the reason for their inactivity?

16. What is the lateral connection behind the creation of tenpin bowling, mime artistry and ice-cream sundaes?

17. A group of people pay to go into a dim room for an hour to look at a blank screen, yet they come out happy afterwards. How come?

18. Which very successful 1995 film, based on a children's book, had to change its lead role 48 times during filming?

19. Greg and Tony were both playing football. When one of Greg's shots touched but didn't completely cross the goal line, it was not deemed to be a goal. However, when Tony managed to get only part of the ball to cross his opponents' goal line, he scored for his team. There were no offsides or similar infringements during play. Can you explain this?

20. A farmer died and left behind him three sons and nineteen horses. In his will, the worthy man gave directions that the eldest son was to inherit half the horses; the next son was to have a quarter of the nineteen horses; and the youngest son was to have a fifth of the nineteen horses. But – and this was laid down very emphatically – none of the horses was to be slain in order to help in the division. Of course, it is not easy to divide 19 into two, four or even five parts without a remainder. Nevertheless, it was done in a few moments by a neighbouring farmer who happened to ride up just as the brothers were at their wits' end. How did he do it? (*Foulsham's Fun Book*)

21. This is a section of a printed map. What type of map is it?

22. Why might cautious drivers in the USA be insulted by this (real) car licence plate?

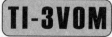

23. In some foreign restaurants and bars, it is possible to order large amounts of beer in very tall glasses. Why does the glass come with a set of numbers round the rim?

DETECTIVE STORIES

In these long-form mysteries featuring our dogged crime-fighting duo Hartland and Barlow, can you spot the vital clues that solve the case?

Detective story 1

Detective Hartland and Police Officer Barlow had been called to the airport.

'Thank you for coming, Detective. It's that pilot over in the corner. He's going to be flying the New York plane in around an hour's time.' The airport manager was sweating slightly. 'I've just received a tip-off over the telephone so I thought you could check him out for me.'

'Certainly. Follow me, Barlow.' Hartland stepped over towards the pilot and introduced himself.

'Pleased to meet you,' said the pilot, who was looking at a fold-out flight chart on the coffee table. 'I'm Steven Parker. I'm just looking over the flight plan for today.'

'Going to be a good trip, I hope,' offered Barlow.

'Yes,' said the pilot, 'the control tower has advised me of the weather forecast and it looks like it's almost clear skies all the way, so it's going to be a direct flight for the most part.' The pilot took out a pencil and ruler from his top pocket and drew a straight line across the Atlantic.

'Is that the route you'll be taking?' asked Hartland.

'Well, not exactly, but that's our planned flight path. Of course, it's mainly down to computerized navigation and some radio contact nowadays, but it helps to get an idea of the visual landmarks, just for my own peace of mind. Of course, the co-pilot helps also.'

'So how long have you been a pilot, sir?' asked Barlow.

'Around 12 years now. Bit of an old hand at these transatlantic flights. I've worked for all the major companies including British Airways and American Airlines.' The pilot took a sip of his coffee. 'Well, I'm afraid I have to go, gentlemen, because we have to do numerous pre-flight checks before we take off. Don't want to take any risks now, do we!' he chortled.

'I'm afraid that won't be necessary, Mr Parker, because you'll be answering some questions back at the police station.'

Can you spot what had particularly aroused Detective Hartland's suspicions about the 'pilot'?

Detective story 2

Just as the two policemen were about to leave the airport, where their last case had been solved, the airport manager confronted them again. 'Here we go again,' said Barlow under his breath. 'I don't know if you could possibly ...' began the manager. 'Help you again?' suggested Hartland. 'Yes, I don't see why not. We have a special two-for-the price-of-one offer on today.' Hartland's sarcasm was lost on the manager.

'We have a man held in Custody Room 3. He tried to take over the plane on a flight from India,' explained the manager. 'I was wondering if you could question him. You'd be better at it than any of the security staff we have here.' Barlow and Hartland went to see the man in the room where he was being held. 'Policemen?' asked the man. 'Thank goodness. I've been framed, I tell you. About fifteen minutes after take-off the pilot started to announce the details of the flight, like they normally do.'

'Indeed. So what happened?'

The man continued. 'Well, when the pilot was speaking I thought I recognized his voice as that of Jack Delaney, a friend of mine. You see, I used to be a pilot. I've been retired for around five years now. Anyway, I asked the stewardess if I could go and meet him. She said "Yes", so I got up out of my seat and went forward to the pilots' cabin, knocked on the door and said hello. At that moment, these two security goons knocked me down and sat on me for the rest of the journey, threatening to break my jaw off if I said so much as a word. I don't understand it.'

At that moment the airport manager entered the room. 'How are the investigations going, Detective?'

Hartland was puzzled. 'Is it usual to have security guards aboard a plane?'

'Yes, sky marshals are pretty standard for most commercial

flights. We even put an extra man on this flight as there were a couple of Bollywood celebrities on board.' 'Well,' concluded the detective, 'I think your staff should be better trained. This man you are holding has done nothing wrong and this whole situation is an unfortunate mistake on the part of the security guards. They should listen more carefully.'

Can you work out what the man had done unintentionally to alarm the guards so much?

Detective story 3

As Detective Hartland was driving towards the police station, the radio buzzed into action. The detective returned the call. 'Yes, go ahead, Penny.'

'Morning, sir. Can you go to the building site at Kensington Yard? Builders have found the body of a young woman. No name yet but we're still getting details,' the radio crackled.

Hartland was there within five minutes. He was met by the site foreman.

'Hello, sir, my name is Pete Norris. We've got a rather nasty situation on our hands. The second shift had just started work when one of the lads discovered a body at the bottom of a long shaft in the building.'

'Could I see where this shaft is?' asked Detective Hartland.

'Certainly.' At that moment the foreman spotted a man leaving the site. He called over to him. 'Oi, Geoff! Can you show this gentleman the same thing you showed me earlier?' He turned to address Hartland again. 'Geoff will have to show you round. He's the only one who's working on that section at the moment.'

Geoff said, 'Follow me, if you would.' He led Hartland up the stairs to the fourth floor of the building-to-be. 'Quite a lot of the work is unfinished, so watch your step. Here we are. I was here for the first shift this morning and the situation was exactly like this. But if you look here ...' The builder went to open a nearby door and pointed downwards to indicate the gaping hole in the floor. 'This shaft is going to be a lift, but before that's installed we use it as a hatch for a pulley system. Near the end of my shift I was raising a few planks that I wanted to bring up to this floor when I noticed this body at the very bottom.'

The Detective looked down the shaft and saw the shape of a body which the builders had covered in a blanket. 'Nasty. What do you reckon happened?' The builder thought for a moment. 'Well, either she was suicidal – it does happen in our business – or she was one of those "urban exploration" kids that got a bit too nosy and fell without realizing there wasn't a floor on the other side of the door.' 'Yes, those are possibilities, but I know it was murder and so do you!'

How did the detective know that there had been foul play?

Detective story 4

Hartland and Barlow arrived at 63 The Parkway to meet a distressed Mrs Edge. An ambulance was already on the scene.

The detective introduced himself and the officer to the woman. 'Do you think you could tell me what happened, Mrs Edge? Of course, if you're too distressed ...'

'No, I think I can manage, thank you. Frank – that's my husband – was attending to his bees, just as he always does. He looks after them regularly and he was out in the garden collecting some honey. Well today, for some reason, they decided to turn on him, and he came bursting through the back door with the whole swarm in chase. I couldn't understand why after ten years they would attack him like that.'

'Well, I think things can just occur like that. Nature will have its own way.' The detective tried to find a more kindly way of putting it, but there was no point in avoiding the truth. Sometimes these things happen. Hartland went to talk to the ambulance crew, leaving Barlow to talk to the woman.

'It's such unfortunate timing as well,' the woman added.

'What do you mean, Mrs Edge?' asked Barlow.

'Well, it was his 50th birthday just yesterday. He was looking so cheerful, opening his presents and having the family round him. Daniel and Mary, our children, had just come back from six months in Malaga. He was so pleased to see them, and they bought some lovely duty-free presents for Frank. We had a lovely tea and then later that day …'

'Ha! Sorry to interrupt you, Mrs Edge, but … Oh, here comes the detective now.'

Hartland returned to say his goodbyes. 'The ambulance crew say that your husband should be fine, Mrs Edge. But I must say this – spending two minutes in that ambulance has given me an idea that the action of his bees is more understandable than it first seemed.'

Can you deduce what Frank Edge did wrong to make the bees attack him?

WEIRD SCIENCE

*These brain-ticklers invite you to dig out your school
knowledge of a wide variety of scientific subjects: biology,
geology, mathematics, astronomy, physics, information
technology and chemistry are all covered.*

1. Rick's body weight is well over 20 stone, which is a problem because his bathroom scales only go up that high. However, he can still accurately weigh himself every day. How?

2. Some aeroplanes use a system whereby a number of identical computers work in parallel to determine exactly how the plane should respond to the pilot's control input. The number of computers is always odd. Why?

3. Here's a surprising fact: a 30 g serving of corn flakes contains exactly the same number of calories as a 30 g serving of corn flakes that have been covered in sugar frosting. How can this possibly be correct?

4. Peter Pernickety likes things to be 'just so'. Each morning he puts his coffee into the microwave for 64 seconds to heat it up. He doesn't mind how hot his coffee is as long as it's been microwaved for around a minute, so why did he choose a very specific number of seconds?

5. Which famous North American landmark will have moved by approximately 150 metres in 100 years' time?

6. Conveyor belts are often used to transfer manufactured parts around factories. What is often done to the conveyor belt so that each side of the belt receives an equal amount of wear and tear?

7. Ufologist Wolf Starman recently took this snapshot of the night sky over the infamous UFO hotspot Area 51. As well as the Moon and eleven stars, it also shows a UFO – but unfortunately, the spaceship looks exactly like a star. Despite this, see if you can still identify it.

8. In many supermarkets, yellow bell (sweet) peppers are more expensive than green peppers, even though they are the same variety of vegetable. Why is this?

9. At the airport, there are two large unfuelled jet planes of the same model and make, with identical internal fittings. There are no cargoes or people on board. Yet the captain can clearly tell that one is approximately a quarter of a tonne heavier than the other. How?

10. A ball bearing is to be dropped into each of these beakers. In which experiment (A, B, C or D) will the ball travel the slowest?

WATER (20°F)   MILK (40°F)   OIL (60°F)   TAR (80°F)

11. A chauffeur has ten pairs of leather gloves in his glove compartment: two pairs of tan, three pairs of brown and five pairs of black. If he draws the gloves out without looking at the colour, how many must he take before he has a matched left–right pair of any colour?

12. I need to put on a pair of rubber gloves before I can perform an experiment. I have 50 gloves in a drawer – 24 are for the left hand and 26 are for the right hand. If I select gloves at random, what is the least number of rubber gloves that I need to pick in order to have a usable pair?

13. A coin is inside a corked bottle. How could you extract the coin from the bottle without breaking anything or removing the cork from the bottle?

14. Which chemical element of five letters can be found in this list? (Lloyd King)

SILICON
HELIUM
NEON
HYDOGEN
LEAD
OXYGEN

15. Marvo the Magician takes any basic drinking straw and, without any preparation or other equipment, pushes it straight through a raw potato. How does he do it?

16. A woman uses a ball-point pen to compose a message, even though it had run out of ink and the nib made no visible indentation. How could this be?

17. Pakistan's pace bowler Shoaib Akhtar became the first man to bowl a cricket ball at 100 miles per hour. How can the average person propel something at this speed without using any equipment?

18. Make a third star appear without altering the diagram in any way:

19. What's wrong with the design of this model car racing circuit?

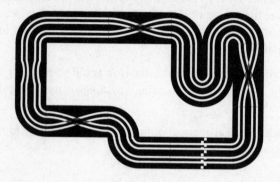

NOB'S FINAL PUZZLE

This incredible, seemingly innocuous, puzzle by Japanese puzzler Nob Yoshigahara has been much admired by his peers. Look before you leap!

What is the missing number?

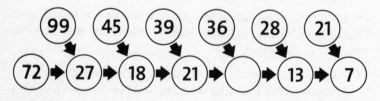

CHAPTER 8

Sudoku War

It's been called 'the twenty-first-century Rubik's cube', 'the perfect puzzle' and 'Viagra for newspaper circulation'. It's spread to virtually every corner of the planet in less time than it would take a pandemic. But despite its rapid rise to full-blown craze, its story takes in 220 years of history and a journey through at least six countries.

The sudoku is a humble-looking puzzle that has adorned the puzzle pages of thousands of publications since its dramatic surge to worldwide popularity in April 2005. The idea of the game is relatively straightforward: fill in a 9 × 9 grid in such a way that each row, column and 3 × 3 region – usually marked by thicker lines on the grid – contains the digits from 1 to 9 once each. What is remarkable is how such a simple idea has led to so much discussion, ingenuity, a little commercial hostility and, for some, millions in earnings.

LATIN SQUARE DANCING

The story of sudoku begins with a Swiss-born mathematician called Leonhard Euler (pronounced 'oiler'). If there is one word that sums up his life it would be 'determination', for he authored 886 books and yet still found the time to father thirteen children. Perhaps these two things are not intractable; as he once said, 'I made some of my most important discoveries while holding a baby in my arms with other children playing around my feet.' Through disease and cataracts, his eyesight deteriorated over his life. He spent his last twelve years effectively blind, but that still didn't put him off – 'Now I will have less distraction,' he insisted.

In 1783, which was also to be the year of his death, Euler was particularly pleased with something he called *nouveau espèce de carrés magiques* – 'a new type of magic square'. They are now called Latin squares, since Euler originally filled them out using letters of the Latin alphabet. The rule of the Latin square is very simple – it consists of a square grid where no element can be repeated in any row or column. For example, here are the only two possible 4 × 4 groups:

0	1	2	3
1	2	3	0
2	3	0	1
3	0	1	2

I	H	V	R
H	I	R	V
V	R	I	H
R	V	H	I

The diagram on the left demonstrates a simple base 4 arithmetic system, which can be likened to a clock with only four hours marked on it: 0, 1, 2 and 3. If the clock is pointing to 2 o'clock and we wind it forward three hours, it will now point to 1 o'clock, as shown. The diagram on the right is called the Klein four group, and it can be represented geometrically as the possible actions you could perform on a rectangle. We could flip it over horizontally (H), vertically (V), rotate it 180 degrees

(R), or simply leave it alone (I, representing 'identity'). From this diagram, it's easy to see that performing a horizontal flip twice in a row gets us back to where we started from (symbolically, H * H = I), and that flipping it horizontally then vertically, or vice versa, is the same as a 180-degree rotation (H * V = R).

In essence, these Latin squares are simple versions of what mathematicians term a 'group', which is a combination of a set of numbers (such as the whole numbers) together with a special operation (such as addition) which you can perform on those numbers. The research into this area has been so extensive that it holds the world record for the longest mathematical proof. To prove how many groups of a certain type exist and to classify them took over 14,000 pages in 500 research papers published over 35 years.

Groups have been vitally important to mathematics since the nineteenth century, but it is only since the 1960s that they have been studied in the classroom. Part of the reason was the lack of practical applications, until eventually it was discovered that group theory was useful in genetics. In the design of scientific experiments, if you're testing five different pesticides on five different crops, you can plant the crops in a 5 × 5 Latin square formation. This reduces the amount of cross-pollination and helps to ensure a fair result.

LE SUDOKU IS BORN

And so our story leaps forward to today, right? Well, no. Recent research has turned up an interesting period in the late nineteenth century when number puzzles were popular in many European newspapers. As well as the typical numerical brainteasers, some French papers ran puzzles where the readers were invited to complete a partially filled magic square so that each row, column and diagonal added up to the same total (called the 'magic constant'). Variations on this theme were published during the 1890s. In 1892 a Parisian newspaper called *Le Siècle* published a partially completed 9 × 9 magic square, featuring the nine 3 × 3 sub-squares that are now part of the standard sudoku. But this puzzle was not a sudoku as it had to be solved mathematically. An inherent feature of the modern sudoku is that it is a purely logical exercise. One could replace the numbers with letters, colours or symbols and, indeed, all of these variations have been produced. Arithmetic has no place in a sudoku.

In 1895, *La France* printed a *carré magique diabolique* by B. Meyniel, which readers had to complete in such a way that each row, column and both main diagonals contained the numbers 1 to 9, giving a magic constant of 45. This makes it an almost-ran in sudoku history, as it lacks the 3 × 3 subregions. Nevertheless, magic square puzzles such as this had a good run – they appeared in several titles on a weekly basis until the onset of World War II, when they appear to have died out with the arrival of more pressing matters.

U.S. SUDOKU

At this point, the trail goes cold until 1979. The American publisher Dell Magazines had begun to print a new puzzle feature they called Number Place. The rules were exactly the same as the modern sudoku – each row, column and 3 × 3 region must contain the numbers 1 to 9. The puzzles would be familiar to

The first sudoku

us now except in one main regard – they were much easier, with more clues given in the grid than was strictly necessary to solve them.

When puzzle fans tried in the 2000s to track down the author of the first sudoku, they hit a problem. Dell Magazines didn't print the authors' names beside the puzzles, preferring instead – as many magazines do – to list all the contributors together at the back. Luckily, there was a way through this thanks to a cunning piece of magazine archaeology. The Number Place puzzle appeared only in certain editions of Dell's *Pencil Puzzles & Word Games* magazine, and coincidentally the only name that appeared in all those editions was one Howard Garns. Furthermore, his name did not appear in any other issues. Thanks to this research by American enigmatologist Will Shortz, it seems that we had our man.

Not much is known about Garns other than he was a retired architect residing in Indianapolis who constructed puzzles for fun. In 1979 he would have been 74 years old; he died in 1989, and so did not live to see the commotion that his puzzle was to cause. Nevertheless, he now has a place in history of being the first compiler of a sudoku.

The original instructions for the puzzle in the May 1979 edition of *Pencil Puzzles & Word Games* were a little more complex than the usual rubric we see today: 'In this puzzle, your job is to place a number into every empty box so that each row across, each column down, and each small 9-box square within the large square (there are 9 of these) will contain each number from 1 through 9. Remember that no number may appear more than once in any row across, any column down, or within any small 9-box square; this will help you solve the puzzle. The numbers in circles below the diagram will give you a head start – each of these four numbers goes into one of the circle boxes in the diagram (not necessarily in the order given).' Over time, Garns dropped the complication with the circles, and the rules became identical to those we know today.

TURNING JAPANESE

In August 1980 a Japanese company called Puzzle Communication Nikoli began to publish a magazine specializing in games and, especially, logic puzzles. It was founded by Maki Kaji, a gambling-mad entrepreneur who named the company after Nikoli, the horse that won the Irish 2000 Guineas race that

Nikoli founder Maki Kaji

year. The company's eponymous quarterly magazine *Nikoli* has since become one of the world's most prolific sources of inventive puzzles.

Nikoli discovered Dell's Number Place and published some puzzles of their own in April 1984 under the title of *Suuji wa dokushin ni kagiru* – which means, loosely translated, 'the numbers must be solitary', referring to the rule of digits never repeating in a row, column or region. The game caught on. Kaji decided to abbreviate the title to *su-doku* – 'single number' – and he trademarked this new name in Japan. In a decision he almost certainly now regrets, Kaji didn't consider protecting the name in other territories, and so the puzzle title later became generic outside of its home country. Other Japanese puzzle companies used the name *nanpure*, which is their version of the original title Number Place. Sometimes the actual text 'Number Place' is printed on the cover of Japanese puzzle magazines, giving rise to the absurd situation that the English-speakers are using the Japanese name, and Japanese-speakers are using the English name.

In 1986, Nikoli made some refinements to the puzzle. The positions of the given clues were changed to a symmetrical distribution, like that of modern crossword grids, making the puzzle more pleasing to the eye. In addition, an upper limit of 32 clues was imposed. The puzzle continued to be a great success in Japan, with at least five current sudoku magazines having a combined circulation in excess of 600,000 copies – it suited a country whose language makes crosswords difficult to construct, but where thought, logic and hard work are immensely valued. However, it did not become the No. 1 bestseller, that title going to *kakuro*, the Japanese version of the number crossword.

LAW AND ORDER

In 1982 Wayne Gould, a lawyer in Matamata, New Zealand, moved to Hong Kong, where he eventually became a Chief District Judge. After Britain handed over Hong Kong to China in 1997, he retired from the legal profession. Later that year he took a holiday to Japan. In a Tokyo bookshop he found a number crossword puzzle – or so he thought (he did not speak or read Japanese). In fact, it was a sudoku. His interest was piqued: 'I felt very tempted to fill them in,' he later explained. He worked on and off on a computer program that would be able to make up millions of puzzles on the spot.

However, there was a problem to overcome. Whether we like it or not, computers are much better than humans at many things. Logic and number-handling come pretty high up that list. A computer can easily create a solvable puzzle in the blink of an eye, but it might take several hours for a poor human to scribble in all the numbers. There's still worse – even if it is solvable by our pink, squishy brains, how could one develop a sensible system of grading the puzzle's difficulty, thereby providing a suitable learning curve for puzzle fans to progress from beginner to sudoku samurai?

And when you consider all the variables involved, the full horror becomes apparent. Suppose we tried filling in thirty-two numbers at random and hoped for the best. Even if a fast computer could get through several million potential puzzles every minute, the chances that we'd end up with a valid sudoku are slim. Furthermore, even if we struck lucky there's no guarantee that the puzzle's difficulty was suitable. Worse still, the odds that the puzzle is symmetrical reach preposterous proportions.

THE TALE OF THE
RED THREAD

The solution to this hi-tech problem comes from an unlikely source – classical mythology. According to the well-known legend, King Minos of Crete attacked the city of Athens to avenge the death of his son, Androgeus. The Athenians capitulated, and agreed to send seven young men and seven maidens for sacrifice. They were fed to the Minotaur, a hideous creature that lived in the middle of a specially built labyrinth. However, one year Minos's daughter, Ariadne, instantly fell in love with Theseus, one of the young men sent for sacrifice, and gave him a ball of thread. When he entered the Minotaur's labyrinth, he used the thread to mark his route. It was difficult for him to become lost because, if at any point he reached a dead end, he could simply retrace his steps and try an alternative route that wasn't marked by the thread. Eventually he managed to find the middle of the maze, slayed the Minotaur, and followed the thread back to the arms of his girlfriend.

The point of interest to us here is the use of Ariadne's thread. The method allows us to attack a difficult problem in a systematic way. It's still essentially a case of trial-and-error, but we don't waste any time going down paths we've already discounted. Furthermore, it allows us to retrace our steps and try again at a very early stage in the process. This means that we can now program a computer to solve any sudoku we like, and it will find the solution in a relatively short period of time – certainly quicker than most humans could achieve. Furthermore, if there are enough possible sudoku puzzles out there – exits to the maze, if you will – then it's reasonable to assume that it's now feasible for a computer to create a sudoku puzzle from scratch by finding just one of those exits.

But how many sudokus are there? Mathematical researchers Bertram Felgenhauer and Frazer Jarvis have worked out that the number of standard 9 × 9 sudoku puzzles is 6,670,903,752,021, 072,936,960. Of all the possible 9 × 9 Latin squares that we could construct, it turns out that only 0.00012% of them happen to be valid sudokus. These two statistics show that sudokus can be constructed by a computer program, but that they are still relatively difficult to hit upon by blind luck. In fact, many sudokus are mathematically identical to one another, either due to rotation, reflection or simply relabelling the numbers for different digits – that is, you could replace the digits 123456789 with 234567891 respectively (or any other arrangement) to get a new-look puzzle that's solvable in exactly the same way as the original. If you allow for other permutations, such as swapping the first two rows (which effectively doesn't give you a new challenge), the number of genuinely unique sudokus comes down to a much more reasonable 5,472,730,538.

As an aside, we still don't know how few given numbers – the ones already filled in on a sudoku grid – can still lead to a unique solution. It's an interesting example of how slippery, frustrating and surprising mathematical proofs can be. Many examples of solvable sudoku containing just seventeen given numbers have been found, and in the darkest, deepest recesses of the Internet you can download web pages containing all 36,628 known examples, if you have enough bandwidth to kill. However, just because a puzzle with sixteen or fewer givens hasn't been found doesn't mean it isn't out there. So many extensive random searches by several independent mathematicians have been performed that it seems unlikely that a sixteen-number sudoku will be found, but the conclusive proof remains elusive.

So we now know that a computer program using the Ariadne's thread technique can be used to find any one of the billions of possible sudoku puzzles in a few moments. The computer can fill in numbers on the grid at will, and if for any reason it reaches a logical dead end, it can retrace its steps – like Theseus did – and try another set of numbers. Eventually a solution will be found. Even if other constraints are added, such as a symmetric layout or a particular level of difficulty, the computer will get there in the end.

PERFECT PITCH

Perhaps because of the above complications, it took six years for Wayne Gould to perfect his sudoku compilation program. He worked out a way for the computer to test each sudoku as it was found and assign it a level of difficulty according to the particular tricks and techniques required to solve it. When asked why it took him so long to complete the program, Gould replied: 'The trouble is that I'm a perfectionist. I'm slowed down by that. It's a terrible combination, having an interest in everything and being a perfectionist.'

Eventually, Gould was ready to sell his puzzles to newspapers. He had small successes in the USA, but he was after a major paper to take on the puzzle and run with it. On a visit to London in 2004, he decided to try his luck with a British paper, knowing that they had a tradition of running puzzle-based promotions such as crosswords and bingo. In the manner of a door-to-door salesman, he bowled up to the main reception desk of *The Times*, home of the famous cryptic crossword, and asked to see features editor Mike Harvey. Harvey recalls that 'He came in off the street. I had a call from the front desk who said a man had a puzzle to show me. I asked one of my staff to get rid of him but he said he was too busy, so I went down myself.'

Gould pitched the idea to Harvey with the aid of a page of his newspaper mocked up to show how the sudoku could fit into the *Times* layout. Instantly, Harvey knew that he wanted the puzzle. An unusual deal was struck – Gould would supply the paper with free sudoku puzzles in return for a mention of his website from which he would sell his sudoku program to members of the public.

And that's when the war began.

PUZZLE PANDEMONIUM

Before the first sudoku was even printed in a British newspaper, rivals to *The Times* knew that something was afoot. The *Daily Mail* and the *Telegraph* began to cast around for suppliers of sudoku puzzles. They'd heard that *The Times* was going to splash a sudoku promotion, and it was a useful exercise, both in morale and readership figures, to run with a similar 'spoiler' feature as soon as possible afterwards. The *Daily Mail* searched in vain for a few days until they eventually twigged that they had a tenuous corporate link to Dell Magazines themselves, so some Number Place puzzles were sourced. Michael Mepham, a long-serving puzzle compiler, recognized that there was an inherent similarity between sudoku and magic squares, so he speedily reworked one of his existing programs for producing magic squares to generate the new puzzles. Though it's fair to say they weren't as elegant as those produced by Gould's program, they were valid sudokus and they did the job.

The Times ran with its first Wayne Gould puzzle on 12 November 2004, which they styled Su Doku, and the *Daily Mail* followed three days afterwards. While they caught the zeitgeist, the *Mail* managed a spectacular own goal by entitling its puzzle Codenumber, at a time when several other British papers were using the sudoku name, which Nikoli hadn't trademarked for use outside Japan. Over a period of weeks, the *Mail* changed the title, first to Codenumber Sudoku, and then, finally admitting defeat, fell in line with Sudoku. Michael Mepham's puzzles began running in the *Telegraph* in February 2005. However, an early glitch in his program created a puzzle that had more than one solution: 'By golly, did I get some mail,' he said, but 'I've never seen anything in the puzzle industry that's caused such a fuss. It's just one of those things that catches on.'

While the puzzle was certainly noticed, it took a few months for full-blown sudoku fever to grip Britain. In April 2005, only four national newspapers were regularly printing sudoku. The BBC's nightly news review programme, *Newsnight*, not usually one to pick up on the latest goings-on in the puzzle world, ran a feature on sudoku. Various players of the game confessed to the BBC that they were becoming addicts. Bernard Stay from St Albans was quoted as saying: 'I never thought I had an addictive personality, but sudoku is definitely bad for me. If I don't complete a puzzle before noon I get suicidally depressed for the rest of the day and even lose sleep fretting on what I've missed.'

THREE-FIFTHS

There was then a piece of good timing. In the early months of 2005, most British newspapers were preoccupied with Tony Blair's attempt to win a third consecutive General Election. The election took place on the fifth of the fifth of the fifth: 5 May 2005. When it was over, newspaper editors had a double head-ache: not only were there no more election stories with which to fill their pages, but an unusually warm spell brought out an early 'silly season' feeling. All told, it was a fairly dull time in the press.

To perk up circulation, a second wave of sudoku promotions was ordered, and this time almost all the national papers jumped on the bandwagon. It was now impossible for anyone to be unaware of sudoku, not least newspaper editors themselves, who noticed that 'Sudoku' on the front page boosted sales. Columnists were delighted to be able to write puff pieces about the new phenomenon, most of them telling how they'd first found the puzzle difficult, then got the hang of it, only for their nine-year-old son to point out that they'd put two 7's in the top-right box.

The Times retaliated with copious sudoku promotions, interviews with Wayne Gould, and making their puzzles more difficult. The *Independent* upped the stakes by printing several a day with different degrees of difficulty, then added another quick sudoku on the back page for good measure. Even the out-and-out tabloid *Sun* ran its own version of the puzzle, Sundoku, and an online edition featuring topless Page 3 girls. The fad reached farcical proportions, each paper trying to outdo its rivals by printing more sudokus than anyone else. The editor of the *Observer* mused: 'I'd put one on every page if I knew it'd raise the circulation – but I don't know if it will yet.' Little did he know that his sister paper, the *Guardian*, would later take the trend to its natural conclusion and print a sudoku on every single page of its *G2* supplement.

However, the *Guardian* was somewhat late to the party – it was the last major national to cotton on to the puzzle that one editor had called 'Viagra for newspaper circulation'. How could it stand out in the crowded market? Its solution was to call upon the puzzle's Japanese popularizer, Nikoli. An editorial sniffily proclaimed that 'The *Guardian* has already occupied the moral high ground in the battle of Sudoku by becoming the only newspaper to publish puzzles hand-crafted by the game's original Japanese inventors (as opposed to the risibly inferior versions spewed out by computer programs).' Nikoli's manually created puzzles, it said, contained so-called 'imperceptible witticisms' which aficionados of the puzzle were sure to appreciate. The computer programmers scoffed at such claims – and, if truth be told, such witticisms have yet to be found.

Nevertheless, a sudoku craze was now in full flow. The sudoku was a highly copiable format, with no legal protection. The argument went that the idea behind sudoku can't be protected, in the same way that it would be unreasonable for the creator of the first crossword to have a monopoly on the idea. Therefore, anyone who could generate publicity on the back of sudoku had a go. The BBC Radio 4's conservative-with-a-small-c *Today* programme even tried out a radio sudoku, with the presenter reading out the numbers to be filled into the grid. New sudoku-only puzzle magazines launched with print runs of 200,000-plus.

Other media joined the bandwagon. On 1 July 2005, the satellite channel Sky One broadcast a one-hour special sudoku game show presented by self-confessed fan Carol Vorderman, with teams competing to solve a sudoku puzzle against the clock. Several other sudoku-themed game shows followed, as did sudoku games for computers, handheld consoles and mobile phones.

And the rest is history. Once news of the British craze spread, all corners of the world were conquered. Multiple variations and themes of the basic puzzle have since surfaced, but it seems likely that the basic sudoku will be around for a very long time to come. Only one mystery remains – why was it this particular puzzle that caused such a sensation? As we've already seen, the puzzle has journeyed from Switzerland, through France, the USA, Japan, Hong Kong and Britain, and then throughout the world, but its birth was far from smooth.

The phenomenon of sudoku is an example of a meme (rhymes with 'cream'), a word coined by the evolutionary scientist Richard Dawkins in 1976 to describe those ideas that get passed between minds, such as tunes, fashions, methods and words, as opposed to the biologically transmitted genes. The sudoku is in fact a type of mental pandemic which lives in the minds of everyone it is shared with. In her book *The Meme Machine*, Dr Susan Blackmore says that 'This puzzle is a fantastic study in memetics. It is using our brains to propagate itself across the world like an infectious virus.' Anything new, exciting and trendy – whether it be an exciting piece of new gadgetry or a humble little number puzzle with eighty-one squares – has the potential to spread this way.

Some psychologists have suggested that the sudoku taps into the addictive part of our brain. The first hook is that the puzzle is already half-complete, and so – just as Wayne Gould felt when he first laid eyes on the puzzle – there is an inherent compulsion in our human nature to fill in the gaps. American puzzle writer Will Shortz calls sudoku 'the perfect puzzle – if a puzzle person sees empty squares, he can't turn the page until he's filled them in.' Then, once you've started, the clockwork nature of the solving process takes over, and the mind is continually rewarded as more and more of the squares are filled in until, hopefully, a glow of satisfaction is gained when the blank squares are banished from the page. But perhaps this addictive nature knows no bounds – as one reader of *The Times* confessed, 'I dreamt of square fields last night, each one with a different number in the middle. Should I be worried?'

And, as with any new invention, there come new moral dilemmas. 'Every day my wife does the crossword and I attempt sudoku,' writes another reader. 'I know she cheats using her electronic solver but she thinks I am unaware. I also cheat by using a computer but she does not know this. Should I mention that her cheating is known and also confess mine?'

The Puzzles

MINI SUDOKU

In these beginner puzzles, every row, column and 3 × 2 rectangle (marked by the heavier lines and shading) must contain all the digits from 1 to 6 inclusive. Beware: the puzzles get more difficult later on and may require a few minutes' pause for thought.

Mini sudoku 1

	4				
			2		1
	3	6	5		
		5	1	6	
6		4			
				1	

Mini sudoku 2

				1	
	1	3			2
			4		1
5		1			
1			2	4	
	5				

Mini sudoku 3

			4		2
4			3	5	
		4			
			1		
	4	6			5
5		3			

Mini sudoku 4

	1			6	
	5				
1			6		
		3			2
				2	
	6			4	

Mini sudoku 5

		6			5
1			2		
6	4				
				4	6
		5			2
2			6		

Mini sudoku 6

5	1				
		4		5	
	6	3			
			6	3	
	5		2		
				6	5

Mini sudoku 7

			5	4	
					3
		3		1	
	1		2		
6					
	4	1			

Mini sudoku 8

	2			5	
		5			
		4			1
1			4		
			6		
	3			2	

In the classic sudoku puzzle, the aim is to fill in all the empty squares so that every row, column and 3 × 3 region (marked by the heavier lines and shading) contains all the digits from 1 to 9 inclusive.

If you're a beginner, try considering each digit in turn – consider all the 1's, then the 2's, 3's, 4's, and so on. Or begin with the digit that appears most frequently among the numbers already in the grid.

Remember the rule that each 3 × 3 box must contain 1 to 9. Many beginners forget about this rule by concentrating too much on the rows and columns.

Classic sudoku 1

		1	3	6	9			7
3	7	2			5			4
2		9	5	7				8
				3				
4				9	2	7		6
1			4			6	5	9
9			7	5	8	4		

Classic sudoku 2

	7	9		4	5			
	4		1	8				2
								1
	6	5						9
9		1	6		8	7		3
3						6	2	
6								
2				6	7		1	
			8	1		2	9	

Classic sudoku 3

4		2			9		7	
	7	9		6	3		2	
						8		
						3		5
	9		4		2		6	
3		7						
		8						
	4		3	8		5	1	
	5		1			7		4

Classic sudoku 4

5				3			2	
				8	2	4		
	4					8		9
1	8		2					
9			7		6			2
					1		5	6
7		4					9	
		2	3	1				
	5			6				4

Classic sudoku 5

3	1		5			8		
4		2	8					
	7							6
	2		9	1				
1		3				4		7
				3	4		5	
6							2	
					9	1		8
		5			6		3	9

Classic sudoku 6

	9				2			1
	3	5						
2			3					
8				9	6	4		3
		4				1		
3		1	8	5				9
					8			5
						6	9	
7			2				4	

Classic sudoku 7

8		9		4				
5	7		9			6	4	
3	2				4			
1				2				8
			1				6	3
	9	6			8		7	4
				7		8		9

Classic sudoku 8

		3	4		9			1
2		4			6			
7			8				6	9
					5		8	
			2	7	8			
	3		9					
3	6				4			2
			5			6		3
1			3		2	5		

Classic sudoku 9

							6	
			3	2	4	5	7	
5		1				9		
	7		1	9				2
3				6	8		9	
		3				6		4
	2	6	4	5	1			
	8							

Classic sudoku 10

				2			1	
	3	7	8		5			
		1	7		4	9		
3			2			1		
1								9
		5			8			4
		4	9		3	8		
			4		1	6	9	
	7			8				

Classic sudoku 11

	6		2	4	5		1	
	1				8	9		
				7				2
	5	1				3		
				8				
		4				5	2	
1				3				
		2	7				6	
	7		9	2	1		3	

Classic sudoku 12

1						8		
		5		1		6	4	
	4				7			
7		3	5			9		
	8	1				2	3	
		2			3	5		8
			3				5	
	1	7		2		3		
		8						2

Classic sudoku 13

6		5		4		1	3	
7			6					
	3	1						4
1	4		7			2		
		2			5		1	8
8						3	7	
					7			2
	7	9		2		6		1

WORD SUDOKU

In this word version of the popular Japanese pastime, every row, column and 3 × 3 box (marked by the heavier lines) contains the nine letters indicated under the puzzle title. When the grid is complete, find the hidden seven-letter word.

Word sudoku 1

ADEGQRSTU

U	R				T			E
S		T			G			
	A		D	R				
						E	D	
E								A
	U	G						
				U	Q		G	
			R			S		D
R				E			T	Q

Word sudoku 2

ACEILRTUV

C	L		U	I				
					A			
		T	C	R				
	R			U			A	L
L	T						I	E
A	I			C			V	
			A	C	V			
			R					
				E	L		R	I

These 16 × 16 sudokus require concentration, but provide a good challenge if you find the classic puzzle too easy. Every row, column and 4 × 4 region (marked by the heavier lines and shading) must contain 0, 1, 2, 3, 4, 5, 6, 7, 8, 9, A, B, C, D, E and F.

Monster sudoku 1

This first puzzle has slightly more clues than are necessary to solve it. The subsequent puzzles require more of a train of thought.

C		F	0	5	7		E				3	8	A		
1	5				0		A	F	E	B				7	3
9	A		6	1	3		C			2			D	4	F
			6	D			1		A		B				5
D		9		4	E	3					B	7	F		0
3	F	A					0	C		7			5		
	0			A	5			F	3						4
	E		5	7						4	D	B			
		E	8	B						F	0		2		
F				C	9			8	6				D		
		1			8		3	2				4	F	A	
0		2	9	E				3	D	1		8			C
5			F		4		8			0	9				
E	7	C			6			8		4	A	3		9	B
A	9				2	E	B	7		F				8	D
		4	3	A				E		C	2	F	7		6

Monster sudoku 2

			4	9		B	0		8	1					
A	9						F			E			2	0	
					4		2	B	D				1		7
	5			8	7				3				D		9
8	1								7				B	5	
7		4		2	3			9					0		E
		9			C	D			6	5					8
2	F	C			6	8	7		1		E				4
5				F		4		8	E	3			6	7	0
4				C	7			5	9				8		
F		A				9				6	0		4		3
	2	E			6									B	C
3		1			0					D	5			F	
D		2			E	1	7		4						
	A	7		F				1						9	2
				2	3		A	0			C	D			

Monster sudoku 3

3	5	8						9	6	F				2	
		C				F			E	8			1	3	6
	4		E				3	B			D		F	7	
			F				B		5		0			8	
				E			A		B		7			D	
	E	B		3	9	4	5			D					
			0				7	4		6	8	A		C	
		9	C			2	0	A							4
E							4	8	1			3	6		
	C		8	7	0		1	E				5			
				5				0	7	C	4		2	A	
	1			A		9		F			3				
	3			B		5		6				1			
	7	0		8			F	1				D		6	
9	F	2			4	1			3				7		
	B				C	0	2						4	F	3

Monster sudoku 4

			A	7				B				F	2		E
			9					5		2				B	
		6	A			3		4		F		0	8		
	D	2		1	E	6		7		9	C				
			3		A		C			8	B				
	7	0		B		5	9	E				D			
		E			7	F					8		9		
8	D			4		2			5		3			0	1
C	4			5		8			A		D			6	7
	F		3				E	8			A				
		2			3	A	F		9		0	8			
			8	6			7		B		4				
			F	E		B		1	D	C		2	7		
	5	4		C		1		8			7		F		
	7			A		4					2				
0		1	6				8				A	3			

In this simple variation on the classic puzzle, every row, column and 3 × 3 region (marked by the heavier lines) contains all the digits from 1 to 9 inclusive. In addition, both main diagonals (marked by the shading) also contain all the digits from 1 to 9.

Sudoku X 1

Sudoku X 2

				1	6			
		5				1		
	3			2			6	
				3				9
6		2	7		8	4		3
1				9				
	2			7			4	
		7				5		
			5	4				

Sudoku X 3

	2	3			8			
					4			7
								6
6	4			1				
				3			2	5
7								
2			5					
			2			1	5	

Sudoku X 4

Sudoku X 5

ONE AWAY SUDOKU

As before, every row, column and 3 × 3 region (marked by the shading and heavier lines) contains all the digits from 1 to 9 inclusive. The white dots mark all the places where two adjacent squares contain digits that are one away from each other – e.g. 1 and 2, or 8 and 7.

One away sudoku 1

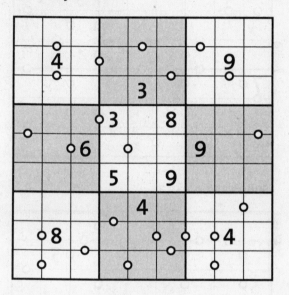

One away sudoku 2

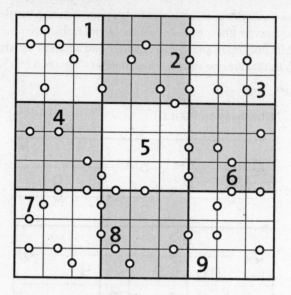

One away sudoku 3

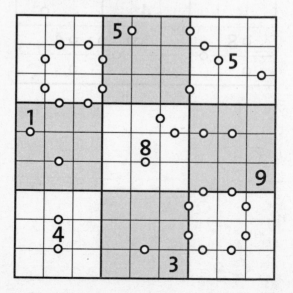

One away sudoku 4

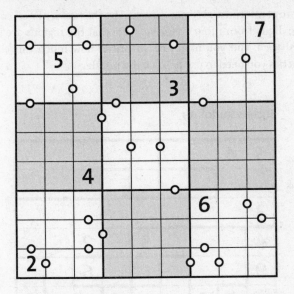

One away sudoku 5

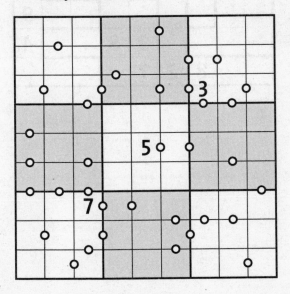

JIGSAW SUDOKU

Every row, column and region (marked by the heavier lines) contains all the digits from 1 to 9 inclusive. Note that the regions are irregularly shaped, and you might be surprised how much this changes the tactics you need to use to solve the puzzle.

Jigsaw sudoku 1

Jigsaw sudoku 2

			6		7		3	4
		9		3			8	5
					4			
			5					
							9	6
		6			5		1	
			1	2				
			7				5	1

Jigsaw sudoku 3

	7				5			
3	4	5					7	
8		2				4		
		3						8
			8				3	
5		1						
9				7				
	2			1				4
				3				

Jigsaw sudoku 4

Jigsaw sudoku 5

ODD/EVEN SUDOKU

Every row, column and 3 × 3 region (marked by the heavier lines) contains all the digits from 1 to 9 inclusive. The shaded squares contain odd digits – namely 1, 3, 5, 7 and 9. The white squares contain even digits.

Odd/even sudoku 1

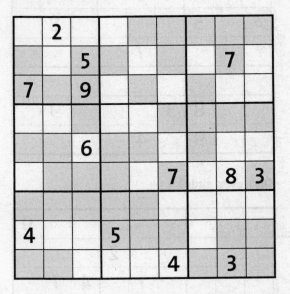

Odd/even sudoku 2

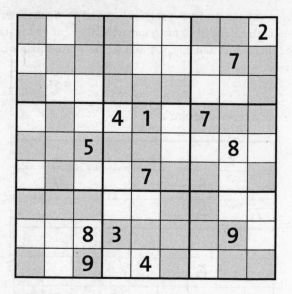

Odd/even sudoku 3

Odd/even sudoku 4

			1					
		9						1
						8		
		2		6	7			
3				5	2			
				2				6
						7		
				7				

Odd/even sudoku 5

		1						
				2			4	9
				6				
7								
2	7	5					1	
	6							
1							9	

147 SUDOKU

Every row, column and 3 × 3 region (marked by the shading and heavier lines) contains all the digits from 1 to 9 inclusive. Plain cells contain either 1, 2 or 3. Cells containing a dotted circle contain 4, 5 or 6. Cells containing a dotted square contain 7, 8 or 9.

147 sudoku 1

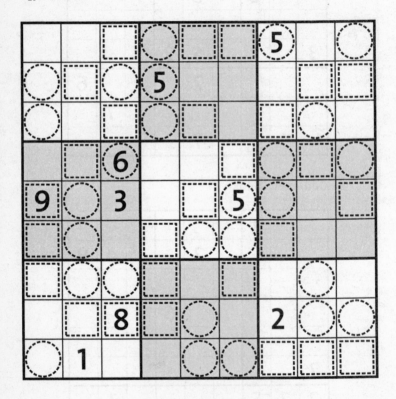

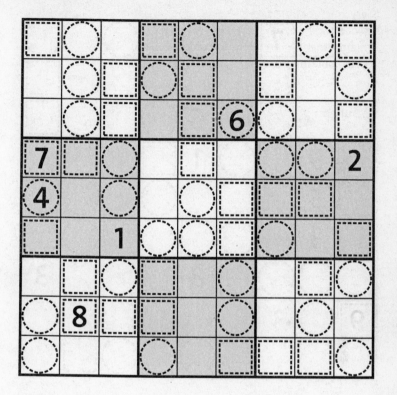

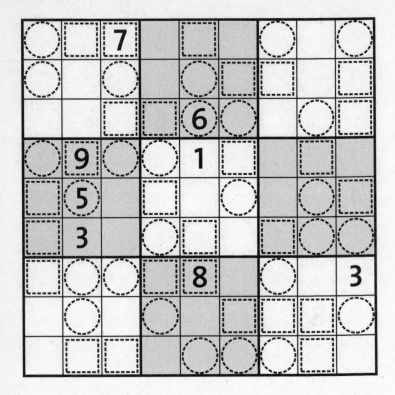

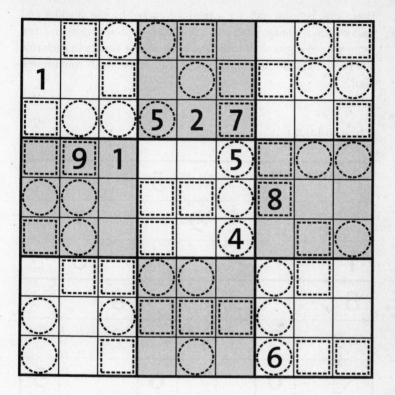

O TO 9 SUDOKU

Every row, column and 3 × 3 region (marked by the shading and heavier lines) contains all the digits from 0 to 9 inclusive. Since there are ten digits to fit into nine squares, one square in each row has been divided into two halves, and each half is to contain one digit.

0 to 9 sudoku 1

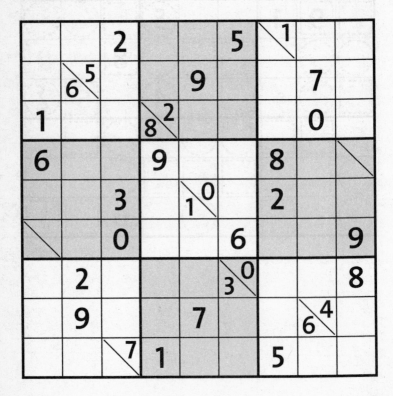

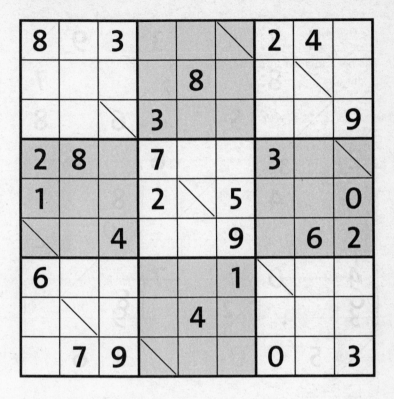

0 to 9 sudoku 3

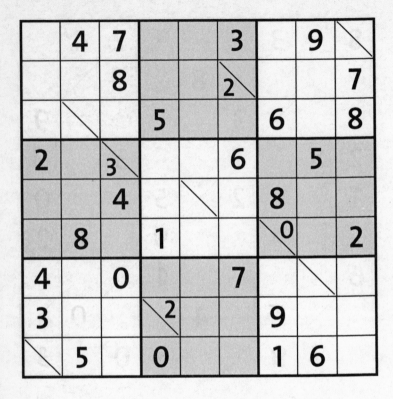

o to 9 sudoku 4

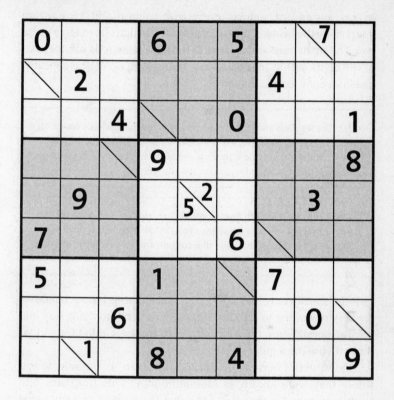

KILLER SUDOKU

As per a standard sudoku, every row, column and 3 × 3 region (marked by the heavier lines) contains all the digits from 1 to 9 inclusive. The small number beside each dashed region tells you the total of the digits within that boundary. **Important**: no digit is repeated inside any one dashed region.

> *Tip* The smallest and largest numbers give you most readily accessible information. For example, a 3-cell dashed region adding up to 7 must contain the digits 1, 2 and 4 in some order. It can't be 1, 3 and 3 because each digit inside a dashed region must be different.

> *Tip* It may be useful to bear in mind that because each row, column and 3 × 3 region contains the digits 1 to 9, by the standard sudoku rules, it immediately follows that each row, column and 3 × 3 region must total 45 (the sum of the digits from 1 to 9).

Killer sudoku may look and sound intimidating, but such puzzles are very rewarding to do. They unravel in a very satisfying way and breathe new life into the sudoku format. However, don't forget that they still use the regular sudoku rules.

These puzzles became established in Japan in the mid 1990s, where they were known as *samunamupure*. This translates into English as 'sum number place', Number Place being an early name for sudoku.

Killer sudoku 1

Killer sudoku 2

Killer sudoku 3

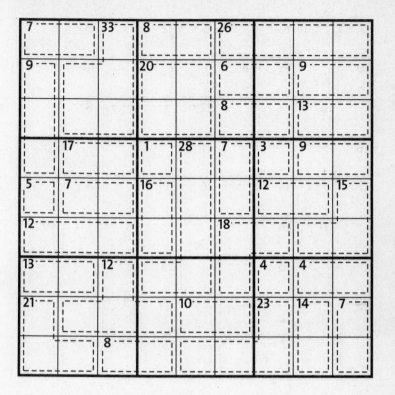

Killer sudoku 4

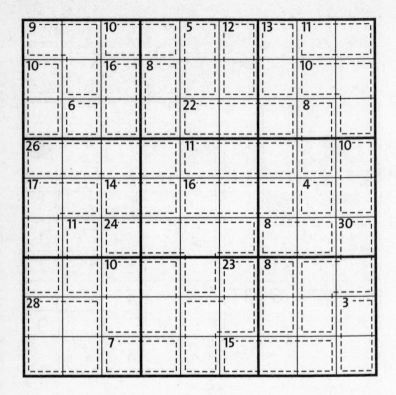

BLACKOUT SUDOKU

Every row, column and 4 × 3 region (marked by the shading and heavier lines) contains all the digits from 1 to 9 inclusive as well as exactly three black squares. No two black squares are adjacent to each other, horizontally or vertically.

OVERLAPPING SUDOKU

Here, two separate classic sudoku puzzles have been overlapped so that they share a common corner. In all other respects, the standard rules apply.

Japan Rediscovered

PLAYBOY MEETS PUZZLES

One question remains in our survey of modern puzzling – why did it take the rest of the world so long to discover the varied delights and inventions of Japanese puzzling? After its protracted evolution, the sudoku virus infected the world in a matter of months – and this explosion was triggered by a chance meeting between a puzzle fan and a newspaper editor in London. How come it took a happenstance to give publishers the courage to try out the sudoku, and other Japanese-influenced puzzles?

This doesn't quite give the full picture – in fact, sections of the puzzle community have been using ideas from the East for quite some time. The newspaper market, which provides most of us with our exposure to puzzles on a daily basis, is inherently conservative – if a new feature is introduced at the cost of a much-loved favourite, the editor who has made such a foolhardy decision can expect the full force of the (albeit polite) outrage heading their way. It has been known for hundreds of crossword fans to complain if their favourite puzzle is printed on a different page or even in a different format. With this in mind, it's very rare for newspaper puzzles to be dropped, and new formats rarely last long.

However, without the pressure of millions of readers,

smaller specialist magazines have been able to run new ideas in puzzles including sudoku and its friends. One of the most famous is *GAMES* magazine, which was started in 1977 by the same company that published *Playboy* – something of a puzzle in itself. With no one but hardcore puzzle fans to satisfy, its mixture of firm-but-fair puzzles allowed it to showcase new puzzles when most newspapers round the world were quite happy with their anagrams and quick crosswords.

CROSS-CZECH

The keenest puzzle-doers take their solving quest out into the big wide world in search of new challenges. At a former event called the International Crossword Marathon, teams of word-smiths spent a day trying to compile a crossword against the clock. The event was usually the preserve of Eastern European countries, but in 1989 an American team captained by the then *GAMES* editor, Will Shortz, brought its own little piece of glasnost to Brno, now the second city of the Czech Republic. Each team worked from 8 p.m. to 8 p.m., trying to generate the largest puzzle. As each country used its own language and rules, there was little point in comparing results, particularly when, for example, the average German word is longer than its English equivalent. When political upheaval caused the 1991 crossword-fest to be cancelled, Shortz put the wheels in motion for a new type of puzzling event.

In 1992, the first World Puzzle Championship saw teams from around the world, but still with a bias towards former Communist countries, converge on New York to battle over sets of brainteasers for several days. The format of the cham-

Will Shortz

pionship, held annually ever since, varies slightly from year to year but the basic elements are the same: teams have to solve a series of puzzle-related challenges, mainly as individuals but sometimes cooperatively, under examination conditions. Some physical brainteasers are put into the mix to give the participants a break from the pencil and paperwork. Points are awarded for correctly solved puzzles, optimal solutions and speed; points are deducted for mistakes. At the end of it all, the brainiest competitors compete to solve a series of extra-tough problems on flipcharts against the clock in front of an audience, until a victor is crowned. A trophy is also awarded to the highest-scoring country.

With teams from virtually every corner of the globe taking part, one of the key considerations is how to test puzzle solving ability when the participants speak different languages. The first casualty is word puzzles, naturally. If you were hoping to take part thanks to your amazing vocabulary and anagram solving ability, you're in for a disappointment. Nevertheless, a surprising range of largely logic-based problems remain. Puzzles are translated into various languages before the event, and meetings are held each evening giving an outline of the questions that await the following day to ensure that no linguistic misunderstandings occur.

As far as possible, cultural bias is ironed out. Peter Ritmeester, the General Secretary of organizers The World Puzzle Federation, recalls 'a huge argument once, about a puzzle the Czechs wanted to include. It was all about a building with windows, where the lights could be on or off. It turned out that the puzzle relied on knowing Morse code! This is a question of general knowledge, not logic. But the Czechs didn't realize that. It turned out that Morse code was taught to all primary school children in Czechoslovakia.' In 2005, a team from India were baffled by a puzzle concerning a jigsaw – they had never seen such a puzzle before. While some word puzzles are included, they are limited to varieties such as wordsearches and letter fits, where vocabulary and comprehension are unimportant and, as a final dollop of fairness, languages such as Swahili are sometimes employed so that they are equally unfamiliar to all competitors.

MULTIPLE PERSONALITIES

Competitors tend to be of a type – bright 20- and 30-somethings with technical backgrounds, sometimes with curious but harmless social eccentricities, and a good sense of humour, as typified by four-time individual champion Wei-Hwa Huang (who now works for Google). The most striking demographic is the male/female ratio. 'Not very many women enter,' says Ritmeester. 'Maybe seven out of every hundred people who enter are women. I think there are many women who do puzzles, but they are not competitive in the same way as men.'

Living under the same roof with a crowd of puzzle obsessives for a week brings about its own topics of conversation. Mechanical toys and magazines from around the world are exchanged, clever hybrid puzzles are discussed, and jokes are shared in the style of the competition's ultra-precise rules. Chris Dickson, a UK representative at the 2004 championship, recalls: 'An ongoing joke of that week was "not even diagonally", normally a reference to the ways in which things may or may not be permitted to touch each other in a puzzle. The phrase "not even" lost all meaning to us outside that context. When we were told before Round 1 that "puzzlers may not smoke inside the building, not even …", the rest of the sentence became immediately obvious.'

With restrictions on the palette of challenges available to them, the Championships have been quicker than most to adopt new ideas from other countries. Puzzles such as sudoku and kakuro had featured in their test papers several years before they appeared in newspapers around the world. It is not a coincidence that Asian puzzles were suitable for use in the WPC. With a complicated, ideogram-based language most unsuited to the formats such as crossword, the Japanese people have been left to their own devices and arrived at different places. Similar partings of the ways have happened before with other media, such as Superman and manga comics. Even the shorthand of comic interpretation is different – characters in Western comics convey the emotion of lust through wide-open eyes and a sticking-out tongue; Japanese comics show it with a nosebleed (from a housewife's tale that if a boy stares at a pretty woman, he would get a bloody nose). Each image makes sense to its own audience, but doesn't always travel well internationally. Such is the case for puzzles too: Japanese puzzle magazines are colourful, highly illustrated and littered with characterful dogs, cutesy rabbits and impish children – a world away from the austere black-and-white grids that dominate the magazines and newspapers seen by Western puzzlers.

Once the rules are translated into English, Japanese puzzles turn out to be not significantly harder than most puzzles in the current Western arsenal. Numbers, lines and shading are combined with an economy of logic to bring about a stunning variety of puzzles. The Japanese publishing company Nikoli have been leaders in the field, and have had so many ideas over the years they have been able to fill a catalogue with around two hundred of their different puzzle formats. Some are minor variants, some are works-in-progress and admittedly not all are winners, but what remains is an impressive array of ingenuity.

CASTY OR KOKI?

One thing that is very evident in Japanese magazines is a sense of authorship. All Nikoli's sudoku puzzles are handmade, not computer-generated, a continuation of a culture where workmanship is highly valued. In some Nikoli magazines, little bylines in the form of nicknames or symbols are used so that the reader knows whether they are pitting their wits against Casty or Koki. Nikoli claim that their hand-tooled approach allows them to vary the levels of difficulty much more effectively than computer algorithms can, and produce puzzles with a smattering of individuality that offer some clues to the psyche of their creators. Nikoli's founder, Maki Kaji, is keen that his puzzles should present a fair range of challenges to his 50,000 readers: 'A good puzzle used to be one that only one in a hundred or one in a thousand people could solve. Or there were other ones that were so easy you didn't even have to try. My idea was to make something that wasn't already being offered and hope that it would sell. I wanted puzzles to be for a change of mood, to kill time, just to make your mind go blank and help you forget everything else.'

Most World Puzzle Championship competitors are now sponsored by a puzzle-related company in their home country, and the WPC is run as an altruistic exercise to exchange new ideas and form new friendships. It's too early to say whether the interest in mind games will continue to such an extent that a full Olympics of the Mind becomes a viable proposition, but if it does, then Will Shortz and Peter Ritmeester will be ready and waiting. In the meantime, you can get in training for your call-up with the wonderful array of Japanese puzzles that follow.

The Puzzles

FUTOSHIKI

The aim here is to complete each row and column of squares so that they contain the numbers 1 to 5 inclusive. That's for a 5 × 5 grid; in a 7 × 7 puzzle, use the numbers 1 to 7, and so on.

- Each digit must appear exactly once in each row and each column (the long diagonals do not have to obey this rule).
- Where you see the 'greater than' (>) or 'less than' (<) sign, the pointed end always points towards the square containing the smaller number. For example, 5 > 3 and 1 < 2. (The name *futoshiki* means 'not equal'.)

The illustration shows how a completed puzzle might look:

Futoshiki 1   **Futoshiki 2**

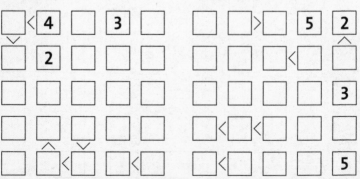

Futoshiki 3

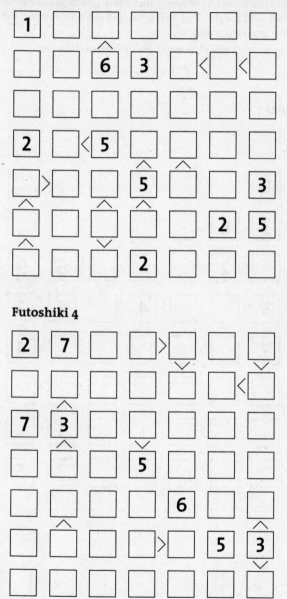

Futoshiki 4

Futoshiki 5

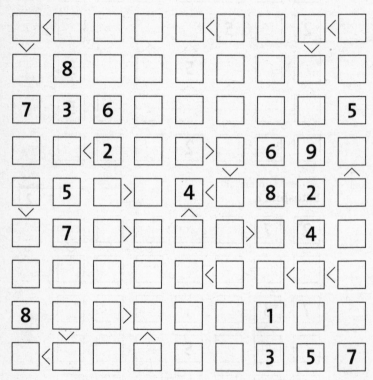

KAKURO

Kakuro are a form of numerical crossword which have almost emulated the popularity of sudoku. Like a standard letter-based crossword, each line of white squares is provided with an across and/or down clue, which you can see in the black areas. The aim of the puzzle is to enter numbers in the grid to satisfy a set of rules.

- Each cell must contain a digit from 1 to 9.
- The clues in the black areas signify the total of all of the digits in the adjacent horizontal or vertical line of white squares.
- No individual across or down answer can contain the same digit more than once.
- However, it is possible for a row or column to contain two identical digits if they are in separate clues.

To clarify this final point, take a look at the example below showing a completed puzzle. The middle column contains two 9's, which is allowed, but no individual clue contains a repeated digit.

In Japan, these numerical crosswords are more popular than sudoku. The name *kakuro* is an abbreviation of the Japanese *kasan kurosu*, meaning 'addition cross'.

Kakuro 1

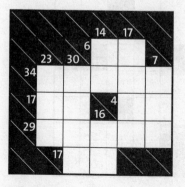

Kakuro 2

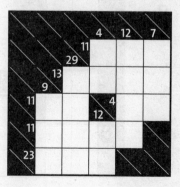

Kakuro 3

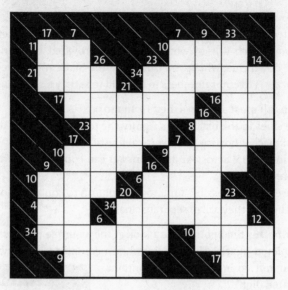

Kakuro 4

Tip The smallest and largest totals usually give you the most useful information. For example, if a line of five cells totals 34, it must contain 4, 6, 7, 8 and 9 in some order because that is the only way of making up 34 when no digit can be repeated. Even if the total were 33 or 32, you can still deduce most of the digits required.

Kakuro 5

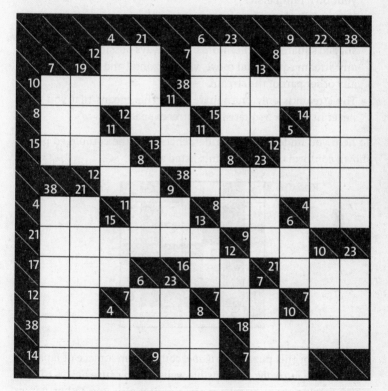

NURIKABE

Nurikabe are intriguing logic puzzles which involve a pictorial element. You have to shade in the correct cells according to a number of simple rules. Think of it as filling in a dark stream which flows around a number of white islands

- The given numbers tell you how large each island is, in squares. There is only one number on each island, and you cannot add your own numbers.
- No two islands can touch, except possibly at a corner point.
- There is only one stream, formed from continuous lines of shaded squares. In other words, it is always possible to travel from any stream square and move, via horizontal and vertical steps, to any other part of the stream.
- The stream is only one square wide. This means that you must never have a 2 × 2 square full of stream spaces.

To help you understand the rules, check that the completed puzzle shown conforms to all the points listed above:

The name for this puzzle, *nurikabe*, comes from a piece of Japanese folklore. The *nurikabe* are invisible walls which cause delays to travellers, forcing them to take more circuitous routes. Other names used for this puzzle include 'Cell Structure' and 'Islands in the Stream'.

Nurikabe 1

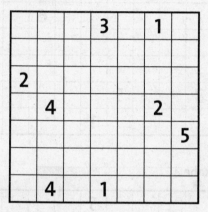

Nurikabe 2

Nurikabe 3

3			8					
	2							
		1				2		
						6		4
4								1
	3		5					
				1				6

Nurikabe 4

					5			
								1
			2					
				1		6		
		2						
5						4		7
				3				
							1	
4		2			4			

Nurikabe 5

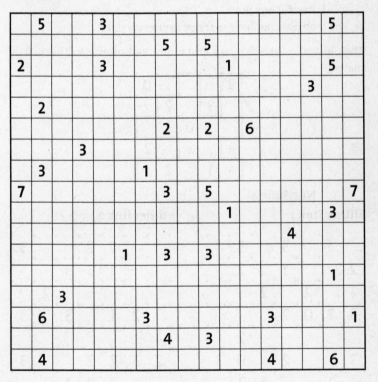

SLITHER LINK

With these puzzles you have to complete a circuit on the grid provided, drawing horizontal and vertical lines between pairs of dots so that one complete loop is formed.

- The number inside a square tells you exactly how many of its four sides (0, 1, 2 or 3) form part of the loop.
- The loop cannot have any dead ends, and must never cross or touch itself at any point.
- The loop does not have to travel over every dot.

The illustration shows how a grid might look after it has been completed:

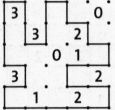

Slither link 1   **Slither link 2**

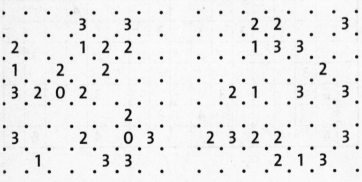

Tip It can be just as useful to identify spaces between dots where a line cannot be drawn. Try using a small cross to mark these locations.

Slither link 3

```
.  .  .  .  .  .  .  .  .  .  .  .
      1                 2  3  3
.  .  .  .  .  .  .  .  .  .  .  .
      1  3  2  2  2  2        1
.  .  .  .  .  .  .  .  .  .  .  .
   1     1  2                 2
.  .  .  .  .  .  .  .  .  .  .  .
            2  3  3        2  1
.  .  .  .  .  .  .  .  .  .  .  .
         1  2        2        3
.  .  .  .  .  .  .  .  .  .  .  .
         2  3        3  1  0
.  .  .  .  .  .  .  .  .  .  .  .
   2     1                 2  2
.  .  .  .  .  .  .  .  .  .  .  .
   2     2     1        2  2  2
.  .  .  .  .  .  .  .  .  .  .  .
         1  2  1  3  1  3
.  .  .  .  .  .  .  .  .  .  .  .
      3  2                       3
.  .  .  .  .  .  .  .  .  .  .  .
```

Slither link 4

```
.  .  .  .  .  .  .  .  .  .  .
   3        1  2        1     1
.  .  .  .  .  .  .  .  .  .  .
   2  2     2     2        2
.  .  .  .  .  .  .  .  .  .  .
   3  2  3        1  1     1
.  .  .  .  .  .  .  .  .  .  .
   1  2     2     1  2  2
.  .  .  .  .  .  .  .  .  .  .
   2           2  2     3
.  .  .  .  .  .  .  .  .  .  .
         3        3              2
.  .  .  .  .  .  .  .  .  .  .
      2  3        0  3     2
.  .  .  .  .  .  .  .  .  .  .
   2  1     1     2     2  1  2
.  .  .  .  .  .  .  .  .  .  .
      2              2
.  .  .  .  .  .  .  .  .  .  .
   3     2        3  3
.  .  .  .  .  .  .  .  .  .  .
```

Tip If you get stuck on a section of the loop, try somewhere else and see if you can join up the two sections later. In harder puzzles, you might have to build up short individual segments and gradually join them together.

Slither link 5

```
·  ·  ·  ·  ·  ·  ·  ·  ·  ·  ·  ·  ·  ·  ·  ·  ·
   2  1     2  3     2  3  3     2  2
·  ·  ·  ·  ·  ·  ·  ·  ·  ·  ·  ·  ·  ·  ·  ·  ·
      2     3                 3  1  2  1
·  ·  ·  ·  ·  ·  ·  ·  ·  ·  ·  ·  ·  ·  ·  ·  ·
   1           1     3
·  ·  ·  ·  ·  ·  ·  ·  ·  ·  ·  ·  ·  ·  ·  ·  ·
      2        3     3  1     1  1  2  2
·  ·  ·  ·  ·  ·  ·  ·  ·  ·  ·  ·  ·  ·  ·  ·  ·
   2  1     3           1                 1
·  ·  ·  ·  ·  ·  ·  ·  ·  ·  ·  ·  ·  ·  ·  ·  ·
2     3           3        2     0
·  ·  ·  ·  ·  ·  ·  ·  ·  ·  ·  ·  ·  ·  ·  ·  ·
      0              1     3  2  1
·  ·  ·  ·  ·  ·  ·  ·  ·  ·  ·  ·  ·  ·  ·  ·  ·
   2     3           3     0  3     2
·  ·  ·  ·  ·  ·  ·  ·  ·  ·  ·  ·  ·  ·  ·  ·  ·
   1  3     2  1  1     2        1
·  ·  ·  ·  ·  ·  ·  ·  ·  ·  ·  ·  ·  ·  ·  ·  ·
            2  2  1        2
·  ·  ·  ·  ·  ·  ·  ·  ·  ·  ·  ·  ·  ·  ·  ·  ·
   2  2  2     2        3           2
·  ·  ·  ·  ·  ·  ·  ·  ·  ·  ·  ·  ·  ·  ·  ·  ·
3        1  2  1  2        2
·  ·  ·  ·  ·  ·  ·  ·  ·  ·  ·  ·  ·  ·  ·  ·  ·
   3  2     2     3  2  2     0  1     2
·  ·  ·  ·  ·  ·  ·  ·  ·  ·  ·  ·  ·  ·  ·  ·  ·
2        2           3        3     3
·  ·  ·  ·  ·  ·  ·  ·  ·  ·  ·  ·  ·  ·  ·  ·  ·
      3     2           1        1  2
·  ·  ·  ·  ·  ·  ·  ·  ·  ·  ·  ·  ·  ·  ·  ·  ·
```

BRIDGES

You are presented with a diagram containing numbered circles representing islands which are, at the moment, unconnected. Your aim is to join them up with bridges.

- All bridges must run horizontally or vertically, starting on one island and ending on another.
- The number on each island tells you exactly how many bridges are to be attached to each island.
- Each pair of islands could be connected by 0, 1 or 2 bridges. In other words, at most an island could be connected by eight bridges, two in each direction.
- No bridge ever crosses another bridge.
- All the islands must be connected. When all the bridges have been built, it must be possible to travel from one island to any other island via the bridges. You can't have two separate sets of bridges.

Take a look at this example, which has already been completed:

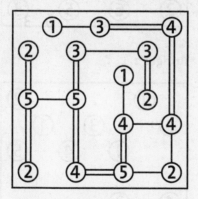

The Japanese name of this puzzle, *hashiwokakero*, literally means 'build bridges'. The first one was published in 1990.

Bridges 1

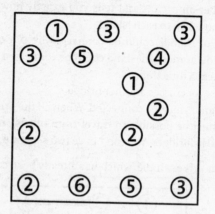

Bridges 2

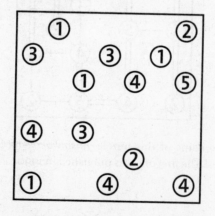

Bridges 3

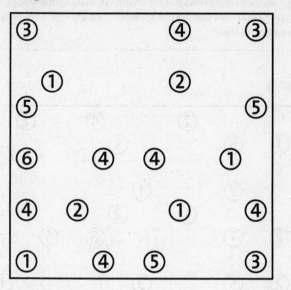

Bridges 4

Tip By the nature of odd and even numbers, islands containing 3, 5 and 7 must have at least one direction where a single bridge is connecting it to an adjacent island.

Bridges 5

NUMBER LINK

In this game, imagine you are an electrical engineer wiring up a circuit board. Can you make all the right connections without causing a short circuit?

- Each line must connect a different pair of matching numbers: 1 to 1, 2 to 2, 3 to 3, etc.
- All connecting lines must run horizontally or vertically through the middle of the grid squares. You can change direction at a square's centre if desired.
- All the connections are single lines, with no branches or dead ends.
- Each connection must start and end at its relevant number. It cannot extend at either end.
- No connection touches or crosses any other line.
- You will find that all the squares will be used.

The illustration shows a simple completed puzzle. Note that all the puzzles can be completed using basic logic; guesswork and advanced analysis shouldn't be necessary.

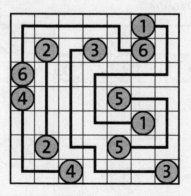

Tip Be wary of number pairs that lie close to each other. Although it is tempting to suppose that they must be connected by a short line, it may be the case that they are in fact joined by a line that takes a tortuous path around the grid.

Number link 1

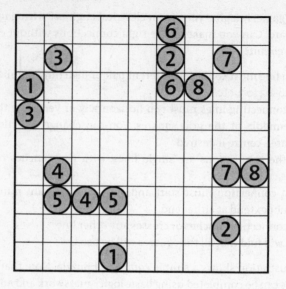

Number link 2

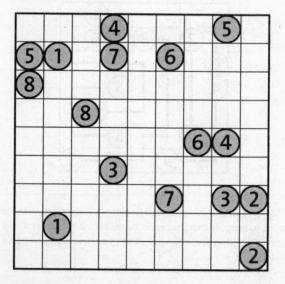

Number link 3

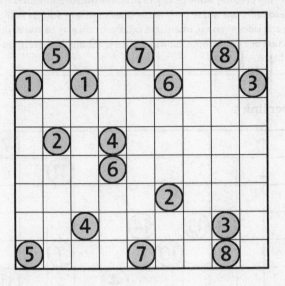

Number link 4

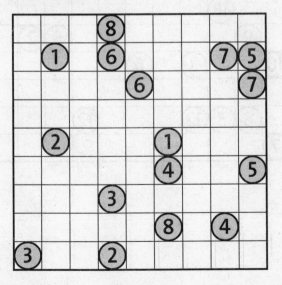

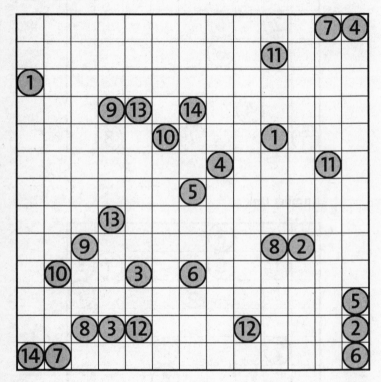

Tip You probably won't be able to guess the path of entire lines at once. Instead, work out where parts of the lines must go – such as at the corners and sides – and see where that takes you. You may be able to deduce a section of a line without knowing which of the numbered terminals it's leading to.

Number link 5

HITORI

The full Japanese title of this puzzle is *hitori ni shite kure*, literally meaning 'let me alone', an apposite name as you will see in a moment. In essence, it's like an overfull sudoku which you have to correct by removing repeated digits.

- Sufficient squares must be shaded in so that no row or column contains the same digit twice.
- Shaded squares cannot be next to each other, horizontally or vertically. However, they can touch at corners.
- When the puzzle is complete, all the white unshaded squares must remain connected. In other words, it must be possible to travel from one white square to any other white square via white squares, by horizontal or vertical moves only.

Take a look at this completed grid shown before you begin:

Tip If a number is next to a shaded square, it cannot itself be shaded. Therefore, all other instances of that number in its row and column must be shaded out.

Hitori 1

4	8	1	1	4	7	6	5
3	6	8	7	4	4	5	2
3	3	2	7	8	4	7	6
2	7	2	4	6	8	3	1
8	1	1	3	4	6	1	4
5	4	7	8	3	6	1	7
7	2	4	6	3	1	6	2
6	3	7	5	1	5	4	8

Hitori 2

7	2	5	3	4	2	2	1
1	7	6	5	3	5	4	5
6	4	2	8	6	6	5	5
4	1	5	6	2	4	5	3
8	2	7	1	7	2	6	5
3	8	1	7	5	4	2	6
7	3	7	2	8	5	1	4
2	5	3	2	6	1	7	5

Hitori 3

2	8	9	6	5	4	2	4	7
4	7	6	7	3	8	5	2	4
5	9	3	8	7	1	4	6	2
2	6	1	3	2	1	7	9	3
7	4	5	4	3	6	6	8	1
5	1	4	4	9	8	3	2	6
3	5	5	9	4	2	6	1	7
9	3	2	1	7	7	8	5	4
6	5	8	3	2	9	3	7	7

Hitori 4

6	5	3	9	8	3	1	7	2
1	1	8	1	6	9	7	2	1
7	2	9	6	4	8	5	4	3
1	6	6	1	3	3	7	4	9
4	1	7	8	9	9	8	5	5
3	8	6	3	2	4	9	5	1
2	5	5	3	1	7	1	9	6
9	7	3	2	2	1	4	8	6
5	5	1	5	7	6	2	5	8

Hitori 5

8	11	3	2	5	3	8	4	6	9	1	4
8	10	6	4	3	1	2	7	2	12	3	9
9	7	11	9	3	7	12	2	9	3	6	10
1	6	4	6	7	8	2	12	9	11	10	2
2	9	3	7	8	7	6	11	10	3	11	5
8	2	5	7	11	9	7	6	3	6	4	8
6	5	9	12	2	9	10	9	9	8	3	4
3	8	9	5	3	2	6	10	1	6	7	6
5	4	7	9	9	11	4	9	12	2	9	1
4	12	6	3	6	10	2	1	1	7	5	4
3	1	2	11	3	12	1	6	7	5	9	8
7	1	6	9	4	6	11	12	8	1	2	2

LIGHT UP

You'll find this Japanese puzzle very illuminating. How quickly can you spot the techniques used to light up the grid?

The aim is to place a number of lanterns – represented by circles – into the grid so that every square is illuminated by at least one lantern.

- A lantern on a square lights all the white squares above, below, to the left and to the right of it. The light does *not* travel diagonally.
- The black squares are solid walls which block the light.
- No lantern may shine light upon any other lantern.
- The numbers in the black squares indicate exactly how many lanterns are directly adjacent to that square, horizontally and/or vertically.
- Subject to all the above rules, you are allowed to place a lantern wherever you like.
- The puzzle is complete when every white square is horizontally or vertically in sight of a lantern, without a black square in between.

The illustration below should make these rules clear:

Light up 1

Light up 2

Light up 3

Light up 4

Light up 5

TENTS

Is it safe to camp next to trees? A tree provides shade for sure, but what if one blows over onto your tent? It matters not, because in this puzzle pitching next to a tree is what you have to do.

- The numbers on the outside of the grid indicate how many tents must be pitched in that row or column.
- A tent must be pitched directly next to a tree, horizontally or vertically. Each tent must have its own tree.
- You need plenty of room from your neighbours, so no two tents can be in adjacent squares – not even diagonally.
- Suffice to say, you can't camp *in* a tree.

Have a look at the sample puzzle. Notice how well spaced the tents are – this is most important to solving the puzzle.

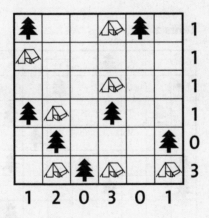

Tents 1

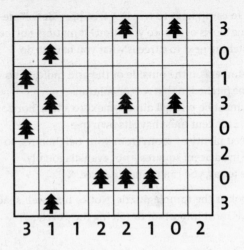

Tents 2

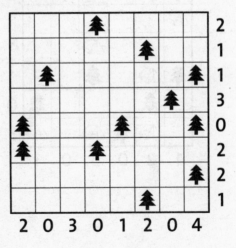

Tents 3

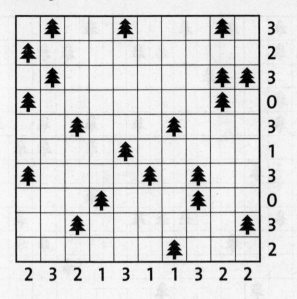

Tents 4

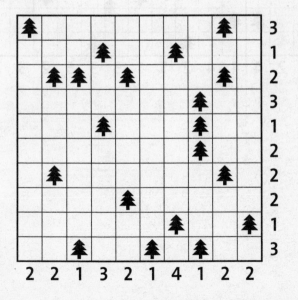

Tents 5

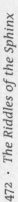

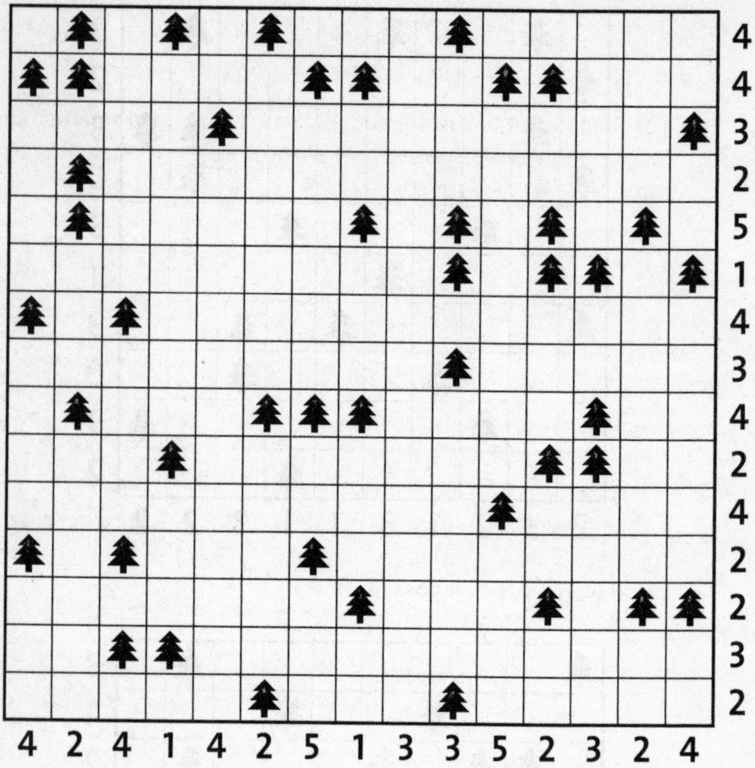
4
4
3
2
5
1
4
3
4
2
4
2
2
3
2
4 2 4 1 4 2 5 1 3 3 5 2 3 2 4

MASYU

As in the Slither Link puzzles earlier in this chapter, the aim in this game is to form a loop around the grid using horizontal and vertical lines only. However, the logic used here is very different.

- The loop must be drawn through the middle of grid squares, and be formed from horizontal and vertical lines only. The line can make a 90-degree turn at a square's middle.
- The loop can have no dead ends, and must never touch or cross itself.
- The loop has to pass through every circle, but not through every square.
- *Black circle rule*: Where the loop enters a black circle, the line must take a 90-degree turn in that square. Furthermore, a 90-degree turn cannot happen in the square immediately before or after a black circle.
- *White circle rule*: Where the loop enters a white circle, the line must keep going straight on. However, it must make a 90-degree turn in the square either immediately before the white circle, or immediately after, or possibly both.

The illustration shows how the two rules are applied. Note that the circles are not placed at every possible point. Instead, the minimum number of circles is given that allows you to deduce the unique path of the loop.

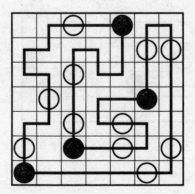

This puzzle was originally called by the Japanese *shiroshinju kuro-shinju* ('white pearls and black pearls'). However, one day the president of puzzle company Nikoli misread the end of the title as *masyu*, and the new, shorter name stuck.

Masyu 1

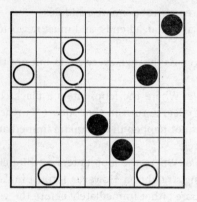

Masyu 2

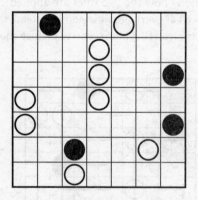

Masyu 3

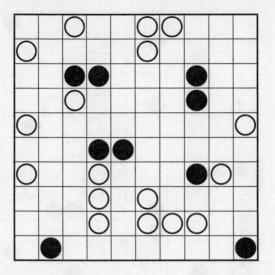

Masyu 4

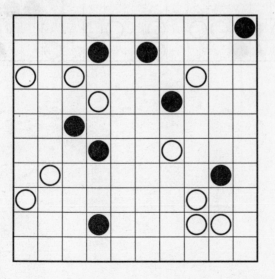

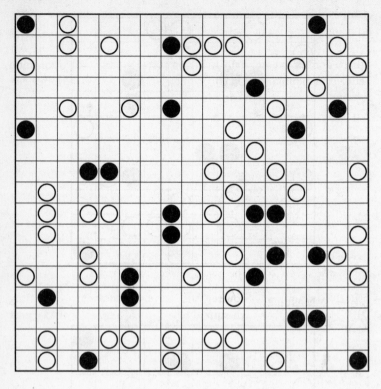

FILLOMINO

This is a straightforward number logic game. The name is an extension of the mathematical term 'polyomino', which describes a combination of squares that are joined at the sides – in the same way that a domino is essentially made up of two squares with a common edge. The popular 1980s computer game *Tetris* uses tetrominoes, shapes made from four conjoined squares.

- The aim is to complete the grid so that each square contains a whole number.
- Each square must belong to a group of squares of exactly that number. For example, a 1 will be an individual square, two 2's will form a domino, three 3's will form either a straight line or an L-shape of three squares, and so on.
- Regions of the same size cannot touch, except possibly at corners. For example, two dominoes cannot lie side by side but may touch at a point.
- All the squares must be used and accounted for.

The illustration shows how regions can vary in shape. The only thing that matters is that each square belongs to a region of the correct size.

1	2	3	3	5	5	5
4	2	3	6	6	6	5
4	4	2	3	6	6	5
4	1	2	3	6	2	2
5	5	5	3	2	1	4
5	2	2	4	2	4	4
5	1	4	4	4	1	4

Tip It may help to draw thicker lines between the squares to mark each region.

Fillomino 1

2		3			1	2
5		5		1		
5					4	6
2		2				
		2	1			
				5		1
3		1	5	5	4	

Fillomino 2

					5		
3			2	1	2		
	4		3				
3	1	6		3	6		
	3		2	4			
		3			1		
6					4		

Fillomino 3

3				1			1
		3				3	
			3	2			
3		2				3	3
	2		2		6		6
	3	3				1	3
			1	3			
	3					3	
3				1			3

Fillomino 4

						5		4
5		2	8			4		
8				1			1	
		5			8		4	
		1		5		1		
	8		8			4		
	2			1				4
		2			6	2		8
1		6						

Fillomino 5

1			8								5	
			2			3	4	5			1		1
			1							2	6		
6	8	4			2		3						
				4				4			7		
		3		2	4	1		4		4			
	2									2			
	4		3		2	1	6		2				
	3			3				4					
				8		4				5	2	3	
	3	8							1				
4		2		1	8	1			2				
	8								3			3	

DIVIDE BY SQUARES

We're softening you up for the big finish with one of the easier games in our collection of Japanese puzzles. This time you have to divide a field into a number of rectangles ... so the Japanese-English title of this game is not exactly accurate.

- Draw rectangles along the gridlines so that each rectangle contains the number of squares indicated by the number inside it.
- Each rectangle must contain exactly one number. You cannot add numbers of your own.
- Every square must be accounted for and belong to one of the numbered rectangles.

The illustration shows how a completed puzzle might look. Just for clarity, in mathematics squares count as rectangles, so if you see a number 4, 9 or 16 it is possible – but not guaranteed – that you need to enclose it with a 2 × 2, 3 × 3 or 4 × 4 square, respectively.

Divide by squares 1

Divide by squares 2

Divide by squares 3

				6			8	
4			6			8		
8					4		4	
				6				
			4					
	4		4					6
		6			4			6
	3		9					

Divide by squares 4

	6						6	
		4		4				
	3						6	
			2		3			
						3		4
4		8						
		8		6				
	3						6	
			6		8			
	4						6	

> **Tip** The numbers do not give you any information about the dimensions or orientation of the rectangle. For example, does '6' represent a 1 × 6 or a 2 × 3 rectangle, and should it lie horizontally or vertically?

Divide by squares 5

	6						9					10			4
	4			2					4						
													6	3	
		6		4	6		2								
								10	6		5				
8		3	8				8							5	4
4					6				4						
									4		4				
	6	4						4					3	2	
				6		2									
						4					6				4
3	3							6				3	4		8
				4		4	2								
								4			6	3		4	
	4	4													
						4					12			4	
3			6				8							4	

GOKIGEN NANAME

It's fair to say that this puzzle isn't seen as frequently as some of the others, and with a name like *gokigen naname*, is that surprising? Never mind, because it's still quite fun and differs enough from the previous puzzles to make it worthy of inclusion.

- Each square must have entered in it a diagonal line, either from top-right to bottom-left, or top-left to bottom-right.
- A number in a circle indicates how many diagonal lines must enter that circle.
- The diagonal lines never form a loop or a closed circuit anywhere in the diagram. (Note: the horizontal and vertical grid lines are to aid the eye only.)
- Unlike some of the previous puzzles in this chapter, it is *not* necessary for the diagonal lines to be all connected together in one network. It is quite acceptable to have separate webs of diagonals.

This illustration shows a completed puzzle:

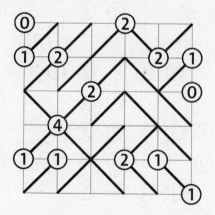

Tip   0's and 4's are the ones to go for first.

Gokigen naname 1

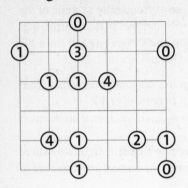

Gokigen naname 2

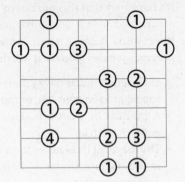

Gokigen naname 3

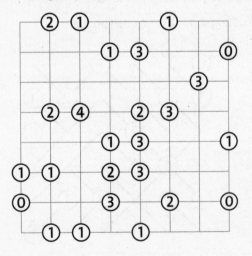

Gokigen naname 4

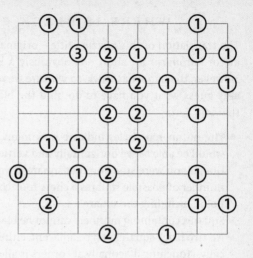

Gokigen naname 5

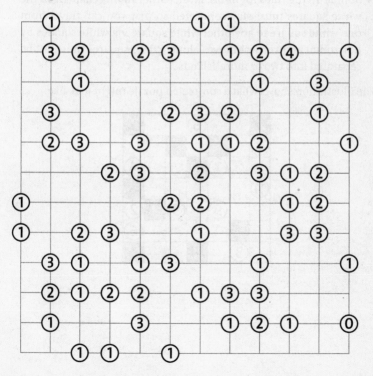

The translation of this puzzle's title – originally *kuromasu wa doko da,* or *kuromasu* for short – is obviously a little rough and ready. However, the name has stuck, so who are we to argue? You can probably guess what you have to do: find the black squares and shade them in.

- The numbered circles indicate how many different squares you would be able to see horizontally and vertically, without interruption, if you were stood on that square. If you prefer, it is the total number of possible squares a chess rook could move to from that point, including the square it is on.
- Squares containing numbers cannot be black.
- No two black squares can be adjacent, either horizontally or vertically. (Touching diagonally at corners is allowed.)
- Similar to the rules for *hitori*, given earlier in this chapter, all the white squares must stay connected so that you can travel from one white square to any other white square via white squares by horizontal and vertical moves alone. White squares must not be separated into two or more 'islands'.

The illustration shows what a completed puzzle might look like:

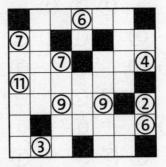

Where is black cells? 1

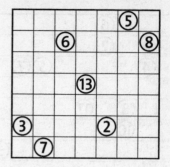

Where is black cells? 2

Where is black cells? 3

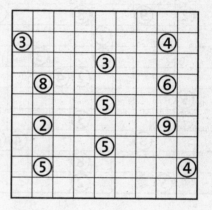

Where is black cells? 4

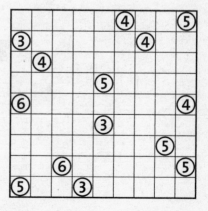

Where is black cells? 5

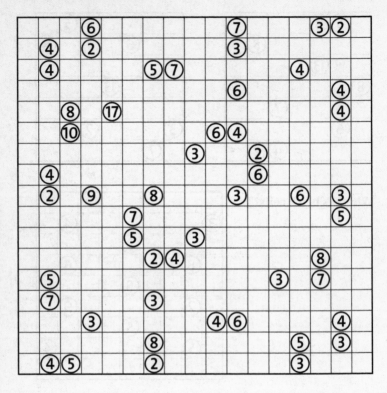

Solutions

CHAPTER 1
The Puzzle Kings

THE SQUAREST GAME ON THE BEACH

Mark off 25, 6 and 19 = 50.

....

PATCH QUILT PUZZLE

Loyd's original solution lists: Lena, Dinah, Edna, Minnie, Anna, Mary, Nancy, Jane, Carry, Jennie, Mae, Judy, Hannah and Eva, and the somewhat dated Jule, Maud and Nan. Jean, Jenny and Macy are also permissible.

....

PUZZLING SCALES

In the first instance we see that a top and three cubes weigh equal to twelve marbles. In the second equation, a top alone equals a cube and eight marbles. Now let us add three cubes to each side of the second scales, and as the addition of equal quantities to both sides of an equation does not change their relative values, we have the same equilibrium. By the addition of three cubes to the second pair of scales we have produced the identical values as shown by the first scales. In the first case a top and three cubes = twelve marbles; in the second illustration we have proved that a top and three cubes = four cubes and eight marbles; therefore, if four cubes and eight marbles weigh the same as twelve marbles, four cubes = four marbles, so a marble weighs just as much as a cube. It proves therefore that one cube and eight marbles, or nine marbles weighs equal to the top!

....

A PUZZLE IN OIL AND VINEGAR

That vinegar merchant sold the 13 and 15 gal. kegs of oil at 50 cents per gal. = $14. He also sold 8, 17 and 31 gals. of vinegar at 25 cents = $14. So he had the 19 gal. barrel left, which was worth $4.75, or $9.50, according to whether it contained vinegar or oil.

REAL ESTATE PUZZLE

There were eighteen lots, bought at $13.50 a lot, and sold at $18, making a profit of $81, which is the cost price of six lots.

MOTHER'S JAM PUZZLE

Like good Mother Hubbard we will solve the problem by inspection, and prove the quantities in the different jars. Knowing that each shelf contains just 20 quarts, let us begin by cancelling off six little jars from the two lower shelves. The result proves that two big jars equal four medium ones, or one large one equals two medium size. Replace the jars and cancel the two large ones from the middle shelf and equalize the top shelf by removing the large one and two of the medium size. This shows that the one medium sized jar must hold as much as three little ones.

Now multiply all the large jars by two and they are changed to mediums, and multiply the number then representing all the mediums by three to reduce them to the smallest size, and when we add them all together we find that the entire amount could be contained in 54 of the small size, 18 of the medium, or 9 of the largest. As a large jar would contain one-ninth of 60 quarts, we see that it would hold just six and two-third quarts.

THE GUIDO MOSAICS

The mosaic is cut into four pieces as shown. The two fragments on the left can form a 4 × 4 square, and the other two can form a 3 × 3 square.

Hence, 3 squared and 4 squared equal 5 squared:

THE GREAT COLUMBUS PROBLEM

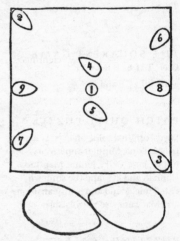

The secret of winning in a contest to see who can place the last egg upon a square napkin as described in the Columbus puzzle, turns upon placing the first egg exactly in the center of the napkin, as shown in the square diagram. Then, no matter where your opponent places an egg, duplicate his play on the opposite in a direct line through egg No. 1. The numbers given illustrate the beginning of the game, proceeding in regular order of play, viz.: 1, 2, 3, 4, 5, 6, 7, 8, 9, etc.

The placing of the first egg in the center would not win, if simply laid on the table, for, owing to the oval form of the egg, the second player might place an egg in close proximity to the conical end, as shown in the last illustration, which could not be duplicated.

The only way to win, therefore, as discovered by the great navigator, according to popular history, is to flatten one end of the first egg played so as to make it stand erect, so as to represent a circle.

A LIP-READING PUZZLE

Out of the thousands of persons who were interested in the scientific feature of that curious lip-reading puzzle the ease and unanimity with which they picked out little Matthew as the first boy on the top row encouraged them to tackle the next, and by a large majority Matthew, Alfred and Eastman were located on the top row, Richard, Theodore, Luke and Oom on the second row, with Hisswald, Shirmer, Fletcher, Arthur and Alden below.

THE NEW STAR

The diagram shows how the French astronomers would locate the new celestial find which proves to be of such heroic dimensions as to cast the other little stars quite in the shade. [The 'still more appropriate anagram' Loyd alludes to is probably MOONSTARERS.]

THE HOD CARRIER'S PROBLEM

The feat can be performed in nineteen steps, as follows: First go to step 1, then back to ground, and proceed by the steps 1, 2, 3, 2, 3, 4, 5, 4, 5, 6, 7, 6, 7, 8, 9, 8, 9. Every step has been used twice and the ground as well as the top has been reached twice.

The answer to the schoolboy's problem: if a brick weighs three-quarters of a brick and three-quarters of a pound, then 'three-quarters of a pound' describes the weight of one-quarter of the brick. Therefore, the entire brick weighs four times this amount = three pounds.

THE CANALS ON MARS

The solution is to literally trace out the message 'THERE IS NO POSSIBLE WAY'.

PUZZLING PRATTLE

In that puzzling prattle it is evident that the children were so befogged over the calendar that they had started to school with their books on Sunday morning! For it is plain that when the day after tomorrow is yesterday, to-day will be three days hence, just as when the day before yesterday was tomorrow carries us back three days from now, which must be Sunday, to be midway between the two 'to-days'.

PUZZLELAND GINGERBREAD

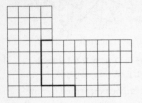

PUZZLE OF THE EDUCATED CATS

The words are: sparkling, sparking, sparing, spring, sprig, prig, pig, pi, I.

THE MOTOR CAR RACE

The first point is to appreciate the fact that, in a race round a circular track, there are the same number of cars behind one as there are before. All the others are both behind and before. There were thirteen cars in the race, including Gogglesmith's car. Then one-third of twelve added to three-quarters of twelve will give us thirteen – the correct answer.

A REMARKABLE PLANT

TOBACCO.

THE CHALKED NUMBERS

This little jest on the part of Major Trenchard is another trick puzzle, and the face of the roguish boy on the extreme right, with the figure 9 on his back, showed clearly that he was in the secret, whatever that secret might be. I have no doubt (bearing in mind the Major's hint as to the numbers being 'properly regarded') that his answer was that depicted in the illustration, where boy No. 9 stands on his head and so converts his number into 6. This makes the total 36 – an even number – and by making boys 3 and 4 change places with 7 and 8, we get 1 2 7 8 and 5 3 4 6, the figures of which, in each case, add up to 18. There are just three other ways in which the boys may be grouped:
1 3 6 8 – 2 4 5 7, 1 4 6 7 – 2 3 5 8, and 2 3 6 7 – 1 4 5 8.

THE THIRTY-THREE PEARLS

The value of the large central pearl must have been £3,000. The pearl at one end (from which they increased in value by £100) was £1,400; the pearl at the other end, £600.

AN EASY DISSECTION PUZZLE

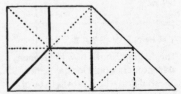

Divide the figure up into twelve equal triangles, and it is easy to discover the directions of the cuts, as indicated by the dark lines.

BICYCLE TOUR

Our puzzlists report that the only possible route by which all of the towns can be visited but once is to take them in the following sequence, according to the designated numbers: Philadelphia to 15, 22, 18, 14, 3, 8, 4, 10, 19, 16, 11, 5, 9, 2, 7, 13, 17, 21, 20, 6, 12 and then to Erie, which completes the trip after having visited the twenty-two towns.

MILITARY TACTICS

That lesson in military tactics, wherein a military division was to enter the park at one gate, go through the sixty-four squares and out at the other gate after passing under the triumphal arch in the center of the field, was sufficiently difficult to amuse and interest our young puzzlists, who found that there was but one way to perform the feat in fifteen moves, as shown, although there are a thousand and one routes which call for just one extra turn.

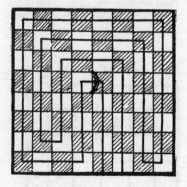

MILKMAN'S PUZZLE

Let us call one of the ten gallon cans A and the other B, and proceed as follows to show how the milkman supplied

his two customers with two quarts each:

Fill 5 qt. pail from can A
Pour 5 qt. pail into 4 qt. pail
Empty 4 qt. pail into can A
Pour 5 qt. pail into 4 qt. pail
Fill 5 qt. pail from can A
Fill 4 qt. pail from 5 qt. pail
Empty 4 qt. pail into can A
Fill 4 qt. pail from can B
Pour 4 qt. pail into can A

which fills can A, leaving 2 quarts in 4 qt. pail. Thus the milkman has supplied each of his customers with exactly two quarts of milk, and solved his perplexing problem.

THE PATROLMAN'S PUZZLE

Clancey's route is shown on the following diagram:

THE MOVING DAY PUZZLE

First move the whisky flask 1, scrubbing brush 2, flat-iron 3, whisky flask 4, pepper box 5, mouse trap 6, whisky flask 7, flat-iron 8, scrubbing brush 9, pepper box 10, flat-iron 11, whisky flask 12, mouse trap 13, flat-iron 14, pepper box 15, scrubbing brush 16, whisky flask – and the feat is accomplished.

BACK FROM THE KLONDIKE

That puzzling return trip from the Klondike proved to be no easy task for our young puzzlists, and but few succeed in getting out of the woods with their treasure. For the benefit of such as could not escape the endless whirlpool of numbers which held them in its vortex we will say that the only escape leads through the backward and forward sequence of S.W. to 4, S.W. to 6, N.E. to 6, N.E. to 2, N.E. to 5, S.W. to 4, S.W. to 4, S.W. to 4, and a bold strike via N.W. to liberty! Those who failed to master it readily discovered that one false step at any stage of the game throws one into the whirlpool from which there is no egress.

ALICE IN WONDERLAND

Many good mathematicians fell into the error of attempting to solve Alice's cryptogram of 'Was it a cat I saw,' upon the basis of there being twenty-four starting points and the same number of endings. They reasoned that the square of 24, viz: 576 different ways, would be the correct answer. They overlooked the branch routes which give exactly 252 ways of reaching the center, C, and as there are just as many ways of getting out to the Ws, the square of 252 gives the correct answer as 63,504 different ways.

OUTWITTING THE WEIGHING MACHINE

It can readily be shown that there could be just ten different combination couples weighed, and that their separate weights must have been 56, 58, 60, 64 and 65 pounds to produce weights as given of 129, 125, 124, 123, 122, 121, 120, 118, 116 and 114. The two lightest together must weigh 114, and as we find by comparison of the weights of the third weight with the lightest and the second, that the lightest is two pounds lighter, we know that she weighs 56 and the next 58, after which it is easy to tell the rest.

RIP VAN WINKLE PUZZLE

To retain the championship of Sleepy Hollow, Rip should now knock down pin No. 6, so as to divide the row into groups of 1, 3 and 7. Then, no matter what play the little fellow makes, he will surely be beaten if Rip continues to make the best plays. To have won the game at the start, the little man of the mountains should have knocked out pin No. 7 so as to divide the row into two groups of 6. Then, whatever Rip knocked out of one group he would duplicate on the other, and thus win by a sure rule.

A STUDY IN EGGS

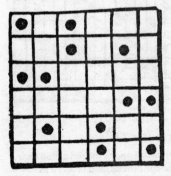

THE LAKE PUZZLE

In this remarkable problem we find that the lake contained exactly eleven acres, therefore the approximate answer of 'nearly eleven acres' is not sufficiently correct. This definite answer is worked out by the Pythagorean law, which proves that in any right-angle triangle the square of the longest side is equal to the sum of the squares of the other two sides.

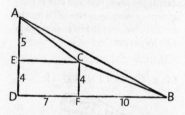

In the illustration ABD represents our triangle, AD being 9 units long and BD 17, because 9 × 9 equals 81, which added to 17 × 17 (289) equals the 370 acres of the largest field. AEC is a right-angle triangle, and the square of 5 (25) added to the square of 7 (49) shows that the square on AC equals 74. CBF is a right-angle triangle, which shows that the square of its sides 4 and 10 prove the square estate on BC to equal 116 acres. The area of our triangle ADB is clearly the half of 9 × 17, which equals 76.5 acres, and as the areas of the oblong and two triangles can plainly be seen to be 65.5, we deduct the same from 76.5 to prove that the lake contains exactly 11 acres.

BABY'S WEIGHT

Mr. Dobson, the baby, and the dog together weighed 180 lb. As Mr. Dobson and the baby weighed 162 lb. more than the dog, it is clear that the dog weighed 9 lb. And since 9 lb. is 70 per cent less than the weight of the baby, the infant must have weighed 30 lb. and Mr. Dobson 141 lb.

THE WAY TO BERLIN

The thick line in the illustration shows a route from London to Berlin in eighteen stages. It is absolutely necessary to include the stage marked 'North Sea' in order to perform the journey in an even number of stages.

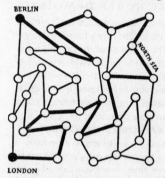

A BANK HOLIDAY PUZZLE

The simplest way is to write in the number of routes to all the towns in this manner. Put a 1 on all the towns in the top row and in the first column. Then the number of routes to any town will be the sum of the routes to the town immediately above and to the town immediately to the left. Thus the routes in the second row will be 1, 2, 3, 4, 5, 6, 7; in the third row 1, 3, 6, 10, 15, 21, 28; and so on with the other rows. It will then be seen that the only town to which there are exactly eighty-four different routes is the seventh town in the fourth row. This town was therefore the cyclist's destination.

MRS. HAMILTON'S HOLIDAY TOUR

There are just eight different routes (counting reverse routes as different), by any one of which Mrs. Hamilton would avoid both tunnels; but the route that also delays her visit to D as long as possible is as follows: HISTLKBCMNUQRGFPODEAH. This is therefore her best route.

THE NOBLE DEMOISELLE

'Some here have asked me,' continued Sir Hugh, 'how they may find the cell in the Dungeon of the Death's-head wherein the noble maiden was cast. Beshrew me! but 'tis easy withal when you do but know how to do it. In attempting to pass through every door once, and never more, you must take heed that every cell hath two doors or four, which be even numbers, except two cells, which have but three. Now, certes, you cannot go in and out of any place, passing through all the doors once and no more, if the number of doors be an odd number. But as there be but two such odd cells, yet may we, by beginning at the one and ending at the other, so make our journey in many ways with success. I pray you, albeit, to mark that only one of these odd cells lieth on the outside of the dungeon, so we must perforce start therefrom. My masters, the noble demoiselle must have been wasting in the other.'

The drawing will make this quite clear to the reader. The two 'odd cells' are indicated by the stars, and one of the many routes that will solve the puzzle is shown by the dotted line. It is perfectly certain that you must start at the lower star and end at the upper one; therefore the cell with the star situated over the left eye must be the one sought.

THE ENGLISH TOUR

It was required to show how a resident at the town market A might visit every one of the towns once, and only once, and finish up his tour at Z. This puzzle conceals a little trick. After the solver has demonstrated to his satisfaction that it cannot be done in accordance with the conditions as he at first understood them, he should carefully examine the wording in order to find some flaw. It was said,

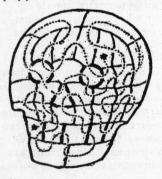

'This would be easy enough if he were able to cut across country by road, as well as by rail, but he is not.'

Now, although he is prohibited from cutting across country by road, nothing is said about his going by sea! If, therefore, we carefully look again at the map, we shall find that two towns, and two only, lie on the sea coast. When he reaches one of these towns he takes his departure on board a coasting vessel and sails to the other port. The annexed illustration shows, by a dark line, the complete route.

NELSON'S COLUMN

A   B

If you take a sheet of paper and mark it with a diagonal line, as in Figure A, you will find that when you roll it into cylindrical form, with the line outside, it will appear as in Figure B. It will be seen that the spiral (in one complete turn) is merely the hypotenuse of a right-angled triangle, of which the length and width of the paper are the other two sides.

In the puzzle given, the lengths of the two sides of the triangle are 40 ft. (one-fifth of 200 ft.) and 16 ft. 8 in. Therefore the hypotenuse is 43 ft. 4 in. The length of the garland is therefore five times as long – 216 ft. 8 in. A curious feature of the puzzle is the fact that with the dimensions given the result is exactly the sum of the height and the circumference.

THE NUMBER-CHECKS PUZZLE

Divide the ten checks into the following three groups: 7 1 5 – 4 6 – 3 2 8 9 0, and the first multiplied by the second produces the third.

THE MILLER'S PUZZLE

The way to arrange the sacks of flour is as follows: 2, 78, 156, 39, 4. Here each pair when multiplied by its single neighbour makes the number in the middle, and only five of the sacks need be moved. There are just three other ways in which they might have been arranged (4, 39, 156, 78, 2; or 3, 58, 174, 29, 6; or 6, 29, 174, 58, 3), but they all require the moving of seven sacks.

THE RIDDLE OF THE TILED HEARTH

No tile is in line (either horizontally, vertically, or diagonally) with another tile of the same design, and only three plain tiles are used. If after placing the four Lions you fall into the error of placing four other tiles of another pattern, instead of only three, you will be left with four places that must be occupied by plain tiles. The secret consists in placing four of one kind and only three of each of the others.

....

THE SPIDER AND THE FLY

Though this problem was much discussed in the *Daily Mail* from 18th January to 7th February 1905, when it appeared to create great public interest, it was actually first propounded by me [Dudeney] in the *Weekly Dispatch* of 14th June 1903.

Imagine the room to be a cardboard box. Then the box may be cut in various different ways, so that the cardboard may be laid flat on the table. I show four of these ways, and indicate in every case the relative positions of the spider and the fly,

and the straightened course which the spider must take without going off the cardboard.

These are the four most favourable cases, and it will be found that the shortest route is in No. 4, for it is only 40 feet in length (add the square of 32 to the square of 24 and extract the square root). It will be seen that the spider actually passes along five of the six sides of the room! Having marked the route, fold the box up (removing the side the spider does not use), and the appearance of the shortest course is rather surprising. If the spider had taken what most persons will consider obviously the shortest route (that shown in No. 1), he would have gone 42 feet! Route No. 2 is 43.174 feet in length, and Route No. 3 is 40.718 feet.

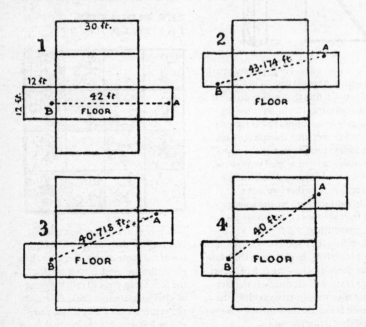

THE TWICKENHAM PUZZLE

Play the counters in the following order: K C E K W T C E H M K W T A N C E H M I K C E H M T, and there you are, at Twickenham. The position itself will always determine whether you are to make a leap or a simple move.

THE MOUSE-TRAP PUZZLE

If we interchange cards 6 and 13 and begin our count at 14, we may take up all the twenty-one cards – that is, make twenty-one 'catches' – in the following order: 6, 8, 13, 2, 10, 1, 11, 4, 14, 3, 5, 7, 21, 12, 15, 20, 9, 16, 18, 17, 19. We may also exchange 10 and 14 and start at 16, or exchange 6 and 8 and start at 19.

THE SIXTEEN SHEEP

The six diagrams show solutions for the cases where we replace 2, 3, 4, 5, 6, and 7 hurdles. The dark lines indicate the hurdles that have been replaced. There are, of course, other ways of making the removals.

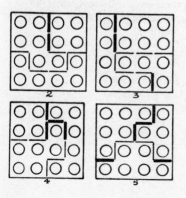

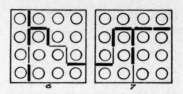

THE ROOK'S TOUR

The only possible minimum solutions are shown in the two diagrams, where it will be seen that only sixteen moves are required to perform the feat. Most people find it difficult to reduce the number of moves below seventeen.

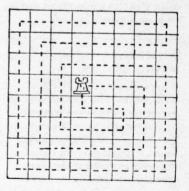

THE ROOK'S JOURNEY

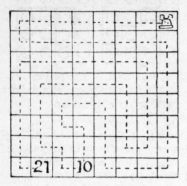

I show the route in the diagram. It will be seen that the tenth move lands us at the square marked 10 and that the last move, the twenty-first, brings us to a halt on square 21.

ANCIENT CHINESE PUZZLE

Play as follows:

Move 1: White's right-hand rook moves one square right (Black must move his king one square right).

Move 2: White's king moves up-left diagonally (Black moves his king one square down).

Move 3: White's left-hand rook moves two squares right (checkmate).

DOMINOES IN PROGRESSION

There are twenty-three different ways. You may start with any domino, except the 4–4 and those that bear a 5 or 6, though only certain initial dominoes may be played either way round. If you are given the common difference and the first domino is played, you have no option as to the other dominoes. Therefore all I need do is to give the initial domino for all the twenty-three ways, and state the common difference. This I will do as follows:

With a common difference of 1, the first play may be any of these: 0–0, 0–1, 1–0, 0–2, 1–1, 2–0, 0–3, 1–2, 2–1, 3–0, 0–4, 1–3, 2–2, 3–1, 1–4, 2–3, 3–2, 2–4, 3–3, 3–4. With a difference of 2, the first domino may be 0–0, 0–2, or 0–1. Take the last case of all as an example. Having played the 0–1, and the difference being 2, we are compelled to continue with 1–2, 2–3, 3–4, 4–5, 5–6. There are three dominoes that can never be used at all. These are 0–5, 0–6, and 1–6.

A CHAIN PUZZLE

To open and rejoin a link costs three-pence. Therefore to join the nine pieces into an endless chain would cost 2s. 3d., whereas a new chain would cost 2s. 2d. But if we break up the piece of eight links, these eight will join together the remaining eight pieces at a cost of 2s. But there is a subtle way of even improving on this. Break up the two pieces containing three and four links respectively, and these seven will join together the remaining seven pieces at a cost of only 1s. 9d.

CHAPTER 2
The World of Words

FORE WORDS

1. GOLF, FLOG.
2. V, which rhymes with all the others. Z would also be acceptable if you pronounce it as an American 'zee' rather than the British 'zed'.
3. (a) Apricot
   (b) Peach
   (c) Melon
   (d) Date
   (e) Banana
   (f) Fig
4. POTATO (children's nursery rhyme).
5. SYNONYMOUS.
6. 'Reports of my death have been greatly exaggerated' (Mark Twain, after a newspaper had incorrectly published a story that he had died).
7. They are all types of book.
8. 'Run out of luck'.
9. QUEUE; AITCH.
10. SPROCKET (the other words are SOCKET, POCKET and ROCKET).
11. CHEIROMANCY, the art of palm reading. Take the top letter off the pile each time.
12. Taking one of the silent letters from each word spells out TAXIDERMY: HAU(T)BOY, (A)ISLE, TABLEAU(X), BUS(I)NESS, HAN(D)SOME, TWITCH(E)D, FO(R)ECASTLE, (M)NEMONIC, PRA(Y)ER.
13. NOON.
14. The past tenses rhyme: BOUGHT, BROUGHT, CAUGHT, FOUGHT, SOUGHT, TAUGHT, THOUGHT, WROUGHT.
15. ORANGE.
16. Monday becomes Dynamo.
17. Peter Piper picked a peck of pickled peppers.
18. NORTH, EAST, SOUTH, WEST.
19. The Nato phonetic alphabet: Alpha, Bravo, Charlie, Delta, Echo, Foxtrot, Golf, Hotel, India, Juliet, Kilo, Lima, Mike, November, Oscar, Papa, Quebec, Romeo, Sierra, Tango, Uniform, Victor, Whisky, X-ray, Yankee and Zulu.
20. Eileen.

DOUBLE CROSSING

1.	PET	CARESS
2.	GROOVE	RUT
3.	SHED	BARN
4.	LIE	RECLINE
5.	SAVE	SALVAGE
6.	WHIRLED	SPUN
7.	SOUR	TART
8.	FAT	PLUMP
9.	CUT	CARVE
10.	SLOPES	HILLS

RHYME AND REASON

1. Too few
2. Big pig
3. Posh nosh
4. Seal deal
5. Prime time
6. Eve's leaves
7. Stuck truck
8. Heart chart
9. Spare chair
10. Bread spread
11. Ceased beast
12. Bears' chairs
13. Narrow arrow
14. Moral quarrel
15. Redeem esteem

16. Summit plummet
17. Smitten kitten
18. Racquet jacket
19. Frighten Titan
20. Cheddar shredder
21. College knowledge
22. Dwelling selling
23. Gruesome twosome
24. Stricken chicken
25. Fleeting meeting
26. Listeria hysteria
27. Teacher's features
28. Stitches britches
29. Fleeting greeting
30. Twilight highlight
31. Matrimony acrimony
32. Defective directive
33. President's residence
34. Launch launch

SYNONYM CROSSWORDS

Synonyms 1
ACROSS: Fraud, Sting, Con, Flimflam.
DOWN: Dodge, Trick, Swindle, Fiddle, Scam.

Synonyms 2
ACROSS: Wary, Quiet, Afraid, Coy, Retiring.
DOWN: Reserved, Reticent, Shy, Timid.

Synonyms 3
ACROSS: Shade, Indicator, Tone.
DOWN: Pigment, Wash, Dye, Paint, Stain.

Synonyms 4
ACROSS: Bullock, Livestock, Oxen, Steer.
DOWN: Calf, Bovine, Taurus, Cattle.

Synonyms 5
ACROSS: Crook, Malefactor, Robber.
DOWN: Criminal, Outlaw, Felon, Thief.

SEARCH ME

Search 1

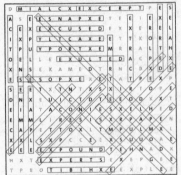

Search 2

Search 3

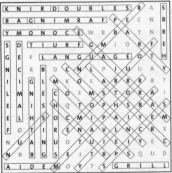

The unscrambled words are:

ABILITY	DOUBLES	LANGUAGE
BAG	DRINK	MARRIAGE
BATHING	ECONOMY	MEDIA
BLESSING	FARMING	METAPHOR
BUNCH	FEELINGS	METAPHOR
CHORUS	FOURSOME	NUMBER
COMPANY	FRUIT	NUTS
CRYSTAL	GRILL	PARTY
DECIMAL	HERBS	SPICES

MILK OF MAGNESIA	$Mg(OH)_2$
POTASH	K_2CO_3
PROPANE	C_3H_8
QUARTZ	SiO_2
QUICKSILVER	Hg
RUST	Fe_2O_3
SODA WATER	H_2CO_3
SUGAR	$C_{12}H_{22}O_{11}$
TABLE SALT	$NaCl$
TALC	$Mg_3(Si_4O_{10})(OH)_2$
VINEGAR	CH_3COOH
VITAMIN C	$C_6H_8O_6$

Search 4

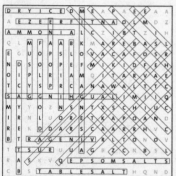

ALCOHOL	C_2H_5OH
AMMONIA	NH_3
ANTIFREEZE	CH_2OHCH_2OH
ASPIRIN	$C_9H_8O_4$
BAKING SODA	$NaHCO_3$
BATTERY ACID	H_2SO_4
BLEACH	$NaClO$
BORAX	$Na_2B_4O_7.10H_2O$
BRIMSTONE	S
CAFFEINE	$C_8H_{10}N_4O_2$
CITRIC ACID	$C_6H_8O_7$
DRY ICE	CO_2
EPSOM SALTS	$MgSO_4.7H_2O$
FOOL'S GOLD	FeS_2
GRAPHITE	C
GYPSUM	$CaSO_4$
LAUGHING GAS	N_2O
LIME	CaO
MARBLE	$CaCO_3$

Search 5

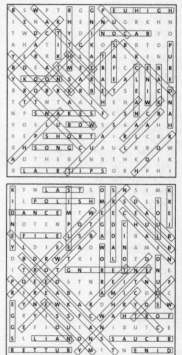

The pairs are:
ALPHA and OMEGA
ASSAULT and BATTERY
BACK and FORTH

BACON and EGGS
BALL and CHAIN
BED and BREAKFAST
BLACK and WHITE
BODY and MIND
BOW and ARROW
BREAD and BUTTER
BREAKING and ENTERING
CAT and MOUSE
CLEAN and JERK
COUNTRY and WESTERN
CUP and SAUCER
FIRST and LAST
GIN and TONIC
HAND and FOOT
HEART and SOUL
HERE and NOW
HIGH and LOW
HOOK and EYE
HUE and CRY
KIT and CABOODLE
NOOK and CRANNY
PURE and SIMPLE
RACK and PINION
RANK and FILE
RHYTHM and BLUES
SAFE and SOUND
SHORT and SWEET
SNAKES and LADDERS
SONG and DANCE
SPIT and POLISH
STEAK and KIDNEY
TOOTH and NAIL
TRIAL and ERROR
WATTLE and DAUB
WEAR and TEAR
WINE and DINE

Search 6

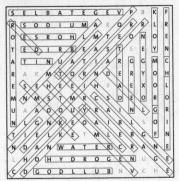

Clue	Words to find
BRINE	WATER and SALT
BROWN	RED and GREEN
BUBBLE AND SQUEAK	CABBAGE and POTATOES
CEMENT	CHALK and CLAY
COMMON SALT	SODIUM and CHLORINE
DRY MARTINI	GIN and VERMOUTH
HEN'S EGG	YOLK and ALBUMEN
FRACTION	DENOMINATOR and NUMERATOR
FRANGLAIS	FRENCH and ENGLISH
MARRIAGE	BRIDE and GROOM
MULE	HORSE and DONKEY
PEWTER	TIN and LEAD
PIT BULL	BULLDOG and TERRIER
RAGOUT	MEAT and VEGETABLES
SMOG	SMOKE and FOG
STAIR	RISER and TREAD
WATER	OXYGEN and HYDROGEN

The unused letters spell BREAKFAST and LUNCH, which can be combined as BRUNCH.

BEFORE AND AFTER

1. ALIMENTAL
2. METRONOME
3. RECAPTURE
4. ICELANDIC
5. HEARTACHE

ARS MAGNA

1. The eyes
2. Pittance
3. Families
4. Postponed
5. Masculine
6. Punishment
7. Mince pies
8. Dormitory
9. Execution
10. Athletics
11. Steaminess
12. Remuneration
13. Catalogues
14. Endearments
15. Norwegians
16. The Mona Lisa
17. Sean Connery
18. Suggestion
19. Adolf Hitler
20. Decimal point
21. Destination
22. Conversation
23. Upholsterers
24. Hermaphrodite
25. Statue of Liberty
26. Slot machines
27. The countryside
28. Softheartedness
29. Tower of London
30. Fame and fortune
31. Garage mechanics
32. Surgical instruments
33. The Leaning Tower of Pisa
34. *Ivanhoe* by Sir Walter Scott
35. The international Morse code
36. The assassination of President Abraham Lincoln

JIG SQUARE

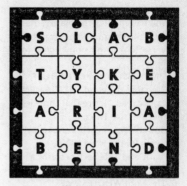

LOST IN TRANSLATION

1. He who laughs last, laughs longest.
2. Work expands to fill the time available (Parkinson's law).
3. Once bitten, twice shy.
4. Fools rush in where angels fear to tread.
5. One small step for man, one giant leap for mankind (Neil Armstrong's first words as he stepped onto the Moon).
6. One swallow doesn't make a summer.
7. Spare the rod and spoil the child.
8. A picture is worth a thousand words.
9. I have nothing to declare except my genius (Oscar Wilde).
10. Faint heart never won fair lady.
11. Should auld acquaintance be forgot, And never brought to mind? (Robert Burns, 'Auld Lang Syne').
12. Necessity is the mother of invention.
13. Marry in haste, repent at leisure.
14. Out of sight, out of mind.

HALFWAY HOUSE

1. DENIM, MINED.
2. You had to fill in the blanks, literally: blank cheque, blank page, blank verse, look blank, point blank, total blank.
3. UNDERSTUDY, or OVERSTUFF.
4. T, so that the word ENTITLEMENT can be read. Notice that three letters are used twice.
5. Both halves of each word are synonyms for the word itself – e.g. 'bath' and 'tub' both describe a bathtub.
6. The word WHOLESOME.
7. 9th – taking the 4th letter of March, the 1st letter of April, etc. spells CALENDAR.
8. HIS GREAT AUNT (anagram of TRISTAN HAGUE, in the same way that KATHERINE EDGE is an anagram of HER TEENAGE KID).
9. It doesn't contain an 'e' – nor are there any in the remaining 50,000 words of this 1939 book.
10. Add 'ten' each time: written, batten, often, hearten, kitten, christen, flatten, mitten, rotten, bitten, forgotten. This forms the number '10'.
11. The sign read 'YREKA BAKERY' – a palindrome.
12. PRINCES.
13. (Seventh) HEAVEN is probably the best known example. The other terms are whole number, half board, third world, quarter day, fifth columnist and sixth sense.
14. (a) Cut your coat/clothes according to your cloth.
    (b) Empty vessels make most sound.
    (c) A fool and his money are soon parted.
    (d) Fine feathers make fine birds.
15. BYSTANDER.
16. STRENGTHS.
17. ONE BILLION, which contains ten letters and ten digits (1,000,000,000).
18. BOOKKEEPER.
19. They all alternate vowel–consonant–vowel–consonant or consonant–vowel–consonant–vowel.
20. The word TON.

DITLOIDS

1 Flew Over the Cuckoo's Nest
1 Foot in the Grave
2 Humps on a Bactrian Camel
2 Strokes Under Par is an Eagle
3 Blind Mice, See How They Run!
3 Coins in a Fountain
3 Strikes and You're Out
3 Segments on the Body of an Insect
4 Presidents Carved on Mt Rushmore
4 Years Between Olympic Games
5 Fluid Ounces in a Gill
5 Words in the Answer
6 Players in an Ice Hockey Team
6 Points on the Star of David
7 Wonders of the Ancient World
7 Years of Bad Luck for Breaking a Mirror
8 Minutes for Sunlight to Reach Earth
8 Pints of Blood in an Average Adult
9 Cat's Lives
9 Months to Have a Baby
10 Pins in a Strike in Bowling
11 Players in a Cricket Team
12 Labours of Hercules
13 Stripes on the American Flag
14 Lines in a Sonnet
15 Minutes of Fame per Person, According to Andy Warhol
16 Tons and What Do You Get?
17 Syllables in a Haiku
18 Holes on a Golf Course

19 Gun Salute for the Vice President of the United States
20 Years Slept by Rip Van Winkle
21 Key of the Door
22 Yards in a Cricket Pitch
23 Pairs of Chromosomes in a Human Cell
24 Carats in Solid Gold
25 Years of Marriage for a Silver Anniversary
26 Letters of the Alphabet
27 Books in the New Testament
28 Dominoes in a Set
29 Days in February in a Leap Year
30 Days Hath September, April, June and November
32 Degrees Fahrenheit at which Water Freezes
36 Black Keys on a Piano
46 Chromosomes in a Human Cell
50 Ways to Leave Your Lover, According to Paul Simon
54 Cards in a Pack with the Jokers
57 Heinz Varieties
60 Degrees in Each Angle of an Equilateral Triangle
66 Books in the King James Bible
76 Trombones Led the Big Parade
78 Cards in a Tarot Pack
88 Constellations in the Sky
94 Length of a Basketball Court in Feet
99 Bottles of Beer on the Wall
116 Years in the Hundred Years War
147 Maximum Break in Snooker
200 Pounds for Passing Go in Monopoly
206 Bones in the Human Body
212 Degrees Fahrenheit at which Water Boils
221 B Baker Street Address of Sherlock Holmes
235 Isotope of Uranium in the Atomic Bomb
451 Degrees Fahrenheit at which Books Burn

500 Sheets in a Ream
666 Number of the Beast in the Book of Revelation
969 Years Lived by Methuselah
1000 Words that a Picture is Worth
1296 Square Inches in a Square Yard
1600 Pennsylvania Avenue, Address of the White House
2001 A Space Odyssey
10000 Duke of York's Men
20000 Leagues Under the Sea
86400 Seconds in a Day

....

WORD TARGET

AFRESH	HORSE
AHEM	HORUS
ASHER	HOSE
ASHORE	HOUR
FARMHOUSE	HOURS
FRESH	HOUSE
HAMS	HOUSER
HARE	HUES
HAREM	HUMS
HAREMS	MARSH
HARES	MASH
HARM	MASHER
HARMS	MESH
HEAR	MUSH
HEARS	MUSHER
HEMS	OHMS
HERA	RASH
HERO	RHEA
HERS	RHEAS
HOAR	RHEUM
HOARSE	RUSH
HOER	SHAM
HOERS	SHAME
HOES	SHARE
HOME	SHEAF
HOMER	SHEAR
HOMERS	SHOE
HOMES	SHORE
HORS	USHER

507 · · Solutions for page 96

WORD TRACKER

Word tracker 1
CONSIDERABLY

Word tracker 2
UNFORGIVEABLE

Word tracker 3
HOUSEWARMING

Word tracker 4
AMBIDEXTROUS

Word tracker 5
LEXICOGRAPHY

Word tracker 6
METALWORKING

Word tracker 7
SUBNORMALITY

Word tracker 8
STENOGRAPHIC

CRYPTANALYSIS

1. Ice cube
2. Swiss roll
3. Invest ('in vest')
4. Deck hand
5. Get set
6. Fig leaf
7. Medicine man
8. News (N, E, W, S are the main compass points)
9. Beer belly
10. Are ('are' is the modern form of 'art', as in 'thou art')
11. Element (He = helium, I = iodine)
12. Seascape (rollers are waves)
13. Foster parents
14. Post mortem
15. Space bar
16. Electricity bill
17. Last of the Mohicans (name of a novel; a 'last' is a holding device used to fashion or repair shoes)
18. Scrambled eggs
19. Double agent (twice 007)
20. Stow (S to W)
21. Water (H to O = H_2O)
22. Circular letter
23. Manx cat (cat without a tail)
24. I haven't got a clue

STAIRCASES

Staircase 1

A							
A	S						
S	A	T					
O	A	T	S				
C	O	A	S	T			
C	O	S	T	A	L		
S	T	O	I	C	A	L	
V	O	C	A	L	I	S	T

Staircase 2

O							
T	O						
R	O	T					
T	O	R	E				
O	U	T	E	R			
R	O	U	T	E	D		
D	E	T	O	U	R	S	
O	U	T	S	I	D	E	R
S	U	B	E	D	I	T	O	R

Staircase 3

A								
A	T							
A	T	E						
T	E	A	L					
L	A	T	E	R				
R	E	T	A	I	L			
R	E	C	I	T	A	L		
A	R	T	I	C	L	E	D	
C	U	R	T	A	I	L	E	D
L	U	B	R	I	C	A	T	E	D

Staircase 4

Staircase 5

....

ACROSTICS AND ASSOCIATES

1. THOMAS EDISON:

```
T o r E
H e a D
O m n I
M a s S
A n n O
S h u N
```

2. Radio
3. Koala
4. Problem
5. Planet
6. Ought
7. Conundrum (Co.-nun-drum)
8. Washington

3 × 3 TRACEWORDS

Traceword 1

ALE	SAVE
ALERT	SAVER
ALES	SEA
ARE	SEAL
ART	SEAR
AVER	SENT
AVERT	SET
EAR	SIN
EARN	SINE
EARNS	SINTER
ERA	SLAVE
ERAS	SLAVER
INERT	TEA
INSERT	TEAL
INSET	TEALS
INTER	TEAR
INTERVAL	TEAS
INTERVALS	TEN
ISLE	TENS
ISLET	TERN
LASER	TERNS
LEA	TESLA
LEAR	TRAVEL
LEARN	TRAVELS
LEARNS	VALE
LEARNT	VALES
LEAS	VALET
LENS	VASE
LENT	VEAL
LET	VEIN
NEAR	VEINS
NET	VENT
RASE	VENTRAL
RAVE	VET
RAVEN	
RAVENS	**Traceword 2**
RAVES	AIM
REAL	AMINO
REIN	AMP
REINS	AMPS
RENT	CAM
RESIN	CAMP
SALE	CAMPION
	CAMPIONS

CAMPS
CAP
CAPS
CHAIN
CHAINS
CHAMP
CHAMPION
CHAMPIONS
CHAMPS
CHAP
CHAPS
CHI
CHIMP
CHIMPS
CHIN
CHINS
CHIP
CHIPS
COIN
COINS
CON
CONS
HAM
HIC
HIM
HIP
HIPS
HIS
ICON
ICONS
IMP
IMPS
INCH
ION
IONS
MAC
MACHO
MAIN
MAINS
MAP
MAPS
MIC
MICA
NIM
NIP
NIPS

PAIN
PAINS
PICA
PIN
PINCH
PINS
PION
PIONS
SIC
SIN
SIP
SNIP
SPA
SPAM
SPIC
SPIN

Traceword 3
ADO
ADORN
AND
ANT
ANY
ARM
ARMY
ART
ARTY
DAN
DARN
DART
DORA
DORM
DORMY
DORY
DRY
LYRA
MOD
MORAN
MORDANT
MORN
MYNA
MYRA
NARD
NARY
RAD
RAN

RAND
RANDOM
RANDOMLY
RANT
ROD
TROD
TRY
TYRO

Traceword 4
APT
ART
ARTS
ATE
EAR
EAST
EAT
EATS
OAR
OAT
OATS
ORATE
ORATES
PAR
PAROQUETS
PARQUET
PARQUETS
PART
PARTS
PAST
PASTE
PAT
PATE
PATES
PATS
PRAT

PRATE
PRATES
PRATS
PRO
QUART
QUARTS
QUEST
RAP
RAPT
RASE
RAT
RATE
RATES
RATS
ROAST
SAP
SAT
SATE
SEA
SEAR
SEAT
SET
STAR
STRAP
TAO
TAP
TAR
TARO
TARP
TAU
TEA
TEAR
TEAS
TRAP
TSAR

4 × 4 TRACEWORDS

Traceword 5

ACNE	ALEX	MOILER	RELAX
ACTS	ALIT	MOIRE	RELIT
ANEW	AXEL	MORE	REMIT
BANE	AXLE	MOREL	RIEL
BANK	BRIE	MORT	RILE
CANE	BRIM	MOTILE	RIME
CITE	BRIO	NILE	RIOT
ENACT	BRIT	NITRE	ROIL
ENACTS	BRITON	NITRO	ROME
FACE	BROIL	NOIR	TIER
FACET	ELINOR	NOME	TILE
FACETS	ELIOT	OILER	TILER
FACT	EMIR	OMIT	TIME
FACTS	EMIT	ORIEL	TIMER
FANE	EQUAL	PLAQUE	TIMON
FITS	EQUALITY	PLEA	TIRE
GETS	EQUITY	PLIER	TIRO
GUST	ERIN	PRELIM	TOIL
GUTS	ILEUM	PRIM	TOILER
KEGS	IRON	PRIME	TOME
KNEW	KLEIN	PROM	TONI
NEGUS	LAXER	PYRE	TONIER
NETS	LEMON	QUALITY	TORE
PICA	LIEU	QUERY	TORI
PICT	LIME	QUIRE	TORY
PICTS	LIMN	QUIT	TRIM
PITS	LIMO	QUITO	TRIO
RUGS	LINO	REAL	TYRE
RUST	LION	REALITY	TYRO
RUSTIC	LIRE	REIN	
RUTS	LITRE		
STEW	MEAL		
SUET	MERINO		
SURGE	MERIT		
URGE	MERLIN		
UTICA	MILA		
VICE	MILE		
WEAN	MILER		
WETS	MILK		
	MINOR		
	MIRE		

Traceword 6

AERY	MIRY
ALERT	MITRE
	MOIL

WORD LADDERS

Word ladder 1

EYE, dye, die, did, LID. In two links: EYE, lye (caustic chemical), lie, LID.

Word ladder 2

PIG, wig, wag, way, say, STY.

Word ladder 3

COAL, coat, moat, most, mist, mint, MINE. Alternatively: COAL, cool, cook, conk, monk, mink, MINE.

Word ladder 4

NOSE, note, cote, core, corn, coin, CHIN. Alternatively: NOSE, pose, pore, core, corn, coin, CHIN.

Word ladder 5

POOR, boor, book, rook, rock, rick, RICH.

Word ladder 6

FOUR, foul, fool, foot, fort, fore, fire, FIVE.

Word ladder 7

WOOD, wold, weld, weed, feed, fled, flee, TREE. Alternatively: WOOD, wool, tool, toot, trot, troy, trey, TREE.

Word ladder 8

TEARS, sears, stars, stare, stale, stile, SMILE.

Word ladder 9

FLOUR, floor, flood, blood, brood, broad, BREAD.

Word ladder 10

CROSS, crops, coops, corps, carps, harps, harpy, HAPPY.

Word ladder 11

GRASS, crass, cress, tress, trees, frees, freed, greed, GREEN.

Word ladder 12

BLACK, slack, stack, stalk, stale, shale, whale, while, WHITE. Alternatively: BLACK, blank, clank, clink, chink, chine, whine, WHITE.

Word ladder 13

HANDS, wands, wants, waits, gaits, grits, grips, gripe, grope, grove, GLOVE.

Word ladder 14

WINTER, winner, winder, wander, warder, harder, harper, hamper, damper, damped, dammed, dimmed, dimmer, simmer, SUMMER.
Alternatively: WINTER, winder, wander, warder, warper, harper, hamper, hammer, hummer, SUMMER.

KANGAROO WORDS

1. Round
2. See
3. Sue
4. Dead
5. Lie
6. Tomb
7. Save
8. Tutor
9. Rain
10. City
11. Apt
12. Rim
13. Urge
14. Mates
15. Rules
16. Spots
17. Rest
18. Lies
19. Rascal
20. Ere
21. Sin
22. Idle
23. Debate
24. Superior
25. Fiction
26. As
27. Ugly
28. Nth
29. Ruin
30. Can, tin

RIDDLE-ME-REE

1. The Moon.
2. An anchor.
3. A pack of cards.
4. Your breath.
5. The word WHOLESOME.
6. A secret.
7. Your lap.
8. A stamp.
9. A dictionary.
10. Lighting (add N for lightning).
11. A joke.
12. A shadow.
13. The word FEW.
14. Key (keystone in an arch, Florida Keys, map key, musical key, door key with combinations, essential nature).
15. A shoe.
16. Stable.
17. The letter V.
18. Salt and pepper.
19. Eye.
20. An egg.
21. Counterfeit money.
22. A glove.
23. Dust.
24. Trust.

25. VIOLET, composed chiefly of Roman numerals.

....

HARSH WORDS

1. Missing letters are all the SAME: diSArMEd, eScArpMEnt, gosSA-MEr, hiStAMinE, SAMplE, teStAMEnt.

2. It's the longest word that can be made without repeating any letter of the alphabet.

3. They are all pronounced differently when spelled with an initial capital letter.

4. HYDRAULIC.

5. Zzuf (i.e. fuzz backwards).

6. Turn 'nop' upside-down to complete 'hazardous'.

7. Placing the words in alphabetical order makes the sentence make sense:

ARNOLD BROWN CAN DO EVACUATION FOR GERRARD'S HARBOR IN JERSEY. KEEP LOW MONDAY NIGHT OR PATROL QUICKLY – RECKONS SOME TROUBLE UNDERWAY. VICTORY WEDNESDAY, XAVIER! YOURS, ZACK.

8. Animal (lamina in reverse).

9. Long time, no see (no C).

10. (a) Hyena   (b) Okapi
(c) Lemur   (d) Caribou
(e) Chamois   (f) Tapir

11. By playing D, E flat, E on a piano keyboard.

12. FIFTY, THIRTEEN and O (zero).

13.

S	O	L	V	E	S
O	R	I	O	L	E
L	I	T	T	E	R
V	O	T	I	V	E
E	L	E	V	E	N
S	E	R	E	N	E

14. HE, HER, HERO, HEROINE.

15. One solution is 'break' and 'brake', which can both mean 'stop'.

16. FRANKINCENSE, giving FRANTIC, BANDAGE, VIKINGS, GLANCED, PROGENY and PROMISE across.

17. Indivisibilities.

18. CABBAGE; in letter position terms, this is $3 + 1 + 2 + 2 + 1 + 7 + 5 = 21$, and $21/7 = 3$.

19. EIGHTHS (since two-eighths is normally referred to as a quarter, etc.)

20. Enlightening.

CHAPTER 3
Codes and Ciphers

A TYPEWRITER CRYPTOGRAM

Dudeney writes: The one letter words, P and g, must be taken from a, I and o, and P cannot be A because the second word begins with a vowel, while it is unlikely to be O. If we make P equals I, and g equals a, then we can assume the sentence begins 'I am', in which case kz will be 'me' or 'my' – probably 'my', because then ngz would end in 'ay'. Call this last 'say', since then pn will be 'is'. Now, either e or t in et must be o or u, but as we know that the second letter in ezhpne is y, the e is most probably a consonant. Make t stand for o; then we immediately get et equals 'to'. We now have found the following, where the dots stand for letters not yet found: 'I am so.y to say my ty.ist is a ......t .oo.' Here 'sorry' and 'typist' are seen at a glance, and then we have the p and r for 'perfect' which gives us the f for 'fool'. The full answer is therefore: 'I am sorry to say my typist is a perfect fool'.

DOUBLE VISION

Reading every other letter, ignoring the distracting pattern, gives:
WHAT DOES THIS MEAN
and
JUST SKIP EACH TIME

CRYPTOGRAMS

Cryptogram 1
The story so far: In the beginning the Universe was created. This has made a lot of people very angry and has been widely regarded as a bad move. – Douglas Adams, *The Restaurant at the End of the Universe*

Cryptogram 2
If the reason for climbing Mt. Everest is that it's hard to do, why does everyone go up the easy side? – George Carlin

Cryptogram 3
Always get married early in the morning. That way, if it doesn't work out, you haven't wasted a whole day. – Mickey Rooney

Cryptogram 4
The advantage of a bad memory is that one enjoys several times the same good things for the first time. – Friedrich Nietzsche

Cryptogram 5
Only two things are infinite, the universe and human stupidity, and I'm not sure about the former. – Albert Einstein

Cryptogram 6
I can forgive Alfred Nobel for having invented dynamite, but only a fiend in human form could have invented the Nobel Prize. – George Bernard Shaw

Cryptogram 7
When you go into court you are putting your fate into the hands of

twelve people who weren't smart enough to get out of jury duty.
– Norm Crosby

Cryptogram 8
One of the universal rules of happiness is: always be wary of any helpful item that weighs less than its operating manual. – Terry Pratchett, *Jingo*

Cryptogram 9
I had a dream last night; I was eating a ten pound marshmallow. I woke up this morning and the pillow was gone. – Tommy Cooper

Cryptogram 10
Computers will never take the place of books. You can't stand on a floppy disk to reach a high shelf. – Sam Ewing

Cryptogram 11
If Dracula can't see his reflection in a mirror, how come his hair is always so neatly combed? – Steven Wright

---

A CRYPTIC WORD

The word is EXCOMMUNICATION. Roman numerals are the key: convert 10 = X, 100 = C, 1000 = M (or vice versa).

A LITTLE ADVICE

'One ought to wait for tea' (One, nought, two, eight, forty).

DATE WITH DESTINY

The key to decoding the message lies in the date, July Fifth. By reading every fifth letter, beginning with the salutation ('Dear Will …'), the message is seen to read WATER TOWER ON THAMES TARGET FOR TWENTIETH.

ALTERNATELY

1. He is *uneasy* about his business.
2. Don't tell *lies*.
3. I see what *the* problem is.
4. He has a good *head* on his shoulders.
5. I know that *that* is right.
6. A good friend *wears* well.
7. Go to the top of *the* class.
8. The king wore a *crown* of gold.

The phrase is: Uneasy lies the head that wears the crown.

NEXT!

To decipher the code, substitute for each letter the one that immediately follows it in the alphabet. The decoded sentence reads:

> EARLY TO BED, EARLY TO RISE, MAKES A MAN HEALTHY, WEALTHY AND WISE.

In the second sentence, take the letter before the one quoted to obtain:

> WHAT HATH GOD WROUGHT?

Quoting Numbers 23:23 from the Bible, this was the first modern telegram message sent by Samuel Morse in 1844.

WORDS OF WAR

Start at the lower right-hand corner, and read up. Then progress to the line next to last, and read down. Continue in this fashion until you reach the letter in the upper left-hand line. The message is THE ENEMY IS SENDING AEROPLANES, BOMBS AND POISON GAS.

CODEWORDS

Codeword 1

```
F A S T   T W E E Z E R S
L   H   U   O   X   Q   T
A C R O N Y M   C A U S E
P   U   I   B   E   I   W
J U G   T H A I L A N D
A     E   T       O     B
C O M E D Y   E L I X I R
K   A     G   A         A
  M E N S W E A R   A R C
B   S   E   Y   Y   C   E
A C T O R   S E N S U A L
N   R   V   E   X   T   E
G E O M E T R Y   D E B T
```

Codeword 2

```
S T A C C A T O   S P A T
O   R   O   H   F   R   A
L E M U R   O V A T I O N
I     G   R   J   C     G
T E Q U I L A   I B E X
U   U     X   T   L     W
D E A D L Y   G A Z E B O
E   D   I   A     S     N
  D R A M   B E M U S E D
I   I   B   S   I       R
B E L I E V E   G E C K O
I   L   R   I   H   U   U
S E E D   P L A T Y P U S
```

Codeword 3

```
A D H E S I O N   S P A R
V   A   P   B   A   R   E
O C C U R   T U R M O I L
I   K   E   U   C   O   A
D Y S P E P S I A   F A X
    A     E   N         E
S E W I N G   H A Z A R D
Q     A   J     M
U S E   P L A U S I B L E
E   X   K   R   T   I   N
A M A Z I N G   Y I E L D
K   C   N   O   L   N   O
Y E T I   U N D E R T O W
```

Codeword 4

```
M A H A R A J A   A Q U A
O   Y   O   U   S   U   T
D R E S S E R   H O I S T
E   N   E   I   O   C   O
  W A T T   S N O O K E R
V     T   T       E     N
E L E V E N   T W I N G E
N   D     Z   H         Y
G L I M P S E   O P A L
E   T   O   P   O   R   V
F L I C K   H I P B O N E
U   O   E   Y   E   S   R
L Y N X   G R E E N E R Y
```

Codeword 5

```
N E P H E W   C Y B O R G
  X   O   I   H   A   Y
S T U B   S Q U I R R E L
  R     T   G   R
B O O G I E     A C I D
  V   A   R   C   C   N
V E N T R I L O Q U I S M
  R   E   A   N   D   P
E T C H     F L A X E N
      O   D   E       C
A D J U T A N T   K I T E
  U   S   Z   T   I   O
C O H E R E   I M P U R E
```

HARDLY THE BARD

The couplet, which comes from Shakespeare's Sonnet 57, reads:

SO TRUE A FOOL IS LOVE, THAT IN YOUR WILL

THOUGH YOU DO ANYTHING, HE THINKS NO ILL.

THE 'CAN INN ALE' CODE

Say the words out loud, beginning with the last 'if' and working backwards. You will hear the following phonetic message:

If I should be in boat off Aquia Creek at dark tomorrow Wednesday evening, could you, without inconvenience, flesh [meet] me and pass an hour or two with me?
– A. LINCOLN

Note that flesh = 'meat' = meet. The code was not intercepted by the enemy. However, the meeting turned out to be fruitless. Lincoln offered a new plan but it was deemed to be impractical by Burnside who, instead, returned to meet his wife in Falmouth for Thanksgiving.

WHAT A TEASE

Insert the letter T repeatedly to obtain: ALTHOUGH THE TWO TOTS TITTERED, THEY TOLD THE OFT TOLD TALE.

RIGHT THIS WAY

Each set of arrows draws out a different letter. If you figured this out for yourself, the answer to the question would indeed have been YES:

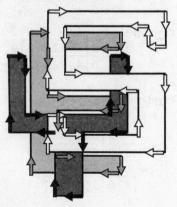

MISSING WORDS

Did you solve the puzzle? If so, it's MIRACULOUS!

COMPLETE
WITH
WORDS
WHAT
CAN
YOU
LOCATE
DOWN
COLUMN
SHOWN

COLLECTED CODES – PART 1

1. AGE CANNOT WITHER HER NOR CUSTOM STALE HER INFINITE VARIETY
   (written backwards then arranged in groups of five letters).

2. IF I SAID YOU HAD A BEAUTIFUL BODY WOULD YOU HOLD IT AGAINST ME
   (arranged in groups of five letters, and the groups given in reverse order).

3. THERE ARE NONE SO BLIND AS THOSE THAT WILL NOT SEE
   (ignore the first and last letters of each group).

4. BETTER THE DEVIL YOU KNOW THAN THE DEVIL YOU DON'T
   (A becomes B, B becomes C, etc.)

5. TO TRAVEL HOPEFULLY IS A BETTER THING THAN TO ARRIVE
   (B becomes A, C becomes B, etc.)

6. ONCE MORE UNTO THE BREACH DEAR FRIENDS ONCE MORE (A becomes N, B becomes O, etc.)

7. Thirteen different letters are used in the keyword UNPREDICTABLY. If you write the unused letters of the alphabet (FGHJKMOQSVWXZ) underneath the keyword, you arrive at a one-to-one code correlation where U = F (and vice versa), N = G, P = H, and so on to Y = Z. This code can be used to decode the five coded words to give this message: NEUROSCIENTIST TRANQUILIZED – UNINTERRUPTED INTERROGATION REQUISITIONED.

8. ACCIDENTS WILL HAPPEN IN THE BEST REGULATED FAMILIES (A becomes Z and vice versa, B becomes Y, C becomes X, etc.)

A FAIR COP

If XX multiplied by XX produces MMCC, then XX can only be 88 and MMCC is 7744. So we have to find the square of 22, which is 484.

CRYPTARITHMS

Cryptarithm 1

```
    2 3
    2 3
    2 3
+   2 3
    9 2
```

Cryptarithm 2

```
      5 8 1
      5 8 1
+   9 2 3 1
  1 0 3 9 3
```

Cryptarithm 3

```
        8 1
        8 1
+   1 9 8 7
    2 1 4 9
```

Cryptarithm 4

```
      8 5 0
      8 5 0
+ 2 9 7 8 6
  3 1 4 8 6
```

Cryptarithm 5

```
        1 0 6
      1 9 7 2 2
+     8 2 5 2 4
  1 0 2 3 5 2
```

Cryptarithm 6

```
    9 5 6 7
+     1 0 8 5
  1 0 6 5 2
```

Cryptarithm 7

```
      3 9 4
    8 0 9 1
    1 3 9 4
+   1 0 9 9
  1 0 9 7 8
```

Cryptarithm 8

```
    6 5 6 8 2
+   9 8 1 8 4 9
  1 0 4 7 5 3 1
```

Cryptarithm 9

```
    1 2 7 5 0 3
    5 0 2 3 5 1
  3 9 4 7 5 3 9
+     4 6 5 7 8
  4 6 2 3 9 7 1
```

Cryptarithm 10

```
    8 6 2 9 0 3
+ 1 6 2 7 3 4 2
  2 4 9 0 2 4 5
```

Cryptarithm 11

```
    7 0 8 8 0 6 2
+ 1 7 5 3 1 9 0 8
  2 4 6 1 9 9 7 0
```

Cryptarithm 12

```
        1 3 8
    x   1 3 8
  1 9 0 4 4
```

Cryptarithm 13

```
        1 2 5
    x     3 7
        8 7 5
      3 7 5
      4 6 2 5
```

Cryptarithm 14

```
      5 7 0 1 4 0
    x           6
    3 4 2 0 8 4 0
```

LETTER-FIGURE PUZZLE

Here is Dudeney's explanation: It is
clear that A must be 1, and that B and
C must be either (6 and 2) or (3 and 5).
In the third equation they are shown
to be 3 and 5, since D must be 7. Then
E must be 8 in order that D × E should
show C = 5. Then the rest is easy, and
we find the answer as follows:
A = 1, B = 3, C = 5, D = 7, E = 8, F = 9,
H = 6, J = 4, K = 2, L = 0.

ON THE TIP OF YOUR TONGUE

Say it aloud quickly and you'll get
All spies should protect their secrets.

....

CON-SEQUENTIAL

Simply respace the words as follows:
PUT THE MONEY OUT OF FRONT
WINDOW NOW.

....

DRIVEN DOTTY

The riddle reads What has no wings,
no rotors and yet can fly? Turn the
book 90 degrees, look at what you
have traced and the answer becomes
obvious: TIME.

SENSE OF DIRECTION

The arrows point to the compass
directions N, S, E, W and the hands
point Up (U), Down (D), Left (L) or
Right (R). In this manner, the arrows
and hands spell out WE SURRENDER.

....

KEY WORD

The word is UNSPORTSMANLIKE.
It happened because the Num Lock
key on the computer was active.
Therefore, instead of letters appearing, the equivalent number characters
from the numerical keypad were
entered.

KEY CODE

4 means the fourth letter of the question ('What is the key…'), so the first letter is T. Continuing in this manner for all the other numbers gives THE CLUE IS IN THE QUESTION. Indeed it is.

ALL KEYED UP

Transpose each letter one position to the right on the keyboard, so that UD becomes IF. The message reads:

If 'typewriter' is not the only longest word using letters from the top row, then the others must be …?

Valid answers to this question include perpetuity, proprietary and repertoire.

ANACROSTICS

Anacrostic 1

WHY	GET	MARRIED
AND	MAKE	ONE	MAN
MISERABLE	WHEN	I
CAN	STAY	SINGLE
AND	MAKE	THOUSANDS
MISERABLE	?

A. CAYENNE
B. ADDENDA
C. ROARS
D. RAN
E. IMMERSIBLE
F. EYELASHES
G. STALEMATE
H. NIGHTHAWK
I. OMBUDSMAN
J. WINEMAKING
The initial letters read CARRIE SNOW.

Anacrostic 2

THE	TROUBLE	WITH
UNEMPLOYMENT	IS
THAT	THE	MINUTE
YOU	WAKE	UP	IN	THE
MORNING	YOU'RE	ON
THE	JOB

A. SMITH
B. LABYRINTHINE
C. AWE
D. PHOEBE
E. PUTTI
F. YOGHURT
G. WHEREUNTO
H. HONEYMOON
I. INKJET
J. TUTU
K. EMOLUMENT
The initial letters read SLAPPY WHITE.

Anacrostic 3

WHAT	DO	YOU	CALL
FIVE	HUNDRED
LAWYERS	LYING	ON	THE
THE	BOTTOM	OF	THE
OCEAN?	A	GOOD
START	(FROM	"THE
WAR	OF	THE	ROSES")

A. DELETE
B. ALL
C. NEWSWORTHY
D. NORTHWEST
E. YARBOROUGH
F. DOGCATCHER
G. EMERALD
H. VOODOO
I. INHUMANITY
J. TAFFETA
K. OFFSHOOTS
The initial letters read DANNY DE VITO.

Anacrostic 4

E	M	P	L	O	Y	E	E	■	O	F	■	T	H	E	■
M	O	N	T	H	■	I	S	■	A	■	G	O	O	D	■
E	X	A	M	P	L	E	■	O	F	■	H	O	W	■	■
S	O	M	E	B	O	D	Y	■	C	A	N	■	B	E	■
B	O	T	H	■	A	■	W	I	N	N	E	R	■	A	N	D
A	■	L	O	S	E	R	■	A	T	■	T	H	E	■	■
S	A	M	E	■	T	I	M	E	■	■	■	■	■	■	■

A. DEAN
B. ENTOMBMENT
C. MEASLES
D. EPITAPH
E. TWOSOME
F. RHEA
G. ICHTHYOLOGY
H. MOONBEAM
I. AWASH
J. ROAD
K. TOFFEE
L. IBEX
M. NOODLE
The initial letters read DEMETRI MARTIN.

Anacrostic 5

M	Y	■	N	E	I	G	H	B	O	U	R	■	A	S	K	E	D
I	F	■	H	E	■	C	O	U	L	D	■	U	S	E	■	M	Y
L	A	W	N	M	O	W	E	R	■	A	N	D	■	I	■	■	■
T	O	L	D	■	H	I	M	■	O	F	■	C	O	U	R	S	E
H	E	■	C	O	U	L	D	,	■	S	O	■	L	O	N	G	■
A	S	■	H	E	■	D	I	D	N	'	T	■	T	A	K	E	■
I	T	■	O	U	T	■	O	F	■	M	Y	■	G	A	R	D	E	N

A. EGGSHELL
B. RACOONS
C. INAUGURATION
D. CHUMMY
E. MUFFLES
F. OUTLOOK
G. ROADWORTHY
H. EDDO
I. CHOOSY
J. ANTIHISTAMINE
K. MIDWEEK
L. BEFUDDLED
M. END
The initial letters read ERIC MORECAMBE.

Anacrostic 6

M	Y	■	G	R	A	N	D	M	O	T	H	E	R	■	■
S	T	A	R	T	E	D	■	W	A	L	K	I	N	G	■
F	I	V	E	■	M	I	L	E	S	■	A	■	D	A	Y
W	H	E	N	■	S	H	E	■	W	A	S	■	S	I	X	T	Y
S	H	E	'	S	■	N	I	N	E	T	Y	-	S	E	V	E	N
N	O	W	■	A	N	D	■	W	E	■	D	O	N	'	T	■
K	N	O	W	■	W	H	E	R	E	■	T	H	E	■	■
H	E	L	L	■	S	H	E	■	I	S	■	■	■	■	■

A. EXTRAVAGANT
B. LIONFISH
C. LOWDOWN
D. EYEWASH
E. NIHILISM
F. DRAWN
G. ELEVENTH
H. GNASHED
I. EKED
J. NETHERMOST
K. EYEWITNESS
L. RHYTHM
M. ENDWAYS
N. SKEWS
The initial letters read ELLEN DEGENERES.

....

MONOCHROME CODE

The key words in play are WHITE and BLACK. The digits refer to the letter you must take from either word. For example, the first three letters are: the fourth letter of WHITE, the second letter of WHITE and the third letter of BLACK. Continuing in this vein and adding punctuation gives: THAT'S THE WAY THE COOKIE CRUMBLES

....

SCENE AND HERD

Extract the words which phonetically match letters of the alphabet, like so: see, why, pea, are, eye, oh, tea, queue, you, aye, tee, owe. These spell out CYPRIOT who should be met in Ecuador's capital, QUITO.

PHONEY

(a) PICASSO
(b) YOGHURT
(c) CANVASS
(d) FORTUNE
(e) VARNISH
(f) ECLAIRS
(g) ALCOHOL

SECRET SHOPPER

white grapes

chicken breasts

chocolate ice cream

boysenberry cheesecake

COLLECTED CODES – PART 2

1. A telephone number: phonetically, it spells out 4258980.

2. On a typewriter, Q is next to the 1 key, W is next to 2 and so on. The 9 is above the letter O.

3. The Hollies. If you type 5317704 in a calculator and turn it upside down, it says hOLLIES.

4. Alternate letters spell THERE'S NO TIME LIKE THE PRESENT and NEITHER ONE THING NOR THE OTHER.

A NOVEL CODE

If the stencil is placed over the letter grid in all four orientations, as shown, the novel TWENTY THOUSAND LEAGUES UNDER THE SEA is spelt out.

CHAPTER 4

Cruciverbalism

WORD SQUARES

Word square 1

L	O	I	N
O	G	R	E
S	L	O	W
T	E	N	T

Word square 2

S	T	E	M
C	O	V	E
A	R	E	A
M	E	N	D

Word square 3

S	L	E	W
H	O	M	E
I	B	I	S
P	E	R	T

Word square 4

T	A	L	C
A	L	O	E
C	L	O	D
T	Y	K	E

Word square 5

A	D	M	I	T
P	R	O	N	E
R	O	O	T	S
I	N	S	E	T
L	E	E	R	Y

Word square 6

S	H	U	S	H
P	A	S	T	A
A	S	H	E	N
S	T	E	E	D
M	E	R	R	Y

Word square 7

S	M	A	R	M
L	E	V	E	E
O	R	I	E	L
B	L	A	D	E
S	E	N	S	E

Word square 8

S	T	A	S	H
P	A	U	L	A
A	S	T	I	R
S	T	O	M	P
M	E	S	S	Y

Word square 9

G	O	S	P	E	L
A	C	T	I	V	E
S	T	A	P	E	S
B	A	K	E	R	S
A	V	E	R	S	E
G	O	D	S	O	N

Word square 10

M	U	S	C	A	T
A	L	C	O	V	E
S	T	A	V	E	S
S	I	L	E	N	T
E	M	E	R	G	E
D	A	R	T	E	D

LETTER FITS

Letter fit 1

Letter fit 2

Letter fit 3

BLACKOUT

SPLIT DECISION

SMALLEST AND HARDEST

Small and hard 1

F	O	P	
A	K	I	N
T	R	E	E
	A	R	T

Small and hard 2

C	I	A	O
O	M	N	I
M	A	N	N
A	M	O	K

Small and hard 3

E	G	I	S
T	O		O
A		W	U
L	E	A	K

Small and hard 4

N	E	R	D
O	X		A
U		A	N
S	I	C	K

QUICK CROSSWORDS

Quick crossword 1

ACROSS: 1 Marching song, 8 Yawning, 9 Circa, 10 Omit, 11 Flambeau, 13 Eleven, 14 Tremor, 17 Augustus, 19 Iris, 21 Clown, 22 Stencil, 23 April showers.

DOWN: 1 Maypole dance, 2 Rawhide, 3 Hail, 4 Niggle, 5 Sycamore, 6 Nurse, 7 January sales, 12 Helsinki, 15 Miracle, 16 Pulses, 18 Group, 20 Keno.

Quick crossword 2

ACROSS: 1 Top priority, 9 End on, 10 Emeriti, 11 Tonneau, 12 Youth, 13 Middle-age, 15 Girth, 17 Block in, 19 Galilei, 20 Barge, 21 Bottom heavy.

DOWN: 2 Ogden, 3 Pinhead, 4 In equilibrium, 5 Reedy, 6 Tribune, 7 Left-luggage, 8 Right-minded, 13 Morello, 14 Amoebae, 16 Holst, 18 Kirov.

Quick crossword 3

ACROSS: 1 Dino, 4 Hobbes, 9 Orangeman, 10 Obi, 11 Aviator, 12 Novak, 13 Dick Dastardly, 16 Evils, 17 Mr Magoo, 20 Ren, 21 Assiduous, 22 Tintin, 23 Mayo.

DOWN: 2 Iraqi, 3 Ought, 4 Homer J. Simpson, 5 Bonanza, 6 Evolved, 7 Tom and Jerry, 8 Mickey Mouse, 14 Chianti, 15 Distant, 18 Madam, 19 Goofy.

Quick crossword 4

The theme words are letters of the Nato alphabet (the radio code which begins Alpha, Bravo, Charlie, Delta)

ACROSS: 1 Nato alphabet, 9 Her, 10 Come again, 11 Sierra, 12 Rococo, 13 Yankee, 15 Effuse, 18 Victor, 20 Juliet, 23 Crash diet, 24 One, 25 Saddle of lamb.

DOWN: 2 Agree on, 3 Oscar, 4 Lima, 5 Head off, 6 Bravo, 7 Tango, 8 Whisky, 14 Epochal, 16 Uniform, 17 Esther, 18 Vices, 19 Chard, 21 Until, 22 Kilo.

Quick crossword 5

The clues in italics are anagrams of their answer, as well as being a valid clue, e.g.: I'm dot in place = Decimal point.

ACROSS: 1/5 Decimal point, 8 Hermaphrodite, 9 HMS Pinafore, 11 United, 13 Retort, 15 Now and again, 17 Impersonation, 20 Epics, 21 Stipend.

DOWN: 1 Doh, 2 Christian, 3 Miami, 4 Lehman, 5 Promote, 6 Ici, 7 The Hilton, 9 Housewife, 10 Evocative, 12 Edwards, 14 Undoes, 16 Atari, 18 Phi, 19 Nod.

U.S.-STYLE CROSSWORDS

U.S.-style 1

U.S.-style 2

U.S.-style 3

GENERAL KNOWLEDGE CROSSWORDS

General knowledge 1

ACROSS: 1 Apocalypse Now,
8 Knossos, 9 Preview, 11 Loofah,
13 Yearlong, 15 Manes, 16 Orpheus,
18 Baptist, 19 Lamia, 21 Aversion,
23 Italic, 25 Outpost, 26 Two-step,
28 Hercule Poirot.

DOWN: 2 Pronoun, 3 Cos, 4 Lisp,
5 Pepperpots, 6 Emeer, 7 Ominous,
8 Kilimanjaro, 10 Wightman Cup,
12 Aesop, 14 Horizontal, 17 Eclat,
18 Breathe, 20 Mulatto, 22 Stoic,
24 Stop, 27 Oui.

General knowledge 2

ACROSS: 1 Willow pattern, 8 Deplete,
9 Proverb, 11 V-necks, 13 Maverick,
15 Laser, 16 Premium, 18 Ravioli,
19 Ideal, 21 Inscribe, 23 Emboss,
25 Natural, 26 Czarina, 28 Down's
syndrome.

DOWN: 2 Impress, 3 Lee, 4 Wren,
5 Alphabetic, 6 Those, 7 Rhenium,
8 Devaluation, 10 Baked Alaska,
12 Kirov, 14 Spoonbills, 17 Idiom,
18 Risotto, 20 Egotism, 22 Rerun,
24 Icon, 27 Air.

General knowledge 3

ACROSS: 8 Crowfoot, 9 Phobia,
10 Adam's apple, 11 Lapp,
12 Crisis, 14 Nepotism, 15 Fascism,
17 Columns, 20 Cephalic, 22 Thebes,
24 Star, 25 Abbreviate, 27 Bronze,
28 Richmond.

DOWN: 1 Trader, 2 Swim, 3 Molasses,
4 Stipend, 5 Upkeep, 6 Cos
lettuce, 7 Diapason, 13 Saccharine,
16 Aperture, 18 Outreach, 19 Iceberg,
21 Loaves, 23 Extant, 26 Iamb.

General knowledge quickie

The numbers in brackets denote the wedding anniversary of the clued material or gift.

ACROSS: 1 Paper, 4 Emerald, 8 All, 9 Base metal, 10 Lace, 11 Platinum, 13 Canvas, 14 Pelota, 17 Yet again, 19 Otis, 22 The Old Vic, 23 Bee, 24 Leather, 25 Coral.

DOWN: 1 Pearl, 2 Pelican, 3 Ruby, 4 Easily, 5 Enmities, 6 Alton, 7 Dilemma, 12 Nargileh, 13 Crystal, 15 October, 16 Silver, 18 Theta, 20 Steel, 21 AC/DC.

....

CRYPTIC CROSSWORDS

Cryptic crossword 1

Cryptic crossword 2

Cryptic crossword 3

ACROSS: 1 Metabolism, 6 Wisp, 9 Good temper, 10 Scar, 12 Land of plenty, 15 Stand-pipe, 17 Crier, 18 Elite, 19 Sideburns, 20 Double-dealer, 24 Nail, 25 Postulated, 26 Yeti, 27 Stands down.

DOWN: 1 Mugs, 2 Took, 3 Bath and Wells, 4 Lamed, 5 Sheffield, 7 Incendiary, 8 Party dress, 11 Black-beetles, 13 Ascendancy, 14 Manicurist, 16 Inside out, 21 Act on, 22 Otto, 23 Aden.

Cryptic crossword 4

ACROSS: 1 Spinal, 4 Space out, 9 Mussolini, 11 Orate, 12 Trident, 13 Tussaud, 14 Chapter and verse, 17 Does it on purpose, 19 Weak tea, 21 Entitle, 23 Riper, 24 Insistent, 25 Pleading, 26 Kaiser.

DOWN: 1 Semitic, 2 Instigate, 3 Awoke, 5 Printing press, 6 Cross over, 7 Omaha, 8 Treadle, 10 Interrogation, 15 Twittered, 16 Roof trees, 17 Dewdrop, 18 Elector, 20 Apple, 22 Tosca.

Cryptic crossword 5

ACROSS: 1 Dutch auction, 8 Arsenal, 9 Summing, 11 Diocese, 12 Trivial, 13 Chest, 14 Ordinance, 16 Litheness, 19 Snuff, 21 Guilder, 23 Overlie, 24 Entries, 25 Frantic, 26 Dragon's teeth.

DOWN: 1 Disrobe, 2 Tangent, 3 Hellebore, 4 Upset, 5 Tompion, 6 Opinion, 7 Eau de Cologne, 10 Golden Fleece, 15 Discomfit, 17 Twister, 18 Eddying, 19 Seepage, 20 Unlatch, 22 Risen.

Cryptic crossword 6

```
S T A L K E R · D O G S T A R
H · A · X · D · N · E · V ·
R E S T · C H I F F O N I E R
P · H · U · S · I · S · R ·
S I R I U S · C O L L I E R Y
T · · A · R · E · T · E ·
A S M O U L D E R · W I N D Y
· B · · T · · · V ·
S M A S H · W I M B L E D O N
· C · E · S · O · U · P ·
B E A R S K I N · L A S S I E
N · V · E · A · L · O · N ·
D R E A M W O R L D · R A I N
O · N · E · Y · O · B · O ·
C E N T U R Y · A G R O U N D
```

SKELETON CROSSWORDS

Skeleton 1

```
L A R D E R · D · H O N E S T
I · H · · · M · W
· · A Z U R E · · · M ·
G L O V E R · S · I N H E R E
H · N · V E N T U R E · R · N
T H E M E · O · S · T R Y S T
H · · R E T R A C T · Y
O U N C E · U · G · L A P S E
U · O · S U P R E M E · O · I
S P O R T S · O · A D D I N G
E · S · E Q U A L · S · H
S E E P E D · T · T A L E N T
```

Skeleton 2

```
O · S · F I T N E S S · P · P
P O K E R · E · A · H O U R I
A · U · E S P A R T O · L · E
L E A V E · O · T · P A L E R
I · · M A R S H A L · X ·
A D E L A · I · I N D E X
E · S H E R I F F · A ·
B R A V O · A · M · T R O T H
A · R · N O T A B L E · M · I
L E M U R · E · U · R E E L S
E · Y · Y A N K E E S · N · S
```

Skeleton 3

```
D I L E M M A · P O A C H E R
I · A · M · R · L · E · U
A · V · R U B S O U T · A · B
L E A S T · I · N · E A R L Y
· C · I N T E G E R · O ·
P L A I N · A · N E G U S
A · · G E O R G I A · G ·
S T U K A · C · O · T I G H T
M · N · L E C T U R E · O · E
U · D · E · U · R · L · N
G R O S S E R · D R Y N E S S
```

ADVANCED CRYPTICS

Advanced 1

```
S C A M P I S H D I G S
C A L A I S P A I D L E
A V O G R W A D S E T B
L I N G O T H I C A P A
A T G M U D I S R U P T
D Y S A E S T H E T I C
E P I S T O L A T O R Y
R I D O T T O B E S O P
O Y E R E W S I R D A R
W P T E R I S L E A S E
T A U T I T C L E F T S
H O N E R E D E L E S S
```

Advanced 2:
Printer's devilry

```
E P I S T O L E R W E P
R I M A R O U G H A G E
A N I L A N N E A L E D
R A T L I N E O P E R A
I F A Y N E T C H I N G
N O B L E S T C E R I O
G R L A E P E E L I N G
S E E T H E R L K S E U
M A C A W N R E N A M E
A N A B A S I S O T I C
L A V E M E N T W E L D
L N E G E R M A N D E R
```

The diagonal line indicates where the word was extracted from, e.g.: 23 down (answer: ATABEG) is indicated by th/inner to give 'that a beginner'.

ACROSS: 1 th/rough, 11 g/irl, 12 th/at, 13 mi/ke, 14 or/gie, 15 B/en's, 16 d/id, 17 sk/imp, 20 Gre/w, 24 rap/ers, 25 s/es, 27 o/f, 30 Si/r, 31 rot/ter, 32 forg/e, 33 S/ally, 34 flo/or, 35 rug/by.

DOWN: 2 ma/st, 3 cla/ssing, 4 to/urs, 5 Boro/din, 6 mo/del, 7 Ar/nold, 8 Sho/g, 9 al/e, 10 h/osts, 15 b/et, 18 la/dy, 19 A/sian, 21 hi/ves, 22 'twi/ll, 23 th/inner, 26 Ba/con, 28 be/d, 29 pa/st.

Advanced 3: Right and left

W	H	O	R	T	L	E	B	E	R	R	Y
R	A	S	U	R	E	G	O	B	I	E	S
I	N	U	L	I	N	G	U	I	N	E	A
N	A	I	L	E	D	B	R	A	G	L	Y
K	P	A	I	R	S	I	N	S	T	E	E
L	O	B	O	S	E	R	E	T	A	R	D
E	L	A	N	E	T	D	E	R	I	D	E
S	O	T	S	O	I	B	G	I	L	L	A
C	L	A	M	B	E	L	E	G	I	O	N
A	L	B	I	O	N	A	R	O	U	S	E
P	O	L	L	E	N	K	I	P	P	E	R
A	P	E	R	S	E	E	A	S	I	L	Y

Advanced 4: Spot the theme

The 13 words contain, as their 4th and 3rd letters, the complete alphabet in pairs, thus: caBAret, maDCap, afFEer, …, paXWax, enZYme.

M	U	J	I	K	C	A	B	A	R	E	T
A	M	E	N	M	U	F	F	N	U	C	I
D	E	T	S	A	R	E	I	N	N	A	N
C	A	S	E	R	N	E	D	A	T	U	M
A	B	A	C	O	L	E	E	T	I	D	E
P	E	M	T	Q	O	R	T	O	L	A	N
P	A	R	Q	U	E	T	I	H	I	T	P
U	R	E	D	I	N	E	N	E	M	E	A
L	I	V	E	N	Z	A	U	S	P	E	X
K	N	U	B	B	Y	H	E	T	O	S	W
H	G	E	A	A	M	O	S	I	R	M	A
A	S	H	G	R	E	Y	L	A	T	E	X

Advanced 5: Playfair

B	I	G	G	I	N	B	X	C	M	L	N
R	E	A	R	H	O	R	S	E	I	I	E
O	Q	U	I	N	T	A	L	D	T	O	M
B	E	D	E	L	T	V	P	A	T	N	A
D	A	Y	G	P	D	E	C	R	E	E	T
I	M	P	A	V	E	S	H	I	N	T	O
N	O	R	E	A	S	T	L	D	T	S	P
G	R	I	L	L	T	S	B	O	R	A	H
N	I	M	A	C	I	N	Q	U	E	S	O
A	N	A	N	U	N	A	T	A	K	K	R
G	I	L	D	Q	E	P	E	R	S	U	E

S	W	I	T	Z
E	R	L	A	N
D	B	C	F	G
H	K	M	O	P
Q	U	V	X	Y

CHAPTER 5

Gatherings for Gardner

EASY AS 1, 2, 3, ...

1. Many of the numbers in the fractions listed cancel each other out, so the question readily simplifies to 'What is one-sixth of 12?' Hence, the answer is 2.

2. 12 inches.

3. The Roman numeral IX (9).

4. In space number 87 – if you look at it upside down, the series goes: 86, ?, 88, 89, 90, 91.

5. 12½ and 12½.

6. Q for 'Quarter' – first letters of 1024, 512, 256, 128, 64, 32, 16, 8, ...

7. 52 + 66 = 118.

8. 8 inches.

9. 22 + 2, or 3³ – 3.

10. One method is: divide the powder evenly, then divide one half into two piles of 25 g. Now weigh out 7 g (5 + 2) as normal. 50 + 25 + 7 = 82. What remains equals 18 g.

11. 275 posts.

12. 19 and 91.

13. 0.585 = 585/1,000. Pure gold is 24 carats, so the answer is (585 × 24)/1,000 = 1,404/100 = 14.04, so it is 14 carat gold.

14. 1000, since XL = 40, L = 50 and M = 1,000 in Roman numerals.

15. Six – two of each kind.

16. By Pythagoras' theorem, each fish is 10 metres away from the starting point. If they swam in opposite directions, they would now be 20 metres apart.

17. The only possible solution is 2, 3 and 6 (i.e. 1/2 + 1/3 + 1/6 = 1).

18. 1,200 feet.

19. One large snowman, five medium snowmen and three small snowmen.

20. 54 years old.

PYRAMIDS OF PERPLEXITY

Pyramid 1

	120		
	68	52	
	36	32	20
17	19	13	7
5	12	7	6	1

Pyramid 2

	265		
	143	122	
	92	51	71
63	29	22	49
41	22	7	15	34

Pyramid 3

	90	
41	49	
22	19	30
14	8	11	19

Pyramid 4

	119	
	53	66
24	29	37
11½	12½	16½	20½
3	8½	4	12½	8

Pyramid 5

Replace the unknowns with A and B:

We obtain two equations:
3 = (5/6 + A) + (A + B),
hence 2A + B = 13/6,
or 12A + 6B = 13.

$2\frac{1}{2} = (A + B) + (B + 5/12)$,
hence $A + 2B = 25/12$,
or $12A + 24B = 25$.

Comparing the two equations, we see that adding 18B has increased the total by 12 (from 13 to 25). Hence, $B = 2/3$. You can now work out that $A = 3/4$.

Pyramid 6

		105		
	31		74	
	8	23	51	
2	6	17	34	
7	−5	11	6	28

Pyramid 7

		331		
	172		159	
	86	86	73	
37	49	37	36	
12	25	24	13	23
3	9	16	8	5	18

Pyramid 8

Call the missing three numbers on the bottom row A, B and C. This gives us these three equations:

$36 = (15 + A) + (A + B)$,
hence $2A + B = 21$.

$16 = (A + B) + (B + C)$,
hence $A + 2B + C = 16$.

$36 = (B + C) + (C + 11)$,
hence $B + 2C = 25$.

Adding the first and last equations together gives $2A + 2B + 2C = 46$, so $A + B + C = 23$. Comparing this to the second equation shows that B must be −7, since it has another B but the total is 7 lower. Now that we know B = −7, it's easy to see from the other equations that A = 14 and C = 16. The rest of the pyramid can now be completed:

		104		
	52		52	
	36	16	36	
29	7	9	27	
15	14	−7	16	11

Pyramid 9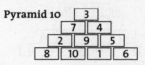

Complete the pyramid as shown. Since it is given that X + Y = 11, the top number = 4(X + Y) + 29 = 44 + 29 = 73.

Pyramid 10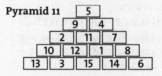

Pyramid 11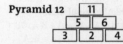

Pyramid 12

	11	
5		6
3	2	4

Pyramid 13

D, E and F all contain exactly five letters. That means they must be one of 3, 7, 8, 40, 50 or 60. It is easy to discount the last three options since A must be a two-digit result (E = 40 or FORTY doesn't work because C's result cannot contain a curved line in word form). Hence, D, E and F must be 3, 7 and 8 in some order. The only way of adding two numbers from (3, 7, 8) and getting a prime result is 3 + 8 = 11. Hence, D and E must be 3 and 8 in some order. If A is to be the biggest result possible, we'd better put 8 in the E slot. That leaves 7 in the F box. Hence, E + F = 7 + 8 = 15 = FIFTEEN – which, thankfully, has no curved lines and completes the solution.

Pyramid 14

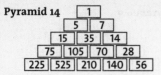

The top number is 1, because 5 and 7 have no common factors other than 1.

Pyramid 15

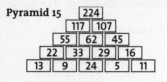

....

NUMBER CRUNCHING

1. If the number is X, then $(X + 3)/2 = 2X$. Rearranging, $4X = X + 3$, or $3X = 3$, and so $X = 1$.

2. Expressing the two-digit number as $10A + B$, the calculation becomes $3(10A + B) + A + B = 10B + A$, which simplifies to $5A = B$. A cannot be 0 (otherwise it would not be a proper two-digit number), nor can A be larger than 1 (because B would be 10 or greater and therefore not a digit). Hence $A = 1$, $B = 5$, and the number we seek is 15.

3. The highest common factor of 2, 3, 4, 5 and 6 is equal to $2 \times 5 \times 6 = 60$. Therefore, likely candidates are 61, 121, 181, 241, 301, 361, etc. Of these, 301 is the first that divides evenly by 7.

4. $X = 2$, $Y = 4$, $Z = 9$ (note: 2 is the only even prime, 9 is odd but not prime).

5. If the missing numbers are X and Y, with X being the smaller, then $2(X - 1) = Y + 1$ and $3X + 4Y = XY$. Rearranging the former equation gives $Y = 2X - 3$. Substitute this into the second equation:

$3X + 4(2X - 3) = X(2X - 3)$, so $11X - 12 = 2X^2 - 3X$, or $X^2 - 7X + 6 = 0$. Factorizing this gives $(X - 6)(X - 1)$. X cannot be 1 (because 'If one less than the smaller of two numbers is doubled ...' in the question wouldn't work) so $X = 6$, and therefore $Y = 2X - 3 = 9$.

6. Let X be one of the sides, and $34 - X$ be the other. By Pythagoras' Theorem, $26^2 = X^2 + (34 - X)^2 = X^2 + (1156 - 68X + X^2)$. Rearranging: $676 = 2X^2 - 68X + 1156$, or $X^2 - 34X + 240 = 0$. Factorizing this gives $(X - 24)(X - 10) = 0$, so the solutions are 10 and 24 units.

7. The number is 12, and the parts are 1, 2, 3 and 6.

8. 42 and 6.

9. Define X to be the result we get each time. Then $A = X - 4$, $B = X + 4$, $C = 4X$ and $D = X/4$. Adding these together: $100 = A + B + C + D = (X - 4) + (X + 4) + 4X + (X/4) = 25X/4$ If $100 = 25X/4$, then $X = 16$. Putting this back into our original equations, $A = 12$, $B = 20$, $C = 64$, $D = 4$.

10. The numbers are 6 and 10. The difference between their squares is $10^2 - 6^2 = 100 - 36 = 64 = 4^3$. On the other hand, the difference between their cubes is $10^3 - 6^3 = 1000 - 216 = 784 = 28^2$.

11. 3, 4 and 5; or −1, 0, and 1.

12. 35 and 36.

13. Note that $a^2 - b^2$ is the same as $(a - b) \times (a + b)$. Hence, $(34 \times 100)/(2 \times 100) = 34/2 = 17$.

14. (a) $4 \times 2,178 = 8,712$; (b) $9 \times 1,089 = 9,801$.

15. 219,438,657.

16. Note that $10^6 = 2^6 \times 5^6$. The 2's and 5's must be kept separate, otherwise a 0 forms at the end of the result (since $2 \times 5 = 10$). Hence, the numbers are $2^6 = 64$ and $5^6 = 15{,}625$. For the second part, just use the '9' repeatedly as follows:
999.999… × 999.999…
= 1,000,000. Mathematically, 999.999… is exactly the same as 1,000.

17. $1/2 = 7{,}293/14{,}586$
$1/3 = 5{,}823/17{,}469$
$1/4 = 7{,}956/31{,}824$
$1/5 = 2{,}973/14{,}865$
$1/6 = 2{,}943/17{,}658$
$1/7 = 5{,}274/36{,}918$
$1/8 = 9{,}321/74{,}568$
$1/9 = 8{,}361/75{,}249$

....

MAGIC SQUARES AND FRIENDS

Magic 1

In a 3 × 3 magic square, the central number is always one-third of the magic number. Given that the central number is 3, the magic number (i.e. the number to which each row, column and diagonal must add up) must be 9. From here, it's easy to work out. Note the negative number in the right-hand column.

0	5	4
7	3	−1
2	1	6

Magic 2

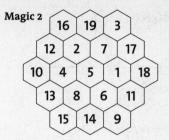

Magic 3

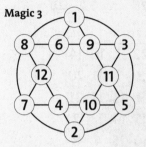

Magic 4

In a 3 × 3 magic square, the central number is always one-third of the magic number. Given that the magic number is 17, the central number must be 17/3. From here, it's easy to fill out the rest.

10	⅔	19⁄3
2	17⁄3	28⁄3
5	32⁄3	4⁄3

Magic 5

Use the 4d stamp twice – on one occasion it's used on its own, on the other it appears in the same square as the ½d stamp.

2½	5	1½
2	3	4
4½	1	3½

Magic 6

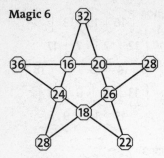

Magic 7

18	22	1	10	14
24	3	7	11	20
5	9	13	17	21
6	15	19	23	2
12	16	25	4	8

Magic 8

The solution explains itself. The columns, rows, and two diagonals all add up alike to 6,726, and nine of each of the figures 1, 2, 3, 4 have been employed.

2243	1341	3142
3141	2242	1343
1342	3143	2241

MONEY, MONEY, MONEY

1. 14 cars were sold at £1,500 each.

2. £27. Strangely, it doesn't actually matter on which races he won and lost – the result's always the same.

3. Mr A owes £50 + £20 and is owed £30, so he must repay £40 to be even. Similarly, Miss B is owed £40 net (10 – 50), Mr C is owed £20 net (10 – 30 + 40) and Mrs D owes £20 net (20 – 40). Hence, two trans-actions are needed – Mr A should give Miss B £40, and Mrs D should give £20 to Mr C.

4. There will be ½ × (13 × 12) = 78 matches, with £100 given out for each match regardless of the out-come, so the total will be £7,800.

5. Comparing the deals, 21p buys three more apples. The raw cost per apple is 21/3 = 7p; the profit on either deal is 6p.

6. Let b = bank and c = courtiers. b – 4c = 18, and b – 7c = –21. Subtract one from other: 3c = 39, so c = 13. Hence, b = 18 + (4 × 13) = 70.

7. The answer is not $6,000 because he would also be taxed on that amount. The correct compensa-tion is 6,000 × (100/80) = $7,500.

8. They spent £6/2 = £3 on average over all their male customers, and similarly £9/3 = £3 on their female customers. Since these values are the same, the total spend = 3 × 500 = £1,500.

9. Let stonkingrich.com's value be represented by X. Then: X + (X – 15) + (X – 7) + (X – 12) = 154, so 4X – 34 = 154, giving 4X = 188. So X = 47, and the others are worth $32m, $40m, $35m respectively.

10. Divide 8,268 into its prime fac-tors: 2 × 2 × 3 × 13 × 53. The only way you can obtain a number in the right range is 53 × 2 = 106 (receiving £78 each).

11. If the buckle is worth G groats, then (7/12) × (100 + G) = 20 + G, hence 700 + 7G = 240 + 12G. This simplifies to 5G = 460, so G = 92.

12. Let B = basic salary and A = Peter's age. Paul is A + 6 years old. We can form two equations: 1,411 = B +

$(A + 6)^2 = B + (A^2 + 12A + 36)$, and $1075 = B + A^2$. Subtracting one equation from the other gives $336 = 12A + 36$, so $A = 25$. Peter is therefore 25, Paul is 31 and the salary is $450.

13. Taking the hint from the question, $(100D + L) − 118 = 2 \times (100L + D)$. This is $98D = 199L + 118$, or $D = (2L + 1) + [(3L + 20)/98]$. The bit in square brackets must be whole, and $L < 100$, so $3L + 20 = 98$, and $L = 26$, $D = 54$. The cheque was for £26.54.

14. £12.37. Calculation: If Z is the pounds amount, then the pence amount is $3Z + 1$. Hence, ($3Z + 1$ pound and Z pence) equals $3 \times$ (Z pounds and $3Z + 1$ pence) plus one penny. Converting everything to pence, $100 \times (3Z + 1) + Z = 3 \times (100Z + 3Z + 1) + 1$. This simplifies to $8Z = 96$, hence $Z = 12$.

SOVEREIGN LAND

Henry Dudeney writes: The large majority of competitors who tried to solve the puzzle in the *Daily News* succeeded in securing bags containing only £45. The correct answer is £47 contained in ten bags, all deposited on outside plots, thus: 4, 5, 6 in the first row, 5 in the second, 4 in the third, 3 in the fourth, 5 in the fifth, and 5, 6, 4 in the bottom row. If you include 5 bags containing £6 each, you can secure only nine bags, and a value of £46.

TWODOOR'S TOWN HOUSE

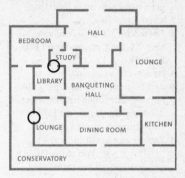

....

HALFWAY HOUSE

1. Golf – in normal stroke play golf the player who performs best always wins. In the other sports, where matches are divided into sets, it is possible for the player who has won the most points to lose (tennis example: 7–6, 0–6, 7–6 is a 2–1 set win by 14–18 games).

2. TEN – these are the final letters of 1 to 10: onE, twO, threE, fouR, fivE, siX, seveN – and eighT, ninE and teN.

3. 3 to the power of (3 to the power of 3) = 3^{27} = 7,625,597,484,987.

4. $888 + 88 + 8 + 8 + 8 = 1,000$.

5. One way is to make a cut parallel to the table top, providing two identical slices. The other solution is to cut along the line from the middle of the cheese to the middle of the rectangle.

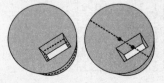

6. Rotate '8' by 90 degrees to give ∞, the symbol for infinity – you can't get a bigger increase than that!

7. 3,801 – 2,586 = 1,215.

8. Swap A for 1, B for 2 (and vice versa), C for 3, etc. and you obtain $E = MC^2$.

9. $(17 × 4 = 68) + 25 = 93$.

10. By 1,600 per cent. Enlarging the area by four times has the effect of doubling the perimeter for any two-dimensional shape.

11. The series goes $81 – (8 × 1) = 73$, $73 – (7 × 3) = 52$, and so on. Since $10 – (1 × 0) = 10$, all the remaining terms will be 10.

12. Only fourteen. No matter how you cut the fourteen planks, the final piece is a 2 ft by 2 ft square at best.

13. Any pair of adjacent numbers along the track sum to a square number: $4 + 32 = 36$, $32 + 17 = 49$, etc.

14. If you convert all the numbers to Roman numerals, you get a palindromic result: I IV III V X II VI IX VIII VII.

15. $9/12 + 5/34 + 7/68 = 1$.

....

CROSSNUMBERS

Crossnumber 1

1	6	7	6
2	4	4	9
9	6	1	0
6	9	1	0

The values are: a = 3, b = 12 and c = 4.

Crossnumber 2

1	3	3	4	0	2
4	2	8	5	7	1
6	7	6	2	0	1
4	6	9	1	8	2
1	8	1	3	3	5

Crossnumber 3

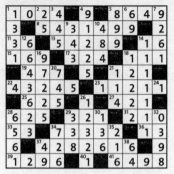

The starting point is 18 across: the three similar figures must be 111, 222, 333, etc. As 26 down is 18 across squared, then 18 across must be 111 or 222 because the larger possibilities are longer than five digits. Now consider 34 across …

....

TIME AND MOTION

1. 4 hours and 17 minutes. When multiplying by 60, the minutes become hours and the seconds become minutes.

2. Daniel reloaded four times in 10 seconds (average = 2.5 s), while Dennis reloaded nine times in 20 seconds (average = 2.222… s). So Dennis is slightly quicker.

3. He would have to travel at an infinite speed on the second lap. If he averaged 60 mph for two laps, they would take precisely two minutes. The two minutes have already been used up in the first lap at 30 mph.

4. The year 2028. Only leap years can possibly have five Tuesdays (or five of any other day) in February. A five-Tuesday leap-year comes one every seven leap years, i.e. once every 28 years.

5. If the time from now until 11 a.m. is X minutes, then the time from 8 a.m. to now is $3X - 20$. The total of these times must be 180, the minutes from 8 a.m. to 11 a.m., i.e. $180 = 3X - 20 + X$. Therefore, $200 = 4X$, so $X = 50$. The current time must be 10.10.

6. M minutes per mile = $(60/M)$ mph = $(60 \times 1.6/M)$ kph = M kph. This simplifies to M being the square root of 96 (approx. 9.8). In other words, around 9.8 minutes per mile is the same rate as 9.8 kilometres per hour.

7. Ambiguities can only occur in the first 12 days of a month. From the 13th onwards, one can deduce the exact date. However, note that each month has 11 ambiguities, not 12, because 1 January, 2 February, 3 March, and so on are not ambiguous. Therefore there are $12 \times 11 = 132$ ambiguous dates.

8. 8 p.m., since this is one hour later than the midpoint between 1 p.m. and 1 a.m., namely 7 p.m.

9. After X hours, $5,000 + 250X = 12,000 - 100X$. Hence, $350X = 7,000$, so X=20. The numbers will be identical in 20 hours.

10. (a) The stairs lift him by three steps every 6 seconds, and he climbs at the rate of one step every 6 seconds. His total speed is therefore four steps for every 6 seconds, so twenty-four steps would take $6 \times 6 = 36$ seconds.

(b) Fifty steps per minute. His tota speed is now two steps every 6 seconds, so the journey now lasts 72 seconds. This is exactly long enough for the first step he touches to travel the 36 steps on the escalator's unseen underside back to the top.

11. In the first case, there are 77 goat-days of food. However, the second case implies that there are 80 goat-days of food with one more day allowed. Hence, enough grass grows each day to sustain three goats, so the answer is 'for ever'.

12. He does his patrols when his digital clock is displaying a palindromic time: 01:10, 02:20, 03:30, 04:40, 05:50, 10:01, 11:11, 12:21.

13. They start and end with the same letter:
9:57   Nine fifty-seveN
8:23   Eight twenty-threE
1:32   One thirty-twO
11:25   Eleven twenty-fivE
9:13   Nine thirteeN
2:48   Two forty-eighT

14. Relative speed of satellites = 15 + 35 = 50 km/s. Hence, 10,000/50 = 200 seconds will elapse before they collide. In that time, the signal will have travelled 300×200 = 60,000 km.

15. Work rate = Area/Time. Suppose the lawn is of area A. Then Mungo's work rate = Rate of both minus Mary's rate = $A/(2.4) - A/4$ = $10A/24 - 6A/24 = 4A/24 = A/6$. Hence Mungo would take 6 hours by himself.

16. Work rate = Bricks/Time. Effective work rate = $B/3 + B/4 - B/12$ = 6B/12. Time taken = Bricks/Work Rate = $B/(6B/12)$ = 2 days.

17. The man was born in 1856 and died in 1920, aged 64 years. Let X = age at death. Then 29X = date of birth. The date of birth + age = date of death, so that $29X + X = 30X$, or date of death. Now, from the question the man was clearly alive in 1900 and is dead now (in 1930). So death occurred during or between

those dates, and, as the date is 30X, it is divisible by 30. The date can only be 1920, which divided by 30 gives 64. So in 1900 he was 44 years of age.

18. There were 129 years between the birth of Cleopatra and the death of Boadicea; but as their united ages amounted to 100 years only, there must have been 29 years when neither existed – that is, between the death of Cleopatra and the birth of Boadicea. Therefore Boadicea must have been born 29 years after the death of Cleopatra in 30 BC, which would be in the year 1 BC.

19. Runner A requires a 44-yard start, and runner C requires a 40-yard handicap.

20. It's trickier than you might think because so many of the digits have constraints: the first and seventh digits must be 0, 1 or 2; the third and fifth digits must be less than 6; and so on. The earliest time and date possible turns out to be 17:48:59 on 26/03. The latest time is 17:56:43 on 28/09.

21. He must have been born in 1892. He was 44 years old in the year 1936 (= 44²).

22. The evil twist here is that '3 knots per hour' is an acceleration, not a speed, because 3 knots per hour = (3 nautical miles per hour) per hour = a constant acceleration of 3 nautical miles per hr². Distance = ½ × (Acceleration × Time²), so Time = √((216 × 2)/3) = √144 = 12 hours.

23. 1 January 1920. The fact that they're on a train narrows the field to after the train was invented. As the two are different ages, their years of birth must be in two different centuries. The ticket inspector knows the current date and year. For him to be certain, the situation must be unique. There are only two years that fit the bill. One is during World War I, which the Paris–Berlin information rules out. This leaves 1920, and it can be true in that year only if both speakers have not yet had their birthday – hence it must be January 1st for the ticket inspector to speak with certainty. One was born in 1905, the other in 1896.

MATCHSTICK PUZZLES

Matchsticks 1

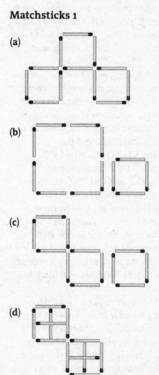

(a)

(b)

(c)

(d)

(e)

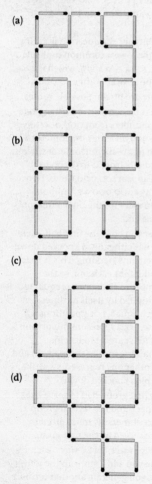

There are other possible
arrangements.

Matchsticks 2

(a)

(b)

(c)

(d)

(e)

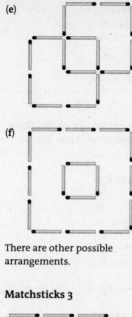

(f)

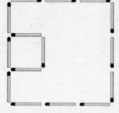

There are other possible
arrangements.

Matchsticks 3

Matchsticks 4

Matchsticks 5

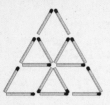

There are three small triangles, three medium triangles and one large triangle.

Matchsticks 6

(a)

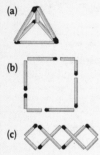

(b)

(c)

Matchsticks 7

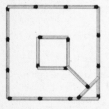

Matchsticks 8

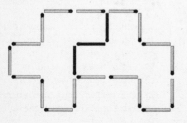

COMBINATION SALAD

1. Assuming that the fare from station A to station B is the same as that from B to A, then (25 × 24)/2 = 300 fares are required.

2. If you answered 47, that's incorrect. The worst-case scenario occurs when Ernie takes all the 5 amp and 13 amp fuses first (since there are more of these), followed by 5 of the 3 amp fuses. 23 + 28 + 5 = 56 fuses.

3. Essentially, the question is asking for the lowest common multiple of 1, 2, 3, 4, 5, 6 and 7, which is 420, so the answer is after 420 days.

4. There are fifteen possible routes.

5. The total is 27,000,001. Imagine the numbers from 000,000 to 999,999 on a car's mileometer. For each of the six mileometer wheels, the digits from 0 to 9 (total 45) will appear 100,000 times. Hence: 6 × 45 × 100,000 = 27 million. Then add 1 for the final '1 million' at the end.

6. After you bowl the first ball, each pin has either been knocked down or remains standing. This is independent for each pin, so the number of situations is equal to 2 multiplied by itself 10 times, which equals 1,024 positions. Of these, 1,023 represent opportunities for spares (1 to 10 pins remaining for the second ball) and the other one represents a strike (all pins knocked down).

7. The first group had to serve 1,365 dinners, and the second group 1,330 dinners: 35 more dinners were served by the first group.

8. (a) Five ways; (b) 89 ways. Each time you add a stone to the journey, you generate another term in

the Fibonacci series (1, 2, 3, 5, 8, 13, 21, 34, 55, 89, …) where each term is the sum of the two previous terms.

9. There are 30 different possible cubes. Suppose we are painting a gaming die, with its faces bearing the numbers 1 to 6. Choose any colour for face 1 (six choices) and any remaining colour for face 6 (five choices) on the opposite side. There are six arrangements for the other four colours running around the middle of the cube. This gives $6 \times 5 \times 6$ arrangements. However, we could repeat this process starting with the face numbered 2, 3, 4, 5 or 6 instead. Therefore, we need to divide by six to get the number of truly different cubes. Hence, $(6 \times 5 \times 6)/6 = 30$ cubes.

OUT OF THIS WORLD

Out of this world 1
Planet A travels through 360/10 = 36 degrees each year. The figure for planet B is 360/9 = 40 degrees. Therefore, B is 4 degrees faster than A. Planet B will be on the line between Planet A and the sun in 300 degrees time (with A and B on the same side of the sun), which will occur in 300/4 = 75 years' time. (In this time, A will have done 7½ orbits, B will have done 8 and one-third.)

Out of this world 2
Planet D travels 360/5 = 72 degrees around the circle every year. Planet C travels 360/3 = 120 degrees around the circle every year. Hence, C gains on D by 120 − 72 = 48 degrees every month. In order for planets to be in line with the sun again, C needs to advance by 180 degrees so that it now lies on the opposite side of the sun.

This happens in 180/48 = 3.75 years (3 years and 9 months).

Out of this world 3
The simplest method is to consider in which years the planets will hit the collision point. Planet A will reach that point in years 5, 13, 21, 29, 37, 45, etc.; Planet B will reach that point in years 9, 19, 29, 39, 49, 59, etc. Since 29 is common to both lists, the planets will collide in 29 years' time.

Out of this world 4
Because the orbits are not in the same plane, G and H will be on the same line with the sun only after each half of an orbit. The answer is 70 years, because 70 is the lowest common multiple of 14 and 10 (i.e. half of 28 and 20). (In this time, G will have done 2½ orbits, H will have done 3½.)

CHANCE WOULD BE A FINE THING

1. One-quarter of the length of the original stick. Because the breaking point is random, the shorter piece could be anywhere from almost nothing to almost half of the length. Therefore, on average it will be a quarter of the length.

2. Suppose that you have X-ray vision and are able to choose a cup that has a marble under it. The chance that the remaining marble is in an adjacent cup is 2 out of 4, or 50 per cent.

3. There are six possible ways of arranging three cards. The probability that they are picked in increasing order of importance is therefore 1/6.

4. Imagine that the spy's twin is on the exact opposite side of the

Pentagon, the same distance away. If one spy sees three sides, his twin will see two, and vice versa. Therefore, the chance that the original spy sees three sides is exactly ½.

5. By symmetry, there is no difference between having the bucket in the third or fourth position, so move it to the left. The left half is now covered by buckets. So, also by symmetry, half of the 100 balls will go in the buckets.

6. The numbers are 1, 1, 3 and 7. Mode = the most common, mean = the arithmetic average, median = the middle number(s) when listed in increasing order (and taking the average of the middle two, if there are an even number of numbers in the list).

7. If tea drinkers = X, coffee drinkers = 2X. Total of people who drink tea and/or coffee = 3X − 24 (to avoid double counting) = 100 − 7 = 93. Hence, 3X = 93 + 24 = 117, so X = 39.

8. For those women who form the 97 per cent, half wearing two earrings and half wearing none is equivalent to each one wearing a single earring. Therefore, overall we have 800 women wearing 800 earrings in total.

9. Mrs Tabako puts one cultured pearl in jar A and all the other pearls in jar B. Then the chances of Mr Tabako picking a cultured pearl from jar A are 99/99, and the chances of him picking one from jar B are 49/99. Cumulatively, the chances of picking a cultured pearl are the average of these two figures = 148/198 = 74 out of 99.

10. There are 15 cards. The odds of picking two of the same suit are

(15 × 4)/(15 × 14) = 2/7. After the spades are added, the odds are [(15 × 4) + (13 ×12)]/28 × 27 = 216/(28 × 27) = 2/7.

11. It's a certainty – because if the first 1,001 people had 0 to 1,000 freckles inclusive, the final 1,002nd person must match with someone else.

12. The chance that all three numbers are different is 5/5 × 4/5 × 3/5 = 12/25. There is a 1/3 chance that Ziggy's number is the middle one, so the answer is 4/25, or 16 per cent.

13. Zero. The only way you can pick two out of four cards and have a 50 per cent chance of a red pair is if there are three red cards and one black card. Therefore, it is impossible to pick a pair of black cards.

14. (a) There are 6 × 6 × 6 = 216 different possible rolls. Suppose we roll one die first. This has six different possibilities. Now we roll the second die. We want this to be different to the first. This gives us 6 × 5 = 30 desirable outcomes so far. For the third die, it must be different to the first two, so there are 6 × 5 × 4 = 120 outcomes. Therefore, the probability that all three dice show different symbols is 120/216, which works out at 55.55 per cent. (b) The even money bet is fair. However, when a double or three of a kind turns up, only two or one of the symbols are winners. This could still be a fair game if the fair odds are offered. However, a specific double should pay out 13.4 to 1, and three of a kind at 215 to 1. This gives the bookmaker a profit margin of just under 8 per cent.

15. To win the game, the final card must be a King. An easy way to see this is to imagine that there are only 13 cards of one suit used. If you turn over the middle card first, you follow the chain of cards until you find the King. There are no cards left in the middle pile, so the King has to be the final card in the chain. The probability of the final card being a King is simply 1/13, so that's the answer.

16. Surprisingly, the probability is 2/3. The counter inside the bag is either black (B) or white (call it W1). We now add a white counter (W2) to the bag and withdraw one counter. There are only three situations: we draw W1 (leaving W2 in the bag), we draw W2 (leaving W1 in the bag) or we draw W2 (leaving B in the bag). Of these three situations, a white counter remains inside the bag for two of them.

17. Believe it or not, 100 per cent. The likelihood of the number containing a '3' increases with digit length: one-digit numbers, 10 per cent; two digits, 19 per cent; three digits, 27.1 per cent; etc. As you approach numbers of infinite length, the probability that the number contains a '3' gets closer to 100 per cent. Such are the problems of percentages used with infinite sets of numbers. (By a similar argument, the chance that a number does not contain a 3 is also 100 per cent!)

HARD QUIZ

1. One of the Egyptians must be up on high – for example, they could be standing at the points of a triangle-based pyramid.

2. 53 matches, because each match knocks out one person, leaving one winner at the end. This rule works regardless of the number of competitors.

3. In each case, the relevant mathematical symbol is rotated 90 degrees anticlockwise to obtain the relevant Roman numeral: < and V (5), – and I (1), × and X (10), = and II (2). If you rotate the intersection symbol used in set theory ($\cap$), you obtain C (100).

4. 50, because FIFTY does not contain the letter E (i.e. Eban = 'E is banned').

5. 8 and 4.

6. $(35/70) + (148/296) = 1$. It looks scary until you realize that it's just a long-winded way of writing $\frac{1}{2} + \frac{1}{2}$.

7. 25 and 52.

8. One way is: (GROSS/DOZEN) + EIGHT = SCORE, since $(144/12) + 8 = 20$. Other answers using the same kind of trick exist.

9. One answer is $4,539,281,706 \times 2 = 9,078,563,412$. If you divide the first number into pairs – 45, 39 etc. – these can be arranged in any order so long as the 06 is not at the beginning or the 45 at the end.

10. The statement relates to a conversion between binary to decimal numbers: 'If 10101010 = 170, then 1010 = 10.' (In binary, the place values are worth 1 2 4 8 16 32 64 … from right to left.)

11. $7 \times 63,492 = 444,444$. The method is to divide 7 into a string of 4's until you get no remainder (i.e. 7 into 44 gives 6 remainder 2, 7 into 444 gives …).

12. $2,572 \times 4 = 10,288$.

13. Note that if $4 + C + D = 16$ and $C + D + E = 16$, then $E = 4$. By a similar argument on the other side, $G = 3$. Therefore, $16 = E + F + G = 4 + F + 3$, so $F = 9$.

14. 512 carrots. To solve, simplify the expression thus: $1/(1 - (¾)^4) \times 350 = 512$.

15. Raising both sides to the 15th power gives 10 cubed versus 4 to the power of 5, which are 1,000 and 1,024 respectively. Hence, the right-hand number is larger.

FOR OUR FINAL NUMBER

1. Let x = total number of CDs. $(x - 6) + (x - 6)/2 = (x + 8)$, so $3(x - 6) = 2(x + 8)$. Rearranging: $3x - 2x = x = 16 + 18 = 34$ CDs.

2. The packaging must weigh 40 g (2 per cent of 2 kg). After pouring the cereal, this 40g accounts for 1/20th of the weight. The total pack weight is now $40 \times 20 = 800$ g, so I ate 1.2 kg of cereal (the diet starts tomorrow).

3. One weighing is sufficient. Take one coin from the first box, two from the second, three from the third, and so on, up to ten coins from the tenth box. The 45 coins should weigh 450 g. If they actually weigh 449 g, then box 1 contains the fakes because there is one lighter coin in the pile. If the coins weigh 448 g, then box 2 contains the fakes, and so on.

4. The farmer planted 12 onions, 36 potatoes, 24 radishes, 30 tomatoes and 27 beets.

5. Mrs Wilkinson bought seven ice lollies. Tom ate four lollies, since half of seven is 3½ and the extra half makes four. Dick ate two and Harriet had the remaining one.

6. She buys four of each shape of balloon plus one extra for three of the shapes. The four of each shape would cost a total of $(1 + 2 + 3 + 5 + 7 + 10) \times 4 = £1.12$. Since we know that the total amount was a multiple of 20p, possible totals for all the balloons include £1.20, £1.40, £1.60, £1.80, and so on. The extra three balloons must therefore have cost a total of 8p, or 28p, or 48p, or 68p, and so on. Using three of the values 1, 2, 3, 5, 7 and 10, the only possible total is 8p. Hence the mother spent £1.20. Therefore, she bought four 3, 7 and 10 pence balloons and five 1, 2 and 5 pence balloons.

7. She carefully cuts each tablet in half. On Saturday, she took one half from each tablet, which must be two 'B' halves and two 'C' halves. She took the remaining halves on Sunday.

8. 30 are playing basketball, 42 are playing netball and 22 are playing hockey. It's possible to split 94 into other sums of multiples of 5, 7 and 11, but all other combinations result in either one sport not being played or an odd number of teams playing two sports, each with no opponent to face.

9. If John received 'J' votes, then total votes cast $= J + (J - 18) + (J - 27) + (J - 41) = (4 \times J) - 86 = 142$. Hence, $J = (142 + 86)/4 = 57$. Results: John: 57 votes, Albert 39, Brian 30 and Charlie 16.

10. It's not possible since the knight will alternate between black and white squares along his route. If there are 64 squares on the board, an even number, he must therefore finish on a black square if he started on a white one, and vice versa.

11. Every number from 2 to 10 can divide into its lowest common multiple, which is: $2 \times 2 \times 2 \times 3 \times 3 \times 5 \times 7 = 2,520$. Since there is always one left over, there must be 2,521 sweets.

12. Sally is a cow and Peter is a bull. If X is the number of cows and Y is the number of bulls, then the equations $X - 1 = Y$ and $2(Y - 1) = X$ can be formed. The solution to these equations gives the answer four cows and three bulls.

13. If a silver coin is taken out with a copper coin, it is immediately replaced. So silver coins can only be taken out in pairs. As we started with an odd number of silver coins, the final coin must be silver.

CHAPTER 6
Truth Will Out

LOGIC WARM-UPS

1. The right way around also. The mirror reverses the word, but looking at it from the other side of the window reverses it back.

2. Five swaps. This worst-case situation occurs if (for example) letters A, B, C, D, E and F are delivered to households B, C, D, E, F and A respectively.

3. RF for royal flush (poker hands: high card, one pair, two pairs, three of a kind, straight, flush, full house, four of a kind, straight flush, royal flush).

4. (a) The bulb is on if only switch B is on.
   (b) The bulb is never on.
   (c) The bulb is on if exactly one switch is on.
   (d) The bulb is on if only B and C are on (and the others are off).

5. Eight. One way is A sends a message to B, D to E, A to D, C to F, C to D, A to F, E to F, and B to C.

6. Neither would hit the ground first, because halfway during a transatlantic flight the plane would be over water.

7. 14 – you need seven to take account of all the different days on which 1 January can fall, and another set of seven to account for leap years.

8. Second. Many people jump to the conclusion that overtaking the person in second position means you've won the race.

9. The name of each number gives the first letter of the next highest whole number: zerO, OnE, EighT, TeN, NineteeN, NinetY. There are no English numbers beginning with Y.

10. (1) B, (2) B, (3) A, (4) B.

11. Go first and subtract a 4 to take the score to 96. Thereafter, if your rival subtracts X, you subtract 8 – X. Eventually, the score will be 8 with your opponent to go next – you can't lose.

12. 26 cards, made up of 13 pairs of cards. Holding a 27th card will give you three of a kind, making a full house.

13. Probably not – if you buy me two beers and I fail to buy three back, you've won the original bet for one beer. I'm now a beer up on the deal. Cheers!

14. The outgoing message tape was a loop with a half-twist put in it (a Möbius strip). Once the message had been played, the tape would keep going until it found the start of the message again, ready for the next caller.

15. None – ducks can't speak …

16. 2 – they are the powers of 2 (2, 4, 8, 16, 32, 64, 128, 256, 512, …) regrouped as pairs of digits.

17. Four under par (or −4). The second round is ten shots better than +3, which is −7. The cumulative score of −7 and +3 is −4.

18. The only order that works is B then C then A. The third sentence eliminates ACB, the fourth eliminates BAC, and the fifth eliminates ABC, CAB and CBA.

19. V – they are the letters on a watch or clock face featuring Roman numerals, reading clockwise from 9 o'clock (IX).

20. It is Robyn, looking at herself in the mirror. You can deduce that she is an only child.

21. In lower case, q is b turned upside-down. Likewise, u becomes n and p becomes d. Hence, the missing letter is W.

22. Five. For brevity, let the person who met X people be called 'Mr X'. Mr 1 must have met Mr 9 (who met everyone); Mr 2 must therefore have met Mr 8 (who met everyone except Mr 1) and Mr 9. By pairing off 1 & 9, 2 & 8, 3 & 7 and 4 & 6, you're left with Mr 5. So you must have met five people too.

....

IQ ASSAULT COURSE

1. The fourth one reads ILLEGIBLE when upside down. Note that the other numbers also form words.

2. 8, so that each part of the number uses one more calculator 'segment' than the previous term.

$$-174368$$

3. None, because the spout is at the same height. The top quarter of coffeepot B cannot carry any liquid.

4. Move the third and sixth characters so that it reads as follows:

$$10 \text{ TO } 10 = 9.50$$

5. Thirteen.

6. The top-right square, because the 7 would be seven squares away (i.e. 4 horizontally + 3 vertically) from the previous number. The same logic applies to the other numbers.

7. Fourteen. No matter how they are cut, each plank consists of a square of each colour. Note that there are only 14 black squares, so that must be the answer.

8. One of each pair of arrowheads points towards one other square containing an arrow, except for the up/down arrow in the final column on the right.

9. A and B because they have the same length of rod. The weight of the bob or the angle of swing don't have a significant effect on the rate.

10. The bottom digit to the power of the right-hand digit results in the remaining number: 5 to the power of 2 = 25, 3 to the power of 4 = 81, 2 to the power of 6 = 64. Hence, insert 7 and 2 to give 7 to the power of 2 = 49.

11. E does not have half-turn symmetry – in other words, it looks significantly different when turned upside down.

12. The middle two cards. It's clear why the striped card must be turned over. The 2 of clubs must be turned over because we need to check it doesn't have a striped back. We don't care about the Ace – the question didn't require that every Ace must have a striped back.

13. One – pour the contents of the fifth glass into the third glass then place this glass (now empty) to the left of the first glass.

14. The leftmost two are linked together:

15. The near-horizontal line near the bottom isn't perpendicular to any other line. The rest of them cross one other line at right angles:

16. It will remain the same, since the volume of water displaced equals the weight of the ice cubes (Archimedes' principle).

17. Fifteen. There's no way of visiting the whole board, no matter which route you take.

18. Square 1 gives a guaranteed win, forcing your opponent to make a line of three crosses. Any other move leads to a tie or loss.

19. Here's one of the possible ways:

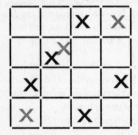

20. 102, because 88 + (number of digital segments in 88) = 88 + 14 = 102.

21. The spoke at four o'clock would be empty because FOUR doesn't contain E, N, S or W. This is why other spokes have been labelled as oNE, tWo, fivE, Six, Eight, NiNE, tEN, etc.

22. The diagram at the top left. There is nothing unique about it or, if you prefer, it is the only one that is not the odd one out so that makes it the odd one out!

23. It should be shaded because the two cubes below it are the same. If they were different, it would be black.

24. Each row, column and main diagonal adds up to 7 hours 30 minutes. This is really a magic square in disguise. The missing clock should read 12:30.

25. Paint the second space in the top row black, the right-hand space in the third row shaded, and the bottom space white:

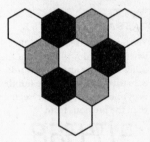

26. The minute hand should point to the four o'clock position, because there are four letters in the number that the hour hand is pointing towards (FOUR, as it happens).

27. The minute hand points to the 8 (the only remaining even number), the hour hand points to the 5 (the only remaining odd number).

28. The ratio of the large triangle to small triangle is 4:1, and so it's the same for the large circle and the small circle.

29. Four times as large – easily seen if you ignore the circles and divide the large square into four quarters.

30. The numbers refer to the corners in the outline of each letter's shape.

31. C (least dense), E, B, D, A (densest).

32. One solution is as follows:

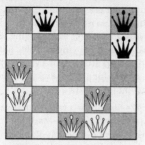

33. B and C are contradictions, so either statement must be true. If C is true, this leads to a contradiction. Hence, C is lying, B is true and A (also lying) is guilty.

34.

L	P	H
I	A	C
N	G	O

35.

U	E	S
Q	A	T
O	R	P

36.

P	K	E
A	R	T
M	S	U

37. Time. One method is to consider the physical units used by each item, then cancel them out, which would leave just time at the end. Alternatively, you can use some school physics: Fc²/VIa = mc²/VI [using F = ma] = E/VI [via E = mc²] = (Power × Time)/Power [using P = VI] = Time.

38. Imagine the numbers 1 to 6 clockwise around each cell, with 1 at the top. The arrow indicates the number of cells that are adjacent. There are three cells bordering the empty cell, so its arrow should point down-right.

39. Six – simply arrange them to form a cube.

40. The only possibility is 12 minutes past 2.

FILM FUN

The film on screen 1 doesn't start at 7.00 (clue 1), 7.30 (2) or 7.10 (3), so is at 7.20. The action movie is on screen 2 (4), starting at 7.10, and the film on screen 3 starts at 7.00. The sci-fi film is on screen 4 (1) and starts at 7.30. Screen 3 isn't showing the comedy (3), so is showing the musical. Screen 1 is showing the comedy. Thus:

Screen 1 – 7.20pm – comedy
Screen 2 – 7.10pm – action
Screen 3 – 7.00pm – musical
Screen 4 – 7.30pm – science fiction

FLYING VISITS

Tuesday's flight doesn't leave at 8.00 (clue 1), so is at 7.00 (3), and the flight to Vienna is on Wednesday (4). The Madrid flight doesn't leave on Thursday or Friday and doesn't leave at 7.00 (1), so is on Monday. The flight to Rome leaves half an hour earlier in the day than Wednesday's flight (2), thus Wednesday's flight isn't at 6.30. So the Copenhagen flight isn't on Tuesday (5), and nor is the Brussels flight (3), thus Tuesday's flight is to

Rome and Wednesday's is at 7.30 (2).
The Copenhagen flight is on Thursday
and the 6.30 flight on Friday (5), thus
it's to Brussels. The 8.00 flight is to
Copenhagen (1) and the Madrid flight
is at 8.30. Thus:

Brussels – Friday – 6.30am
Copenhagen – Thursday – 8.00am
Madrid – Monday – 8.30am
Rome – Tuesday – 7.00am
Vienna – Wednesday – 7.30am

....

GAME GIRLS

The woman who watches tennis
isn't Jilly (clue 1), Milly (2) or Tilly (3),
so is Lily. Ted plays rugby (4). Jed's
girlfriend has watched him 9 times
(1) and Jilly has watched 7 times. The
woman who has seen 10 games isn't
Tilly (3) or Lily (4), so is Milly. Tilly has
seen 6 games (3) and Lily 9 games.
Ted's girlfriend is Milly (4). Jilly's
boyfriend isn't Ned (5), so is Ed. Tilly
is Ned's girlfriend. Ned doesn't play
football (2), so plays hockey. Ed plays
football. Thus:

Ed – football – Jilly – 7 times
Jed – tennis – Lily – 9 times
Ned – hockey – Tilly – 6 times
Ted – rugby – Milly – 10 times

....

COPY-CATS

Ricky is from Northton (clue 2).
Danny, who has been studying for
either 1 or 3 years, isn't from Easton
(clue 1) or Weston (3), so is from
Southton. Louisa isn't from Easton (2),
so is from Weston. She hasn't been a
student for 4 years (2), so has been for
2 years (3). Eliza is from Easton. The
man copying Deloire isn't Danny (4),
so is Ricky. The Martine isn't being
copied by Danny or Louisa (1), so it

must be Eliza. The artist who has been
studying for one year isn't Eliza (2)
or Ricky (4), so is Danny, who isn't
copying Rouleau (5), so is copying Van
Loda. Louisa is copying Rouleau. Eliza
hasn't been a student for 3 years (3),
so has been for 4 years. Ricky has been
a student for 3 years. Thus:

Danny – Southton – 1 year – Van Loda
Eliza – Easton – 4 years – Martine
Louisa – Weston – 2 years – Rouleau
Ricky – Northton – 3 years – Deloire

....

PRESENT TIME

The present wrapped in bell-pat-
terned paper was bought for the
birthday on the 17th (clue 1). The
gift for the birthday on the 21st isn't
gloves (3), perfume (4) or a CD (5), so is
a scarf. Dawn's sister's birthday is on
the 17th (2). Her gran's is on the 12th,
and the CD was bought for her sister
(5). Her mum's birthday isn't on the
21st (3), so is on the 8th. Thus Dawn's
niece's birthday is on the 21st; and
her gift isn't wrapped in plain (4) or
star-patterned paper (6), so is in floral
paper. Dawn's gran's isn't in star-patterned paper (6), so is in plain paper,
and her mum's gift is perfume (4). So
the gloves were bought for Dawn's
gran and the perfume is wrapped in
star-patterned paper. Thus:

8th – mum – perfume – stars
12th – gran – gloves – plain
17th – sister – CD – bells
21st – niece – scarf – floral

....

ON THE BOTTLE

Bella chose either 6 or 12 bottles of
wine which wasn't from England (clue
2), Australia (1) or Chile (3), so was
from France. Roger bought either 8 or

10 bottles (4). The person who bought 6 bottles wasn't Tina (3) or Eric (5), so was Bella, who chose white (5). Roger bought 8 bottles (4). Someone bought 12 bottles of English wine (2). Tina's wasn't from Australia (1) or Chile (3), so was from England. By elimination, Eric bought 10 bottles. Both his and the English wine are red (2), so Roger bought white. The Australian wine is red (1), so was chosen by Eric. Roger bought the wine from Chile. Thus:

Bella – 6 bottles – France – white
Eric – 10 bottles – Australia – red
Roger – 8 bottles – Chile – white
Tina – 12 bottles – England – red

....

UP IN FLAMES

The couple who brought sausages don't live at No. 12 (clue 4) and have names that begin with the same initial. These names don't include Laura (1) or James (4), so (by elimination) they're Boris and Bette. Boris and Bette live at No. 9 (2), and the couple who brought steak live at No. 12. Leo lives at No. 11 (3). He isn't married to Jenny (3) or Laura (4), so his wife is Delia. James's wife isn't Jenny (4), so must be Laura. George is thus married to Jenny. They don't live at No. 12 (3), so are at No. 10; and James lives at No. 12. George didn't bring hamburgers (3), so brought prawns. Leo brought hamburgers. Thus:

Boris – Bette – sausages – No. 9
George – Jenny – prawns – No. 10
James – Laura – steak – No. 12
Leo – Delia – hamburgers – No. 11

....

AGES AND AGES

The boy aged 18 (the oldest) isn't the brother of Pam (clue 1), Jan (3), Sue (4) or Fay (5), so is Ann's brother. The girl aged 11 (the youngest) isn't Pam (1), Jan (3), Sue (4) or Ann (5), so is Fay. Pam is either 15 or 16 (1), so Ann and Sue (4) aren't 15 and 16 – thus Ann is 12 and Sue is 13. Jan is 16 (3) and Rob's sister is 15; so Rob is Pam's brother. Rob is either 13 or 14 (1), so (2) Dan is either 14 or 15 – in other words, the boy aged 14 is either Rob or Dan. Guy is 15 (4) and Sue's brother is 14; so Rob is 13 and Dan is Sue's brother. Jan's brother is 17 (3) and Ann is Bob's sister. Jan's brother is Ian (3) and Guy is Fay's brother. Thus:

Bob – Ann – 18 – 12
Dan – Sue – 14 – 13
Guy – Fay – 15 – 11
Ian – Jan – 17 – 16
Rob – Pam – 13 – 15

....

BOOK REVIEW

The thriller is either B or C (clue 1). The crime book is either A or B, and *High Life* is either C or D (2). *Somewhere* isn't B, nor is it immediately next to *High Life* (3), so it's A, the thriller is B (1) and Gail Wright's book is C. The crime story is at A (above). The biography is C and Carla Scribe's book is B (6). By elimination, the romance is D. The book written by Emma Taylor is further to the right than *Night Falls* (5), so it's D. Book A is written by Anna Penn. *Night Falls* isn't written by Gail Wright or Emma Taylor (5), so it's B. Thus *Full Time* is C (4) and *High Life* is D. Thus:

Anna Penn – *Somewhere* – crime – A
Carla Scribe – *Night Falls* – thriller – B
Emma Taylor – *High Life* – romance – D
Gail Wright – *Full Time* – biography – C

PANCAKE DAY

The child at C had syrup (clue 3), so the boy who ate four pancakes (1) isn't at A (1 and 3) or B (3), so is at C or D, and the child who had lemon juice is at A or B (1). The child who had one pancake is at B or C (1). The child at B is either Melissa (3), who didn't have one pancake (4), or the child who had two pancakes (3), so one pancake was eaten by the child at C. The boy who ate four pancakes is at D, and the child who had lemon juice is at B (1). Child C didn't have maple syrup (2), so had golden syrup. Thus child D had orange juice (2), and child A is the girl who had maple syrup. Girl A isn't Jessica (4), so is Melissa. The child at B ate two pancakes (3), so Melissa ate three. Jessica ate one pancake (4). Angus isn't at D (5), so is at B, and Connor is the boy at D. Thus:

A – Melissa – 3 – maple syrup
B – Angus – 2 – lemon juice
C – Jessica – 1 – golden syrup
D – Connor – 4 – orange juice

....

IT FIGURES

	1	2	3	4	5	6
1	3	7	2	3	8	7
2	1	6	3	4	7	3
3	5	8	4	5	9	2
4	2	9	1	6	2	1
5	4	5	6	7	8	9
6	6	4	9	8	5	1

....

RELATIVE CHANGES

Georgie's uncle's body has his sister's legs (clue 2). His brother's body and aunt's feet haven't his uncle's legs (clue 3), so they have his mother's (5). Georgie's sister's legs aren't with his brother's feet (2), so are with his mother's. His uncle's head and brother's legs (1) are thus with his sister's feet. Georgie's uncle's legs have his brother's feet, and his uncle's feet have his aunt's legs. His brother's body has his sister's head. His sister's feet aren't with his aunt's body (4), so are with his mother's. His aunt's body has his uncle's legs and mother's head. His aunt's legs are with his brother's head and sister's body. Georgie's aunt's head has his uncle's body. Thus (head – body – legs – feet):

Aunt – uncle – sister – mother
Brother – sister – aunt – uncle
Mother – aunt – uncle – brother
Sister – brother – mother – aunt
Uncle – mother – brother – sister

....

FALL OUT

Trotter was ridden by Richard, who was 4th (clue 3), so (4) Stella was 2nd, Maybelle 3rd, and the rider unseated at the hedge was 1st. David, on Amity, was (2) 1st, and Stella was thrown at the 4-bar gate. Campari threw a rider at the water jump (1), so Stella rode Nemesis (5) and Campari was 5th. Barbara was thrown at the 5-bar gate (1), so she rode Maybelle. Kevin (intro) rode Campari. Richard fell at (5) the wall. Thus:

Amity – David – hedge – first
Campari – Kevin – water – fifth
Maybelle – Barbara – 5-bar gate – third
Nemesis – Stella – 4-bar gate – second
Trotter – Richard – wall – fourth

....

FIT FOR ANYTHING

Ballet classes are in the scout hut (clue 2), and the classes in the theatre are on Tuesday evenings (3). Boxing classes on Monday (2) aren't in the community centre (1) or church hall (5), so are in the sports centre (6). Jane is the mother (5), so Isabel (intro) is the daughter whose classes are at the church hall. Thus the community centre classes (1) are on either Thursdays or Fridays, and, since Sean's are on Wednesdays (4), Isabel's are also on either Thursdays or Fridays. Sean attends ballet classes (4) on Wednesdays. Jujitsu classes (5) are on Tuesdays and Isabel's are on Thursdays, so the community centre classes are on Fridays. Brendan is the father and doesn't go to jujitsu (5) or to the classes at the community centre (3), so he goes to boxing. The son at jujitsu (5) is Lenny (intro). Jane's classes are on Fridays. Aerobics are (1) on Thursdays, so judo classes (6) are on Fridays. Thus:

Brendan – boxing – Mondays – sports centre
Isabel – aerobics – Thursdays – church hall
Jane – judo – Fridays – community centre
Lenny – jujitsu – Tuesdays – theatre
Sean – ballet – Wednesdays – scout hut

ON THE CARDS

The cards total 81 (intro), so the 10 is missing. Thus card F isn't the king (clue 3) and K isn't the 8 (4) so the queen isn't G (2). B isn't the king or queen and F isn't the 3 or ace (3), so C isn't the king (1) or queen (2). So the king is either D, G or H (1). Thus the queen is either D, F or H (2) and the 3 is either G, I or K (2). If the ace is K, then (2) the 3 is I, which (4) leaves no possible value for C. So the ace isn't K (4). If the ace is J, then the 5 is K (1)

and the king is G, leaving no place for the 3 or 8 (2). Thus the ace is G (1), the 5 is H and the king of spades is D. The 3 of diamonds is I (2), the 8 is J and the queen is F. B is the 9 (3) of clubs (intro), J is a spade, L is a club, K is a heart, C is a diamond and A is a heart. G is a club (3), so E is a spade (intro). E is the 6 and L is the 7 (4). C is the 4 (4) and K is the 2; thus A is the jack. Card F is a heart (5) and H is a diamond. Thus:

JH – 9C – 4D – KS
6S – QH – AC – 5D
3D – 8S – 2H – 7C

....

ON LOCATION

On location 1

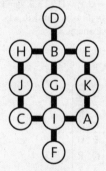

On location 2

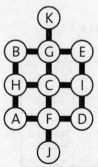

FIGURE IT OUT

F	E	I	R	G	U
E	U	F	I	R	G
I	G	R	F	U	E
U	F	E	G	I	R
R	I	G	U	E	F
G	R	U	E	F	I

The letter in squares 6 and 19 (clue 2) is U. The letter in 15 and 32 (clue 3) is different to that in 16, 21, 26 and 31, so from diagonal 6–31 the letter in 15 and 32 is the same as either 6 or 11, thus it's R. 1 = F and from 1–31, 25 = R. The letter in 5 and 31 (clue 1) is G, thus 7 = E, 3 = I and 4 = R. In 6–31, 26 = I, so 27 = G, 9 = F and 21 = E. In 6–31, 16 = F, so in 2–32, 20 = F, 8 = U and 14 = G. Thus 10 = I, 12 = G, 17 = U, 18 = E, 23 = I and 24 = R. In 1–36, 29 = E and 36 = I, so 28 = U, 34 = E and 35 = F.

ALL SQUARE

E	R	S	A	U	Q
U	A	R	Q	S	E
S	Q	U	E	R	A
Q	S	A	R	E	U
A	U	E	S	Q	R
R	E	Q	U	A	S

WHERE THE L?

Where the L? 1

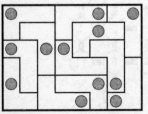

Where the L? 2

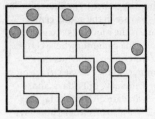

CALIBAN'S CONUNDRUMS

Caliban 1

Hubert Phillips writes:
Of statements (2) and (4), one must be true. And, if (2) is true, either (1) or (4) must be true also. So (4) is the true statement and the other three are false, i.e. Mr Driver is the guard, Mr Fireman is the driver and Mr Guard is the fireman.

Caliban 2

You have to consider every possibility. If you draw eight marbles, the stipulated conditions will probably be fulfilled, but 'probably' is not good enough. To draw eight marbles may leave all eight blue ones, and only two of each of the other colours. To draw seven, however, covers all contingencies.

Caliban 3

The possible colour distributions are:

(a)	8	4	3	2
(b)	7	5	3	2
(c)	6	5	4	2

But to ensure that at least two of one colour and at least one of a second colour are drawn, the numbers which it is necessary to draw differ. In case (a), twelve must be drawn; in case (b), eleven; in case (c), ten. Hence the actual distribution is (b), and there are seven green marbles. So to make sure of drawing at least one green marble, it is necessary again to draw eleven.

Caliban 4

A very simple puzzle! Only a Lemon can say that he's not White; for a White, if he said so, would be lying; and an Orange would be telling the truth. So Mr White is the Lemon; and Mr Lemon, who says he is not a Lemon, must be the White. Hence he tells the truth about Mr Yellow. Hence, Mr Yellow is a White.

Caliban 5

Here are the data:

Owner	Daughter	Yacht
Spinnaker		*Iris*
Buoy	Iris	*Daffodil*
Luff		
Gybe		*Anthea*
Windward	Lalage	*Jonquil*

Obviously, Mr Luff's yacht is the *Lalage*. What is Mr Luff's daughter's name? Clearly, not Iris or Lalage. Nor yet Daffodil, for Daffodil's father would then own the *Daffodil*; nor yet Jonquil, for Daffodil would then be Mr Windward's daughter. So Mr Luff's

daughter is Anthea, and Mr Gybe's daughter is Daffodil. It follows that Jonquil's father is Mr Spinnaker.

....

CARROLL'S SYMBOLIC LOGIC

1. No pencils of mine are sugar-plums.
2. No hedge-hog takes in *The Times*.
3. No M.P. should ride in a donkey-race, unless he has perfect self-command.
4. Guinea-pigs never really appreciate Beethoven.
5. No bird in this aviary lives on mince-pies.
6. No plum-pudding that has not been boiled in a cloth can be distinguished from soup.
7. All your poems are uninteresting.
8. No heavy fish is unkind to children.
9. No engine-driver lives on barley-sugar.
10. Rainy days are always cloudy.
11. No badger can guess a conundrum.
12. I cannot read any of Brown's letters.
13. I always avoid a kangaroo.

CHAPTER 7

Thinking Sideways

CATCH QUESTION COMPILATION

1. Handel.
2. Downstream.
3. None – they're uninhabited.
4. Monday.
5. Halfway – after that, it is running out of the forest.
6. Four and five make nine.
7. To make the lift go to another floor.
8. None – Noah took animals onto the Ark.
9. The letter O.
10. The outside.
11. Examples are lunch, tea, dinner and supper.
12. Vincent van Gogh.
13. A complete circle – we don't see the rest of it because the horizon gets in the way.
14. The window.
15. A whip – the 'crack' of a whip is a small sonic boom.
16. Not really – it's better to get down feathers from a duck.
17. None – if you have a widow, you'd be dead.
18. A haircut.
19. A snail, or a leg.
20. Because a camera does the job much better.
21. All of them.
22. In the ground.
23. More people live in England than in Scotland.
24. Time to get a new clock.
25. One big pile.
26. You'd prefer the cheetah to attack the leopard, rather than you.
27. Your left wrist (or hand, or elbow).
28. There's no such thing as a female bull.
29. A $5 bill, because it is more valuable than a $1 bill.
30. None, because how can their numbers be unlisted if they're in the telephone directory?

WORDS AND NUMBERS

1. Place letters in the spaces to get six longer words: ACTOR, BISHOP, CURATE, DIRECTOR, ENSIGN, FRANTIC. As it is not a job position, FRANTIC is the odd one out.
2. Simply use the word CARAVAN six times.
3. All of them – any number can be divided by seven. Whether a remainder is left over is another matter.
4. ARROWROOT, which uses the A, W and T once, and the R and O three times each.
5. Pewter is made from tin and lead mixed together; TAILEND is made from TIN and LEAD mixed together.
6. The letter A: A5 × 4 = A3 is correct because one sheet of A3 paper makes 4 sheets of A5, and so on.
7. Three – cut into quarters (two cuts), stack those four pieces into a pile, and finally cut through the middle of the pile.
8. Replace X with C and Y with F to give 10C = 50F, 20C = 68F and 30C = 86F (temperature conversions from Celsius to Fahrenheit).
9. Crossing out THE UNNECESSARY LETTERS does indeed leave A COMMON PHRASE.

10. The right-hand cube bears the digits 0 to 5. The left cube has 0, 1, 2, 6, 7 and 8. To obtain a 9, turn the 6 upside down.

11. The Greek letter PI, to form the word CAPITAL.

12. Footstool is indeed a palindrome, but only when tapped out in Morse code.

13. DIX (10 in French) = DIX (509 in Roman numerals).

14. Two-thirds of ELEVEN is EVEN!

15. Figure A, to continue the numerical sequence 3, 4, 5, 6, 7:

16. By turning the u and p upside down and making use of the ambiguity of I, you can form:

Ireland

17. None – rearrange the ones you already have into a 2 × 2 × 2 cube.

18. None – instead, pick up both hoops and move them completely away from the counters so that they both contain none.

19. Three pieces – even a neat, deliberate cut in one link will leave you with two halves of the chain and the broken link.

20. The answer is 51. A vertical line gradually moves from one side of the 5 to the other, as shown:

21. The complete sequence is: ACE, TWO, THREE, FOUR, FIVE, SIX, SEVEN, EIGHT, NINE, TEN, JACK, QUEEN, KING.

22. They all appear in the statement 'How are all these letters related?'

23. Pronounce the first letter of each word as an individual syllable to get a new word: ceiling (or sealing), derive, effort, emotion, estate.

24. E and F (on their side, with their prongs interlocking):

25. WHAT. In fact, the question tells you the answer. The first 17 letters are repeated in the same order.

26. A gaming die:

27. *Sebiro* is a corruption of 'Savile Row', the famous street for tailoring.

28. The statement doesn't use any letters with descenders, i.e. those with 'tails' that fall below the base line – g, j, p, q and y.

29. The 16th cube is the number 729 (9 × 9 × 9), which is formed by the cubes' darker sides.

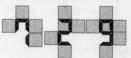

30. They are all contained somewhere in the question: '*Can y*ou figure out what *all of t*hese words *in* particular ha*v*e *in* common?'

31. Move one of the lines forming the equals sign over to the minus (effectively changing the positions of the equals and minus signs). Then turn the book upside down! The equation then reads 569 – 288 = 281, which is correct.

$$569 - 288 = 281$$

32. It is possible to read the calculation as a correct computation without changing anything. Just hold the book up to a mirror so that it reads as follows:

$$508 = 102 \times 5 - 2$$

33. There's 90 cents and another 90 cents, which is paid for by one dollar bill and 80 cents in coins. In other words: 'Cents and cents, a bill eighty' (*Sense and Sensibility*).

....

THINK ABOUT IT

1. Chicken and egg.
2. On the same day that the fewest people are born – 29 February.
3. Coals for a fire.
4. Pac-Man – the pizza with a slice missing inspired the familiar shape.
5. Baby elephants.
6. That of US President (at the time of writing, four out of 43 assassinated).
7. If they were a foreign coin collector, then £8.88 would give them one specimen of each UK coin currently in circulation, including one £5 'crown'.
8. A dictionary.
9. Cain (killed Abel).
10. Serve chips or mashed potatoes.
11. They are all things that can be bought in left-handed versions.
12. The second customer had placed $3 on the bar in change. The first customer had used three dollar bills.
13. Oz (as in *The Wizard of Oz*), said to have been inspired by the label 'O–Z' on a filing cabinet drawer.
14. It's easily possible if you've turned your trousers inside out first.
15. The statement describes Mount Rushmore, the memorial of four former Presidents (Washington, Jefferson, Lincoln, Roosevelt) carved into the granite rock face.

....

TIGHT CORNERS

1. She was on a blind date but didn't know what he looked like – she looked to see who answered his mobile to identify him.
2. The bird from the inner city will have a noticeably louder chirp or song. This is because it is used to singing over the top of traffic noise.
3. On a telephone keypad, 123580 would form a T shape. It was thought that this would be an easy number for inebriated people to remember to call for a cab, rather than risk driving home.
4. They are attracted by the electrical buzzing noise, thinking bees are around.
5. Her real birthday is 25 December, so she has a 'half birthday' celebration to ensure that she doesn't miss out on a party (or presents).
6. They signed their names on a circular piece of paper so that no one was at the top of the list. The device was called a *ruban rond*, or 'round ribbon', from which we obtain the English term 'round robin'.
7. They are pilots on the same aircraft, who aren't allowed to eat the same meal in case of food poisoning.
8. He kept ducks.
9. During a period of hyperinflation, when money would devalue so quickly that it effectively became worthless.
10. The company knew that everyone who responded must have an

illegal installation that bypassed any pay-per-view scrambling. The company sent the T-shirts – each with a lawsuit.

11. The winner is decided on the distance travelled. The second car began further back on the starting grid, so it had actually covered a greater distance in the same time than the apparent 'winner'.

12. They are 'narkhitels' (empty articles), false entries added as an anti-copying device. If the fictional entries appear in other reference works, it proves copyright theft. The same trick is used by mapmakers, who add false towns and roads, and lexicographers invent new words for their dictionaries.

13. This countdown is used by the armed forces, or anyone testing missiles, explosives. etc. The '5' is omitted because it sounds too much like 'fire'.

14. 'That way, the caption will read "(your name) is pictured here with …", ensuring you top billing every time.'

15. The batsman on strike had 98 runs and wanted a century. If he ran a single, the match would end immediately and he'd only be credited with 99 runs. Since they had plenty of wickets in hand, they stood still until a boundary was hit.

16. They were all created as workarounds to legal bans. Tenpin bowling was introduced when ninepins was banned; mime artistry was created in France when the emperor prohibited plays; and when ice-cream sodas were prevented from being sold on Sunday, the vendors sold them without the soda – 'The Sunday-soda', now

known as the ice-cream sundae, was born.

17. They have been watching a film at the cinema. During the projection process, the screen is blank between frames, for a total of around an hour during a typical film. A phenomenon called 'persistence of vision' fills in the gaps.

18. *Babe*, which starred 48 different piglets.

19. They were playing two different games. In soccer, the ball has to completely cross the line to count as a goal. In American football, which Tony was playing, any part of the ball needs to cross the goal line for a touchdown.

20. The farmer rode up, jumped off his own horse and put it with the nineteen, making twenty. Then he gave half the horses (10) to the eldest brother, a quarter (5) to the second brother, and a fifth (4) to the youngest brother. The 10, 5 and 4 horses made 19. The twentieth horse was his own, upon which he remounted and departed. Now the question is: How was it possible for him to add his own horse to the others, do the dividing exactly as required by the will, and have his own horse returned to him at the end? Simply because a half, a quarter, and a fifth do not add up to unity.

21. A so-called upside-down map (officially named 'McArthur's Universal Corrective Projection') which puts Australasia at the top. It was designed by Australian student Stuart McArthur.

22. A slow driver will see MOVE-IT in their rear-view mirror.

23. To enable several people to share the same glass (so long as everyone

remains sober enough to drink from their number each time).

DETECTIVE STORIES

1. 'Direct flights' between two places at different latitudes over the Earth's spherical surface usually looked curved when projected onto flat maps. Therefore the pilot could not have plotted the flight plan using 'a pencil and ruler'.

2. If you didn't spot this one, get ready to groan. Earlier in the story you are told that the man thought the pilot was a friend of his, Jack Delaney. When the man reached the pilots' cabin, he knocked on the door and said 'Hi, Jack!'

3. The builder was clearly lying. He had been the one working on that section and he himself said that the scene was as the detectives first saw it. The man then 'opened the door' – impossible, since the woman could not have closed the door behind her since there was no floor on the other side.

4. Among the duty-free goods the beekeeper received was some cologne. He wore some the next day, and the bees did not recognize his scent, and so they attacked the 'stranger' to their hive. When Hartland went into the closed space of the ambulance he could smell the cologne.

WEIRD SCIENCE

1. Rick has two scales. He places one foot on each and sums the readings.

2. If there were an even number and some computers malfunctioned, 'ties' would be possible where (e.g.) half the computers vote to make the plane climb and the other half vote for it to descend.

3. All carbohydrates, whether starch (cereal) or sugar (frosting), contain four calories per gram.

4. Peter's microwave turntable takes 16 seconds to make one revolution, so when the 64 seconds are up the cup will still be in the right position for Peter to take it out by the handle.

5. The Horseshoe Falls on the Niagara River, due to erosion. The American Falls also erode, at the slower rate of 15 cm per year.

6. A half-twist is put into the belt – making it into a Möbius band – which causes all of the belt to get the same amount of use.

7. If the dot indicated was a star, it would be obscured by the dark side of the Moon. Therefore, this spot must be the UFO. (Lloyd King)

8. Green peppers eventually ripen to yellow peppers. Farmers justify the higher price because yellow peppers take longer to produce.

9. One was painted, the other was left naturally metallic. The coat of paint on a large jet weighs around 250 kg.

10. Experiment A, because water at 20 degrees Fahrenheit is ice!

11. Although he isn't looking at the gloves, he can feel whether they are for the left or the right hand.

The most he has to draw out is nine left-handed gloves and one right-handed glove, or vice versa.

12. Two – even if you pick two left-hand or two right-hand gloves, you can turn one inside-out to make a left–right pair.

13. Push the cork *into* the bottle. It's now easy to tip the bottle upside down and remove the coin.

14. Argon, because the 'R has gone' from HYDROGEN.

15. He squeezes one end of the straw shut. The trapped air strengthens the straw significantly.

16. She was using it as a stylus to tap the pressure-sensitive screen on her palmtop computer.

17. By sneezing (unpleasant, but true).

18. Cross your eyes until the stars overlap – you can now see three stars even though you know there are really only two.

19. The odd number of cross-over pieces has created a Möbius loop – i.e. there is only one track, not two. Either controller would move both cars.

....

NOB'S FINAL PUZZLE

It seems that the answer ought to be 15, given that each circle is the difference between the two circles that lead into it. However, if you look carefully you'll notice that the 'logic' seems to break down at the last hurdle: 21 – 13 is 8, not 7. So we must revisit our assumption and start again. Looking at the first step (99 and 72 give 27), notice that 9 + 9 + 7 + 2 = 27. Likewise, 4 + 5 + 2 + 7 = 18. In fact, adding the digits works for each stage. Therefore the missing number is 12, because 3 + 6 + 2 + 1 = 12.

CHAPTER 8
Sudoku War

MINI SUDOKU

Mini sudoku 1

2	4	1	6	3	5
5	6	3	2	4	1
1	3	6	5	2	4
4	2	5	1	6	3
6	1	4	3	5	2
3	5	2	4	1	6

Mini sudoku 2

6	2	5	3	1	4
4	1	3	5	6	2
3	6	2	4	5	1
5	4	1	6	2	3
1	3	6	2	4	5
2	5	4	1	3	6

Mini sudoku 3

3	5	1	4	6	2
4	6	2	3	5	1
6	1	4	5	2	3
2	3	5	1	4	6
1	4	6	2	3	5
5	2	3	6	1	4

Mini sudoku 4

3	1	4	2	6	5
2	5	6	4	1	3
1	2	5	6	3	4
6	4	3	1	5	2
4	3	1	5	2	6
5	6	2	3	4	1

Mini sudoku 5

3	2	6	4	1	5
1	5	4	2	6	3
6	4	3	5	2	1
5	1	2	3	4	6
4	6	5	1	3	2
2	3	1	6	5	4

Mini sudoku 6

5	1	2	3	4	6
6	3	4	1	5	2
1	6	3	5	2	4
2	4	5	6	3	1
4	5	6	2	1	3
3	2	1	4	6	5

Mini sudoku 7

3	2	6	5	4	1
1	5	4	6	2	3
2	6	3	4	1	5
4	1	5	2	3	6
6	3	2	1	5	4
5	4	1	3	6	2

Mini sudoku 8

6	2	1	3	5	4
3	4	5	2	1	6
2	6	4	5	3	1
1	5	3	4	6	2
5	1	2	6	4	3
4	3	6	1	2	5

CLASSIC SUDOKU

Classic sudoku 1

8	4	1	3	6	9	5	2	7
6	9	5	2	4	7	1	8	3
3	7	2	1	8	5	9	6	4
2	6	9	5	7	1	3	4	8
7	1	8	6	3	4	2	9	5
4	5	3	8	9	2	7	1	6
1	8	7	4	2	3	6	5	9
5	3	4	9	1	6	8	7	2
9	2	6	7	5	8	4	3	1

Classic sudoku 2

1	7	9	2	4	5	3	6	8
5	4	6	1	8	3	9	7	2
8	3	2	9	7	6	4	5	1
4	6	5	7	3	2	1	8	9
9	2	1	6	5	8	7	4	3
3	8	7	4	9	1	6	2	5
6	1	4	5	2	9	8	3	7
2	9	8	3	6	7	5	1	4
7	5	3	8	1	4	2	9	6

Classic sudoku 3

4	8	2	5	1	9	6	7	3
5	7	9	8	6	3	4	2	1
6	3	1	7	2	4	8	5	9
1	2	4	6	7	8	3	9	5
8	9	5	4	3	2	1	6	7
3	6	7	9	5	1	2	4	8
7	1	8	2	4	5	9	3	6
9	4	6	3	8	7	5	1	2
2	5	3	1	9	6	7	8	4

Classic sudoku 4

5	6	8	4	3	9	7	2	1
3	7	9	1	8	2	4	6	5
2	4	1	6	7	5	8	3	9
1	8	6	2	5	3	9	4	7
9	3	5	7	4	6	1	8	2
4	2	7	8	9	1	3	5	6
7	1	4	5	2	8	6	9	3
6	9	2	3	1	4	5	7	8
8	5	3	9	6	7	2	1	4

Classic sudoku 5

3	1	9	5	6	7	8	4	2
4	6	2	8	9	1	3	7	5
5	7	8	2	4	3	9	1	6
7	2	4	9	1	5	6	8	3
1	5	3	6	8	2	4	9	7
9	8	6	7	3	4	2	5	1
6	9	1	3	7	8	5	2	4
2	3	7	4	5	9	1	6	8
8	4	5	1	2	6	7	3	9

Classic sudoku 8

6	8	3	4	5	9	7	2	1
2	9	4	7	1	6	8	3	5
7	5	1	8	2	3	4	6	9
9	4	2	6	3	5	1	8	7
5	1	6	2	7	8	3	9	4
8	3	7	9	4	1	2	5	6
3	6	5	1	8	4	9	7	2
4	2	8	5	9	7	6	1	3
1	7	9	3	6	2	5	4	8

Classic sudoku 6

6	9	7	5	4	2	8	3	1
1	3	5	6	8	7	9	2	4
2	4	8	3	1	9	5	6	7
8	7	2	1	9	6	4	5	3
9	5	4	7	2	3	1	8	6
3	6	1	8	5	4	2	7	9
4	2	6	9	3	8	7	1	5
5	8	3	4	7	1	6	9	2
7	1	9	2	6	5	3	4	8

Classic sudoku 9

2	3	7	5	1	9	4	6	8
8	6	9	3	2	4	5	7	1
5	4	1	6	8	7	9	2	3
6	7	8	1	9	5	3	4	2
9	5	2	7	4	3	1	8	6
3	1	4	2	6	8	7	9	5
1	9	3	8	7	2	6	5	4
7	2	6	4	5	1	8	3	9
4	8	5	9	3	6	2	1	7

Classic sudoku 7

8	1	9	2	4	6	7	3	5
5	7	3	9	8	1	6	4	2
6	4	2	7	3	5	9	8	1
3	2	5	8	6	4	1	9	7
1	6	7	3	2	9	4	5	8
9	8	4	1	5	7	2	6	3
7	3	8	4	9	2	5	1	6
2	9	6	5	1	8	3	7	4
4	5	1	6	7	3	8	2	9

Classic sudoku 10

4	6	8	3	2	9	5	1	7
9	3	7	8	1	5	4	2	6
2	5	1	7	6	4	9	8	3
3	4	6	2	9	7	1	5	8
1	8	2	5	4	6	7	3	9
7	9	5	1	3	8	2	6	4
6	1	4	9	5	3	8	7	2
8	2	3	4	7	1	6	9	5
5	7	9	6	8	2	3	4	1

Classic sudoku 11

9	6	8	2	4	5	7	1	3
2	1	7	3	6	8	9	4	5
4	3	5	1	7	9	6	8	2
8	5	1	4	9	2	3	7	6
6	2	3	5	8	7	4	9	1
7	9	4	6	1	3	5	2	8
1	4	9	8	3	6	2	5	7
3	8	2	7	5	4	1	6	9
5	7	6	9	2	1	8	3	4

Classic sudoku 12

1	3	6	2	5	4	8	7	9
2	7	5	8	1	9	6	4	3
8	4	9	6	3	7	1	2	5
7	6	3	5	8	2	9	1	4
5	8	1	9	4	6	2	3	7
4	9	2	1	7	3	5	6	8
6	2	4	3	9	8	7	5	1
9	1	7	4	2	5	3	8	6
3	5	8	7	6	1	4	9	2

Classic sudoku 13

6	9	5	8	4	2	1	3	7
7	8	4	6	1	3	9	2	5
2	3	1	5	7	9	8	6	4
1	4	8	7	9	6	2	5	3
3	5	7	2	8	1	4	9	6
9	6	2	4	3	5	7	1	8
8	2	6	1	5	4	3	7	9
4	1	3	9	6	7	5	8	2
5	7	9	3	2	8	6	4	1

WORD SUDOKU

Word sudoku 1

U	R	D	S	Q	T	G	A	E
S	Q	T	A	E	G	D	R	U
G	A	E	D	R	U	T	Q	S
T	S	Q	U	A	R	E	D	G
E	D	R	G	T	S	Q	U	A
A	U	G	Q	D	E	R	S	T
D	E	S	T	U	Q	A	G	R
Q	T	U	R	G	A	S	E	D
R	G	A	E	S	D	U	T	Q

Word sudoku 2

C	L	R	U	I	V	E	T	A
U	E	V	T	L	A	I	C	R
I	A	T	C	R	E	L	U	V
V	R	C	E	U	I	T	A	L
L	T	U	A	V	R	C	I	E
A	I	E	L	C	T	R	V	U
R	U	L	I	A	C	V	E	T
E	V	I	R	T	U	A	L	C
T	C	A	V	E	L	U	R	I

MONSTER SUDOKU

Monster sudoku 1

C	B	F	0	5	7	2	E	D	4	9	3	8	A	6	1
1	5	8	D	9	0	4	A	F	E	B	6	C	2	7	3
9	A	7	6	1	3	B	C	5	0	2	8	E	D	4	F
4	2	3	E	6	D	8	F	1	7	A	C	B	9	0	5
D	1	9	C	4	E	3	2	6	5	8	B	7	F	A	0
3	F	A	4	8	B	6	0	C	2	7	D	9	5	1	E
8	0	B	7	D	A	5	1	9	F	3	E	2	6	C	4
2	E	6	5	7	F	C	9	0	A	1	4	D	B	3	8
7	D	E	8	B	1	A	6	4	C	5	F	0	3	2	9
F	3	5	A	2	C	9	4	B	8	6	0	1	E	D	7
6	C	1	B	0	8	D	3	2	9	E	7	5	4	F	A
0	4	2	9	E	5	F	7	A	3	D	1	6	8	B	C
5	6	D	F	C	4	7	8	3	B	0	9	A	1	E	2
E	7	C	2	F	6	1	5	8	D	4	A	3	0	9	B
A	9	0	1	3	2	E	B	7	6	F	5	4	C	8	D
B	8	4	3	A	9	0	D	E	1	C	2	F	7	5	6

Monster sudoku 2

6	7	D	4	9	E	B	0	2	8	1	A	3	F	C	5
A	9	8	B	3	D	1	F	C	5	E	7	4	2	0	6
0	E	3	C	6	4	5	2	B	D	F	9	8	1	A	7
1	5	F	2	8	7	A	C	6	3	0	4	B	D	E	9
8	1	0	6	E	A	9	4	3	7	2	D	C	B	5	F
7	D	4	5	2	3	F	B	9	A	C	8	1	0	6	E
E	B	9	A	1	0	C	D	4	6	5	F	2	7	3	8
2	F	C	3	5	6	8	7	0	1	B	E	A	9	D	4
5	C	B	D	F	1	4	A	8	E	3	2	9	6	7	0
4	3	6	1	0	C	7	E	5	9	A	B	F	8	2	D
F	8	A	7	B	5	2	9	D	C	6	0	E	4	1	3
9	2	E	0	D	8	6	3	F	4	7	1	5	A	B	C
3	4	1	8	A	9	0	6	E	2	D	5	7	C	F	B
D	0	2	9	C	B	E	1	7	F	4	3	6	5	8	A
C	A	7	E	4	F	D	5	1	B	8	6	0	3	9	2
B	6	5	F	7	2	3	8	A	0	9	C	D	E	4	1

Monster sudoku 3

3	5	8	A	4	E	7	C	9	6	F	1	0	D	2	B
B	0	C	2	5	D	F	9	7	E	8	A	4	1	3	6
1	4	6	E	0	A	8	3	B	C	2	D	9	F	7	5
D	9	7	F	2	1	6	B	3	5	4	0	C	E	8	A
4	8	F	3	E	6	C	A	5	B	1	7	2	0	D	9
A	E	B	6	3	9	4	5	2	0	D	C	F	8	1	7
5	2	1	0	F	B	D	7	4	9	6	8	A	3	C	E
7	D	9	C	1	8	2	0	A	F	3	E	6	5	B	4
E	A	5	7	C	F	B	4	8	1	9	2	3	6	0	D
2	C	D	8	7	0	3	1	E	A	B	6	5	9	4	F
F	6	3	9	D	5	E	8	0	7	C	4	B	2	A	1
0	1	4	B	A	2	9	6	F	D	5	3	7	C	E	8
8	3	E	4	B	7	5	D	6	2	0	F	1	A	9	C
C	7	0	5	8	3	A	F	1	4	E	9	D	B	6	2
9	F	2	D	6	4	1	E	C	3	A	B	8	7	5	0
6	B	A	1	9	C	0	2	D	8	7	5	E	4	F	3

Monster sudoku 4

3	8	9	A	7	5	4	D	B	C	6	0	F	2	1	E
7	1	C	4	9	8	F	0	5	3	2	E	6	A	B	D
B	E	6	5	A	2	C	3	D	4	1	F	7	0	8	9
F	0	D	2	B	1	E	6	A	7	8	9	C	4	3	5
4	9	F	1	3	0	A	E	C	6	D	8	B	5	7	2
2	C	7	0	8	B	6	5	9	E	A	1	4	D	F	3
5	6	3	E	1	D	7	F	0	2	4	B	8	C	9	A
8	D	A	B	4	9	2	C	7	5	F	3	E	6	0	1
C	4	E	9	5	F	8	B	2	A	0	D	1	3	6	7
D	F	5	3	2	4	0	1	E	8	7	6	A	9	C	B
6	B	2	7	D	E	3	A	F	1	9	C	0	8	5	4
1	A	0	8	6	C	9	7	3	B	5	4	D	E	2	F
A	3	8	F	E	6	B	9	1	D	C	5	2	7	4	0
E	5	4	D	C	3	1	2	8	0	B	7	9	F	A	6
9	7	B	C	0	A	D	4	6	F	3	2	5	1	E	8
0	2	1	6	F	7	5	8	4	9	E	A	3	B	D	C

SUDOKU X

Sudoku X 1

3	8	5	9	6	2	1	7	4
9	6	1	5	4	7	3	2	8
4	7	2	8	3	1	9	5	6
6	5	7	4	9	8	2	1	3
1	4	3	2	7	6	5	8	9
2	9	8	3	1	5	4	6	7
7	3	6	1	5	9	8	4	2
8	1	4	6	2	3	7	9	5
5	2	9	7	8	4	6	3	1

Sudoku X 2

8	7	9	4	1	6	3	5	2
2	6	5	3	8	7	1	9	4
4	3	1	9	2	5	7	6	8
7	5	4	2	3	1	6	8	9
6	9	2	7	5	8	4	1	3
1	8	3	6	9	4	2	7	5
5	2	8	1	7	3	9	4	6
9	4	7	8	6	2	5	3	1
3	1	6	5	4	9	8	2	7

Sudoku X 3

1	2	3	6	7	8	5	4	9
8	9	6	3	5	4	2	1	7
4	7	5	1	9	2	8	3	6
6	4	2	8	1	5	7	9	3
5	3	7	4	2	9	6	8	1
9	1	8	7	3	6	4	2	5
7	5	4	9	8	1	3	6	2
2	6	1	5	4	3	9	7	8
3	8	9	2	6	7	1	5	4

Sudoku X 4

9	2	7	6	1	3	5	8	4
8	4	1	2	9	5	3	6	7
3	6	5	7	4	8	1	9	2
4	7	2	3	6	9	8	5	1
5	1	9	8	7	4	2	3	6
6	8	3	5	2	1	4	7	9
7	9	8	1	5	2	6	4	3
1	3	4	9	8	6	7	2	5
2	5	6	4	3	7	9	1	8

Sudoku X 5

4	6	2	7	1	9	3	5	8
1	3	8	4	5	6	2	7	9
5	7	9	8	3	2	4	6	1
9	8	7	5	4	3	1	2	6
3	4	1	6	2	7	9	8	5
2	5	6	1	9	8	7	3	4
8	1	5	3	7	4	6	9	2
7	9	4	2	6	5	8	1	3
6	2	3	9	8	1	5	4	7

ONE AWAY SUDOKU

One away sudoku 1

8	3	7	4	9	1	6	2	5
6	4	1	2	8	5	7	9	3
2	5	9	7	3	6	4	8	1
4	9	2	3	6	8	1	5	7
5	7	6	1	2	4	9	3	8
3	1	8	5	7	9	2	6	4
9	6	3	8	4	7	5	1	2
7	8	5	9	1	2	3	4	6
1	2	4	6	5	3	8	7	9

One away sudoku 2

4	5	1	9	3	8	7	2	6
3	6	7	5	4	2	1	8	9
8	9	2	1	7	6	5	4	3
2	4	8	6	1	7	3	9	5
1	3	6	2	5	9	8	7	4
9	7	5	4	8	3	2	6	1
7	8	4	3	9	1	6	5	2
6	1	9	8	2	5	4	3	7
5	2	3	7	6	4	9	1	8

One away sudoku 3

7	1	9	5	4	2	3	8	6
3	2	8	7	9	6	4	5	1
5	6	4	3	1	8	7	9	2
1	7	5	9	3	4	2	6	8
2	9	3	6	8	5	1	7	4
4	8	6	2	7	1	5	3	9
9	3	1	8	2	7	6	4	5
6	4	7	1	5	9	8	2	3
8	5	2	4	6	3	9	1	7

One away sudoku 4

6	3	2	9	8	5	1	4	7
7	5	1	4	2	6	3	8	9
4	9	8	1	7	3	5	2	6
5	7	3	2	9	1	4	6	8
8	2	9	6	5	4	7	1	3
1	6	4	8	3	7	2	9	5
9	4	7	5	1	8	6	3	2
3	8	6	7	4	2	9	5	1
2	1	5	3	6	9	8	7	4

One away sudoku 5

7	2	6	3	8	9	4	1	5
5	3	1	6	4	7	8	9	2
8	9	4	5	1	2	3	7	6
4	7	5	9	3	8	2	6	1
3	1	9	2	5	6	7	4	8
2	6	8	4	7	1	9	5	3
1	5	7	8	9	3	6	2	4
9	8	2	1	6	4	5	3	7
6	4	3	7	2	5	1	8	9

JIGSAW SUDOKU

Jigsaw sudoku 1

5	4	1	6	2	3	8	9	7
2	7	3	8	6	9	4	1	5
3	8	9	1	4	2	5	7	6
4	6	7	9	3	5	2	8	1
9	1	4	5	8	7	6	3	2
7	2	5	3	1	6	9	4	8
8	3	2	4	5	1	7	6	9
1	5	6	7	9	8	3	2	4
6	9	8	2	7	4	1	5	3

Jigsaw sudoku 2

4	3	7	9	1	2	5	6	8
8	5	2	6	9	7	1	3	4
7	1	9	2	3	6	4	8	5
3	6	1	5	8	4	9	2	7
1	2	4	8	5	3	6	7	9
5	7	8	3	4	1	2	9	6
9	8	6	4	7	5	3	1	2
6	9	5	1	2	8	7	4	3
2	4	3	7	6	9	8	5	1

Jigsaw sudoku 3

1	7	9	6	4	5	8	2	3
3	4	5	1	6	8	2	7	9
8	5	2	3	9	1	4	6	7
2	6	3	7	5	4	9	1	8
4	1	7	8	2	9	6	3	5
5	3	1	9	8	2	7	4	6
9	8	6	4	7	3	1	5	2
7	2	8	5	1	6	3	9	4
6	9	4	2	3	7	5	8	1

Jigsaw sudoku 4

5	7	1	3	9	8	6	4	2
2	6	3	9	4	1	8	5	7
3	9	6	2	8	4	7	1	5
4	5	8	1	7	6	2	3	9
8	2	9	5	3	7	4	6	1
7	3	5	4	2	9	1	8	6
1	8	2	7	6	3	5	9	4
9	1	4	6	5	2	3	7	8
6	4	7	8	1	5	9	2	3

Jigsaw sudoku 5

6	7	5	4	2	9	8	3	1
8	3	9	6	7	1	5	2	4
2	6	4	5	1	3	7	9	8
1	4	3	2	9	8	6	5	7
5	1	8	7	3	4	9	6	2
9	2	7	1	8	6	3	4	5
7	9	6	8	5	2	4	1	3
3	5	2	9	4	7	1	8	6
4	8	1	3	6	5	2	7	9

ODD/EVEN SUDOKU

Odd/even sudoku 1

6	2	4	8	7	5	3	1	9
1	8	5	3	2	9	4	7	6
7	3	9	4	1	6	5	2	8
8	4	7	2	6	3	9	5	1
3	9	6	1	5	8	7	4	2
2	5	1	9	4	7	6	8	3
5	1	3	7	9	2	8	6	4
4	6	8	5	3	1	2	9	7
9	7	2	6	8	4	1	3	5

Odd/even sudoku 2

9	4	7	5	8	6	3	1	2
6	5	3	1	2	4	8	7	9
1	8	2	7	9	3	4	6	5
2	9	6	4	1	8	7	5	3
7	1	5	9	3	2	6	8	4
8	3	4	6	7	5	9	2	1
3	7	1	2	6	9	5	4	8
4	2	8	3	5	7	1	9	6
5	6	9	8	4	1	2	3	7

Odd/even sudoku 3

6	1	5	3	7	4	8	2	9
4	7	8	9	6	2	1	3	5
9	3	2	5	1	8	4	7	6
2	9	6	8	3	1	7	5	4
1	5	4	6	9	7	2	8	3
3	8	7	4	2	5	9	6	1
7	2	3	1	5	9	6	4	8
8	6	9	2	4	3	5	1	7
5	4	1	7	8	6	3	9	2

Odd/even sudoku 4

2	5	4	1	8	6	3	9	7
8	6	9	7	3	4	2	5	1
7	1	3	2	9	5	6	8	4
1	4	2	8	6	9	7	3	5
5	9	8	3	1	7	4	6	2
3	7	6	4	5	2	9	1	8
9	3	7	5	2	8	1	4	6
6	2	5	9	4	1	8	7	3
4	8	1	6	7	3	5	2	9

Odd/even sudoku 5

4	9	1	5	6	8	7	3	2
8	5	7	3	2	1	6	4	9
3	2	6	7	4	9	8	5	1
5	8	2	9	1	6	4	7	3
6	1	3	4	8	7	9	2	5
7	4	9	2	5	3	1	6	8
2	7	5	8	9	4	3	1	6
9	6	4	1	3	2	5	8	7
1	3	8	6	7	5	2	9	4

147 sudoku 1

1	3	9	6	8	7	5	2	4
6	8	4	5	1	2	3	7	9
5	2	7	4	9	3	8	6	1
2	7	6	1	3	8	4	9	5
9	4	3	2	7	5	6	1	8
8	5	1	9	6	4	7	3	2
7	6	5	8	2	9	1	4	3
3	9	8	7	4	1	2	5	6
4	1	2	3	5	6	9	8	7

147 sudoku 2

9	4	2	8	5	1	3	6	7
3	6	8	4	7	2	9	1	5
1	5	7	3	9	6	4	2	8
7	9	6	1	8	3	5	4	2
4	3	5	2	6	9	8	7	1
8	2	1	5	4	7	6	3	9
2	7	4	9	3	5	1	8	6
6	8	9	7	1	4	2	5	3
5	1	3	6	2	8	7	9	4

147 sudoku 3

4	8	7	2	9	3	5	1	6
5	2	6	1	4	7	8	3	9
3	1	9	8	6	5	2	4	7
6	9	4	5	1	8	3	7	2
7	5	2	9	3	4	1	6	8
8	3	1	6	7	2	9	5	4
9	4	5	7	8	1	6	2	3
1	6	3	4	2	9	7	8	5
2	7	8	3	5	6	4	9	1

147 sudoku 4

3	8	5	4	9	1	2	6	7
1	2	7	3	6	8	9	5	4
9	4	6	5	2	7	1	3	8
8	9	1	2	3	5	7	4	6
4	5	3	9	7	6	8	1	2
7	6	2	8	1	4	3	9	5
2	7	9	6	5	3	4	8	1
6	1	4	7	8	9	5	2	3
5	3	8	1	4	2	6	7	9

O TO 9 SUDOKU

0 to 9 sudoku 1

0	7	2	6	3	5	9/1	8	4
8	6/5	4	0	9	1	3	7	2
1	3	9	8/2	4	7	6	0	5
6	1	5	9	2	4	8	3	7/0
9	4	3	7	1/0	8	2	5	6
7/2	8	0	3	5	6	4	1	9
5	2	1	4	6	3/0	7	9	8
3	9	8	5	7	2	0	6/4	1
4	0	6/7	1	8	9	5	2	3

0 to 9 sudoku 2

8	5	3	1	9	7/0	2	4	6
9	6	0	4	8	2	1	5/3	7
7	4	2/1	3	5	6	8	0	9
2	8	6	7	0	4	3	9	5/1
1	9	7	2	6/3	5	4	8	0
5/3	0	4	8	1	9	7	6	2
6	3	8	0	7	1	9/5	2	4
0	2/1	5	9	4	3	6	7	8
4	7	9	6/5	2	8	0	1	3

0 to 9 sudoku 3

0	4	7	8	6	3	2	9	5
5	6	8	9	4	2	3	0	7
1	3	9	5	7	0	6	4	8
2	0	3	7	8	6	4	5	9
9	7	4	3	2	5	8	1	6
6	8	5	1	9	4	7	3	2
4	9	0	6	1	7	5	8	3
3	1	6	4	5	8	9	7	0
8	5	2	0	3	9	1	6	4

0 to 9 sudoku 4

0	3	1	6	4	5	8	9	2
9	2	7	3	1	8	4	5	0
8	5	4	7	9	0	3	6	1
1	6	5	9	3	7	0	4	8
4	9	8	0	5	1	6	3	7
7	0	3	4	8	6	9	1	5
5	4	9	1	0	3	7	8	6
2	8	6	5	7	9	1	0	4
3	7	0	8	6	4	5	2	9

KILLER SUDOKU

Killer sudoku 1

1	3	2	5	6	7	8	9	4
6	9	7	8	4	3	5	1	2
5	4	8	1	2	9	3	6	7
2	5	1	9	8	6	7	4	3
8	6	9	7	3	4	2	5	1
3	7	4	2	5	1	6	8	9
9	2	3	6	1	8	4	7	5
4	1	6	3	7	5	9	2	8
7	8	5	4	9	2	1	3	6

Killer sudoku 2

1	4	6	5	8	2	7	9	3
8	2	7	3	1	9	6	5	4
9	5	3	6	4	7	2	8	1
6	1	8	7	9	4	5	3	2
2	9	4	1	3	5	8	7	6
3	7	5	8	2	6	4	1	9
4	8	2	9	5	1	3	6	7
7	3	9	4	6	8	1	2	5
5	6	1	2	7	3	9	4	8

Killer sudoku 3

1	6	4	3	5	9	2	7	8
2	9	7	8	4	1	5	3	6
3	5	8	6	2	7	1	9	4
4	8	9	1	6	5	3	2	7
5	1	6	7	3	2	8	4	9
7	3	2	9	8	4	6	5	1
6	7	5	2	9	8	4	1	3
8	2	1	4	7	3	9	6	5
9	4	3	5	1	6	7	8	2

Killer sudoku 4

1	5	4	6	3	8	7	2	9
8	3	9	7	2	4	6	1	5
2	6	7	1	9	5	8	3	4
7	2	8	9	4	6	1	5	3
3	1	6	8	5	2	9	4	7
9	4	5	3	1	7	2	6	8
4	7	3	2	8	1	5	9	6
5	8	1	4	6	9	3	7	2
6	9	2	5	7	3	4	8	1

BLACKOUT SUDOKU

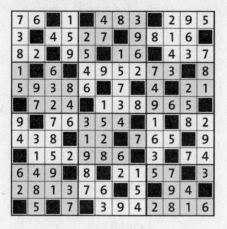

OVERLAPPING SUDOKU

5	4	1	9	8	6	3	2	7						
8	9	3	7	2	1	5	4	6						
2	6	7	5	4	3	8	9	1						
4	7	8	6	5	9	1	3	2						
1	5	9	3	7	2	6	8	4						
6	3	2	8	1	4	7	5	9						
9	8	5	2	6	7	4	1	3	2	5	6	9	8	7
3	1	6	4	9	5	2	7	8	1	3	9	4	5	6
7	2	4	1	3	8	9	6	5	4	7	8	1	2	3
						1	3	9	8	6	2	7	4	5
						8	4	6	7	9	5	2	3	1
						5	2	7	3	1	4	8	6	9
						3	8	1	5	2	7	6	9	4
						7	9	4	6	8	3	5	1	2
						6	5	2	9	4	1	3	7	8

CHAPTER 9
Japan Rediscovered

FUTOSHIKI

Futoshiki 1

2 < 4	1	3	5
1	2	3	5	4
3	5	2	4	1
4	1	5	2	3
5	3 < 4	1 < 2

Futoshiki 2

4	3 > 1	5	2
5	1	2 < 3	4
2	5	4	1	3
3 < 4 < 5	2	1
1 < 2	3	4	5

Futoshiki 3

1	7	2	6	5	3	4
5	1	6	3	2 < 4 < 7
3	5	7	4	6	1	2
2	4 < 5	1	3	7	6
4 > 2	1	5	7	6	3
6	3	4	7	1	2	5
7	6	3	2	4	5	1

Futoshiki 4

2	7	5	4 > 3	1	6
3	1	6	7	2	4 < 5
7	3	1	6	5	2	4
1	6	2	5	4	3	7
5	2	4	3	6	7	1
6	4	7	2 > 1	5	3
4	5	3	1	7	6	2

Futoshiki 5

6 < 9	5	8	1 < 2	7	3 < 4
5	8	3	2	7	4	9	1	6
7	3	6	9	2	1	4	8	5
4	1 < 2	5	8 > 7	6	9	3
3	5	7 > 1	4 < 6	8	2	9
2	7	8 > 3	6	9 > 5	4	1
9	4	1	7	3 < 5	2 < 6 < 8
8	6	9 > 4	5	3	1	7	2
1 < 2	4	6	9	8	3	5	7

KAKURO

Kakuro 1

Kakuro 2

Kakuro 3

Kakuro 4

Kakuro 5

NURIKABE

Nurikabe 1

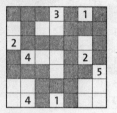

Nurikabe 2

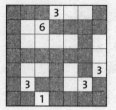

Nurikabe 3

Nurikabe 4

Nurikabe 5

SLITHER LINK

Slither link 1

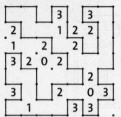

Slither link 2

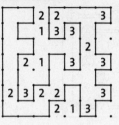

Slither link 3

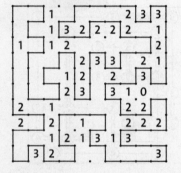

Slither link 4

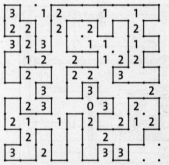

Slither link 5

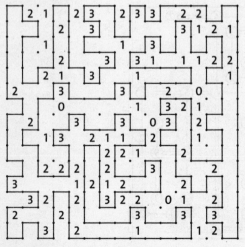

BRIDGES

Bridges 1

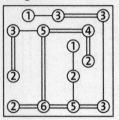

Bridges 2

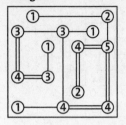

Bridges 3

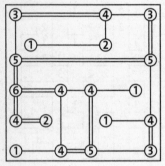

Bridges 4

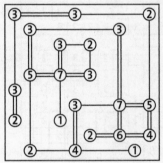

Bridges 5

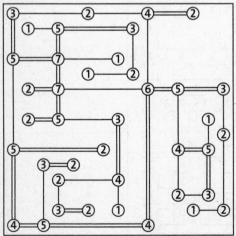

NUMBER LINK

Number link 1

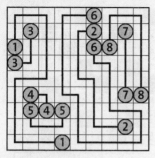

Number link 2

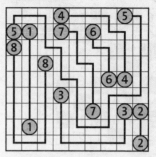

Number link 3

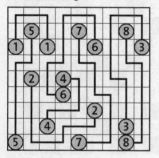

Number link 4

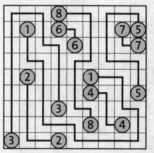

Number link 5

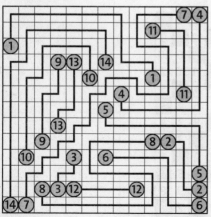

HITORI

Hitori 1

4	8		1		7	6	5
	6	8	7	4		5	
3		2		8	4	7	6
2	7		4	6	8	3	1
8		1	3		6		4
5	4		8	3		1	7
7		4	6		1		2
6	3	7		1	5	4	8

Hitori 2

7		5	3	4		2	1
1	7	6		3	5	4	
	4	2	8		6		5
4	1		6	2		5	3
8		7	1		2	6	
3	8	1	7	5	4		6
	3		2	8		1	4
2	5	3			6	1	7

Hitori 3

	8	9	6	5		2	4	7
4		6	7		8	5	2	
5	9	3	8	7		4	6	2
2	6		3		1	7	9	
7		5	4	3	6		8	1
	1	4		9		3		6
3	5		9	4	2	6	1	
9	3	2	1		7	8	5	4
6		8		2	9		7	

Hitori 4

6	5		9	8		1	7	2
1		8		6	9	7	2	
7	2	9	6	4	8	5		3
	6		1		3		4	9
4	1	7		9		8		5
	8	6	3	2	4	9	5	1
2		5		1	7		9	
9	7	3	2		1	4	8	6
5		1		7	6	2		8

Hitori 5

	11	3	2	5		8	4	6	9	1	
8	10		4		1	2	7		12		9
	7	11		3		12	2	9		6	10
1		4	6	7	8		12		11	10	2
2	9		7	8		6	11	10	3		5
	2	5		11	9	7		3	6	4	
6	5		12	2		10	9		8	3	4
	8	9	5		2		10	1		7	6
5		7		9	11	4		12	2		1
4	12		3	6	10		1		7	5	
3		2	11		12	1	6	7	5	9	8
7	1	6	9	4		11		8		2	

LIGHT UP

Light up 1

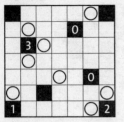

Light up 2

Light up 3

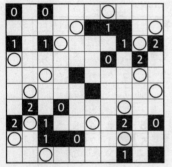

Light up 4

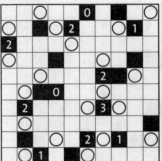

Light up 5

TENTS

Tents 1

Tents 2

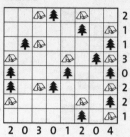

Tents 3

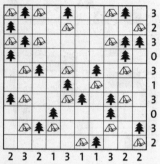

Tents 4

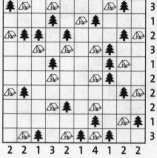

Tents 5

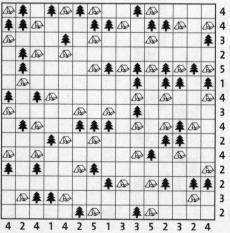

MASYU

Masyu 1

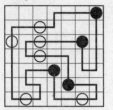

Masyu 2

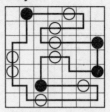

Masyu 3

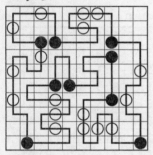

Masyu 4

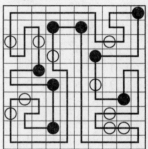

Masyu 5

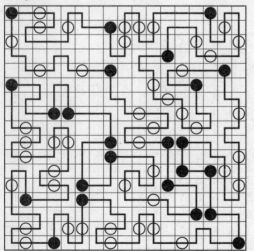

FILLOMINO

Fillomino 1

2	2	3	3	3	1	2
5	5	5	5	1	4	2
5	6	6	4	4	4	6
2	6	2	6	6	6	6
2	6	2	1	5	4	6
3	6	6	5	5	4	1
3	3	1	5	5	4	4

Fillomino 2

4	4	6	2	5	5	5
3	4	6	2	1	2	5
3	4	6	3	3	2	5
3	1	6	6	3	6	6
6	3	6	2	4	6	6
6	3	3	2	4	1	6
6	6	6	6	4	4	6

Fillomino 3

3	3	1	3	1	4	4	3	1
3	1	3	3	4	4	3	3	2
1	3	2	1	3	2	2	1	2
3	3	2	3	3	6	3	3	3
2	2	3	2	6	6	6	6	6
1	3	3	2	3	3	1	3	3
3	4	4	1	3	2	2	3	1
3	4	3	2	2	3	3	1	3
3	4	3	3	1	3	1	3	3

Fillomino 4

2	2	5	5	5	5	5	4	4
5	5	2	8	8	8	4	4	1
8	5	2	8	1	8	8	1	4
8	5	5	8	5	8	4	4	4
8	8	1	5	5	5	1	2	2
1	8	8	8	5	8	4	4	4
2	2	1	8	1	8	8	8	4
3	3	2	2	6	6	2	8	8
1	3	6	6	6	6	2	8	8

Fillomino 5

1	8	8	8	8	3	4	4	4	5	5	5	5
8	8	2	2	8	3	3	4	5	7	1	5	1
6	6	6	1	8	5	5	5	5	7	2	6	6
6	8	4	4	2	2	3	3	3	7	2	7	6
6	8	8	4	4	1	4	4	4	7	7	7	6
6	2	8	3	2	2	4	1	6	4	4	4	6
4	2	8	3	1	6	6	6	6	2	4	2	6
4	4	8	3	2	2	1	6	4	2	5	2	3
4	3	8	8	3	3	3	4	4	6	5	5	3
1	3	2	2	8	8	8	4	6	6	5	2	3
4	3	8	8	8	1	8	8	6	1	5	2	1
4	4	2	2	1	8	1	6	6	2	2	3	3
4	8	8	8	8	8	8	8	3	3	3	1	3

DIVIDE BY SQUARES

Divide by squares 1

Divide by squares 2

Divide by squares 3

Divide by squares 4

Divide by squares 5

GOKIGEN NANAME

Gokigen naname 1

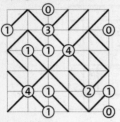

Gokigen naname 2

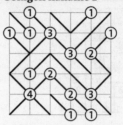

Gokigen naname 3

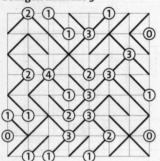

Gokigen naname 4

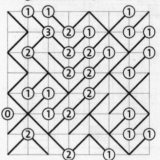

Gokigen naname 5

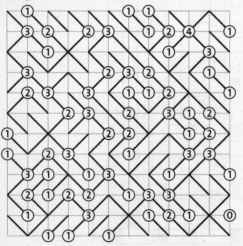

WHERE IS BLACK CELLS?

Where is black cells? 1

Where is black cells? 2

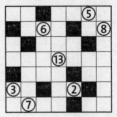

Where is black cells? 3

Where is black cells? 4

Where is black cells? 5

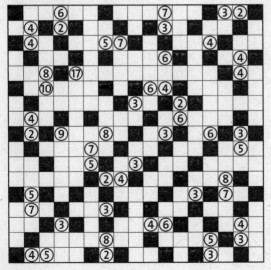

Further Reading

Every effort has been made to acknowledge the authors whose work has been used in this volume, and apologies are made for any omissions that may have occurred. Any such oversights will be corrected in subsequent editions. As well as further reading, this list contains sources used, including those from which material is quoted.

General

Can You Solve It? (1926), Arthur Hirschberg.
Chronology of Recreational Mathematics (unpublished), David Singmaster.
Creative Puzzles of the World (1995), Pieter Van Delft and Jack Botermans.
The Greatest Puzzles of All Time (1988), Matthew J. Costello.
Hoffmann's Puzzles Old & New (1893), Professor Hoffmann.

Chapter 1: The Puzzle Kings

Amusements in Mathematics (1917), Henry Dudeney.
The Canterbury Puzzles (1907), Henry Dudeney.
Cyclopedia of 5000 Puzzles, Tricks & Conundrums with Answers (1914), Sam Loyd Jr.
The 15 Puzzle (2006), Jerry Slocum and Dic Sonneveld.

'Henry Ernest Dudeney: England's greatest puzzlist', by Angela Newing, in *The Lighter Side of Mathematics* (1994), edited by Richard K. Guy and Robert E. Woodrow.
Modern Puzzles (1926), Henry Dudeney.
The Puzzle King: Sam Loyd's Chess Problems and Selected Mathematical Puzzles (1996), edited by Sid Pickard.
A Puzzle-Mine (undated), Henry Dudeney.
Puzzles and Curious Problems (1931), Henry Dudeney.
Sam Loyd and His Chess Problems (1913), Alain C. White.
Sam Loyd and His Puzzles (1928), Sam Loyd.
The Tangram Book (2001), Jerry Slocum.

Chapter 2: The World of Words

Excursions into Puzzledom (1879), the Late Tom Hood and His Sister.

'Lewis Carroll: Mathematician'
(*Scientific American*, April 1956),
Warren Weaver.

Lewis Carroll's Puzzles and Games
(1992), edited by Edward Wakeling.

The Oxford Guide to Word Games
(1984), Tony Augarde.

Rediscovered Lewis Carroll Puzzles
(1995), edited by Edward Wakeling.

*Riddles and Conundrums for All
Occasions* (1924), Paul W. Kearney.

Chapter 3: Codes and Ciphers

The Code Book (1999), Simon Singh.

Chapter 4: Cruciverbalism

A–Z of Crosswords (2006), Jonathan
Crowther.

Anatomy of the Crossword (1963),
Douglas St P. Barnard.

Chambers Crossword Manual (2006),
Don Manley.

The Crossword Obsession (2001), Coral
Amende.

80 Years of Cryptic Crosswords (2004),
Val Gilbert.

How to Do the Times Crossword (2001),
Brian Greer.

How to Solve a Crossword (1988), Colin
Parsons.

The Magic of Lewis Carroll (1973),
edited by John Fisher.

Secrets of the Setters (2005), Hugh
Stephenson.

75 Years of the Times Crossword
(2005), Colin Dexter (foreword).

The Strange World of the Crossword
(1975), Roger Millington.

Ximenes on the Art of the Crossword
(2001), Derrick Macnutt.

Chapter 5: Gatherings for Gardner

Foulsham's Fun Book (n.d.), anon.

Mathematical Recreations and Essays
(13th edn, 1987), W. W. Rouse Ball
and H. S. M. Coxeter.

Mathematics Magic and Mystery
(1956), Martin Gardner.

*The Penguin Book of Curious and
Interesting Puzzles* (1992), David
Wells.

*The Unreasonable Utility of
Recreational Mathematics* (1992),
speech by David Singmaster at the
First European Congress of
Mathematics.

Chapter 6: Truth Will Out

The Lady or the Tiger? (1982),
Raymond Smullyan.

The Riddle of Scheherazade (1997),
Raymond Smullyan.

To Mock a Mockingbird (1985),
Raymond Smullyan.

What is the Name of This Book? (1978),
Raymond Smullyan.

Chapter 7: Thinking Sideways

Amazing 'Aha!' Puzzles (lulu.com,
2005), Lloyd King.

De Bono's Thinking Course (1982),
Edward de Bono.

Lateral Thinking (1970), Edward de
Bono.

Lateral Thinking Puzzlers (1992), Paul
Sloane.

Puzzles for the High IQ (1996), Lloyd
King.

Chapter 8: Sudoku War

'Sudoku variations' (*Mathematical
Association of America*, September
2005), Ed Pegg Jr.

Chapter 9: Japan Rediscovered

'Puzzle maker lays down the rules'
(*The Japan Times*, 3 July 2006),
Barbara Bayer.